POPE PIUS XII LIBRARY, ST. JOSEPH COL.

3 2528 08457 6505

D1527161

The Romances of Chrétien de Troyes

$45.00

01-03-02

The Romances of
Chrétien de Troyes

Joseph J. Duggan

Yale University Press

New Haven and London

Published with assistance from the foundation
established in memory of Philip Hamilton
McMillan of the Class of 1894, Yale College.

Copyright © 2001 by Yale University. All rights
reserved. This book may not be reproduced, in
whole or in part, including illustrations, in any
form (beyond that copying permitted by Sections
107 and 108 of the U.S. Copyright Law and except
by reviewers for the public press), without written
permission from the publishers.

Designed by Nancy Ovedovitz and set in ITC
Veljovic type by Tseng Information Systems.
Printed in the United States of America by
Sheridan Books, Chelsea, Michigan.

Library of Congress Cataloging-in-Publication Data
Duggan, Joseph J.
The romances of Chrétien de Troyes / Joseph J.
Duggan.
    p.   cm.
Includes bibliographical references and index.
ISBN 0-300-08357-2 (cloth)
1. Chrétien, de Troyes, 12th cent.—Criticism and
interpretation.   I. Title.
PQ1448 .D84   2001
841'.1—dc21   00-011726

A catalogue record for this book is available from
the British Library.

The paper in this book meets the guidelines for
permanence and durability of the Committee on
Production Guidelines for Book Longevity of the
Council on Library Resources.

10 9 8 7 6 5 4 3 2 1

For Marie, Kathleen, Joe

Contents

Preface

This book has a double audience: the general reader interested in literature of the Middle Ages who is looking for an account of Chrétien de Troyes's romances set in the context of their period and the specialist in medieval French literature. To satisfy the needs of both is not easy, but I have tried to take no arcane knowledge for granted, have gone to some length in clarifying technical terms, and have provided necessary background. I have endeavored to give the uninitiated access to the results of the research and interpretations of specialists in medieval French literature. For initiates my principal aim has been to emphasize certain important features of Chrétien's works that I considered to be underemphasized—although by no means untreated—in the current critical literature, namely the roles of kinship, societal values, interiority, and myth, and to furnish a synthesis that draws together the many strands of a rich body of critical and philological thought.

For foreign-language citations I have provided English translations, my own unless otherwise noted. The criteria for the translations from medieval French are clarity and faithfulness to the text: I have no illusions as to their elegance. For readers in search of that quality, I recommend the fluid renderings of Burton Raffel published by Yale University Press between 1987 and 1999.

I take it for granted that the reader has read Chrétien's works or is reading them in tandem with this book. Thus I provide no comprehensive summary of the various romances, although interpretive summaries are furnished for some passages under discussion. Line numbering, alas, differs from edition to edition of Chrétien's works, and thus also from translation to translation.

Etymons are indicated by the symbol <, with starred forms representing reconstructed etymons: thus Rhiannon < *Rigantona.

Chrétien de Troyes has been the subject of many studies, as a glance at the Bibliography will show—some of them major works of synthesis, such as Frappier 1982 (1968) and Topsfield 1981. Chrétien is not only important in his own right and read for his intrinsic merits, but his works provide rich supplementary readings in courses on medieval history, culture, and civilization. The principal one-volume bibliography is that of Douglas Kelly (1976), which is supplemented by Sandra Ihle in Kelly 1985: 343–53. Annual recensions are found in the serial bibliographies of the *Bibliographical Bulletin of the International Arthurian Society,* the *Cahiers de Civilisation Médiévale,* the *Zeitschrift für Romanische Philologie,* and the *Year's Work in Modern Language Studies.* Guides to four of the romances have been published in the Critical Guides to French Texts series: Burgess 1984 for *Erec,* Hunt 1986 for *Yvain,* Busby 1993C for *Perceval,* and Polak 1982 for *Cligès.* On Arthurian literature in general, see Lacy 1996. E. H. Ruck's index (1991) of themes and motifs in twelfth-century Arthurian texts includes Chrétien's Arthurian romances. A concordance to the five romances as found in the Guiot manuscript, with lists of words, forms, and rhymes, has been published by Marie-Louise Ollier (1989), who also collaborated with Pascal Bonnefois to produce a lemmatized concordance to *Yvain* (Bonnefois and Ollier 1988). Gabriel Andrieu (1976) has published a concordance to the Lecoy edition of *Perceval.* The achievements of scholarship on Chrétien, a cumulative enterprise, are impressive. The present work is not meant as a guide to scholarship, however, and if references to some studies are lacking, this is no reflection on their value.

Many of the subjects treated here I first took up in my Berkeley classes on twelfth-century French literature and medieval comparative literature, particularly in a seminar on Chrétien in spring 1996, in which I profited greatly from discussions with Gil Anidjar, Kate Bonin, Cristina Guardiola, Michelle Hamilton, Emily Keas, Louisa Mackenzie, and Jennifer Monahan. For help with various questions of detail, I thank Pascal Bonnefois, John Levy, the Rev. John Lynch, C.S.P., and Elaine Tennant. My research assistants Karen Akiyama, Ruth Desmond, and Kim Starr-Reid gave invaluable support with bibliography and databases. Karen Akiyama, Jennifer Miller, and Kristen Lee Over read the manuscript and contributed greatly to its improvement. Annalee Rejhon, on whose expertise in Celtic literature and language I drew abundantly and gratefully and with whom I discussed virtually every idea in the book, made it substantially better. The University of California, Berkeley, granted me the sabbatical leave during which I wrote this study. Finally, I would like to express my gratitude to Berkeley's Committee on Research and above all to Joseph Cerny, Vice Chancellor for Research and Dean of the Graduate Division, for generous support of my research.

Images of the medieval manuscripts are reproduced by permission of the Bibliothèque Nationale de France for plates 1–6, 8, and 10; the Bibliothèque interuniversitaire, Montpellier, for plate 7; and Princeton University Library for plate 9.

Figures and Abbreviations

   The plates follow page 182

Ir.   Irish
L.   Latin
O. F.   Old French
W.   Welsh

The Romances of Chrétien de Troyes

Chapter 1

Chrétien and His Milieu

T he role of Chrétien de Troyes's five romances in literary his-
tory is crucial. His *Erec and Enide* is, to our knowledge, the first
Arthurian romance, whatever was the contribution to that tale
of the professional storytellers that he refers to in his prologue.
In fact, the only extended tales about King Arthur that survive from before
Chrétien's time are the eleventh-century Welsh prose story *Culhwch and
Olwen*, Geoffrey of Monmouth's Latin prose *History of the Kings of Britain*,
Wace's translation of Geoffrey's work into French verse as the *Roman de
Brut*, and possibly other such translations (on the latter, see Tatlock 1950:
456–60). The Latin prose *Story of Meriadoc* (*Historia Meriadoci*) and *Rise of
Gawain* (*De Ortu Waluuanii*) appear to date from the first half of the thirteenth century or the end of the twelfth (Bruce 1913; Day 1984, 1988), and
the French work from which the Swiss Ulrich von Zatzikhoven translated
his romance *Lanzelet* is lost, as are perhaps other works that may have preceded *Erec*. In any case, Chrétien continued traditions of narrative set in
motion by the authors of the medieval romances of antiquity, particularly
the *Roman d'Enéas*. He launched, in the form that later generations would
take up, two of the most widely developed narrative subjects of medieval
and modern literature: the adultery of Lancelot and Guinevere and the
Grail quest. He was translated or adapted in the Middle Ages by authors
writing in German, English, Norse, Swedish, and probably Welsh. His character Erec was appropriated as the protagonist of a fifteenth-century prose
romance in three widely differing versions (Foerster 1890; Pickford 1968)
and his *Yvain* was revised in the sixteenth century by Pierre Sala (Burin
1993). Beyond these versions of his works, he exercised decisive influence
on the development of Arthurian romance written in French, both verse
and prose (see Lacy, Kelly, and Busby 1987–88; and Schmolke-Hasselmann
1998), and, through the intermediary of the French tradition, in other major

European literatures. Insofar as an idealizing representation of the life of medieval nobles influenced behavior, Arthur and his court as depicted in romance played a major role in the self-image of countless men and women of the Middle Ages and later periods. The medieval tradition of Arthurian literature that he helped launch has produced, in addition, a vast postmedieval progeny.

The modern reader of Chrétien de Troyes who wants to view the romances as the author saw them, however, is laboring under two major handicaps. The first is that this reader has the advantage of knowledge and perspectives that were not available to Chrétien. Modern exactness in measurement, for example, allows the use of certain narrative motifs that were beyond Chrétien's reach because they were beyond his world. A simple example is the role of time. Try to imagine the genre of the adventure film without deadlines, without clocks ticking off the hours, minutes, and seconds, without the pervasive temporal pressure of impending time limits. Deadlines are not completely absent from Chrétien, although they are rare and are expressed only in terms of days: in *Yvain,* Lunete has to find a champion to defend her against her three accusers, but only within a limit of forty days (*Yvain* 3687), and when the final day arrives, her captors are prepared to execute her, but at no specified moment of the day. The time of day was a much more fluid construct in the twelfth century, measured only by inexact and undependable means such as the water clock (provided that the water was not frozen) or the sundial (except on cloudy days) or the burning of calibrated candles (but calibrated against what?) (see Duggan 1986a). Chrétien's modern audiences must peel away layers of technological change and try to imagine themselves in a world in which fire was the only source of artificial light, most commodities were acquired by barter rather than by purchase, roads were dependable only in dry weather, medical attention was much more likely to harm than to heal, and the span of human life was brief. But the discrepancies were mental and moral as well as physical and technological: most marriages were arranged, theologians deemed extreme sexual pleasure in the marriage bed to be sinful, there was no central legal authority, maps were extremely rare and full of fantasy, the causes of events were conceived as either divine or demoniac, and judicial guilt and innocence were often decided by combat, the "judgment of God" based on the premise that God would see to it that the unjust would not triumph over the just.[1]

The second handicap is the necessity of replacing the mental structures that we provisionally suppress in our process of reading medieval literature with the structures that Chrétien would have taken for granted and within which his characters carry out their lives. Among these are the high importance accorded to kinship, the nature of the marriage relationship, how renown was acquired, the degrees of human responsibility, and the nascent twelfth-century concept of the interior life.

Several hypotheses are tested in this book. One is that characters in Chrétien's romances, as distinct from characters in the works of other medieval writers of romance and in opposition to what certain critics maintain, are sometimes depicted as changing and developing. An author can, of course, conceive of a variety of motivations for a character to change conduct: the instruction of parents, teachers, and acquaintances, the imitation of models of conduct, the admonitions of ecclesiastical authorities or other forces external to immediate influences, or self-motivation, when the character is shown coming to decisions independently. But whatever the scenario that leads to change, its very existence implies a narrative of interiority. In medieval society, with its pervasive belief in the soul and in the effects of original sin, the distinction between body and mind underlies any examination of motivation. Whether motivation, as depicted in medieval romances, can profitably be studied according to our own theories of the psyche is of great interest to me, but less so than the elucidation of the process of decision-making in Chrétien's characters as he conceived it.

Another hypothesis is that medieval concepts of kinship and genealogy are essential to understanding how Chrétien structures his characters' motivations. Still another is that the system of values operating in northern France in the late twelfth century differs essentially from our own. This may seem obvious to medievalists, but it is seldom articulated in the critical literature except as regards the depiction of medieval institutions. That French authors living in this period, and so the characters they created, should have entertained concepts of secular moral responsibility that differ not only in their accidentals but in essential features from those of the modern reader is one of the keys to understanding Chrétien's romances. Finally, the eclipsing of source study during the past twenty years, understandable within the context of exciting new initiatives in scholarship, has resulted in neglect of an extremely significant aspect of Chrétien's achievement, his subtle integration of myth, particularly Celtic myth, with the depiction of medieval life and medieval motivations.

That the interior life of characters should be the subject of narrative does not go without question. In the major narrative genre of medieval French literature, the *chanson de geste,* characters are typically seen acting according to decisions they have made, but the narrators seldom tell us *how* they have come to be made. Depiction of characters in the chanson de geste is in terms of externals, of who does what, and decisions are the subject of dialogues that are largely contrastive in nature rather than of insights provided by the narrator. It may well be that the poets who created these works had no concept of interiority, although that would be surprising in the context of a set of religious beliefs that placed great weight on the notion of sin. But whether the concept of interiority was readily available to them or not, they do not seem to pay much attention to it.

In twelfth-century French romance that precedes Chrétien, by contrast, beginning with the *Roman d'Alexandre* and continuing through the *Roman de Thèbes*, the *Roman de Troie*, and the *Roman d'Enéas*, poets do attempt to let the reading or listening audience in on what is transpiring in characters' minds. References in Chrétien's romances show that he was acquainted with all four of these works.

WHAT IS KNOWN OF CHRÉTIEN'S LIFE

Chrétien is not a common name in twelfth-century Champagne (Holmes and Klenke 1959: 52–61). The association of Chrétien the writer of romances with the town of Troyes has led to a search among surviving documents for his trace in history. One candidate, a canon of the Augustinian abbey of Saint-Loup in Troyes named Christianus, is mentioned as witness to a charter issued by the bishop of Troyes and dated 1173, preserved in the cartulary of the Premonstratensian abbey of La Chapelle-aux-Planches (Vigneras 1934–35). Another was Christianus chaplain of the collegiate church of Saint-Maclou, a dependency of the count of Champagne in the town of Bar-sur-Aube, who copied a document of 1179 in his own hand (see the photograph in Holmes and Klenke 1959: fig. 1) and is mentioned in another document dated 1172. The Christianus of Saint-Loup in Troyes may or may not be identical with the chaplain of Saint-Maclou in Bar-sur-Aube. The emblem of St. Loup in legend was a mythic animal called the *cocatrix,* which Chrétien may refer to in line 6721 of *Erec* where he says that two *cocadrilles* were carved on the faldstools (folding seats) used in Erec's coronation (Walter 1997: 21–22; 1999: 61–62), but since the cocatrix was carried every year in procession at Troyes, there does not seem to be any particular reason to link the use of this word with a canon of the monastery of Saint-Loup. Although it would be entirely possible for a writer of worldly tales to be a cleric in this period, neither of the clerics named Christianus is referred to as an author or as an associate of the court of Champagne, and the charters of the counties of Champagne and Flanders for this period have yielded no Christianus (Benton 1961: 562).

Nothing, then, is known of Chrétien's life except what can be gathered from his works and the occasional medieval reference (see Van Coolput 1987), and that is extremely little. He refers to himself in his romances: *Erec* 9, 26; *Cliges* 23, 45, 6702; *Lancelot* 25; *Yvain* 6805; *Perceval* 7, 62, in the third person perhaps influenced by the knowledge that the texts were destined to be read aloud to an audience by a reader or perhaps treating the author as a source among several (for this last, see Marnette 1998: 218). Twice Godefroy de Lagny mentions Chrétien as the one who began the romance *Lancelot*, which Godefroy is finishing with Chrétien's permission (7105, 7107). Only once does Chrétien call himself Chrétien de Troyes, in *Erec* 9, the romance in which he also boasts that his tale will be remembered as long as Christianity lasts, which he no doubt thought of as until the Second Coming of Christ. In *Perceval* he speaks of himself as putting his effort and pains (*entant et poine,* 62) into rhyming the best tale ever told in royal court (63–65), and in *Lancelot* he uses the same terms to indicate his own contribution to what his patron has supplied (his *painne* and his *antancion,* pains and effort, 29). Ten mentions of the author's name in more than thirty-six thousand lines are little to go on. Moreover, had those lines not contained references to place and time and, more specifically, to two patrons, we would know virtually nothing about the author. As it is, almost all we know is by inference.

Only one twelfth-century reference to Chrétien by another author has survived, in the *Chevalier à l'épée,* and he was rarely referred to in the thirteenth century (Van Coolput 1987). The fullest references are in Huon de Méry's *Tournoiement de l'Antechrist* (1235), where Huon calls him "he who had such high repute for composing" (*cil qui tant out pris de trover*) and says that Chrétien and Raoul de Houdenc "took the beautiful French language smoothly, just as it came to hand" (*prenoient / Le bel françois trestout a plain, / Si com il lor venoit a main*). Other references are found, naturally enough, in the first and fourth continuations of *Perceval* and in the *Didot Perceval.* (All are cited in Pickford 1981.)

In an ingenious study, Aurelio Roncaglia (1958) made a convincing case for seeing in the *senhal* "Carestia" of the renowned troubadour Raimbaut d'Aurenga, the lord of Orange in Provence, a reference to Chrétien de

Troyes. A *senhal* is a fictitious name or sobriquet that one poet uses to address another. Chrétien's poem "D'amors qui m'a tolu a moi" contains correspondences in imagery, reference, and wording to Raimbaut's "No chan per auzel ni per flor," as well as to Bernart de Ventadorn's famous "Can vei la lauzeta mover." Roncaglia shows that Chrétien is taking a tack contrary to the stances of the two troubadours. The senhal "Carestia," meaning 'rarity, scarcity', would derive from a concept dear to Chrétien, reflected in the phrase *chier tans* 'time of scarcity', in line 42 of Chrétien's poem, in which he exhorts his heart not to abandon faith toward the lady despite the scarcity of love it is experiencing. The idea that a love that is delayed—and thus "scarce"—is all the more enjoyable is found among Gauvain's arguments to Yvain in the *Chevalier au lion* (2515–23). "Carestia" appears also to be a pun on the name "Crestiien." If Roncaglia is right, and in my view he is, then Chrétien would have been active as a poet in the early 1170s, since Raimbaut d'Aurenga died in 1173.

Chrétien's work on *Lancelot* under the patronage of Countess Marie de Champagne (1145–1198) and on *Perceval* under Count Philip of Flanders, known from the prologues of those two romances, makes it clear that he was writing actively between Marie's marriage with Count Henry I "the Liberal" of Champagne (1127–1181, count from 1152) and 1191, when Count Philip died. The earliest reference to Marie as countess of Champagne is in a charter of Henry's dated to 1159 (Holmes and Klenke 1959: 18; Misrahi 1959: 112; Benton 1961: 554). In seeking more precise dates for Chrétien's activity as a writer than the broad period 1159 to 1191, one enters the realm of conjectures and estimates of probability. The most widely accepted theory for the chronology of his works is that put forth by Anthime Fourrier (1950, 1955, 1958), who places Chrétien's first romance in the early 1170s, but Claude Luttrell (1974) has presented a proposal that his early activity was a decade and a half later.

Troyes was in the late twelfth century one of the most prosperous towns in Europe, one of the sites of the fairs of Champagne—along with Provins, Lagny, and Bar-sur-Aube—and the location of one of the palaces of the counts of Champagne. The fairs were held twice a year, one known as the *Foire froide* (the "cold fair," November 2 to January 2), the other as the *Foire chaude* (the "hot fair," from early July to September 13), and were a key commercial event for merchants and travelers from Italy, Spain, and Portugal in the south to Scandinavia, the Low Countries, and Britain in the north. Chrétien presents the portrait of such a commercial center when he has Gauvain view the town of Escavalon in *Perceval:*

And he sees the whole town
Peopled by an attractive crowd,
And the changing-counters all covered
With gold, silver, and coins,
And he sees the squares and the streets
All full of good craftsmen
Plying various trades.
And as their crafts are various,
One makes helmets and the other hauberks,
One makes saddles and the other coats of arms,
One makes reins and the other spurs,
And those furbish swords,
These full cloth and those weave it,
These paint it and those trim it.
Some melt silver and gold,
Others make rich and beautiful objects:
Cups, goblets, and bowls,
And jewels with enamelwork,
Rings, belts, and clasps.
One could well imagine
That there was always a fair in the town,
It was full of so much wealth:
Wax, pepper, and dyes
And gray and shimmering furs
And all types of merchandise.
[Et esgarde la vile toute
Pueplee de molt bele gent,
Et les changes d'or et d'argent
Trestoz covers et de monoies,
Et voit les places et les voies
Toutes plaines de bons ovriers
Qui faisoient divers mestiers.
Si com li mestier sont divers,
Cil fait elmes et cil haubers,
Et cil seles et cil blasons,
Cil lorains et cil esperons,
Et cil les espees forbissent,
Cist folent dras et cil les tissent,
Cil les pingnent et cil les tondent.
Li un argent et or refondent,
Cist font oeuvres riches et beles:
Colpes, hanas et escüeles

> Et joiaus ovrés a esmaus,
> Aniax, çaintures et fremaus.
> Bien poïst l'en cuidier et croire
> Qu'en la vile eüst toz jors foire,
> Qui de tant avoir estoit plaine:
> De cyre, de poivre et de graine
> Et de pennes vaires et grises
> Et de totes marcheandises.]   (*Perceval* 5758–82)

Similar scenes could be viewed in any commercially active town, but all the more so in Troyes, whose revenues greatly enriched the count and countess of Champagne and provided a solid economic basis for their power. Judith Kellogg (1989: ch. 2) has illuminated the economic aspects of *Erec* and *Yvain,* including the themes of debt and credit and their relation to considerations of time. A thriving Jewish community was established in Troyes, one of whose members was Salomon ben Isaac (1040–1105), known as Rashi, one of the greatest of Talmudic scholars, whose work was carried on in the twelfth century by his grandson, Jacob ben Meir (1100–1171), called Rabbenu Tam. A cathedral school taught a curriculum centered on theology and the seven liberal arts (grammar, logic, and dialectic, which made up the trivium, and geometry, arithmetic, music, and astronomy, the quadrivium). Peter Comestor was a teacher there between 1147 and 1164. In addition to the cathedral church of Saint-Pierre, the Augustinian abbey of Saint-Loup was within the walls of Troyes, and just outside, to the east, stood the Benedictine abbey of Saint-Martin-es-Aires. It was in such a town that at least for a time Chrétien worked his own trade, the weaving of texts.

DATING THE ROMANCES

That *Erec et Enide* was the first of Chrétien's romances is indicated by the prologue to *Cliges,* which mentions *Erec* but not *Lancelot, Yvain,* or *Perceval.* In *Cliges* Chrétien does, however, ascribe to himself four projects based on works of Ovid: the "Comandemenz d'Ovide" (*Cliges* 2), taken to be a translation of the *Remedia amoris;* the "Art d'amors" (3), a translation of the *Ars amatoria;* and two tales recounted in book 6 of the *Metamorphoses,* "Le Mors de l'espaule" (4), the story of King Pelops, whose shoulder, eaten by Demeter, was replaced by a marble one (*Metamorphoses* 6.403–11); and "De la hupe et de l'aronde et dou rousignol la muance" (*Cliges* 6–7), the story of Philomena, her sister Procne, and Procne's husband, Tereus (*Metamorphoses* 6.426–674). The dates of these translations and adaptations from

Ovid are unknown, but it is logical to assume that, around the time he produced *Cliges* with its long passages of love casuistry, Chrétien would have
produced his translations of the poet known in the Middle Ages as an ancient authority on amatory behavior.

None of these Ovidiana are extant except for the last tale Chrétien mentions, which was identified by Charles De Boer as the narrative about
Philomena incorporated into a fourteenth-century compilation, the *Ovide
moralisé*. In this 1,468-line poem, published by De Boer (1909), the author
identifies himself, or the compiler identifies him, as "Crestiiens li Gois"
(*Philomena* 734). The word *Gois*, a monosyllable rhyming with *bois*, has
been subject to differing interpretations. Harry F. Williams (1958), for example, took it as a variation on *gais*, so the meaning of the phrase would
be "Chrétien the joyful." Olivier Collet interprets *li Gois* as "the Jew" (1994:
l. 743 and n.), no doubt influenced by the fact that Troyes was the site
of a thriving Jewish community in the twelfth century,[2] but this meaning is extremely unlikely since the putative Hebrew etymon of *goy* designates not a Jew but rather a Gentile, perhaps one converted from Judaism
to Christianity. Finally, *Gois* meaning either "Jew" or "convert from Judaism" is otherwise unknown in Old French. The most likely interpretation is
"Gouais," meaning an inhabitant of the town of Gouaix near Provins in Brie.
In addition to associating himself with Troyes in *Erec*, Chrétien was later
under the patronage of the countess of Champagne, who lived in castles
at Troyes and Provins. But since all we know about Chrétien's identity is
in his works themselves, it is not necessary to think that he was born in
Troyes, and he may well have originated in Gouaix and have identified himself thus in an early work. Anne Berthelot opts for this interpretation in
her translation: "Chrétien de Gouaix" (1994a: 935).

The text of *Erec* tells us nothing about its date and little of the circumstances under which it was written except that the tale or tales on which
it is based circulated in oral tradition (19–22). Certain features, however,
seem to link it to Plantagenet interests. William the Conqueror and the Norman and Breton fighters who accompanied him in the conquest of England
in 1066 introduced to that land Old French as a spoken, literary, and administrative language. The Norman aristocracy in England continued to
speak French until the middle of the thirteenth century, and John Gower
wrote his *Mirour de l'omme* around 1370 (see Price 1984: 217–31; and Short
1979–80). French continued as an artificial language of the courts into the
eighteenth century. When Henry Plantagenet, count of Anjou, became
King Henry II of England in 1154, the Continental holdings of the English

royal family were enlarged substantially to include not only Anjou and Normandy but also the regions that owed homage to Henry's wife, Eleanor of Aquitaine, namely Poitou, Aquitaine, and Gascony, the western parts of France as far south as the Pyrenees. French was the native language not only of Henry II but of his sons, and King Richard I "Lion-Heart" of England spent only a few years of his life in England.

In the course of the late eleventh and early twelfth centuries, the French spoken in England, based on the Norman dialect, developed features that distinguished it from other dialects of French, and gradually an Anglo-Norman dialect emerged. Anglo-Norman produced a vigorous literature, much of it resulting from the support of wealthy patrons. Anglo-Norman literary texts include the following "firsts" in French literature: the earliest written version of a chanson de geste (the Oxford *Chanson de Roland*), the earliest surviving drama (the *Jeu d'Adam*), the earliest adventure narrative (the *Voyage de S. Brendan,* containing the earliest octosyllabic rhymed couplets), the earliest histories (Geoffrey Gaimar's *Estoire des Engleis*), the earliest eyewitness history (Jordan Fantosme's *Guerre d'Ecosse,* containing an account of the rebellion of Henry II's son Henry), the earliest scientific text (Philippe de Thaon's *Comput*), the earliest law text (the laws of William the Conqueror), the earliest translations of the Bible (the *Oxford Psalter,* the *Eadwine Psalter,* and the *Quatre Livres des Reis*), the earliest monastic rules (of the Knights Hospitaler), the earliest significant examples of prose (a translation of the Book of Judges), the earliest woman writer (Clemence of Barking, who wrote a *Vie de S. Catherine*), and the earliest identifiable patrons of literature (Queen Matilda, wife of King Henry I). (On these "firsts," see Short 1992.) French literature obviously thrived in twelfth-century England, and the Plantagenet kings ruled vast areas of western France that were also productive of high-quality literature in both French and Occitan, including some of the finest troubadours.

In *Erec et Enide,* the lands from which the guests present at Erec's coronation come are exclusively those that were in the second half of the twelfth century under the suzerainty of the Plantagenets (Fourrier 1950: 73; Schmolke-Hasselmann 1998: 232–33). Chrétien even refers to France in a slightly pejorative way when he states that the castle of Brandigan could not be taken by all the forces of France and Lombardy combined (*Erec* 5384–87). The names of two historical figures associated with Henry II of England appear in the poem. The first, Brian of the Isles (*Erec* 6722), corresponds to Brian Fitz Count, lord of Wallingford, who died around 1150 (Weston 1924–25, Keats-Rohan 1989: 316–18; Schmolke-Hasselmann 1998:

238–40). The second is the Welsh Owein Cyfeiliog, 1130–1197 (Thomas Jones 1955: 145), who is Yvain de Cavaliot (*Erec* 1705). Moreover, the time and place of the coronation scene, at Christmas in Nantes in Brittany, coincide with those of a court that Henry II as overlord of Brittany held in that town in 1169 (Fourrier 1950: 72). Chrétien's placing of the coronation at Nantes seems to be unmotivated by anything in the rest of the plot of *Erec.* Nantes is not even mentioned elsewhere in the romance—unless under the name Carnant (see Chapter 2). Henry II convoked the court of Christmas 1169 for the purpose of having his third son, twelve-year-old Geoffrey, the half-brother of Marie de Champagne, receive homage from the nobles and prelates of Brittany, the culmination of four years of efforts on Henry's part. In 1166, Geoffrey was betrothed to Constance, daughter and heir of the count of Brittany, an alliance that joined the Plantagenets to the highest Breton nobility. In May 1169, Geoffrey, at the age of eleven, first received homage in the cathedral of Rennes directly from the barons of Brittany who were then present. A possible allusion to the Plantagenets in *Erec et Enide* is that the leopard, heraldic animal of the kings of England, is represented, along with the *cocadrille,* on the set of chairs that Brian of the Isles is said to have presented to King Arthur. Arthur and Erec sit on these chairs during the coronation (*Erec* 6705–27). Earlier in the romance, in preparation for riding off with Enide on their journey of adventures, Erec puts on his armor on a carpet that depicts a leopard (*Erec* 2630). Chrétien might well have written *Erec et Enide* under the patronage of Henry, Geoffrey, or Constance, or someone in their entourage (Schmolke-Hasselmann 1998: 232–42). The epilogue that speaks of Arthur's great generosity at Erec's coronation feast may have been meant as a discreet reminder to the patron of the romance, whoever this might have been (Dembowski 1994b: 119).

Countess Marie de Champagne, for whom Chrétien wrote his *Lancelot,* was kindly enough disposed toward her half-brother Geoffrey to donate an annual revenue to the cathedral of Notre-Dame in Paris in his memory in 1186 (Guérard 1850, 1: 296–97).[3] Henry II of England certainly took an interest in the legend of King Arthur. Constance named Geoffrey's posthumous son Arthur (1187–1203), an indication of the importance of the Plantagenet dynasty's desire to link itself with the Arthurian past. Even the mention of Guivret, king of the Irish, and the presence of Garras, ruler of Cork, at the wedding celebration in *Erec* would be apt shortly after 1169–1170, years that were marked by Norman incursions into Ireland. Henry II himself took armed forces to Waterford in 1171.

These conjunctions of circumstances are indeed fragile as they con-

cern dating (Misrahi 1959). They have been challenged by Claude Luttrell
(1974: 32), who dates *Erec* to the period 1184–1186 on the basis of what he
sees as resemblances between: (1) the portrayal of Enide and the description of Nature in Alan of Lille's *Complaint of Nature* (*De planctu Naturae*);
(2) Enide's worn robe and the robe of Prudence in the same author's *Anticlaudianus;* and (3) the description of Erec's coronation robe, on which are
portrayed the liberal arts of the quadrivium, and the depiction of the liberal arts in the *Anticlaudianus.* Alan of Lille wrote *The Complaint of Nature*
in the late 1170s, and the *Anticlaudianus* was probably composed in 1183, so
Erec, in Luttrell's view, would have been written after that.

Erec's links with the Plantagenets and with Brittany and the attention it
gives to the figure of Enide lead me to think that it was composed for Constance and Geoffrey, betrothed since 1166 and married in 1181. In 1176, Geoffrey was eighteen years old and Constance fourteen; in 1184, he was twenty-
six and she was twenty-two. The Catalan troubadour Guerau de Cabrera,
who was no longer living in October 1170 (Riquer 1957: 339), reproaches his
jongleur in a *sirventes-ensenhamen,* a humorous poem of admonishment,
for not knowing

> about Erec
> how he conquered
> the sparrow-hawk outside his kingdom.
> [d'Erec
> com conquistec
> l'esparvier for de sa reion.]   (Riquer 1957: 344, ll. 73–75)

This may refer to the Conquest of the Sparrow-Hawk in *Erec,* or to an independent tale such as Chrétien refers to in *Erec* 21–23. In either case it shows
that material about Erec was circulating in the earlier of the two periods
here in question.

Whether *Erec* was composed after 1170 or after 1183, it is the earliest extant romance in verse devoted to the Arthurian ambiance, although a lay
about King Arthur written in England, Robert Biket's *Lai du cor* (Dörner
1907; but see Bennett 1975: xxii), may be still earlier. Other French romances preceded *Erec,* but they were devoted to figures and events taken
from classical antiquity: early versions of the *Roman d'Alexandre,* Benoît de
Sainte-Maure's *Roman de Troie,* the *Roman de Thèbes,* the *Roman d'Enéas,*
and perhaps others, such as the two romances by Gautier d'Arras, *Ille
et Galeron* and *Eracle,* composed between 1176 and 1184, and the Anglo-
Norman Hue de Rotelande's *Ipomedon.*

A native Welsh Arthurian prose tale, *Culhwch and Olwen,* however, precedes *Erec et Enide,* perhaps by more than a century, and scattered references to Arthur are found in earlier Welsh texts. But although Chrétien draws heavily upon Celtic lore, none of his narratives correspond to the substance of any work of Celtic literature surviving from before his time. This may be because his primary conduit for Celtic materials was Breton tradition. No substantial Breton literary text from before the fifteenth century has survived (Fleuriot 1987a: 21).

Chrétien claims to have read a book containing the story of the first part of *Cliges,* the tale of Alexandre and Soredamor, in the library of the cathedral of Saint-Pierre in Beauvais. Lucie Polak made a case for the book's containing an analogue to the Persian story *Vis and Ramin,* which includes love between the king's bride and his young kinsman, a talisman that renders the king impotent, and the kinsman's succession to the throne upon the king's death (Polak 1974). Whatever the nature of Chrétien's source, Claude Luttrell (1974: 33–45) has found analogies to elements of the plot of *Cliges* in a series of romances that have been, or could be, dated to the decade of the 1180s: Hue de Rotelande's *Ipomedon* (probably 1187–1188) and *Protheselaus* (probably the late 1180s), Aimon de Varenne's *Florimont* (dated to 1188), and the first revision of *Athis et Prophilias* (after 1186). These romances are set wholly or partially in the ancient Greek world. In many of the analogous passages and motifs, it is a question either of influence or of a common literary ambiance.

Attempts have been made to link *Cliges* to a contemporary political context. *Cliges* has three settings: Constantinople, Germany, and Britain. The details of Byzantine provenance in the romance are few, with the exception of the Greek cities Athens and Constantinople, the Greek personal names Alexandre and Alis (=Alexis), and the Greek-sounding names of Cliges's companions, such as Licorodé, Permenidos, Caron, and Neriolis. The Holy Roman Emperor, however, is found at Regensburg (Reinneborc, 2624; "Ratisbonne" in Modern French) and holds a court at Cologne. The duke of Saxony, whose name is never mentioned, resists the Greek emperor Alis's marriage with Fenice, whom the duke has been promised in marriage, and demonstrates his cowardice in single combat against the young Cliges. The Holy Roman Emperor Frederick I "Barbarossa" held a court at Cologne in June 1171 at which he received envoys from Constantinople who proposed that he marry his eldest son to the daughter of the Byzantine emperor, Manuel Comnenos. Henry the Lion, duke of Saxony and Bavaria, plotted against Barbarossa and impeded the marital arrangement with Byzantium until finally, at a diet held at Regensburg on June 24, 1174, negotiations with the Greeks failed. Henry the Lion refused to accompany his cousin Barbarossa on an expedition to Lombardy, where the emperor was defeated, missing, and rumored to be dead after the battle of Legnano at the end of May 1176. Contemporary chroniclers saw this refusal as the main cause of the rupture between Frederick and Henry (Munz 1969: 347). After Henry subsequently failed to appear at two of Frederick's courts, he was charged with treason and summoned to a judicial battle, but again did not appear. In January 1180, Frederick Barbarossa tried Henry the Lion in a feudal court and divested Henry of his duchies of Saxony and Bavaria.

Chrétien could have heard of the developing hostility between the emperor and Henry the Lion through his attachments to the court of Champagne. Count Henry the Liberal held nine small fiefs from Barbarossa and was an honorary prince of the empire. Barbarossa's wife, Beatrice, was the daughter of the titular duke of Burgundy, Renaud III. The pope was promoting the marriage of Barbarossa's daughter Agnes with the young prince Philip, destined to rule France as Philip II "Auguste," but the papal attempt fell through. The fact that Chrétien avoids citing the names of his German characters with the exception of the symbolic Fenice, "female Phoenix," whereas he uses Greek-sounding names as elements of local color for the Byzantine characters, raises the probability that he is making covert references to contemporary political relations in the Holy Roman Empire. In any event, the court of Champagne was anti-Guelf, and thus antagonistic to Henry the Lion, who was married to Matilda, daughter of Henry II of England. Anthime Fourrier settled on the year 1176 as the most likely time for Chrétien to have become aware of the hostile sentiments that divided Frederick Barbarossa and Henry the Lion (Fourrier 1950: 80), and thus as the most likely date for the composition of *Cligès.* One could equally well defend the proposition that Chrétien was impressed by Henry the Lion's deposition in 1180. In any case, if one believes that Henry the Lion's fate suggested to Chrétien the portrayal of an ignominious duke of Saxony, this could have happened at any time after the events, which would at best provide only a *terminus post quem.*

The same argument applies to an earlier stage of Byzantino-German relations that provides a parallel to the plot of *Cligès* even closer than the events of the 1170s (Misrahi 1959). Manuel, the younger surviving son of the Byzantine emperor John, took the throne in 1143 and married Berta, the sister of the Holy Roman Emperor Conrad III, but only after she had been raised in status by being declared the emperor's daughter by adoption. Henry the Proud, duke of Saxony, was the enemy of Conrad, his victorious rival in the imperial election of 1138. The parallels in *Cliges* involve a younger son, Alis, succeeding to the imperial throne of Constantinople and marrying the daughter of the Holy Roman Emperor, enemy of the duke of Saxony.

In line with his dating of *Erec,* Claude Luttrell has proposed a dating for *Cliges* in the following decade, around 1185–1187 (Luttrell 1974: 26–46).

As for Chrétien's reference to a source book in the library of the cathedral of Beauvais, the count-bishop of Beauvais from 1175 was Philip of Dreux, first cousin of Marie de Champagne, who was to accompany Count Henry the Liberal of Champagne on crusade in 1179 (Fourrier 1950: 81), so access to the cathedral library would not have posed a problem. The nature of the source Chrétien alleges is unknown, but it is likely to have included the character Fenice since her name, meaning "Phoenix," is perfectly appropriate to her fate in the romance—she is disinterred alive—but Chrétien says only that it is fitting because the phoenix is the most beautiful of birds and only one phoenix can exist at a time (2681–85). Consequently, the theme of the false death would also come from the source book.

In my opinion, *Philomena* was composed not long before *Cliges,* in which it is mentioned. The translation of the Ovidian tale contains a long disquisition on love of the type that one finds in *Cliges,* and whereas *Erec* betrays little influence from the Roman poet, *Cliges* certainly does. I see no reason to consider *Philomena* a piece of juvenilia. This view would place it in the period around 1175.

Chrétien's next two romances, *Yvain* and *Lancelot,* are linked in that reference is made three times in *Yvain* to the action of *Lancelot,* the first by the imprisoned Lunete (*Yvain* 3702–11), the second by the noble who is married to Gauvain's sister (3914–23, 3933–35), and the third by the narrator, who tells that the queen had returned from captivity but that Lancelot remained imprisoned in the tower (4734–39). This last is a detail unknown to the characters of *Lancelot,* who have no idea why Lancelot is absent from Arthur's court, and also corresponds to the episode during which Chrétien ceased composing his romance and gave it over to Godefroy de Lagny to finish. Since Gauvain is present in *Yvain* when the hero runs off as a madman to live in the woods and fights a duel against Yvain at the end of the romance, the entire plot of *Lancelot* takes place within the time limits of *Yvain.* It would appear on first analysis, then, that *Lancelot* precedes *Yvain.*

Basing himself first on the characters' apprehension of the boastful but ultimately incompetent nature of Keu, Arthur's seneschal (the highest court official) in *Lancelot,* which makes no sense unless the audience is aware that Keu has already acted flauntingly in *Yvain,* Fourrier made the case (1950: 83–85) that Chrétien began *Yvain* and interrupted it just before the episode of the daughters of Noire Espine (which begins at line 4697) to compose *Lancelot.* He would then have entrusted the completion of this romance to his collaborator when he returned to finish *Yvain.* But in fact, Keu also acts boastfully in *Erec* (3947–4071) and pays for it. Fourrier also argues that the reference to the tower in *Yvain* is not correct if one understands *Lancelot* already to have been completed when it was made, because when the queen returned from captivity, Lancelot was not yet imprisoned in the tower that Meleagant had caused to be built. David Shirt (1975, 1977) built on this inconsistency an elaborate hypothesis about the stages and rewrites in the composition of *Lancelot,* rejected by Evelyn Mullally (1984), who thought the reference was simply a mistake on the author's part.

That *Yvain* and *Lancelot* were composed around the same time is plausible, and Fourrier posits this time as the period 1177–1181, Luttrell as 1186–1189. In *Yvain,* the feast of St. John, June 24, is said to take place two weeks after Pentecost (664–67, 2087), which happened only twice in the second half of the twelfth century, in 1166 and in 1177, but this is not a determining argument because as a writer of fictions Chrétien would have been free, within the limits of plausibility, to arrange the calendar in accord with the needs of his narrative. A reference in *Lancelot* to knights who were not armed because they were *croisé* (5770)—that is, they bore the cross in anticipation of a crusade they had promised to undertake—again is not decisive. It is true that Philip of Flanders and many of his vassals are absent on crusade to the Holy Land between June 1177 and October 1178, that Henry II Plantagenet and Louis VII of France promise at Nonancourt on September 25, 1177, to undertake a crusade together, and that Count Henry the Liberal of Champagne goes on crusade from June or July 1179 to March 1181. An author writing about the past would, however, have only to conceive of crusading as a perennial phenomenon in order to refer to knights taking the cross at any period. Chrétien's reference to crusaders in the distant past when King Arthur lived is an anachronism in any case and does not depend on current crusading activities. And yet, as Luttrell points out, in late 1188, Count Philip of Flanders, Count Thibaut of Blois, and other nobles promised not to use arms against other Christians until they returned from what became the Third Crusade (Luttrell 1974: 30), producing a closer parallel to the wording of the passage in *Lancelot.* Fourrier dates

Yvain and *Lancelot* to the later 1170s or the very early 1180s. In keeping with his theory that Chrétien was influenced by the *Anticlaudianus* of Alan of Lille, Luttrell believes that Chrétien begain *Yvain* in 1186 or 1187, stopped to write *Lancelot* in 1187–1188, and returned to *Yvain,* finishing it in 1188 or 1189.

The patron of *Lancelot* was Marie de Champagne, identified in the first line of that romance as *ma dame de Chanpaigne.* Marie was of royal lineage, daughter of King Louis VII of France and his first spouse, Eleanor of Aquitaine. As Eleanor's child she was also the half-sister of the children of King Henry II of England: Henry "the Young King," Matilda (duchess of Saxony as the wife of Henry the Lion, until Henry's removal in 1180), Richard "Lion-Heart" (later Richard I of England), Geoffrey (duke of Brittany), Eleanor (queen of Castile), Joanna (queen of Sicily), and John (later king of England).

Marie's husband, Henry the Liberal, was the nephew of King Stephen of England and the great-grandson of William the Conqueror. Henry of Blois, his uncle, was from 1126 until his death in 1172 the abbot of Glastonbury and from 1129 the bishop of Winchester, both towns rich in memories of King Arthur—particularly Glastonbury. Henry of Blois officiated at the consecration of Thomas Beckett as archbishop of Canterbury (Fourrier 1960: 115). Henry the Liberal's sister, Adela, was queen of France as the second wife of King Louis VII, whom she married in 1160. From that union, which joined the lineage of Charlemagne through Adela with the lineage of Hugh Capet, was born Philip, the future King Philip II "Auguste," who was also Marie's half-brother. Her brother-in-law Guillaume "White Hands" occupied the most powerful ecclesiastical position in France as archbishop of Rheims from 1176. The count of Champagne was one of the lay peers of France, along with the counts of Flanders and Toulouse and the dukes of Normandy, Burgundy, and Aquitaine. These six and the count of Anjou were the highest feudal princes in France next to the king himself.

The court of Henry the Liberal and Marie welcomed men of letters. Among them was Master Nicolas of Clairvaux, author of sermons, letters, and sequences, as well as commentaries on the Psalms lifted from Hugh of St. Victor. Gautier d'Arras, a noble at the court of Flanders, dedicated his romance *Eracle* to Marie, her brother-in-law Thibaut V of Blois, and her son-in-law Baudouin, count of Hainaut (Raynaud de Lage 1976: 53, 61, 6523, 6528, 6530, 6559). Peter of Celle (d. 1183), bishop of Chartres, dedicated his *De disciplina claustrali* to Henry the Liberal. A Master Simon Capra Aurea, identified as a canon of Saint-Victor in Paris, wrote a 430-line poem in Latin for Count Henry on the Trojan War (Boutémy 1946). After Henry's death, Marie continued her association with authors, including the anonymous translator of Psalm 44, *Eructavit* (Jenkins 1909), and Evrat, from whom she commissioned a translation of Genesis into French (Grimm 1976). Evrat's work, more than twenty thousand lines long, was finished after Marie died in 1198. Two *trouvères* mention Marie in their poems: Gace Brulé, a knight, says that she asked him to sing (Benton 1961: 567; Dyggve 1951: 396, and discussion at 18–23, esp. 21), and Conon de Béthune, who was from Artois but was also a vassal of the count of Champagne, mentions her in "Mout me semont Amors" (Wallensköld 1921: 5). Andreas, a chaplain at the royal court and author of the renowned *Art of Courtly Love* (*De arte honeste amandi,* translated in Parry 1964), which was written in the mid-1180s and quotes a letter purportedly written by Marie, appears as a witness in one of Marie's charters. None of the authors associated with the sophisticated court of Champagne during the lifetimes of Henry and Marie approaches Chrétien in quantity of production, quality of writing, literary progeny, or influence.

An illustrious poet, the troubadour Rigaut de Berbezilh (ca. 1170–ca. 1210), in his poem "Tuit demandon qu'es devengud'Amors" (Varvaro 1960: poem IX, pp. 198–214), mentions Marie in the first *tornada* (envoi):

> Gay and worthy countess, of valiant reputation,
> you who have illumined Champagne completely,
> I want you to know the love and the friendship
> that I bear you, for I leave behind my soul and my sad heart.
> [Pros comtess'e gaia, ab pretz valen,
> que tot'avetz Campaigna enluminat,
> volgra saupsetz l'amor e l'amistat
> que·us port, car lays m'arma e mon cor dolen.]   (Varvaro 1960: 206)

The authenticity of this tornada and the identification of the countess with Marie are confirmed by Rigaut's editor, Alberto Varvaro (1960: 14–16, 213), but more definite evidence for a visit of Rigaut to the court of Champagne is lacking. Andreas Capellanus cites the countess's judgments in love cases and may have frequented the court of Champagne or even have been Marie's chaplain (Benton 1961: 378–82). Geoffroy de Villehardouin, who later composed a celebrated chronicle to defend his role in the Fourth Crusade, was her marshal in 1185.

Henry the Liberal died on March 16, 1181. Between that date and the majority of her son Henri in 1187, Marie was regent of Champagne and one of the ten or so most powerful nobles in France. Luttrell points out that

the form by which Chrétien refers to her in the first line of *Lancelot*, "my
lady of Champagne" (*ma dame de Chanpaigne*), is more appropriate to this
period when Marie was regent than to the time before Henri the Liberal's
death, when, for example, Gautier d'Arras refers to her in his *Eracle* as "the
Countess Marie, the daughter of Louis" (*la contesse Marie, fille Loëi*), a form
similar to that used in Latin documents of the earlier period (Luttrell 1974:
28). If *Lancelot* was composed in the period 1187–1188, Marie would have
been in her mid-thirties when she commissioned it, and playing this role
for a work whose theme was adultery would be less scandalous than when
she was a married woman. If it was composed earlier, as Fourrier conjectured, she would have been in her early thirties.

Marie's court was certainly a key point of contact between troubadours
composing in Occitan and trouvères composing in French, and since Chrétien is the earliest author of chansons written in the troubadour manner, he
may have absorbed elements of the troubadour ethic at the court of Champagne.

That Marie could read texts in French is indicated by Evrat, who also
mentions her library:

> . . . The countess of Champagne
> Who knew how to understand and read it
> Can select it from her book-cabinet.
> [. . . La contesse de Champaigne
> Ki bien lo sout entendre et lire
> Lo peut en son armaire eslire.]   (Cited in Benton 1961: 564n)

This skill is by no means to be taken for granted in the nobility of the period
(see Clanchy 1993: 251–52). Henry I and Henry II of England were reputed
to be learned (*litterati*), but King John is the first king of England who can
be shown to have owned a library (Clanchy 1993: 161). Whether Marie read
Latin is uncertain. Terry Nixon has found that more than half of the manuscripts containing French vernacular texts from before the early thirteenth
century also contain some Latin (Nixon 1989: 85), but women are less likely
than men to have been schooled in Latin.

Chrétien tells us that he wrote his *Perceval* for Count Philip of Flanders
(*Perceval* 11–13). Philip (1143–1191) was one of the most powerful and influential nobles in northern France and a patron of letters (Stanger 1957:
214–16). He had inherited the county of Alsace from his father, Thierry, and
he assumed the duties of count of Flanders in January 1168, although he
had in fact been ruling jointly with his father for a decade before. Through

his union with Elisabeth of Vermandois, he exercised hegemony over the Vermandois, including Amiens and Valois. The territory under his rule exceeded that of Louis VII in the Ile-de-France. Philip was instrumental in the short-lived reconciliation between Henry II of England and Thomas Beckett in 1170 and visited the saint's tomb at Canterbury in 1184. He also journeyed as a pilgrim to Santiago de Compostella in 1172 and to the Holy Land in 1177–1178. In addition to his role as vassal of the king of France, he was a prince of the Holy Roman Empire, a status to which Chrétien may be referring in *Perceval* 11–12 when he calls Philip "the most excellent noble / in the Holy Roman Empire" (*le plus prodome / Qui soit an l'enpire de Rome*).[4] From 1178, during the illness of Louis VII, he advised the king's son Philip, known to posterity as Philip II "Auguste," and attempted to influence him. At the new king's coronation on All Saints' Day 1179, Philip carried the royal sword in procession, and at the feast that followed he served as steward, a high honor. In 1180, he took the office of seneschal of the kingdom of France and knighted the young monarch on June 8, 1180, at a tournament held in Arras.

Champagne and Flanders were rivals for influence over the fourteen-year-old king. Philip II married Philip of Flanders's niece Isabelle of Hainaut in April 1180. The court of Champagne, allied in this case with King Henry II of England and with the young King Philip's own mother, Queen Adela, bitterly opposed this marriage for political reasons because it would weaken the royal family's strong ties with Champagne. Louis VII's daughters had both, after all, married members of the house of Champagne, as had Louis himself in his second marriage. Furthermore, Philip of Flanders had promised Isabelle to Henry, the young son of Henry the Liberal, and had also pledged his nephew, Baudouin of Hainaut, to Henry I's daughter Marie, a set of arrangements he renounced in March 1180. But not long thereafter Henry II arranged the treaty of Gisors on June 28, 1180, and Philip's relations with the king deteriorated, leading him to repair his relations with Champagne. On May 14, 1181, the *journée de Provins*, Philip offered another niece, Yolande of Hainaut, as Henry of Champagne's wife. Hostilities broke out between Philip of Flanders and the king in the fall of 1181, and Philip burned Noyon and besieged Senlis, continuing his campaign in 1182 until peace was arranged at La Grange Saint-Arnoul on April 11, 1182, lasting until November 1184.

In 1182, Philip of Flanders, a widower since the same month that Marie de Champagne had been left a widow by Henry's death, March 1181, proposed marriage to Marie. Philip sent emissaries to the Holy See in 1182 to ask for a dispensation to marry Marie, the second cousin of his deceased wife, Elisabeth of Vermandois, but withdrew his envoys suddenly in the autumn of 1183 and went on to marry Matilda of Portugal. In 1185–1186 the houses of Champagne and Flanders were at long last linked through the marriage of Baudouin de Hainaut and Marie, the young daughter of Marie de Champagne. Philip of Flanders took part in the Third Crusade in 1190 and died in June 1191 during the siege of St. John of Acre.

Two dates in the life of Philip of Flanders, his assumption of the title of count of Flanders and his death, allow the composition of *Perceval* to be situated between January 1168 and June 1191, but when in that long stretch of time? Rita Lejeune (1954; 1957: 95), emphasizing Chrétien's claim that his work was the best told "in royal court," proposed that it was begun while Philip of Flanders was regent, in 1180–1181, and that Philip's purpose in commissioning it was to provide his young charge Prince Philip, whose formation he was supervising, with the example of the young Perceval. Following Wilmotte and Frappier, Lejeune took another passage, the description of the commune of a town in an uproar (ll. 5878–6033), as an indication that Chrétien may have traveled into the lands ruled by Philip of Flanders, as this province was the site of several communal revolts. She noted that the revolts in Ghent, Saint-Quentin, Péronne, and Hesdin occurred in the years 1178 and 1179 (Lejeune 1957: 98). Fourrier pointed out, however, that the scene in Chrétien concerns not a communal revolt but, rather, the commune coming to what it believes is the assistance of its absent lord, and thus fighting in his interests. Lejeune proposed for the composition of *Perceval* the period just after Philip's return from the Holy Land, in October 1178, but before his relations with the house of Champagne turned bitter in the spring of 1180.

In his ties with patrons, Chrétien could not have moved easily between the house of Champagne and the court of Flanders until after peace was established between the two parties in June 1180, and an even more likely period is between May 1182 and the autumn of 1183, when Philip of Flanders was pursuing the project of marrying Marie. This was Fourrier's opinion (1955: 101). Luttrell places the composition of *Perceval* in 1189–1190. Chrétien could have accompanied his patron on the Third Crusade and died in the plague that struck the crusading army before Acre in June 1191.

The unfinished nature of *Perceval*, coupled with the fascination audiences obviously had for the Grail itself and the mystery of its nature, led four authors to write continuations. These are included in the manuscripts along with *Perceval*, typically without any break to indicate the point at which Chrétien ceased to write. The fourth continuator, Gerbert de Montreuil, mentions that Chrétien died before finishing his work.

> Chrétien de Troyes told us this,
> He who began the story of Perceval,
> But death, which overtook him,
> Did not let him carry it to conclusion.
> [Ce nous dist Crestiens de Troie
> Qui de Percheval comencha,
> Mais la mors qui l'adevancha
> Ne li laissa pas traire affin.]   (Mary Williams 1922–25: ll. 6984–87)

Luttrell places the cessation of Chrétien's work on *Perceval* in September 1190, when Philip of Flanders left on crusade (Luttrell 1974: 32). This is an attractive hypothesis, but unfortunately it must remain no more than that.

Lancelot is also unfinished, but there Chrétien evidently allowed Godefroy de Lagny to complete the work (see *Lancelot* 7102–12; I see no reason to doubt the truth of this statement). The reasons that motivated him to abandon his romance have been a matter of much conjecture: Having received the matter and the interpretation of the story from Countess Marie, did he find it not to his liking? One crucial consideration in this regard is that *Lancelot* is the only one of Chrétien's romances in which he presents an adulterous relationship without negative overtones. The question of Chrétien's attitude toward the material of *Lancelot,* a subject on which critics have differed widely (Bruckner 1986), is taken up in Chapter 3.

If Chrétien were to have composed all his works between 1183 and 1190, a relatively short span of time for the production of five major romances, the fact that no rival poets wrote other Arthurian romances during his lifetime would be somewhat more understandable. The reputation of his early works would hardly have had time to become established in literary circles before his death. On the other hand, the writing of five masterpieces in just seven years would be such an extraordinary achievement as to strain credulity. Giving weight to Aurelio Roncaglia's arguments that the senhal "Carestia" used by the troubadour Raimbaut d'Aurenga, who died in 1173, refers to Chrétien, I side with Fourrier in placing Chrétien's early activity in the 1170s but situate *Perceval* in the late 1180s and perhaps as late as 1190.

Godefroy de Lagny says he took up Chrétien's work from the point at which Lancelot was immured in the tower. Godefroy would probably have composed, then, from around line 6133 to the end, or about one-seventh of the entire text. We know nothing of Godefroy aside from what he tells us in the final lines of *Lancelot,* where he says he is a cleric, and although we are free to believe or disbelieve his statement that he finished the romance with Chrétien's consent, critics have overwhelmingly accepted the truth of Godefroy's claim. David Hult (1989b), however, has gone so far as to suggest that Godefroy is a fiction invented by Chrétien to dissociate himself from problems of closure in *Lancelot.* That Godefroy's continuation of *Lancelot* has been accorded a different status from the continuations of *Perceval,* always printed separately from the base romance, is probably justified on the grounds that his work was carried out with Chrétien's consent.

GUILLAUME D'ANGLETERRE

One other romance has been ascribed by some to Chrétien de Troyes, *Guillaume d'Angleterre,* but others have opposed this attribution.[5] In the prologue to this work the author names himself twice as "Crestiiens," yet without further qualification. He claims that the story can be found at the monastery of St. Edmond (Suffolk, England).

Guillaume d'Angleterre is the tale of a king of England living in Bristol who gives away his wealth and leaves the kingship after hearing a heavenly command. He goes into exile, accompanied by his wife, Gratienne. Near the beginning of the journey, the queen gives birth to twin boys. In a series of encounters with traveling merchants, Guillaume, Gratienne, and the boys are separated. The twins are raised by merchants and eventually make their way to the court of the king of Caithness, who makes them knights. Guillaume finds employment with a rich burgher in Galloway and prospers as a merchant. Gratienne contracts a chaste marriage with a knight, an old widower who leaves her his castle and estate. Eventually the characters' paths cross, leading to recognition, reunion, and restoration as the royal family of England.

Although it presents itself as the work of Chrétien and its linguistic characteristics, including dialectal traits, do not differ significantly from those of Chrétien de Troyes (see Holden 1988: Introduction), *Guillaume d'Angleterre* is an inconsistent narrative, following in part the conventions of the saint's life, in part those of the *roman d'aventures,* clumsy in its handling of motivation. It is unworthy of the mature Chrétien de Troyes and unmentioned among the early works cited in the prologue to *Cliges.* The author of *Guillaume d'Angleterre* was perhaps the enigmatic Rogers *li cointes* (meaning probably "the capable" or "the elegant"), whom the epilogue claims told the tale and who would have invoked the name of Chrétien—suspiciously, the

very first word of the romance!—in an attempt to lend his story the weight
of authority. Or perhaps the author's real name was Chrétien, but I do not
think he was Chrétien de Troyes. Accordingly, *Guillaume d'Angleterre* is not
treated in this volume.

THE SONGS

The songs of the trouvères are extant in songbooks, medieval anthologies
that transmit the songs of many poets. Two songs by Chrétien de Troyes
have survived: "Amors tençon et bataille" in two songbooks, and "D'Amors,
qui m'a tolu a moi" in twelve. Both belong to the genre of the *chanson,* the
love song whose author adopts a stance addressing himself to a lady or
speaking as if to be overheard by her. Other songs are ascribed to Chrétien de Troyes in the trouvère songbooks, namely "De joli cuer chanterai,"
"Quant li dous estez decline," and "Joie ne guerredons d'Amors," but these at-
tributions have been rejected by the only scholar to have studied the songs
in all their aspects, Marie-Claire Zai (1974).

In "Amors tençon et bataille," the poetic persona complains of Love (a
feminine personification in medieval French texts), whose champion he
has become but who shows him no pity. He is willing to suffer by taking
on all comers but is fearful, for despite his suffering, he is not inclined to
revolt. None but the courtly can learn about Love, but she wants to charge
entry to her fief, forcing the aspirant to abandon reason and moderation. A
fickle heart cannot learn about Love either, but the poet is steadfast, to the
point that his harm is her benefit. To enter her fief, he has exhausted his
moderation and abandoned reason with no prospect of reneging. There is
no escape, so he must, like a hawk, patiently molt his feathers even if his
constant heart does not change. His struggle with Love will not end soon
unless she takes mercy on him. The dominant metaphor in this song is the
poet's vassalic service to an abstraction that stands, by metonymy, for his
lady. Like most trouvère poems in the genre of the chanson, this text plays
on a limited range of thoughts in allusive ways. But its ultimate, if implied,
aim is to persuade the lady of the poet's good faith so that she will love him.
The poem is composed of six full stanzas, rhyming two by two (the troubadours' *coblas doblas*) and a half-stanza envoi repeating the rhymes of the
last four lines of stanza 6.

"D'Amors, qui m'a tolu a moi" plays for six stanzas upon the same metaphoric keys, but in a slightly more complicated rhyme scheme, although

also in coblas doblas. The poet complains that Love does not want him in her service, although she has ravished him away from himself. He submits willingly, but he sees those who commit treason against her attaining their joy while he is failing. Love should not abandon her own if she wants to convert her enemies. The poet sends her his heart, which is no favor to her because it is hers in any case. Addressing her as his lady, he asks her rhetorically if she is grateful to have him, anticipating that she only puts up with him. Yet he asks her to show him mercy, because he cannot serve another. Never did he drink of the potion that poisoned Tristan, but his pure heart and sincerity make him love even better than Tristan because he was never forced to love. Only what his own eyes have seen constrains him to love. He exhorts his own heart to remain faithful to her, for what is obtained with difficulty and despite its scarcity will be all the sweeter when it comes. He would easily find mercy if it were in his compass, for he, who does not serve Love frivolously, has asked his lady repeatedly for it. Aurelio Roncaglia has analyzed the polemical relationship between this song and "No chan per auzel ni per flor" of the great troubadour Raimbaut d'Aurenga, to which it is a response, as well as Bernart de Ventadorn's "Can vei la lauzeta mover." All three songs evoke the legend of Tristan and Ysolt, in counterpoint to which Chrétien composed *Cliges*. Roncaglia has proposed for Chrétien's poem, convincingly, a date shortly after 1171–1172, when the two songs by troubadours were composed (Roncaglia 1958: 128). Marie-Claire Zai has remarked that, among Chrétien's romances, the language of Chrétien's songs most closely resembles that of *Cliges,* composed around 1176.

Composing love songs of this type already in the early 1170s, Chrétien is the earliest known trouvère to have composed in the troubadour manner, and the two troubadours with whom he is associated, Bernart de Ventadorn and Raimbaut d'Aurenga, are among the most accomplished practitioners of the art of song.

LANGUAGE

Medieval French was not a standardized language, so all texts contain features that can be identified with one or another of the dialect regions of France. Dialects are not spoken within neatly defined geographical limits but, rather, are made up of a series of characteristic sounds and forms—reflected in spelling—and vocabulary that are associated with certain areas.

By studying medieval texts that circulated locally, primarily charters in which propertied people granted privileges or made donations, scholars have arrived at a fairly adequate idea of what sounds, forms, and words were typical of the various regions.

There are, however, several complicating factors. The first is that charters written in French are available in quantity only from the thirteenth century on, and even then not in all regions. Second, beginning in the late twelfth century a literary language slowly developed that incorporated features from several forms of regional speech. The third consideration is that, as a literary work was copied, the scribe tended to introduce features from his own dialect, and as this process continued through several generations of copying, successive layers of scribal language could intrude into the text. As a result, most texts reveal a mixture of dialect traits from various regions. Philological theory posits that the dialect features of the language of the author of a poem of substantial length can be recovered through a careful study of the rhyme words in particular, because scribes are less likely to alter these. Any alteration in a word in line-end position would require a corresponding change in the word with which it rhymes.

By studying the rhymes of Chrétien de Troyes, a series of scholars, beginning with Wendelin Foerster (1884: xlvii–lxxv) and continuing with T. B. W. Reid (1942: xvi–xxii) and Brian Woledge (1986: 17–49), have identified characteristic features of the language in which Chrétien composed his poems. Following a common editorial practice of the period in which he was working, Foerster imposed a uniform dialect orthography in his text, which Reid used in his edition.

Analysis of Chrétien's rhymes shows a number of features that are typically found in champenois, the dialect of Champagne, although most are shared with eastern (Lorraine, Burgundy) and northern (Picardy) dialect regions, too, as one would expect, given the central geographical position of Champagne and the fact that a transdialectal literary language was being formed in this period. This conclusion leads us to think that Chrétien came from Champagne, possibly (though not necessarily) from Troyes itself. He associates Troyes with his name in only one place, and he may well have located there to be in the same town as one of the sites of the court of Henry the Liberal and Marie. If the interpretation of the epithet Gois as "inhabitant of Gouaix" is correct (see "Dating the Romances," above), then Chrétien would have come from a village close to the town of Provins, locus of another of their courts.

LATIN AND FRENCH SOURCES

Chrétien read Latin. His claim to have rendered into the vernacular the commands of Ovid and the art of love, undoubtedly the Roman poet's *Remedia amoris* and his *Ars amatoria,* make this all but certain (pace Vitz 1990 and 1999: 93). He probably derived his paradox that rare love is preferable to abundant love from line 541 of the *Remedia amoris:* abundance takes away love (*copia tollet amorem*). The text of his *Philomena* refers to such figures of ancient civilization as Plato (131), Homer, and Cato (131–32). In the description of Cliges (*Cliges* 2720–26), the counterexample of Narcissus is invoked, which Chrétien would have known from the *Metamorphoses* or the lay *Narcisse* (from the period 1165–1175). Lancelot's love is said to be greater than that of Piramus, "if that is indeed possible" (*Lancelot* 3803), a reference that could be based on the *Metamorphoses* or on *Pirame et Thisbé* (ca. 1160). Intimacy with themes from Ovid is seconded by references to the canonical author Macrobius (*Erec* 6730, 6733), who wrote a commentary on Cicero's *Dream of Scipio.* Three times Chrétien refers to specific sources: the tales that professional storytellers told about Erec, son of Lac (*Erec* 19–22), the book in the collection of Saint-Pierre de Beauvais from which he took the story of Cliges (*Cliges* 20–23), and the book about the Grail that Philip of Flanders gave him (*Perceval* 66–67). The last two would have been written sources.

Chrétien was probably educated in a school attached to an abbey or a cathedral such as the episcopal schools found at Chartres, Paris, and Troyes. He may have been a cleric, at least in minor orders. As any cultivated person of this period would have been able to do, Chrétien refers to such biblical characters as Abel, Noah, Abraham, Esau, Jacob, David, Absolom, and Solomon. He invokes Samson as a model of courage (*Cliges* 3508). His works are marked by frequent use of rhetorical tropes and figures that he would have learned from reading in the canon of *auctores* 'authorities', ancient authors who were the basis of the twelfth-century school curriculum.

Schooled in Latin literature, Chrétien may have been familiar with the ancient texts transmitting the tales of Troy and Thebes and the founding of Rome: the Latin narratives of Dares the Phrygian and Dictys the Cretan, Statius's *Thebaid,* Virgil's *Aeneid.* In *Cliges,* Alis is persuaded to come to a peaceful agreement with his brother by the ominous example of Eteocles and Polinices (2494–95), enemy brothers in Statius's *Thebaid.* Mabonagrain's lady is said to be more lovely than Lavinia (*Erec* 5883) and Helen

of Troy (*Erec* 6336). Cliges tells his lover that she will be received in Britain more joyfully than Helen was in Troy when Paris led her there (*Cliges*
5234–35). Fenice's nurse Thessala boasts that she knows more magic than
Medea (*Cliges* 2985), reference to whose powers is found in a number of ancient authors. Chrétien views Alexander the Great as an example of wealth,
power, and largess (*Erec* 2266, 6665, 6676, *Cliges* 6619), but also as a man
marked by vices (*Perceval* 14, 58–59), and he takes Alexander's horse Bu-
cephalos as an equine paragon (*Lancelot* 6780). On Enide's saddle is carved
the story of the *Aeneid:*

> How Aeneas came from Troy,
> How Dido received him in her bed
> In Carthage with great joy,
> How Aeneas deceived her,
> How she killed herself on his account,
> How Aeneas then conquered
> Laurentum and all Lombardy
> And Lavinia, who was his lady friend.
> [Coment Eneas vint de Troie,
> Coment a Cartage a grant joie
> Dido en son lit le reçut,
> Coment Eneas la deçut,
> Coment ele por lui s'ocist,
> Coment Eneas puis conquist
> Laurente et tote Lombardie
> Et Lavine, qui fu s'amie.]   (*Erec* 5331–38)

In *Perceval* (9059), Queen Ygerne expresses the wish that Gauvain should
marry her granddaughter as Aeneas did Lavinia.

Knowledge of these stories and characters from classical antiquity could
have been gleaned from readings in classical and medieval Latin literature. It probably derives as well, however, from adaptations, fairly recent
in Chrétien's period, of ancient tales into the vernacular, in the series of
poems that constitutes the "matter of Rome the great," namely the *Roman de
Thèbes* (ca. 1150–1155), the *Roman d'Enéas* (ca. 1155–1160), Benoît de Sainte-
Maure's *Roman de Troie* (ca. 1160–1165), *Pirame et Tisbé* (1160–1165), and *Narcisse* (from around 1165–1175, lost but known from a reference). Vernacular
versions of the legend of Alexander the Great were available in the *Roman
d'Alexandre:* an Occitan version by Alberic of Pisançon early in the century,
then an anonymous version in French decasyllabic verse from around 1160,
followed by versions by Eustache, Lambert le Tort, Alexandre de Bernay,

and Pierre de Saint-Cloud. Luttrell maintains that in certain details, Chrétien's *Cliges* reflects the influence of Alexandre de Bernay's *Alexandre,* composed between 1182 and 1190 (Luttrell 1974: 34–35).

Chrétien also knew the literature of his contemporaries. In addition to
references to the legend of Tristan and Ysolt, of which he says he himself wrote a version (*Cliges* 5) and in opposition to which he composed his
Cliges, he refers to other literary characters. The Apoloine of *Philomena* 175
is the hero of *Apollonius of Tyre,* a very popular romance in Latin of which
a lost French version is thought to have been written around the middle
of the twelfth century. Although most of his references are to learned literature, Chrétien also alludes to the *Chanson de Roland:* to Roland in *Yvain*
3236, to Ganelon in *Cliges* 1072, and to Roland's sword Durendart in *Yvain*
3235. He refers as well to five pagans who appear in chansons de geste:
Thiébaut l'Esclavon, Saracen king in the *Prise d'Orange, Foucon de Candie,*
and a number of other songs of the William cycle; Opinel, who is either
a Saracen mentioned in the late works *La Mort Charlemagne* and *Gaufrey*
or, more likely, Otinel, eponymous hero of a chanson de geste; Fernagu, a
Saracen in the *Entrée d'Espagne* and *Floovant* (all three Saracens mentioned
in *Erec* 5770–71); the Saracen king Ysoré, who plays a role in the *Moniage
Guillaume* (*Lancelot* 1352); and Forré, another Saracen king figuring in a lost
song about the capture of Noples but whose name is incorporated into the
idiom "to avenge Forre" (*venger Forré, Yvain* 595).

Belief in Arthur as a historical king is ascribable to Geoffrey of Monmouth's spectacularly influential *History of the Kings of Britain* (ca. 1138),
the work first responsible for presenting Arthur to a non-Celtic public and
for representing him as a monarch rather than merely a leader of lesser
stature. This history was popular in its own right—Julia Crick (1989) has
repertoried 215 extant manuscripts. It was soon also translated into vernacular languages for the benefit of those who could not read Latin: into
French by several writers, including Wace, whose work is known as the
Roman de Brut (Arnold 1938–40; Arnold and Pelan 1962; Weiss 1999), and
into Welsh in several versions (Roberts 1991). Wace's *Roman de Brut* was in
turn translated into English by Layamon (Brook and Leslie 1963–78; Allen
1992; Miller 1998).

Geoffrey, who calls himself Galfridus Monemutensis (Geoffrey of Monmouth, a town in the Welsh marches that was probably his place of birth), is
named as a witness in charters from Oxford dated from 1129 to 1151 and also
in the agreement of Westminster between King Stephen and his soon-to-be
successor Henry Plantagenet in 1153. He died around 1155. Geoffrey twice

uses of himself the term *magister* in charters, suggesting that he taught, perhaps in Oxford at the College of St. George, of which he may have been an Augustinian canon. Late in his life he was ordained a priest and consecrated bishop of St. Asaph. He once refers to himself as Galfridus Arturus, which suggests that his father's name was Arthur. That he was of Breton origin, perhaps descending from one of the many Bretons who came to Great Britain along with William the Conqueror or in his wake, is suggested by the preference he shows for the Breton branch of the kings of Britain from which Arthur springs, as well as by the currency in Brittany of the names Galfridus and Arturus (Lloyd 1942).

Although he is obviously drawing on Gildas's *Destruction of Britain* (*De excidio Britanniae*) and the *History of the Britons* (*Historia Brittonum*) of the writer known as "Nennius" (see Dumville 1975–76), Geoffrey claims as an important source "a very ancient book in the British language that, from Brutus the first king of the Britons to Cadwallader son of Cadwallo, put forth the acts of all of them continuously and in order in very beautiful phrasings" (*Britannici sermonis librum uetustissimum qui a Bruto primo rege Britonum usque ad Cadualadrum filium Caduallonis actus omnium continue et ex ordine perpulcris orationibus proponebat,* Wright 1985: 1). According to an epilogue that appears in some manuscripts, this book was brought *ex Britannia* (Wright 1985: 147; lit. "from Britain"), probably in this case from Wales (see Short 1994). The nature and very existence of the source book, supposedly given to Geoffrey by Walter, archdeacon of Oxford and provost of the College of St. George, has long been debated. "British language" could refer to Welsh, Cornish, Breton, or for that matter the language of the Welsh living in Strathclyde. According to Gerald of Wales, Cornish and Breton were mutually intelligible languages in the twelfth century (J. E. Caerwyn Williams 1991: 254; translated in Thorpe 1978: 231; see also Bromwich 1983: 48).

But Geoffrey appears to have had access to many sources, both written and oral, whose strands he wove into a coherent account of the kings of Britain from Brutus, great-grandson of Aeneas, to Cadwallader, after whom the rule of Britain passed to the Saxons. The idea of carrying British genealogy back to Brutus was already in the *History of the Britons* ascribed to Nennius, and Geoffrey certainly drew upon Bede's *Ecclesiastical History of the English People,* Gildas's *Destruction of Britain,* and early genealogical materials (see Piggott 1941 and Bartrum 1966). Just under a quarter of the history is devoted to Arthur, whose reign is marked not only by success against the Germanic newcomers but also by an invasion of the European continent and victories over Rome. It is cut off in the year 542 by the battle of Camlan and the king's removal to the Isle of Avalon. The story of Merlin and his prophecies is the subject of book 7, which circulated as an independent work as early as 1135, and Geoffrey wrote a verse life of Merlin later, around 1150 (Clarke 1973). The *History of the Kings of Britain* is dedicated in its oldest form to powerful patrons: Robert, earl of Gloucester (d. 1147), bastard son of King Henry I of England and partisan of the Empress Matilda and her son Henry of Anjou (later Henry II of England), and Waleran, count of Meulan (1104–1166). One manuscript bears dedications to King Stephen of England and Robert of Gloucester (see Thorpe 1966: 39–40, n. 7). The *Prophecies of Merlin,* according to Geoffrey, were written at the request of Alexander, powerful bishop of Lincoln, whose diocese included Oxford. The *Life of Merlin* is dedicated to Robert de Chesney, bishop of Lincoln (Clarke 1973: 36–37). Geoffrey probably had in mind to provide a heroic past for the kings of Britain with which the Norman dynasty could associate itself (Gerould 1927).

There is no reason to believe that Chrétien knew Geoffrey's *History of the Kings of Britain* directly, and very little to indicate that he knew its earliest surviving complete French version, the *Roman de Brut* (contrary to Köhler 1974: 11), completed in 1155 by the Norman Wace, who was a native of Jersey and became a canon of the cathedral of Bayeux. That the *Roman de Brut* is found in a number of manuscripts that contain other histories or works on national origins argues that many, perhaps most, medieval readers considered it to have a factual value on the same level as that of the other works (Blacker 1994: 177). Wace also wrote three religious poems early in his career and later the *Roman de Rou,* which traces the genealogy of the dukes of Normandy back to Rollo (O. F. *Rou*). The long but unfinished *Roman de Rou* was written under the patronage of Henry II and Eleanor of Aquitaine, and this may also have been the case with the *Roman de Brut,* which according to Layamon was presented to Eleanor (but see Miller 1998: 97n). To judge by a few resemblances in content and style, above all in descriptions, Wace might have provided for Chrétien a model of narrative about King Arthur written in Old French and a framework for the courtly Arthurian world (see Pelan 1931). At times the likeness appears more specific, as in the rebellion of Angres of Guinnesores (Windsor) in *Cliges,* which may have been inspired by Mordred's revolt in Wace. Wace repeats Geoffrey's statement that Guinevere was living with Mordred, which may have influenced Chrétien's tale about Guinevere's adultery with a knight close to Arthur in *Lancelot.* A description of commercial activities in the town of Escavalon resembles the description of Carleon in the *Brut.* Chrétien's evocation of the state of Britain after the death of King Uther (*Perceval* 442–49, 8740–47) corresponds in sense to Wace's account of the same period (Sturm-Maddox 1984). The only passage from Wace that is generally agreed to show his influence on Chrétien, however, is *Yvain* 575–78, in which Calogrenant recalls how he felt like a fool in returning from his combat at the fountain, echoing a passage not from the *Roman de Brut* but from Wace's *Roman de Rou,* lines 6396–98 (Holden 1973, 3: ll. 6373–98). For further information on the lack of Wace's influence on Chrétien, see page 201, below.

Chrétien's Celtic sources, largely coming to him through oral tradition, are treated in Chapter 5: Celtic Myth, Folklore, and Historical Tradition.

MANUSCRIPTS AND TEXTS

Of new developments in the study of Chrétien de Troyes, none is more promising than the advances in codicology and textual criticism, fields that leave behind them a lasting benefit long after more ephemeral interests have begun to assume a look of quaintness.

Two single-volume editions of Chrétien's works appeared in the same month in 1994. The first was under the general editorship of Daniel Poirion in the elegant Bibliothèque de la Pléiade, *Chrétien de Troyes, Œuvres complètes* (Paris: Gallimard), with texts edited by a team of scholars: Peter F. Dembowski (edition and translation into modern French of *Erec et Enide*), Philippe Walter (edition of *Cliges* and translations of that work and *Yvain*), Karl D. Uitti (edition of *Yvain*), Anne Berthelot (editions and translations of *Philomena, Guillaume d'Angleterre,* and the two songs), and Daniel Poirion (editions and translations of *Lancelot* and *Perceval,* and introduction to the volume). Although all five of the major romances are edited from a codex whose readings had been made available in the past—Paris, Bibliothèque nationale, fonds français 794, copied by the scribe Guiot—the widely used editions of that manuscript in the series entitled *Les Romans de Chrétien de Troyes d'après la copie de Guiot (Bibliothèque nationale, fr. 794)* edited by Mario Roques (Roques 1952b, 1958, 1960; Micha 1957; Lecoy 1973–75—all in the Classiques Français du Moyen Age series) were uneven in faithfulness to the manuscript and in correction of scribal errors, as well as in their annotations. The Pléiade volume furnishes extensive introductions and notes for all the texts. The completion of the Poirion project marked the first time that a medieval author had been the subject of an entire volume in the prestigious Bibliothèque de la Pléiade, extensively available and widely read. It brought Chrétien and his works to the attention of the cultivated French reading public more than ever before.

The other 1994 edition of the complete works was *Chrétien de Troyes, Romans* (Livre de Poche, Classiques Modernes, La Pochothèque; Paris: Librairie Générale Française), under the general direction of Michel Zink. This edition also brought together a team of scholars, consisting of Jean-Marie Fritz (edition and translation of *Erec et Enide*), Charles Méla (edition and translation of *Lancelot* and *Perceval* and, with Olivier Collet, of *Cliges*), David F. Hult (edition and translation of *Yvain*), Marie-Claire Zai (edition and translation of the songs), and Olivier Collet (translation of *Philomena* printed with the edition established in 1909 by Charles de Boer). *Guillaume d'Angleterre* is not included in this edition. With the exception of *Lancelot,* the texts are from manuscripts other than Guiot's copy. The editions of the five romances had appeared as separate volumes in the Lettres Gothiques series. Unfortunately, neither in the collected publication nor in the single-romance volumes are the texts provided with more than an occasional expository note.

Another series of editions appeared in the Garland Library of Medieval Literature, providing texts and English translations of *Erec* (Carroll 1987), *Yvain* (Kibler 1985), *Lancelot* (Kibler 1981), and *Perceval* (Pickens 1990). Based on the Guiot manuscript, these texts are a great improvement over those that appeared under the general editorship of Roques. The latter are noninterventionist, placing their faith in an extremely competent but sometimes creative scribe and correcting only obvious errors. A more interventionist approach, which attempts to establish a critical text with the help of readings from several manuscripts, is taken in the editions of *Cliges* (Gregory and Luttrell 1993) and *Perceval* (Busby 1993b) published under the patronage of the Eugene Vinaver Memorial Trust.

As is the case with other textual traditions of medieval French literature, editors are returning to sounder methods developed primarily by German scholars of the nineteenth and early twentieth centuries that enable us to approach more closely the texts as Chrétien wrote them. Although absolute certainty in this domain is rarely within the realm of possibility, trust in the text of one medieval scribe, such as results from the single-manuscript method espoused by Joseph Bédier in a study (1928) whose wide influence was unjustified, is an expedient that is indefensible when several manuscript versions are available. The pioneering editions of Wendelin Foerster and Alfons Hilka (*Erec:* Foerster 1890 and 1896; *Cliges:* Foerster 1884 and

Foerster and Hilka 1901; *Lancelot:* Foerster 1899; *Yvain:* Foerster 1887; *Perceval:* Foerster and Hilka 1932, 1966) hold a fund of editorial wisdom for those working on Chrétien's texts. For the reader who is interested in learning more about the history of textual criticism as practiced on medieval French literary texts, Alfred Foulet and Mary B. Speer's *On Editing Old French Texts* (1979) provides a valuable orientation.

The most ambitious and finest collaborative achievement in recent scholarly studies of Chrétien is the two-volume set *Les manuscrits de Chrétien de Troyes / The Manuscripts of Chrétien de Troyes,* edited by Keith Busby, Terry Nixon, Alison Stones, and Lori Walters (Faux Titre, 71–72; Amsterdam: Rodopi, 1993). In addition to providing a complete repertory of the medieval textual sources for Chrétien's works, with authoritative codicological descriptions and a series of excellent studies, this publication makes available more than four hundred photographic plates and figures of the manuscripts themselves. In contrast to the methodless "new philology," this work is an achievement that combines sound philological principles with the concerns of art historians and represents a genuine advance in studies of Chrétien de Troyes. The datings of Chrétien's manuscripts in the present book are based on Terry Nixon's invaluable study (1993c).

Chrétien's five romances have survived into the modern period in some forty-three medieval manuscripts, fragments, and excerpts (listed and described in Nixon 1993a and 1993c).[6] Of these forty-three witnesses, fourteen are either excerpts that are deployed in other contexts or fragments, leaving twenty-nine complete or substantial manuscripts in which modern editors can read Chrétien's romances.

In the twelfth and thirteenth centuries, romances or episodes from them were sometimes performed by jongleurs, as can be seen from the list of topics ascribed to jongleurs performing in the wedding scene of the mid-thirteenth-century Occitan romance *Flamenca* (Duggan 1989). But the primary mode of existence of the romance as we define it—a verse narrative of fantasy and adventure written in octosyllabic rhyming couplets—was in manuscript copies. Typically twelfth-century authors would compose their works on wax tablets, boards of wood covered with a thin layer of colored wax that were written on with a sharp stylus of bone or other hard material. The contents of the tablets were then transferred to the more durable medium of parchment, after which the wax was smoothed over for subsequent reuse (Rouse and Rouse 1989; Duggan 2000). When book production moved out of the monastic scriptorium and into a secular context, bookmakers and booksellers set up shops near major cathedrals and in the vicinity of the schools that would soon form the nucleus of the universities. In addition to making school texts, such shops would receive commissions from wealthy patrons who wished to have books made, either in Latin or in the vernacular language. Works would often first be copied in quires of six, eight, or ten parchment folios, which would be bound to form a book (L. *codex,* plural *codices*). The existence of autonomous units within the volumes makes it obvious that those interested in buying books could specify particular combinations of works to fit their needs. Booksellers employed scribes, rubricators, and illuminators, and they often carried out the work of copying, decorating, and binding themselves (Rouse and Rouse 1990). Books were expensive to produce and were acquired mostly by the nobility, by clerics, and by prosperous burghers.

The number of surviving codices containing works by Chrétien varies from romance to romance: for *Erec et Enide,* seven manuscripts, five fragments, and an excerpt; for *Cliges,* eight manuscripts, three fragments, and an excerpt; for *Lancelot,* seven manuscripts and a fragment; for *Yvain,* nine manuscripts, three fragments, and an excerpt; and for *Perceval,* fifteen manuscripts and three fragments. On the basis of this evidence, one might conclude that in the Middle Ages *Perceval* was Chrétien's most popular work, and that was probably the case. The survival of medieval manuscripts, however, owes as much to chance as to the number of copies that originally existed, many of which perished under a variety of circumstances. The most perilous times were, in France, in the sixteenth century during the Wars of Religion and in the eighteenth during the French Revolution, and in Britain during the dissolution of the monasteries in the sixteenth century. Certainly the romances of Chrétien that had the greatest influence on subsequent literature were *Lancelot* and *Perceval.* Major plot elements of both were incorporated into the French prose romances composed in the third or fourth decade of the thirteenth century and known collectively as the Vulgate Cycle or the Lancelot-Grail Cycle: the *Story of the Holy Grail (Estoire del saint graal), Merlin,* the *Lancelot* proper, the *Quest for the Holy Grail (Queste del saint graal*), and the *Death of King Arthur (La Mort le roi Artu).*

No extant manuscript containing Chrétien's romances is contemporary with the author himself. The earliest manuscript dates from the extreme end of the twelfth or the beginning of the thirteenth century, the Tours codex of *Cliges* (Bibliothèque municipale 942; Nixon 1993c: 18–19), which contains no other text. Somewhat later, in the first half of the thirteenth century, two other manuscripts were copied each containing only Chrétien's

Perceval: Clermont-Ferrand, Bibliothèque municipale et interuniversitaire 248,[7] first quarter of the century, and Florence, Biblioteca Riccardiana 2943, first half of the century. In this early period, within a half-century or so of Chrétien's authorial activity, French literary works tended to be copied one, sometimes two, at a time into codices of small or medium format without illuminations, which is the case with all three of these manuscripts. They are likely to have been produced for nobles with relatively meager economic resources.

The Annonay fragments (in private hands, the property of M. Boissonnet in Serrières, France), twenty-six complete and partial large-format folios containing *Erec et Enide* (2 ff.), *Cliges* (15 ff.), *Yvain* (8 ff.), and *Perceval* (1 f.), are from the same period. The scribe's dialect is champenois. Patricia Stirnemann dates the production of the manuscript to which the Annonay fragments belonged to between 1205 and 1220 and on the basis of their decoration includes them in the "Manerius" series produced largely in Champagne between around 1195 and around 1235 (Stirnemann 1993: 205–6). This style is found in a manuscript of the Bible copied by the scribe Manerius (Paris, Bibliothèque Sainte-Geneviève 8–10), hence its name. It is impossible to say, however, whether works by other authors were in the Annonay manuscript as it was originally constituted. If that manuscript also included *Lancelot,* it was one of only three to have contained all five of Chrétien's romances.

The other two, both large-format codices in the fonds français of the Bibliothèque nationale in Paris, are the famous fr. 794, which was copied by the scribe Guiot of Provins in Brie in the second quarter of the thirteenth century, and fr. 1450, copied by an unnamed Picard scribe most likely in the same period.

Guiot's copy is, more than any other, the manuscript upon whose texts Chrétien's editors have based their editions.[8] On f. 105 is found the following colophon (plate 2), referring to *Yvain:*

> He who wrote it is named Guiot.
> In front of Notre-Dame-du-Val
> is his permanent dwelling.
> [Cil qui l'escrist Guioz a non.
> Devant Nostre Dame del Val
> est ses osteus tot a estal.]

The purpose of this colophon, with its mention of the location of Guiot's shop in front of the collegial church of Notre-Dame-du-Val in the faubourg of Fontanet just outside the wall of Provins (Roques 1952a: 189–90), was no doubt primarily to attract other clients. Provins was one of the sites of the renowned fairs of Champagne, and merchants and rich patrons were likely often to pass Guiot's way. Working in Provins, within sixty kilometers of Troyes and ten kilometers of Gouaix, Guiot, although perhaps half a century after Chrétien, would have spoken a dialect not very different from what Chrétien himself spoke. He was a careful and intelligent scribe, although this latter quality has also caused problems, as he often attempted to improve Chrétien's text. The Guiot manuscript is tricolumnar and was copied in three units. The first part contains *Erec et Enide, Lancelot,* which opens with an historiated initial depicting Marie de Champagne (plate 1), *Cliges, Yvain,* and the three-line colophon. The second section consists of the romance *Athis et Prophilias* (Hilka 1912–16), also known as *Le Siège d'Athènes,* a romance of antiquity written in the early thirteenth century by a certain Alexander, perhaps Alexander of Bernay, and more than 20,700 lines long in this version. The third division contains Benoît de Sainte-Maure's *Roman de Troie,* Wace's *Roman de Brut, Les Empereurs de Rome* by the Champenois cleric Calendre (ca. 1219, see Schmidt-Chazan 1979), and Chrétien's *Perceval* followed by its first two continuations. This substantial manuscript was probably commissioned by a patron who had an interest in ancient history, especially the matter of Britain (Schmidt-Chazan 1979: 75); it is likely that most medieval readers believed Arthur to have been a historical figure, and they made little distinction between classical times and Arthurian antiquity. The historiated initial portraying Marie de Champagne is the only illustration, and the decoration is confined to initials. Guiot's text of the *Roman de Brut* was chosen by Ivor Arnold for his edition of the Arthurian section of Wace's work (Arnold and Pelan 1962).

The anonymous scribe of ms. 1450 began his manuscript with the *Roman de Troie* of Benoît de Sainte-Maure and the *Roman d'Enéas,* then proceeded to copy Wace's *Roman de Brut.* Chrétien's five romances were inserted in the middle of the *Brut,* after the point at which Wace mentions the wonders and adventures that tellers of tales have recounted about Arthur and that took place during a twelve-year period of peace. The scribe continues (plate 3):

> But what Chrétien testifies
> You can hear at this point without delay.
> [Mais ce que Crestïens tesmoigne
> Porrez ci oïr sanz aloigne.]

After this line begins *Erec et Enide,* minus the twenty-six lines of its prologue, followed by the *Perceval,* likewise without its prologue, and the *First
Continuation, Cliges, Yvain,* and *Lancelot.* Modifying the end of this last romance, the scribe writes:

> Lords, if I were to say more,
> It would not be good to say.
> [Segnor se jo avant disoie,
> Ce ne seroit pas bel a dire.]

Then he adds the line:

> On this account I return to my matter.
> [Por ce retor a ma matire.]

He then goes back to the text of the *Roman de Brut* and copies it to the end
(see Walters 1985; Huot 1987: 27–32; Putter 1994). The final work in the
manuscript is Herbert's *Dolopathos,* a version of the *Seven Sages of Rome*
(Leclanche 1997). A large foliate initial begins each work. The manuscript
contains a few drawings of humans, animals, and dragons connected to initials.

Manuscript 1450 and Guiot's volume are both large-format codices, and
the selection of works in each reveals an emphasis on history from the
ancient Greeks to the Arthurian world. The amount of copying that each
represents could have been financed only by a patron with substantial economic resources, probably a member of the high nobility (Nixon 1989).
John Benton (1981: 43) thought the patron of Guiot's codex might have been
Blanche of Navarre, countess and regent of Champagne from 1201 to 1222,
who died in 1229.

A more likely possibility along the same lines, raised by Patricia Stirnemann (1993:210), is that Guiot copied his codex for Blanche's son, Thibaut IV "le Chansonnier" of Champagne (1201–1253, r. from 1222), a trouvère of great distinction, who did homage to the king for the county of
Champagne in 1214 and became king of Navarre in 1234. Benton comments
that the third part of the Guiot manuscript is aptly constituted for the period
1226–1227, when Thibaut of Champagne was in a state of hostilities with
King Louis VIII and was even suspected of having poisoned him, all while
contracting an alliance with the duke of Brittany and flirting with the English. The third section of the Guiot manuscript contains works by two
writers associated with England, Benoît de Sainte-Maure and Wace, as well
as a history of Rome by a critic of Thibaut I of Lorraine who was the enemy

of Blanche of Navarre, and Chrétien's *Perceval*, commissioned by the old
enemy of Philip Augustus, Count Philip of Flanders. Manuscript 1450 may
also have been copied for Thibaut IV. He was a cultivated prince (see Grossel 1994), and that he had a taste for ancient history as well as for Celtic
lore can be seen by the references in his lyric poetry to Jason, to Julius
Caesar and Pompey, and to Tristan (Wallensköld 1925, 1: 4, 5: 16, and 23: 34,
respectively). In the serventois "Deus est ensi conme li pellicanz," which
Wallensköld assigns to the period 1236–1239, Thibaut refers directly to an
episode recounted in Wace's *Roman de Brut:*

> We would do well to look, in history,
> At the battle between the two dragons,
> As it is found in the book of the Britons,
> Which caused the castles to fall down.
> That's this world, which it's appropriate to overthrow
> Unless God makes the battle end.
> It was necessary to call upon the intelligence of Merlin
> To guess what was going to happen.
> [Bien devrions en l'estoire vooir
> La bataille qui fu des deus dragons,
> Si com l'en trueve el livre des Bretons,
> Dont il couvint les chastiaus jus cheoir:
> C'est cist siecles, qui il couvient verser,
> Se Deus ne fet la bataille finer.
> Le sens Mellin en couvint fors issir
> Por deviner qu'estoit a avenir.]   (16: 31–38)

The *Roman de Brut* figures in both the Guiot manuscript and ms. 1450.

Of the four continuations of *Perceval* (all in William Roach's great edition, 1949–83), the first two, both anonymous, were written before the end
of the twelfth century and can be read with *Perceval* in sequence. Neither
reaches a conclusion. The *Third Continuation,* written in the first half of the
thirteenth century by Manessier for Jeanne, countess of Flanders, grand-
niece of Philip of Flanders and granddaughter of Marie de Champagne, is
a sequel to the *Second Continuation* and does provide the narrative with an
ending. Gerbert of Montreuil, also author of the *Roman de la Violette,* wrote
the *Fourth Continuation,* an interpolation between the plots of the second
and third continuations. Two other authors, both anonymous, wrote prologues to *Perceval,* entitled *Bliocadran* and *L'Elucidation* (Thompson 1931; on
the *Elucidation,* see Meneghetti 1987–88). Seven manuscripts, all copied in
the century following 1250, are devoted exclusively to *Perceval* and its con-

tinuations or prologues, including the deluxe volume Bibliothèque nationale, fonds français 12577 (plates 5, 6, and 10), from the second quarter
of the fourteenth century containing *Perceval* and the first three continuations, and the extensively illustrated Montpellier, Bibliothèque interuniversitaire, Section Médecine H249 (plate 7; *Perceval,* the *First* and *Second Continuations,* Manessier's *Third Continuation,* fourth quarter of the thirteenth
century).[9]

From the first quarter of the thirteenth century, however, Chrétien's narratives begin to appear in compilations of works by various authors, and
nineteen manuscripts containing romances by Chrétien fall into this category, the Guiot codex and ms. 1450 among them.

The earliest of these miscellanies is London, British Library Additional
36614, which contained initially *Perceval,* the first two continuations, and
the *Vie de Ste. Marie l'Egyptienne,* each copied by a different scribe. The
various parts of this manuscript may have been copied and decorated in
separate workshops (Stirnemann 1993: 203, basing herself on the pen-work
decoration), but the *Perceval* itself, ff. 1–87, is decorated in the "Manerius"
style. This style is associated with Champagne and the scribe's dialect is
champenois. The *Bliocadran* prologue was inserted into the *Perceval* at a
time close to or contemporary with that at which the initial works were
copied. The juxtaposition of the life of a female saint and Chrétien's romance with its appurtenant texts would suggest that the manuscript was
originally designed for a woman who might have read the *Perceval* as a religious quest. Patricia Stirnemann believes that Additional 36614 may have
been copied for or given to Jeanne, countess of Flanders, who, as mentioned above, was the granddaughter of Henry the Liberal and Marie of
Champagne (Stirnemann 1993: 209–12). Additional 36614 includes the first
two continuations: Did reading it inspire Jeanne to commission Manessier
to write the *Third Continuation?*

Another manuscript that might have been compiled at the request of a
female patron, if one is to follow the assumption that women wished to read
about exemplary women with whom they could identify and whom they
could emulate, is Paris, Bibliothèque nationale, fonds français 1374, from
the mid-thirteenth century. This manuscript includes, in addition to *Cligès*
with its prominent female characters Soredamor and Fenice, the chansons
de geste *Parise la duchesse* (unique) and *Girart de Vienne* (in which Roland
is betrothed to Aude), the *Roman de la Violette* by Gerbert de Montreuil,
Florimont by Aimon de Varennes, the *Venjance Nostre Seigneur,* and *Placidas* (unique), which tells the legend of St. Eustace. Four scribes appear to

have copied this codex, one the *Roman de la Violette,* one *Florimont,* one part of the *Placidas,* and the fourth the rest of the texts. The *Cliges* of this manuscript was the base text for Foerster's edition (1884).

The selection of works in several manuscripts seems to point primarily to male patrons and readers. Paris, Bibliothèque nationale, fonds français 1420, for example, from the middle (Nixon 1993c: 37–39) or the third quarter (Gasparri, Hasenohr, and Ruby 1993: 113) of the thirteenth century, adds to *Erec et Enide* and *Cliges* two folios containing the narrative of the battle between Hector and Achilles from the *Roman de Troie.* Escorial, Real Biblioteca del Monasterio M. III. 21, copied in the third quarter of the thirteenth century, has only *Lancelot* and the chanson de geste *Fierabras.* Two other codices from the last quarter of the thirteenth century include the chanson de geste *Garin de Monglane,* Princeton University Library, Garrett 125, with *Lancelot, Yvain,* and the *Chevalerie de Judas Machabee,* illuminated (plate 9), and the finely illustrated Paris, Bibliothèque nationale, fonds français 24403 (plate 8), with *Erec et Enide* and *Ogier le Danois,* copied in Arras (Stones 1993: 253–56).

An important early compilation is Bern, Bürgerbibliothek 354, from the second quarter of the thirteenth century. This manuscript is made up of three sections, the first of which contains four dozen *fabliaux,* a number of *dits,* the *Folie Tristan,* and two romances, *Le Chevalier à l'épée* and *La Mule sans frein.*[10] The second unit is a copy of the *Roman des sept sages de Rome* in prose, and the third consists of Chrétien's *Perceval.* In contrast to Add. 36614, this manuscript has a decidedly secular cast to it (see the detailed description of contents in Rossi 1983). Charles Méla based his edition of *Perceval* (1990) on its text.

Only one surviving manuscript containing a work by Chrétien was copied in medieval England, even though the aristocracy of that country spoke French well into the thirteenth century and read it as late as the fourteenth century, and in spite of the theory that the patron of *Erec et Enide* might have been a noble in the Plantagenet orbit. That manuscript is London, College of Arms, Arundel XIV, localized by Thiolier (1989, 1: 67–69) and Busby (1993b: xviii) to the vicinity of Hereford. The manuscript is in three units copied in different periods, the oldest of which dates to the mid-fourteenth century and contains a number of works of a historical nature, including the *Roman de Brut,* Gaimar's *Estoire des Engleis, Le Lai d'Haveloc,* Pierre de Langtoft's *Chronique, La Lignée des Bretons et des Engleis* (from Brutus to Edward II), and *Perceval* (the only copy of that work in Anglo-Norman dialect). Like the Guiot manuscript and fr. 1450, both of which also contain the *Roman de Brut,* this codex must have been made for a patron with an interest in history and genealogy, and the historical works it contains are ordered according to the sequence of the events they recount (Micha 1939: 265). Presumably *Perceval,* read in this context, would have been considered a historical work.

A codex that also appears to reflect a historical inclination, among other interests, is Paris, Bibliothèque nationale, fonds français 375, an extensive collection in large format, composed of two parts that originally were separate. The second part, copied in an atelier in Arras, four columns to the page, by six scribes between 1289 and 1317, concerns us here, as it transmits *Cliges* and *Erec et Enide,* as well as one of the two extant copies of *Guillaume d'Angleterre.* The manuscript contains Wace's *Roman de Rou* and a genealogy of the counts of Boulogne ending with Robert II (r. 1278–1317), who is characterized as still alive. Other works that may have been viewed as primarily historical are Benoît de Sainte-Maure's *Roman de Troie,* the *Roman de Thèbes,* and the *Roman d'Alexandre,* and Alexandre de Bernay's *Athis et Prophilias.* But poems that we view as principally of entertainment value are also represented—namely, *Floire et Blanchefleur, Blancandin,* Gautier d'Arras's *Ille et Galeron, Amadas et Ydoine,* and *La Chatelaine de Vergi*—along with works of a religious nature: Gautier de Coinci's *Miracle de Théophile, L'épître farcie de saint Etienne,* several miracles of the Virgin Mary, and three works by other authors from Arras—the *Congés* of Jean Bodel and the *Vers de la Mort* and *Louange de Notre-Dame* of Robert le Clerc. The nature of the texts makes it difficult to characterize inclusively the contents of this well-known manuscript (but see Huot 1987: 21–27).

A mid-thirteenth-century manuscript containing three romances of Chrétien, *Yvain, Lancelot,* and *Cliges,* Paris, Bibliothèque nationale, fonds français 12560, acephalic, opens with the last column of a penitential in prose whose explicit identifies it as *Li Ver d'aumone* (for the probable contents of the opening gatherings, see Hult 1998: 26–27). The Foerster edition of *Lancelot* (1899) and the Méla edition of *Cliges* (1994a) are based on this manuscript.

The largest group of manuscripts, on the basis of contents, comprises those that contain secular narratives in verse, for the most part romances.

A codex that contains three of Chrétien's romances and eight others, including unique copies of *Le Bel Inconnu* by Renaut de Bâgé (also known as Renaut de Beaujeu), the anonymous *Hunbaut,* and the *Merveilles de Rigomer* attributed to a certain Jean de Chantilly, is Musée Condé 472, from around the middle of the thirteenth century. This manuscript also contains *L'âtre périlleux,* Guillaume le clerc's *Fergus,* Raoul de Houdenc's *Vengeance Ragui-del, Perlesvaus* (a prose romance), and the *Roman de Renart.* The scribe of *Fergus* identifies himself as Colin le Fruitier. Most of the works begin with a new quire, raising the likelihood that they were copied as separate units and then combined as a book after the buyer had chosen them from among other possible texts. The romances by Chrétien are *Erec et Enide, Yvain,* and *Lancelot.*

Paris, Bibliothèque nationale, fonds français 12576, fourth quarter of the thirteenth century, combines the Perceval cycle (*Perceval* and the continuations, copied without a break) with two works by the Renclus de Moiliens, *Le Roman de Miserere,* from the turn of the thirteenth century, and *Le Roman de Carité* from the 1180s, moralizing works whose purpose is to chastize the worldly and lead them to salvation (Van Hamel 1885). Since the poems by the Renclus begin in a new quire, the Perceval cycle may originally have been intended to stand alone (Busby 1993a: 52). The editions of *Perceval* by Roach (1959) and Busby (1993b) are based on this manuscript, which shares with Bibliothèque nationale, fonds français 6614, the distinction of having contained all four continuations of *Perceval.* Both of these manuscripts were in fact copied by the same scribe from the same exemplar (Busby 1993a: 53–55) in Arras (Stones 1993).

Other codices fit into this category of Chrétien manuscripts containing secular verse narratives. Vatican City, Biblioteca Apostolica Vaticana, Regina Latina 1725, from the turn of the fourteenth century, contains, in addition to *Lancelot* and *Yvain,* Jean Renart's *Guillaume de Dôle* (unique copy) and Raoul de Houdenc's *Meraugis de Portlesguez.* From the same period, Paris, Bibliothèque nationale, fonds français 1376, holds Aimon de Varenne's *Florimont* and *Erec et Enide* and is the base manuscript for the Fritz edition of the latter (1992b, 1994), and Bibliothèque nationale, fonds français 12603 has the *Chevalier aux deux épées, Yvain,* the *Roman d'Enéas,* Wace's *Roman de Brut,* Adenet le Roi's *Enfances Ogier,* the chanson de geste *Fierabras,* Marie de France's *Fables,* and several fabliaux. Bibliothèque nationale, fonds français 1433, a small deluxe illustrated manuscript from the first quarter of the fourteenth century (plate 4), contains *L'âtre périlleux* and *Yvain* and is the basis for the Hult edition of *Yvain* (1993) and the object of a study by Lori Walters (1991). Turin, Biblioteca Nazionale Universitaria L. I. 13, dating from the second quarter of the fourteenth century and damaged in the famous fire of 1904, includes, along with *Cliges, Eracle* by Gautier d'Arras, *Sone de Nansai, Richars li biaus,* and two romances of Jean de Condé, *Le blanc chevalier* and *Le Chevalier a la mance.*

Far removed from the life situations and mentalities of medieval readers as we are, it is often difficult or impossible for us to uncover the motivations behind the selection of works one finds in these manuscripts and their production and purchase. We tend to classify medieval literary works in genres some of which, such as the chanson de geste or certain types of lyric poetry, were medieval realities but others of which were not. In particular, there is no medieval genre term for what we call a "romance" in verse, that is to say, in this period, a sustained narrative in rhyming couplets often containing elements of fantasy. French writers of romance themselves typically call their works "tales" (*contes: Erec* 19, 6950; *Cliges* 8, 45; *Lancelot* 7110, *Perceval* 63, 66) or "stories" (*estoires: Erec* 23; on the meaning of *estoire,* see Damian-Grint 1997). The term *romanz* simply meant any work written in the vernacular language, as opposed to Latin (*Cliges* 23; *Lancelot* 2, 7101, *Yvain* 6805; *Perceval* 8). But whereas modern readers take the greatest pleasure in reading romances, chansons de geste, and saints' lives, medieval readers who had no formal schooling also loved to read translations from the Latin, whether of biblical or secular texts (see Nixon 1989: ch. 4), bestiaries, aviaries, lapidaries, commentaries on religious texts, wisdom literature, and other types of nonnarrative literature that receive vastly less attention from modern scholars, proportionately, than they got from the reading public in the late twelfth century.

The early thirteenth century is a crucial period in the history of reading. Certainly in the twelfth century it was common to have a lector read a book out loud to an audience many of whom were presumably unable to read. A classic depiction of such a scene is, in fact, in Chrétien's *Yvain,* at the point at which the hero and his train have entered the castle of Pesme Avanture. The knight sees, in an orchard, a girl reading to her parents a *roman,* a book written in the vernacular language:

> He saw leaning on his elbow
> A noble man who was lying
> On a silk cloth, and a maiden
> Was reading before him
> From a romance, I don't know whose.
> And to listen to the romance
> A lady had also come to lean down,
> And it was the girl's mother.
> And the noble man was her father.
> And they could well take very great
> Pleasure in seeing and listening to her,

For they had no other children.
And she was not yet seventeen years old.
[Apuyé voit deseur son coute
Un prodomme qui se gesoit
Seur .i. drap de soie, et lisoit
Une puchele devant li
En un rommans, ne sai de cui.
Et pour le rommans escouter
S'i estoit venue acouter
Une dame, et estoit sa mere.
Et li prodons estoit sen pere.
Et se pooient esjoïr
Mout de li veoir et oïr,
Car il n'avoient plus d'enfans.
Ne n'avoit pas .xvii. ans.]   (*Yvain* 5358–70)

A similar scene of a lector reading a work aloud to a noble audience is found
a century or so later in a passage of the romance *Hunbaut* (coincidentally
in Chantilly, Musée Condé 472, along with *Yvain*) from the third quarter of
the thirteenth century, in which Keu and Sagremor arrive at the castle of
Gaut Destroit during a reading:

The girl got up to greet them
As soon as she saw them coming.
She had with her six maidens
And as many as ten knights;
They listen to beautiful lines from a romance.
The girl was having it read aloud.
[La pucele est contre els levee
Si tost conme venir le(s) voit.
O li sis puceles avoit
Et chevaliers desi a dis;
D'un roumant oënt uns biaus dis.
La pucele le faissoit lire.]   (Winters 1984: 3048–53)

If we are to conceive of the hostess as having also commissioned the copying of the romance, presumably it would be for the purpose of this type of
public reading.

That readers also read vernacular works in private, however, is indicated
by the miniatures and decorative features in manuscripts of this period,
the expense of which would be justified only if they were executed for the
gaze of wealthy readers.[11] The richness of illustrations in some of the manu-

scripts containing Chrétien's works can quickly be appreciated through consultation of the plates and figures in volume 2 of *The Manuscripts of Chrétien de Troyes* (Busby et al. 1993). Terry Nixon, reviewing thirty-one manuscripts containing literary works in French verse from the twelfth and early thirteenth centuries, found physical evidence of heavy use, suggesting that these were "personal books, meant for reading and part of the daily life of the seigneury for whom they were probably made" (Nixon 1989: 164). Most are of modest size and thus easily portable, with one or two columns of text to a page, and contain a single work (Nixon 1989: 165). In late antiquity and the early Middle Ages, even reading in private appears ordinarily to have been accompanied by the sound of the reader's voice pronouncing the words, but by the eleventh century those who read in private seem to have done so commonly in silence (Saenger 1972).

Chrétien's works have not attracted constant interest from ordinary readers, scholars, or even antiquarians since they were first composed. David Hult (1998) has pointed out that Chrétien appears almost to have disappeared from readers' ken by the middle of the fourteenth century, when his romances ceased to be copied. The first postmedieval copy of a complete romance, *Yvain,* appeared in 1838 as an appendix to Lady Charlotte Guest's *The Mabinogion, from the Llyf Coch o Hergest and Other Manuscripts.* Hult interprets the chronological distribution of manuscripts containing Chrétien's romances as evidence that the peak of his popularity in the Middle Ages was in the first half of the thirteenth century and that by the following century, his name had fallen into oblivion, only to be revived with the advent of philological interests in the nineteenth century.

However a particular person living in the twelfth or thirteenth century received a romance by Chrétien, each heard or saw it through a filter of medieval experience and with a set of expectations formed by the surrounding society. I will take up one by one a series of areas of experience and expectation that I believe were essential aspects of the phenomenon of reading or listening to the romances of Chrétien de Troyes in that period.

Chapter 2

Kinship and Marriage

Relations among kin bore an importance in Chrétien's society that far outweighs the significance of all but the parent-child relationship in American and Western European societies. Not only were members of kinship groups considered responsible for one another's actions, but political alliances often depended on the extension of such groups through arranged marriages. Understanding the ramifications of kinship and marriage in northern France in the second half of the twelfth century is essential for an appreciation of Chrétien's romances.

The organization of French society in the second half of the twelfth century is idealized as a threefold division: the nobility, the clergy, and the peasants, those who ruled and fought, those who prayed, and those who worked. Into this theoretical schema the burghers and merchants intruded, especially in contexts in which they abounded, such as the thriving commercial towns of Troyes, Provins, Lagny, and Bar-sur-Aube, in which the fairs of Champagne were held.

The nobility preserved its prerogatives in part through a system of inheritance that privileged male over female and firstborn over younger children. If a nobleman had a son, that child would inherit from the father, and only if there were no surviving male heirs would the estate pass to a female child. Younger male children and all female children had to seek advancement by other means. Male primogeniture did not apply in Occitania, where Roman law had long favored the equal distribution of holdings among the children (Lewis 1965: 123, 170–71, 275–76). Fiefs, which in the early Middle Ages tended to be granted for the life of the holder only, came to be hereditary, first for the high nobles around the beginning of the tenth century, then for castellans about a century later, and finally around 1030 among the lower aristocracy. A heightened consciousness of the identity and circumstances of one's ancestors spread through noble society in roughly the same chronological steps, corresponding to the power of lineage and inheritance to determine wealth and status through the male line (Duby 1977).

The term *family* has no exact equivalent in the Middle Ages. Latin *familia*, like Old French *famille*, designates not a couple living with their children and perhaps their parents or other close relatives, but all the dependents, whether related by kinship or not, living under the authority of a head of household, along with the property of that household (Herlihy 1985: 3). A basic living group consisted of two or three *ménages*, each comprising a couple and their descendants, and sometimes took in up to seventy people (Bloch 1949, 1: 68, 370–71, 391). The children would live in the household, even after marrying, and sometimes continued to live together after their parents' deaths, sharing their possessions. The term *mesnie* is used in medieval French texts to designate those serving a lord in the immediacy of his dwelling.

Marriage tended to be an arrangement through which kin groups could seek to increase their wealth and power. A woman would take with her into a marriage a dowry granted by her kin, normally movable goods and sometimes slaves, but rarely real estate. Women did come endowed with their aristocratic status, however, and the combination of nobility and wealth attracted many of the younger sons who were excluded from inheritances and wished to marry up.

In addition, women brought the influence of their biological kin, which was especially useful for the male offspring of the marriage. In particular, a special relationship known as the avunculate existed between a man and his maternal uncle. According to Roland Carron, this relationship is widely mentioned until the beginning of the thirteenth century, when it begins to cede before the father-son relationship. The level of compensation to be paid by a murderer's kin makes it clear that the order of responsibility was: brother, uncle, nephew, cousin. Sons and grandsons are not mentioned (Carron 1989: 9–10). That the ties between a man and his nephew on his sister's side are especially close in both romance and epic of this period is well recognized (see, for example, Carron 1989: 6–10). One reason for the closeness of this relationship was that a man could be more certain that his sister's son was indeed related to him than he would be of his brother's son, whose wife might well have conceived as a consequence of an adulterous act. Another possibility is that the intimacy of this relationship is the remnant of a period in which matrilineality prevailed over patrilineality.

In any case, the avunculate is mentioned as far back as Tacitus, who at the end of the first century remarks in *Germania,* chapter 20, that among the Germans the sons of sisters are as much honored by their uncles as by their fathers and that in certain tribes the relationship between uncle and sister's son was even closer.

During the twelfth century, emphasis came to be placed more and more on the paternal lineage at the expense of the maternal, as families began to conceive of themselves as patrimonies (Brundage 1987: 227; Goody 1983: 103–56). The avunculate thus became less and less important in society, although literature does not reflect this consistently.

Among the characteristics of the kin group in twelfth-century France that distinguish it from kin groups in most Euro-American societies today is collective responsibility. Members of a kin group were responsible for one another's conduct. If one of the kin incurred shame, the others felt some obligation to act so as to remove the blemish from the group. The literary *locus classicus* for the expression of shame extending to the kin group is found in the Oxford version of the *Chanson de Roland,* commonly dated to the end of the eleventh century. There Roland defends his action of refusing to sound his ivory horn by stating that he would not wish his kin to incur shame from such an action:

> "May it not please the Lord God
> That my kin be blamed on my account."
> ["Ne placet Damnedeu
> Que mi parent pur mei seient blasmét."]　　　　　(Short 1997: 1062–63)

Roland justifies his action even though not sounding the horn condemns to death both him and the warriors entrusted to his protection.

Legal sources give ample evidence of the sharing of responsibility for actions committed within the kin group, although the details vary considerably from place to place. In the *Coutumes de Beauvaisis,* which discusses customal law of the region around Beauvais in the late thirteenth century, Philippe de Beaumanoir recognizes that people once had the right to take vengeance on behalf of relatives to the seventh degree of kinship, but he restricts this to the fourth degree, in view of the then recent reduction in the prohibited degrees of consanguinity for marriage, for the boundary of kinship should be the same in respect to vengeance and to consanguinity (Salmon 1899–1900: §1686). Beaumanoir reports that a noble is considered to be in a state of enmity when members of his kin group (in Medieval French his *amis*) commit offensive actions even if he was not present when the actions were committed, unless he is prepared to reject those who did commit them (Salmon 1899–1900: §1684; see also Akehurst 1992: 615–16). Further, when peace is made between the leaders in a situation of private war, it must be observed between the kin groups that are involved on either side (Salmon 1899–1900: §1678).

According to Marc Bloch, in 1260 a knight, Louis Defeux, took a certain Thomas d'Ouzouer to court for having attacked him. Thomas's sole defense was that a nephew of Louis had assaulted him and he was merely taking vengeance, having waited the prescribed forty days before doing so. Louis got no profit from his legal action, because the judges sided with Thomas and the principle of kinship solidarity, in this case between uncle and nephew (Bloch 1949, 1: 197).

Kinship solidarity was thus an essential aspect of the ethics of personal relations. Members of a kin group were expected to respect one another's property and not to make predatory war on one another. Further, relatives were expected to come to one another's assistance in time of need, whether such assistance was military, financial, or moral. In the case of proposed marriage, the ensemble of the lineage was consulted, and marriages that took place without the kin's consent could result in sanctions.

Conversely, kin could be held responsible for the actions of other members of the lineage at least well into the thirteenth century and, in many regions, beyond that. Such responsibilities were often satisfied by gifts, payments, or acts of homage. Although it should not be taken as a model for other areas, the *Livre Roisin* from around 1290 specifies the fines according to the degree of kinship: at Lille, for example, in compensation for a death the killer's brother was expected to give twenty *sous,* the uncle or nephew fifteen, the first cousin ten, the second cousin five, and the third cousin two sous and six *deniers,* with proportional amounts specified for maiming (cited in Carron 1989: 19). Likewise, kin out to the level of cousins could bring cases for compensation to court if one of their own was wronged. Vengeance was a matter of kin, and it was exacted, sometimes reciprocally over a period of generations as each kin group considered itself injured beyond reason or simply resented the punishments meted out. The blood feud (L. *faida,* O. F. *faide*) that resulted was one of the scourges of medieval society, although as time went on, and particularly in the thirteenth century, peaceful means for resolving differences became available to supplant private warfare.

A renowned case of vengence involved Count Philip of Flanders, the patron of *Perceval.* One day in 1175, Philip surprised his wife in the company of a knight, Gautier de Fontaines, whom the count caused to be beaten with swords and staffs and hanged by the feet with his head immersed in a cesspool until he died. Although Gautier's offense, adultery or attempted adultery with the wife of his lord, was of the highest order of gravity under feudal law, his kin avenged his death by attacking and ravaging Philip's lands.

Because members of a lineage were obligated to defend each other, it was sometimes deemed necessary to prevent kin from exercising undue influence in one another's favor. Thus the *Très Ancienne Coutume de Bretagne* forbids first cousins and those of closer kinship from testifying in one another's law cases, except when small sums were at issue, and extends the prohibition in cases of inheritance to the fourth degree of kinship (Planiol 1896: §100).

In literary texts, this attitude toward kinship solidarity extended beyond questions of strict legal responsibility. As Gauvain tells Guiromelant, if he were to love a girl or a lady, he would also love and serve her entire lineage (*Perceval* 8774–76).

Kinship responsibilities were considered to extend as far as one's cousins and their spouses. Cousins are next to brothers in the eyes of the emperor in *Eracle* by Gautier d'Arras, a contemporary of Chrétien:

> Or l'aime tant li empereres
> con s'il li fust cousins u freres.
> [Now the emperor loves him
> as if he were a cousin or a brother.]   (Raynaud de Lage 1976: 1135–36)

First cousins, *cousins germains*,[1] descended from common grandparents, were under canon law linked in the same degree of consanguinity as were nieces and nephews with their uncles and aunts (Carron 1989: 11). In *Guy de Warewic* (second quarter of the thirteenth century), the duke of Saxony deems himself obliged to avenge the death of his first cousin in a tournament, even though it resulted from a legitimate and honorable joust. The duke thus places his own life in jeopardy (Ewert 1932–33: ll. 847–53). According to the *Très Ancienne Coutume de Bretagne,* from the beginning of the fourteenth century, when a crime is committed against a person, it is committed against first cousins and closer relatives, all of whom have the right to demand justice (Planiol 1896: 139, 142). First cousins and those more closely related were exempted from the prohibition against aiding a person who was *forbanni,* banished for legal cause. The *Très Ancienne Coutume de Bretagne* explains clearly the reason for this exception:

Outlaws will be pursued as banished, except by first cousins male and
female and those of closer kin, who are not obliged to shame themselves
and their own blood, for if they shame their cousins and their aforesaid
blood, they shame themselves, for by birth they are of the same flesh and
blood according to custom when they are of such close lineage.

[Les mefferants seront poursuivis comme les forbannis, excepté cousins germains, cousines germaines et dedenz, qui ne sont pas tenuz
à eulx et leur sang honnir, quar se ils honnissent leur cousin et leur
sang dessurdiz, ils honnissent eux-mêmes, quar par nature, ils sont une
meisme char et sang par coustume quant ils sont si près du lignage.]
(Planiol 1896: §110)

Carron (1989: 13) believes that such provisions once extended to any degree
of cousinage but that the *Très Ancienne Coutume de Bretagne* is attempting to
restrict somewhat the extent of the practice. He further observes (14) that
to kill one's cousin would be to destroy the feudal edifice: not only would
the rest of the kin feel threatened in their persons and possessions, but
vassals would be reluctant to continue to serve a lord who showed himself
capable of committing such an outrageous crime in violation of the expectations of society. In other regions, however, attempts were made from the
middle of the thirteenth century to prevent evildoers from taking refuge
with their kin. At the higher levels of the feudal aristocracy, other interests
played stronger roles, since marriage joined many of the great lineages in
kinship.

How far did the kin group extend? The *Summa de omnia facultate* defines parricide as killing one's father, mother, grandparent, brother, sister, brother-in-law, cousin, aunt, wife, son-in-law, or *nourris,* that is, those
brought up in one's household, often nephews (cited in Carron 1989: 16). In
order to head off the temptation of royal officials to intervene in disputes
on the side of their relatives, Louis IX forbade his seneschals and bailiffs
from marrying anyone in the administrative district of the bailiff, and he
extended this prohibition to kin of the officials, including their children,
brothers, sisters, nephews, nieces, and cousins (*Regestrum Curie Francie,*
101, cited in Carron 1989: 12). The kin group ranged, then, as far as one's
cousins and their spouses, although the degree of cousinage to which it extended seems to have been undefined and indefinite. To these degrees of
physical and matrimonial kinship must be added the legal and moral kinship one felt with those brought up in fosterage in one's own household,
the nourris.

The degrees of consanguinity were calculated differently under canon law and civil law. Under canon law, a person was considered to be in the first degree of kinship with his or her parents, siblings, uncles and aunts, and children. The second degree of consanguinity took in one's grandparents, great-uncles and great-aunts, first cousins, nieces and nephews, and grandchildren. Great-grandparents, second cousins, great-nephews and great-nieces, and great-grandchildren were related to one in the third degree. In the fourth degree of kinship were great-great-grandparents, grandchildren of cousins of one's grandparents, and third cousins.

The principles of canon law generally prevailed as far as marriage was concerned. Marriage within the seventh degree of kinship was forbidden by canon law until the Fourth Lateran Council of 1215 reduced the extent of prohibition to the fourth degree (Carron 1989: 16), although some regions, among them Normandy and Brittany, retained the more extensive prohibitions. Jean-Louis Flandrin (1979: 26) has calculated that the reduction of marital prohibition from the seventh degree to the fourth degree enormously widened the possibilities of finding a marriageable partner. If one assumes that in each generation a couple raised one boy and one girl and that both of these married, the number of a person's kin to the fourth degree would be 188, of whom only 88 would be of the same generation, whereas one's kin to the seventh degree would number 10,687! Most of these would probably be living in the same region. Little wonder, then, that the church narrowed the circle of prohibited unions. Dispensations were, of course, often granted, sometimes by local ecclesiastical authorities in the case of more or less distant kinship between members of the higher nobility, sometimes by the Holy See. Affinity, relationship through marriage, was also an impediment in the choice of marriage partners. In general, a husband or wife was related to others in the same lines and degrees of affinity as the spouse was bound to those persons by consanguinity. At the time of Chrétien de Troyes's romances, marriage or sexual relations with any relative out to the seventh degree of kinship would, strictly speaking, have been considered incestuous. In practical terms, however, people could not keep count of such large numbers of kin, and in any case the issue does not arise in Chrétien beyond the fourth degree of kinship.

Dorothea Kullmann sees a distinction between the romances of antiquity, in which father-son ties are significant, and the Arthurian romances, where the uncle-nephew relationship maintains an importance similar to what one finds in the chansons de geste. But unlike the epic poems, in which the uncle often plays the role of hero, the romances tend to place the nephew in this role (Kullmann 1992: 131–34). This is certainly true of Chrétien's romances.

THE ARTHURIAN LINEAGE IN CHRÉTIEN'S WORKS

Chrétien does not set out the lineage of King Arthur systematically in his works, perhaps taking for granted at least a modicum of knowledge on the part of his audiences. This knowledge would most likely have come from Geoffrey of Monmouth's *History of the Kings of Britain* or, for those who did not read Latin or preferred not to, Wace's *Roman de Brut* or another translation. That still other literary paths were open to bring knowledge of Arthur's kin relationships to the French-speaking public in France and England is possible, as witness Robert Biket's *Lai du cor* (Dörner 1907; Bennett 1975), probably composed in England, whose archaic verse form has led some to conclude that it predates Chrétien's *Erec*. Chrétien himself reveals a third source: *cil qui de conter vivre vuelent* ("those who want to live by telling stories," *Erec* 22), professional performers of tales. Marie de France's Arthurian *Lai de Lanval* may also predate *Erec,* but that is not at all certain.

In any case, one has to reconstruct Chrétien's idea of Arthur's kin group, the most important lineage in his romances, by collecting scattered references from the romances themselves. Some of the kinship relations that are found there are traditional, whereas others are of Chrétien's invention. The phenomenon by which the names of formerly independent historical, legendary, or mythological personages accrete around a legendary figure of high renown is well known (see Duggan 1986b), and for Arthur this process began well before Geoffrey of Monmouth and continued in Chrétien.

In Chrétien, Arthur's lineage extends back only to his parents, Uther and Ygerne (fig. 1). In *Erec* and *Yvain,* Arthur is said to be the son of Pendragon.[2] This name corresponds to the epithet "Pendragon" that Geoffrey of Monmouth assigns to Arthur's father, Uther,[3] explaining that, upon assuming the kingship, Uther had two gold effigies of dragons made, one of which he carried when making war. "From that moment onwards," writes Geoffrey, "he was called Utherpendragon, which in the British language means 'a dragon's head' " (Wright 1985: 95; Thorpe 1966: 202). In *Perceval,* Arthur's father is called Uterpendragon (l. 8740). The epithet actually means "chief dragon," a metaphor for a strong battle leader (Bromwich 1978: 520, 1991: 278). There is some evidence, although indirect, that Uther, who is attested

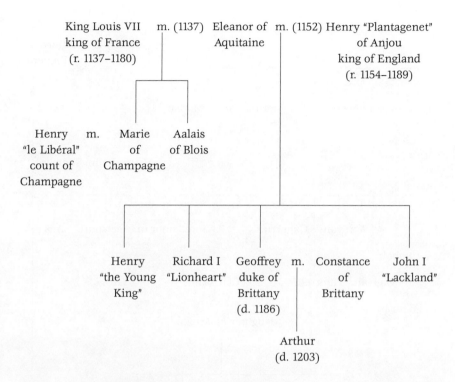

Figure 1. Capetians and Plantagenets

in the pre-Geoffrey tradition in Welsh, was there also identified as Arthur's father (Bromwich 1978: 521–22).

According to Geoffrey, Uther belonged to the Breton branch of the kings of Britain descended from Aeneas's great-grandson Brutus through Constantine I of Brittany. When Vortigern usurped the throne of Britain, the descendants of Constantine invaded the land and their leader, Ambrosius Aurelianus, seized the throne after burning Vortigern in his castle. Wishing to build a monument to British nobles who had been killed by the Saxons, Ambrosius sent his brother Uther to Ireland, along with Merlin, to bring back stones with which to build Stonehenge. Ambrosius was subsequently poisoned, and Uther became king of Britain. With the assistance of one of his most powerful vassals, Gorlois, duke of Cornwall, Uther suppressed a Saxon revolt, but he soon fell in love with Gorlois's surpassingly beautiful wife, Ygerna,[4] to her husband's great alarm. Gorlois retired from the court without Uther's leave, secluding Ygerna in his castle of Tintagel while

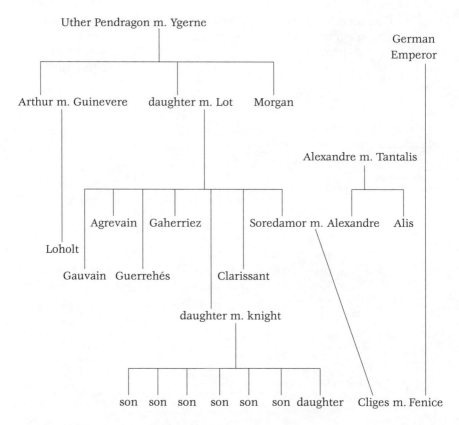

Figure 2. Arthur's lineage in Chrétien's works

himself taking refuge in another stronghold, Dimilioc. Through a potion, Merlin gave Uther the appearance of Gorlois, and to himself and another noble the semblance of two of Gorlois's men; the king was then able to approach Ygerna in Tintagel and make love to her without causing suspicion. Arthur's conception resulted from this deception. Gorlois died in battle that same night, leaving Ygerna a widow, and Uther soon became her husband. Ygerna also bore Uther a daughter, Anna.[5]

Gauvain is Arthur's sister's son in Chrétien (fig. 2), as elsewhere in medieval Arthurian literature, and identifies himself as such in *Perceval* 8833–34: "Are you Gauvain?" — "Yes, King Arthur's nephew" (*"Gauvains iés tu?"*— *"Voire, li niez le roi Artu"*). This relationship that is responsible for his role in the romances as the leading knight of Arthur's court is absent from Wace (Kullmann 1992: 132–33), in whose text Arthur still functions as a hero in his own right. Chrétien leaves the name of the king's sister unreported. Even in *Perceval,* in which Gauvain's mother is present in the castle of the Rock of Champguin and in which his grandmother's name is given as Yguerne (8742), his mother remains nameless and is referred to only as "Gauvain's mother" (*mere Gauvain*), who was the wife of King Lot (8749–53).[6] This line of descent figures in *Perceval* in the conversation between Gauvain and Ygerne. There Gauvain tells the queen that he is the eldest of King Lot's sons and that Agrevain, Gaherriez, and Guerrehés are his brothers (8138–42). Agrevain figures earlier in *Perceval* (4768–74), when he offers, unsuccessfully but in keeping with the principle of kinship solidarity, to defend his brother against a charge of having killed Guingambresil's lord without challenging him. Gaherriez is also mentioned, but not as Gauvain's brother, in *Erec* 1721. These brothers will be retained in the thirteenth-century prose romances. Chrétien never mentions Mordred. Gauvain's sister Clarissant (8269; *Clariant* in three mss.), born after her mother came to the castle, is also present, and Ygerne addresses her as *niece* (8065, 8087, 8275, 8278, 9049), a word that here has retained the meaning of its Latin etymon, *neptia* 'granddaughter'.

Morgan the Fay is once named as Arthur's sister (*Erec* 4214), but nowhere in Chrétien is she associated with King Lot, so for Chrétien she is not Gauvain's mother. Her lover is Guilemer, lord of the Isle of Avalon (*Erec* 1953).

Gauvain has a nephew and a niece in *Yvain,* the son and daughter of his sister (3913), whom Yvain saves by killing the giant Harpin de la Montagne. The sister is, however, not named (see the note in Uitti 1994: 1217).

In *Cliges* the eponymous hero's mother, Soredamor, is Gauvain's sister. That the names of her mother and father are never mentioned points up the nontraditional nature of this kinship relation, which Chrétien seems to have created solely to situate Cliges among Arthur's kin. Gauvain joins Arthur in arranging Soredamor's marriage with Alexandre (2308–11), as would be fitting for those present with the greatest legal kinship obligations, the bride's brother and maternal uncle. Cliges is thus the sister's son of Gauvain, who is in turn the sister's son of Arthur. So Arthur is Cliges's great-uncle, although the term Chrétien uses is simply *oncle* (*Cliges* 5238, 6591). In *Cliges,* the hero is once called Arthur's favorite nephew (4998–99; that is, grandnephew). This reference may be a clue that other nephews of Arthur were mentioned in Arthurian tales that preceded Chrétien but are now lost (Kullmann 1992: 134); this was perhaps true of Gauvain's brothers Agrevain, Gaherriez, and Guerrehés, whom Chrétien mentions only in passing in *Perceval* (8138–42). Those brothers were destined to play significant roles in later works, especially in the prose *Lancelot* of the Vulgate Cycle. It is always possible, however, that Chrétien simply invented them. Gauvain's sisters are probably Chrétien's creations, but unlike the brothers they fill needs of the narrative in *Cliges* and *Yvain,* as well as in *Perceval.* Geoffrey of Monmouth and Wace give Arthur two nephews in addition to Gawain: Mordred and Hoel.

Guinevere is Arthur's wife already in *Erec,* in which Chrétien presents her as a protective figure who replaces Enide's tattered clothing with an expensive tunic and a cloak. Chrétien never mentions the queen's lineage, however, unlike Geoffrey, who identifies her as coming from a Roman family and being raised by Duke Cador of Cornwall. Although she commits adultery with Lancelot in *Lancelot,* Chrétien seems to go out of his way to have Gauvain praise her in *Perceval* (8176–98).

Ygerne is, in *Perceval,* queen of the castle of the Rock of Champguin[7] (8817) in a realm that Gauvain enters by crossing a great stream, typical passage into the Otherworld (see the examples given in Patch 1950: ch. 7). She does not recognize her grandson and poses to him a series of questions about the offspring of Lot, which he answers by designating himself, in the third person, as the eldest, and then naming his three brothers. The castle is a land populated by five hundred ladies and also ruled by women, although there are some male inhabitants.

Arthur's son, Loholt, receives only a perfunctory mention in *Erec* (1728) and plays no narrative role in any of Chrétien's romances. Wace says specifically that Arthur and Guinevere could not have children (Arnold 1938–40: ll. 9657–58).

Because Arthur has no brothers, all of his younger kin are on the female side, related to him through his sister, wife of King Lot. The nephew through whose betrayal, according to Geoffrey and Wace, he was killed, Mordred, as noted, passes unmentioned.

According to Geoffrey (Wright 1985: 106), followed by Wace (Arnold 1938–40: 9617–20), the men with whom Arthur was related by marriage were extremely powerful. In Northumberland were three brothers, Loth, Urianus, and Auguselus, in the royal family of the Scots. When he had consolidated his power, Arthur returned to Auguselus the kingship of the Scots (Wace: Escoce), to Urian the kingship of Moray (Wace: Mureif), and to Loth the dukedom of Lothian (Wace: Loeneis) and adjacent lands. Two of these are mentioned in Chrétien, namely Loth, who is King Lot (*Erec* 1733), specified as Gauvain's father in *Yvain* 6257 and *Perceval* 8135, and Urien, father of Yvain in *Yvain* 1016, 1818, 2124, and 3627, and *Perceval* 8149, but Chrétien registers Lot only as related by marriage to Arthur.

EREC ET ENIDE: CONTRAST WITHIN A KIN GROUP

Erec et Enide presents a lineage that is unknown to Geoffrey of Monmouth and Wace, that of King Lac, Erec's rich and powerful father (Fritz 1992b: ll. 19, 651, 667, 1261, 1688, 1895, 2312, 2682, 3876, 6030), who rules over Estre-Gales (3877), whose chief castle is at Carrant (2311) or Carnant (Dembowski 1992b: l. 2275), and who has more castles and cities than any king but Arthur (3878–79).

These place-names, and thus the location of Lac's kingdom, are problematic. Roger Sherman Loomis, the scholar who did the most to establish Chrétien's debt to Celtic antecedents, conjectured that Carnant or Carrant may be a deformation of "Caerwent" in Monmouthshire (Loomis 1949: 481), but it seems much more likely to me that it is simply a rendering of "Nantes" in a Brittonic form: Old Breton and Middle Welsh *caer,* Modern Breton *ker,* originally 'fortress, stronghold', then 'inhabited place, house, village, town', plus *nant* suggested by "Nantes" but construed as Breton *nant* 'pool, fountain'. Formations of this type are found in Breton place-names: Carfantin and Kerfeunteun, 'place of the fountain', Carfo 'ivy place', Kerbrat 'meadow house', Kerloc'h 'lake village', Keronnic 'village of the ash grove', Kernon 'place of the ash tree' (Nègre 1991: nos. 18744, 18751, 18745, 18747, 18754, 18757, 18763). Four French localities named Ternant are compounds with Gaulish *nant* 'valley' (Nègre 1991: no. 2237). The true etymology of Nantes is *Namnetes,* the name of a Gaulish tribe. Misrahi (1959: 99) interpreted the conjunction of Nantes and Carnant to mean that in the coronation scene "Nantes" is a nonce equivalent of "Carnant," but I think it was the other way around: Chrétien meant to posit Lac as an ancient king of Nantes, and formulated "Carnant" as a form of "Nantes" with Breton flavoring.

"Estre-Gales" may resemble a form used for "Strathclyde" (see Bromwich 1991: 292 n. 23), and Becker thought it referred to Striguil, medieval name of Chepstow in Monmouthshire (Becker 1934: 73), but it is more likely to have represented for Chrétien something like "Outer Wales."

On the level of detail, however, Lac's kingdom is devoid of geographical specificity and corresponds to no historical realm. The lack of a Galfridian past is all the more surprising in that Lac is said to be the most powerful king in the land after Arthur (3878–83). Chrétien must have conceived of Lac as Arthur's vassal because Erec receives the kingdom back from Arthur after his father's death: "For he received his land back from the king" (*"Que dou roi sa terre reprist,"* 6537).

Except for King Lac, the only other kin of Erec mentioned in the ro-

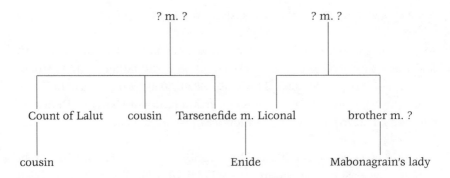

Figure 3. Enide's lineage

mance is *li larges rois de Galvoie,* "the openhanded king of Galloway" (6809, 6820–22), Erec's uncle who attends his coronation but whose name is not given. Galloway is a district in southwest Scotland. This king plays the honorific role, along with Gauvain, who is associated elsewhere with Galloway, of leading Enide into the hall. In *Perceval* Galloway is presented as an Otherworld kingdom from which no knight ever returns (*Perceval* 6602–4). Whether the king of Galloway is related to Erec through his mother or his father is not stated.

The lineage receiving the most attention in *Erec et Enide,* however, is that of Enide herself (fig. 3). Her father and mother are Liconal, a poor vavasor (vassal of low station, from L. *vassus vassorum* 'a vassal of vassals'), and Tarsenefide (*Erec* 6886–88). (Guiot calls Enide's father Licorans.) Her maternal uncle (*Erec* 1275) is the count of Lalut, a town named only in line 6312, although it figures large and early in the story as the castle in which Erec meets and wins Enide. The avunculate was of great importance in this period, but the relation of a man to his sister's daughter was significant also because it guaranteed a blood relationship, like the avunculate but unlike any supposed relation through a kinsman, which was always vulnerable to adulteration if the kinsman's wife was unfaithful. When the count of Lalut discovers Erec's identity, he declares that he considers Erec to be his lord (1264), which appears to mean that Lalut is a fief whose overlord is Lac. Enide has a first cousin in Lalut (1353), who is the count's niece and who gives Enide a horse before she leaves for Arthur's court. Erec promises to give Liconal the castles of Rotelan (1331; Roadan in the Guiot ms., l. 1323) and Montrevel (1335), places that he appears to have from his father. The lady who holds Mabonagrain in thrall in the Joy of the Court is

Liconal's niece through his brother; she and Enide are thus related through the male line.[8]

The two sisters of Guivret le Petit, whose followers are Irish (3862), appear briefly. They live in his castle of Penuris, are skilled at healing, and put Erec on a diet devoid of garlic and pepper. Penuris gives all the signs of an Otherworld kingdom, not the least of which is that Guivret gives Enide a horse whose head is black on one side and white on the other, with a green line separating the two, typical of strangely colored Otherworld horses.

Two important lineages that appear to derive from Celtic mythology figure in passing in *Erec et Enide*. Erec's first conquest, in the Test of the Sparrow-Hawk, is Ydier, son of Nut. That Nut is the avatar of the Celtic god Nodons is recognized by the author of the Welsh analogue to *Erec et Enide, Geraint, son of Erbin*, who calls him Nudd, the Welsh form of Nodons (see pp. 205–6, below). Nodons or Nodens was a sea-god, and his name is cognate with that of the Roman god Neptune.

Mabonagrain, the hero whom Erec defeats, thereby dispelling the enchantment of the Joy of the Court, is the nephew of Evrain, king of Brandigan (6263). Mabonagrain is widely recognized as the avatar of Mabon, the P-Celtic form of the name of the deity Maponos, the "Great Son" of Modron (Brittonic *Matrona*), the "Great Mother" after whom the River Marne is named.[9] In Welsh tradition he is a renowned prisoner, a status compatible with the role he plays in *Erec et Enide*. The place-name Brandigan appears to derive from the name of another Celtic deity, Bran the Blessed (Welsh *Bran Vendigeit* or *Bendigeid Vran*). From this anthroponymic-toponymic tangle emerges the strong possibility that Mabonagrain was in some way connected with Bran, probably in the Breton tradition from which Chrétien took the names Erec and Enide. Rachel Bromwich points out that in *Le Bel Inconnu,* Mabon and Evrayn are guardians of an enchanted castle, and the name Mabonagrain may be a garbled derivative of the two names joined by the conjunction *a(c)* 'and' (Bromwich 1978). Inscriptions from north Britain appear to assimilate the Celtic Maponos with the Greco-Roman deity Apollo, but he is also attested in evidence coming from first- and third-century Gaul, and his name is attached to a fountain in a document of around 1090 from the abbey of Savigny (Rhone) (Bromwich 1978: 433).

Erec's first and last victories are thus both over avatars of Celtic deities. What this means for Chrétien's romance, however, is unclear. He does not appear to be aware of any connections between his characters and mythological figures, which in any case he would probably have interpreted as devils, as he does Pluto in *Philomena*. That the Celtic tale or tales behind

Erec et Enide represented Erec as struggling with the sons of Nodons and Matrona is nevertheless not to be ruled out.

The marriage of Erec with Enide and the couple's subsequent trials form the main narrative subject of the romance. At the beginning, and thus shortly before the time of his marriage, Erec is less than twenty-five years old (90). Although Enide is represented as a young woman in the bloom of her beauty, Chrétien does not give her age at marriage. What is certain, however, is that the union itself is a key element in the romance. Even when Erec is most withdrawn from his bride, just after the bedroom scene at Carnant and as the two of them are about to set off without escort, he obtains his father's consent that if he, Erec, should die and she return alone, Lac should invest her with a freehold consisting of half his kingdom for life (*Erec* 2721–27), an unusually generous arrangement for a childless widow in this period.

When Mabonagrain and his lady tell the story of their alliance and subsequent travails, it is obvious that Chrétien is drawing a contrast between the marriage of Erec and Enide and the union of Mabonagrain and his lady. The first was celebrated with full permission of kin and openly before witnesses:

> he married me
> So that my father knew it well
> And my mother had great joy of it.
> All our kin knew it and were happy,
> As well they should have been.
> [il m'esposa
> Si que mes pere bien le sot
> Et ma mere grant joie en ot.
> Tuit le sorent et lié en furent
> Nostre parent, si con il durent.]   (*Erec* 6286–90)

Mabonagrain and Enide's cousin, by contrast, secreted themselves away from Evrain's court without telling anyone (6279). Mabonagrain subjected himself to the rigors of a *don contraignant* in promising his lady to obey her wish before knowing what that wish was, whereas Erec and Enide's troubles lead to a journey in which each is put to, and passes, a series of tests.

Erec et Enide is thus a work that contrasts two attitudes toward marriage precisely at a time in history when the nature of the marriage relationship was changing. In the eleventh century marriage had been a matter of power of kin groups: the bride's and groom's kin took charge of the union, and the ceremony took place in the house of the bride's father. As ecclesiastical authorities asserted strongly their right to supervise marriages, the ceremony moved out of the house and into the church, where it was celebrated before witnesses (Baldwin 1994: 75). Georges Duby claims that Bernard of Clairvaux (1090–1153) was the first clerical authority to state that marriage was effected by the church (Duby 1983: 198–200). In *Erec,* although Erec declares in Liconal's presence his intention to marry Enide and encounters no opposition (1321–23), the marriage takes place not in the bride's father's house as would have been the case according to earlier customs but, with Arthur's permission, at Caradigan, Arthur's city. Erec first gives lavish gifts to his bride's father and mother (1847–54) and has them transported for the wedding from Lalut to Caradigan (1865–72, 1891–93), where he invests them with two castles that are his father's dependencies (1873–82, 1894–1902). Present at the marriage are all the vassals of Arthur's kingdom. Enide's name is made known to all for the first time, for, says Chrétien, in order to marry her Erec had to name her by her right name (2021–27). The archbishop of Canterbury officiates, in accord with the model of marriage that was new in Chrétien's day, and prelates accompany the couple into their bridal chamber (2028–70).

All this detail contrasts with the union between Mabonagrain and his lady, who, although she is Enide's kinswoman, runs away with her lover, retains him by enchantment as her prisoner (6089), and hides their relationship from the gaze of the kin group. Public marriage was one of the concerns of the reform movement in twelfth-century canon law that endeavored to bring marriage under the rule of ecclesiastical rather than customal law. Bishop Ivo of Chartres (1091–1116) cited authorities in his widely used *Decretum* to the effect that secret marriages were improper and that marriage ideally involved a public exchange of vows, marriage gifts, a wedding ring, and a priest's blessing (Brundage 1987: 189), none of which figure in the relationship between Mabonagrain and Enide's cousin. The union between these two has all the earmarks of a secret marriage, which, however reprehensible, was still considered valid. Above all, the relationship between Mabonagrain and his lady was not sanctioned by their families. As Georges Duby puts it, "A fundamental principle, accepted unconditionally by heads of kinship networks, was that a good marriage was the business not of individuals but of families" (Duby 1983: 131).

Luttrell interprets *Erec et Enide* as a mirror of marriage (1974: 77), in the course of which Chrétien rings the changes of marital possibilities: a balanced love that is marred by excesses (the relationship between Erec and

Enide just after they are married), a proposal for a liaison that would be made possible by betrayal (Count Galoain), forced marriage (the count of Limors), a secret marriage or sustained extramarital relationship (Mabonagrain and his lady), and finally the perfection of marital love in the state that Erec and Enide reach at the end of their journey. Without following Luttrell in his reading of *Erec et Enide* as the narrative parallel of Alan of Lille's *Anticlaudianus,* and adding the context of the evolution of marriage practices in late twelfth-century France, I see much merit in this interpretation. It also raises the possibility that *Erec et Enide,* whose patron is not identified in the text, was composed in the context of a marriage. What is striking, however, is the extraordinary disparity between the treatment of Mabonagrain and his lady in *Erec et Enide* and that of Lancelot and Guinevere in *Lancelot.* Unquestioning love service is, after all, the basis of both relationships. As in many other ways, *Lancelot* stands out in this respect for its differences from Chrétien's other romances.

CLIGES: MARRIAGE AS AN ALLIANCE OF POWERFUL KIN GROUPS

In *Cliges,* King Arthur's kin are linked to two other lineages in marriages that are based on mutual love. The relationship between Alexandre, eldest son of the Byzantine emperor, and Soredamor, sister of Gauvain, joins the imperial lineage of Constantinople with that of Arthur, who is Gauvain's, and therefore Soredamor's, uncle. Cliges, the offspring of that union, is thus Arthur's great-nephew. He is also the nephew of Alis and thus, like Tristan, falls in love with his uncle's wife. The love between Cliges and Fenice eventuates in a marriage that joins Arthur's kin group through Cliges with that of the Holy Roman Emperor, father of Fenice. Both of these marriage alliances are through the female branch of Uther Pendragon's progeny.

The second alliance displaces the abortive union between the Byzantine and German imperial lines brought about when Alis wed Fenice. This marriage was not legitimized by either of the two elements that canonists of the period, chief among them Gratian, considered as conferring validity on a union: consent of the two parties and consummation (Brundage 1987: 235–38). The counselors who seek a bride for Alis succeed in obtaining the German emperor's consent to the marriage of his daughter, an older form of consent that twelfth-century reformers called into question (Brundage 1987: 183). But in contrast to the consent that Soredamor grants to her marriage with Alexandre, Fenice herself is never shown consenting and in fact takes the effective step of Thessala's potion to make Alis think, falsely, that he has consummated the union. Nor is it merely understood that Soredamor gives her permission; Chrétien goes out of his way to emphasize it by having Alexandre raise the possibility that she might not consent to the marriage:

> "But it may be, for some reason,
> That this maiden would not wish
> That I should be hers or she be mine.
> If she grants me nothing of herself,
> Still I grant myself to her."
> ["Mais puet cel estre a nul endroit
> Cele pucele nel voudroit
> Que suens fusse ne ele moie.
> S'ele de lui rien ne m'otroie,
> Toute voies m'oitroi ge a lui."]   (*Cliges* 2285–89)

Soredamor's wedding is in conformity with the new model as Chrétien shows her consenting:

> At this word she [Soredamor] trembled,
> She who does not refuse this gift.
> She betrays her heart's desire
> Both in words and in looks,
> When, trembling, she grants herself to him,
> And says that she will exclude nothing,
> Neither will nor heart nor body,
> And that she will do all he wishes.
> [A cest mot cele tressailli
> Qui cest present pas ne refuse.
> Le voloir de son cuer encuse
> Et par parole et par semblant,
> Quant a lui s'otroie en tremblant,
> Et dit que ja n'en metra fors
> Ne volenté, ne cuer ne cors,
> Et que tout son plesir ne face.]   (*Cliges* 2290–97)

Among the high nobility in northern France, the cultural milieu with which Chrétien would have been most familiar, marriages arranged without the bride's consent were probably in the majority, since it was only in this period itself, during the pontificate of Alexander III (1159–1189), that the church adopted Peter Lombard's thesis that verbal consent between bride and groom was essential to render a marriage valid (Herlihy 1985: 81). Duby sees a line in the *Chroniques des comtes d'Anjou,* written around 1180, of Jean de Marmoutier as the first clear expression of the principle that consent makes the marriage (Duby 1983: 252; Halphen and Poupardin 1913: 101).

That the union of Alexandre and Soredamor is consummated is assured, since she becomes pregnant with Cliges within three months of the marriage (2332–33).

Cliges, then, is the romance of Chrétien that most directly celebrates the new matrimonial practices imposed by the church. Alexandre knows after his victory over the count of Windsor that if he asks Arthur for Soredamor's hand, it will be granted to him, but he wants first to have her consent (*son voloir,* 2216). Perhaps ironically, considering how Chrétien portrays her in *Lancelot,* Guinevere is the one who makes explicit the mutual consent of Alexandre and Soredamor. "I shall put this marriage together" (*"J'asemblerai cest mariage,"* 2270), she says, and after giving the lovers to each other she assists at the public marriage ceremony (*esposailles,* 2311, also referred to as *noces,* 2315) the same day in Windsor, with the consent (*otroi,* 2309) of both King Arthur and Gauvain, the bride's closest male kin, her maternal uncle and her brother.[10] That Fenice and Cliges both consent to the relationship that will fifteen months or so later result in their marriage (see 6281) is clear from their dialogue upon Cliges's return from Arthur's court (5169–70), although the terminology is less direct and more imbued with courtly metaphor than in the case of Cliges's parents.

The age of the characters in *Cliges* points up the fact that much of medieval courtly narrative concerns the adventures—and the emotional lives—of adolescents. When Alis is born, Alexandre is old enough to become a knight and rule the empire should he be so inclined (52–56), but has not yet been knighted, despite his father's wishes. Since the age of majority in most romances of this period is represented as fifteen, Alexandre would have been at least fifteen years older than Alis. Three months after Soredamor marries Alexandre, she conceives Cliges, who was, then, approximately sixteen years younger than his father and only a few years younger than his paternal uncle, a difference in age that renders him all the more plausible as a rival for the love of Alis's wife.

Alis thinks that Alexandre died on his trip to Arthur's court, but when this turns out not to be the case, he cedes the power to his brother, keeping the title and crown of emperor against a promise never to marry. Before Alexandre dies, he advises Cliges to seek out Arthur's court for himself, so the boy is presumably of an age to understand. Although Alis wishes to remain faithful to his promise of celibacy, his counselors soon convince him to marry. They ask the emperor of Germany for the hand of his eldest daughter, Fenice, and this request receives a favorable response even though Fenice had been promised to the duke of Saxony. In the Middle Ages, one's age was not generally regarded as a crucial element of identity unless it was tied to some legal restriction, such as the age of majority, and from the evidence of chronicles, saint's lives, romances, and other medieval narratives it appears that people were little concerned with their precise age and that older men and women may not even have kept track of their own ages. That Chrétien never mentions the age of the Maiden of the Short Sleeves who solicits Gauvain as her champion in *Perceval* even though she is young enough to be carried in her father's arms is indicative of this lack of concern for age as a tally of years. Chrétien does tell us, however, that Cliges is at this time nearly fifteen:[11] "He was in the flower of his age" (*en la flor estoit ses aages,* 2718), and Fenice appears to be around the same age.

Cliges underscores the ties of kinship through two generations of the female line, since Cliges belongs to the Arthurian kin group through his mother, the daughter of Arthur's sister. The tie between Cliges and Arthur is reinforced by the young man's insistence, following the advice of his father, on traveling to Arthur's court, even to the point of refusing Alis's offer to share the government of Constantinople (4172–78) as his father had before him. But whereas Alexandre's journey to the British court was motivated solely by Arthur's reputation, that of Cliges is also an effort to maintain acquaintance with the Arthurian kin as Alexandre had recommended to his son (2576). Cliges's martial qualities are implicitly compared to Alexandre's, as both win resounding victories in service to Arthur. And Arthur's forces are ready to help the king's kinsmen, both father and son, regain the throne of Constantinople against the usurper Alis.

By the end of *Cliges,* Arthur's lineage has been joined to two of the most prestigious and powerful lines of Europe, the imperial lineages of the eastern and western empires. A dynasty that had newly raised itself to royal status, the Angevins, was interested in appropriating to itself the prestige of Arthur's lineage. Who in the decade of the 1170s would have had a special interest in a prestigious link between the Arthurian lineage on the one hand and those of the two empires on the other? The name of Henry "the Young King" (d. 1183), eldest son of Henry II "Plantagenet" of England, springs to mind, but there are two potential impediments to thinking that a Plantagenet was the patron. The first is that Chrétien states clearly in *Cliges* that chivalry and learning came from Greece and Rome to France, and then expresses the wish that they should never leave France, a sentiment unlikely to appeal to a member of the royal family of England, whatever its ties with Anjou, Brittany, and Poitou. The second is that the duke of Saxony is treated with contempt in *Cliges,* written soon after Matilda, daughter of Henry II, had in 1168 married Henry the Lion, duke of Saxony.

Another possible patron is someone in the kin of Brian Fitz Count, the illegitimate son of Duke Alan Fergant of Brittany (1084–1112), although not Brian himself or any direct descendant. The castle of Brian, who was instrumental in bringing Henry Plantagenet and Eleanor of Aquitaine to Britain in 1153 when King Stephen was ill with the sickness that would kill him (Poole 1951: 163), was at Wallingford in England. When Cliges travels to Britain to seek out Arthur and Gauvain, he goes immediately to Wallingford (Galingefort, 4515) on the Thames. Chrétien never explains this destination, which is not a seaport. Winchester, and not Wallingford, was the locus in which King Stephen and Henry of Anjou concluded a treaty under which Henry was made Stephen's heir, enabling him to take the throne of England in 1154 (Poole 1951: 165n). The following year, Henry granted freedom from tolls to Wallingford in gratitude to its inhabitants, who had served him in obtaining the crown (Poole 1951: 163–64n). From Wallingford, Cliges takes part in a tournament on the plains near Oxford (Oxenefort, 4527), where on three successive days, incognito in three colors of arms, he defeats Sagremor, Lancelot, and Perceval and proves himself the equal of his uncle Gauvain. Arthur and his knights are represented as coming from the Oxford side, and the other knights from the Wallingford side.

Brian Fitz Count died without an heir, probably before 1150, and probably after having retired to the monastery of Bec in Normandy (Keats-Rohan 1989: 316–18; see also Davis 1910). He was the most faithful supporter of the empress Matilda, rival for the throne during the time of King Stephen (r. 1135–1154) in the civil strife that wracked England during his reign. An ally of Robert of Gloucester, one of the lords to whom Geoffrey of Monmouth dedicated his *History of the Kings of Britain,* Brian was renowned for his bravery in escaping the siege of Oxford with Matilda in 1142. The two took refuge in Wallingford castle. That the setting and configuration of the tournament in *Cliges* owe something to the events of 1142 is likely, especially because Brian is already mentioned in *Erec* under the name Brianz des Isles (6722)—related to the sobriquet "of the Island," that is, of Britain (*de Insula*), by which Brian Fitz Count was occasionally identified—

who gives Arthur and Guinevere two ivory faldstools carved with images of crocodiles and leopards (Weston 1924–25). The leopard is a heraldic animal of the kings of England (Schmolke-Hasselmann 1998: 240n).

But if Brian had no heirs, what possible patron might have inspired these reminiscences of Wallingford and of him? One possibility is Constance, daughter of Conan IV of Brittany whom Henry II had forced to abdicate in favor of Geoffrey. Constance married Henry's son Geoffrey in 1181. She was nineteen at the time of her marriage, and she and Geoffrey had been betrothed for fifteen years. Constance was the great-grandniece of Brian Fitz Count, through her father, Conan, her grandmother Berthe, and her great-grandfather Conan III, who was Brian's half-brother. If *Cliges* was indeed composed around 1176–1177, as Fourrier posited, then Constance would have been fourteen or fifteen years old at the time and Geoffrey eighteen or nineteen. Geoffrey was the half-brother of Marie de Champagne, for whom Chrétien wrote *Lancelot*, and it is likely that relations between brother and sister were cordial because Marie gave a donation to the cathedral of Notre-Dame in Paris in Geoffrey's memory in 1186 (Guérard 1850, 1: 296–97), as mentioned above in Chapter 1. Although the lack of evidence makes it impossible to conclude for certain, Constance, perhaps along with Geoffrey, seem to me to be the likely patron or patrons of *Cliges*. A son was born to the couple in 1187, after Geoffrey's death. This son of the duke of Brittany, who died aged sixteen at the hands of his uncle King John "Lackland," was called Arthur, a name that could only have been inspired by the memory of King Arthur.

LANCELOT: LACK OF KIN

The hero of *Lancelot* does not have surviving Celtic antecedents and appears to be a character of late invention. The form of his name may owe something to the Breton name Lancelin. Chrétien mentions him in *Erec* (Lanceloz dou Lac, 1690) and has Cliges defeat him at the tournament of Oxford (Lanceloz del Lac, *Cliges* 4701), before writing a romance with him as male protagonist.

Ulrich von Zatzikhoven's romance *Lanzelet*, although written between 1194 and 1203, some fifteen to twenty-five years after the most likely date of Chrétien's *Lancelot*, goes back ultimately to a source earlier than Chrétien's romance, since it does not show Guinevere engaged in an adulterous liaison with Lancelot, or indeed with any other man, a representation that would not have been likely if Ulrich had known of Chrétien's portrayal. Ulrich's source was a foreign book (*welschez buoch,* in this case *welsch* designating 'French') that Ulrich claims to have translated faithfully (Spiewok 1997: ll. 9323–24). The book came to him, Ulrich tells us, through a certain Hugh of Morville who was sent to the German emperor Henry VI as one of the hostages when King Richard Lion-Heart was ransomed. This would have been in 1194. The tale in Hugh's book, probably written in the 1170s or the early 1180s and in Anglo-Norman dialect, to judge by the forms of French words that have come through in the translation, had Arthur himself participate in the queen's rescue.[12] This is in keeping with a tradition attested in three sources: the bas-relief depicting a rescue of Guinevere on the archivolt of the Porta della Pescheria of the cathedral of Modena, dating from around 1125 and bearing names of Arthurian characters with a Breton coloring (see pp. 204–6, below); Caradog of Llancarfan's *Life of Gildas,* which predates Geoffrey's *History of the Kings of Britain;* and the Welsh "Conversation between Arthur and Guinevere" dated to around the middle of the twelfth century but based on more ancient materials. In none of those three sources is Lancelot present. The motif of adultery between Lancelot and Guinevere appears, then, to be one of Chrétien's most significant contributions.[13]

As he is depicted in *Lancelot,* Lancelot is a man without a genealogy. At a point in the narrative in which the hero is trapped in a castle, he looks at a ring on his finger to see that the trap is no enchantment, conjuring up a woman:

> "Lady, lady, so help me God,
> Now I would be in great need
> Of your being able to help me."
> This lady who had given him
> The ring was a fairy,
> And she raised him in his childhood,
> And he had great confidence in her
> That she would assist and aid him
> Wherever he was.
> ["Dame, dame, se Dex m'aït,
> Or avroie je grant mestier
> Que vos me poïssiez eidier."
> Cele dame une fee estoit
> Qui l'anel doné li avoit,
> Et si le norri an s'anfance,

S'avoit an li molt grant fiance
Que ele an quel leu que il fust
Secorre et eidier li deüst.]   (*Lancelot* 2342–50)

Chrétien says no more about this lady. *Lanzelet,* however, tells the story of
how Lancelot was abducted by a water fairy who raised him among women
in a land without sorrow until he reached the age of fifteen, at which time
he received instruction in the skills of knighthood. In *Lanzelet,* the hero
is the son of King Pant of Genewis and his wife, Arthur's sister Clarine
(Spiewok 1997: 4959; see note 12).

In the prose *Lancelot* of the Vulgate Cycle, written around 1225, Lancelot
is presented as the son of King Ban of Benoÿc, a name that derives from
the same eventual source as Ulrich's "Pant of Genewis." [14] Ban's kingdom is
located in the border area between Gaul and Brittany, and his wife, Hélène,
is descended from no less a figure than the biblical King David. King Ban
dies near the shore of a lake called the Lac de Diane (Kennedy 1991: 54),
and shortly thereafter a fairy named Ninienne (94; or in some manuscripts
Vivienne) takes Lancelot from his mother and dives into the lake with him
(76), raising him to manhood in her kingdom inhabited by both men and
women and hidden away by the lake (98). He has two cousins, Lionel and
Bohort, sons of King Bohort of Gaunes, who was his father's brother.

Did Chrétien know in detail the traditions about Lancelot's childhood
and kinship ties that are seen in the *Lanzelet* and the prose *Lancelot?* Aside
from the information he supplies, namely that the hero was brought up by
a fairy, it is impossible to answer this question, but Chrétien writes tan-
talizingly of having received from Marie de Champagne the matter of his
romance, which may have included other details that he has not passed on
to us. Whatever he knew, Chrétien chose not to invoke kin for Lancelot in
his romance.

For an author to pass over the lineage of the principal hero of a romance
is highly unusual and may reflect Chrétien's unease with the task assigned
to him by Marie de Champagne. But Lancelot's lack of kinship relations
also simplifies Chrétien's task of recounting his act of adultery with Guinevere, since the knight has no kin in the romance to advise him against his
course of action or to suffer the consequences of his folly, which constitutes
a felony in the medieval context.

The first kin group that Lancelot encounters is that of Bademagu, king of
Gorre. His son Meleagant, the villain of the romance, is an unusual figure,
an evil character born of a good and kindly father. Bademagu opposes Me-

leagant's actions every step of the way. One of his cities is Bade, that is to say Bath, which is a key to his origin. In the *Roman de Brut* Wace calls him Bladud the magician, founder of the city of Bath (Arnold 1938–40: ll. 1627– 53). Wace derives Bladud from Geoffrey of Monmouth, according to whom he was the son of Hudibras, king of Loegria, who succeeded his father as king and built Kaerbadum, "which is now called Bado," that is, Bath, constructed the hot baths there, and established the temple of Sulis-Minerva. He had fires built for the goddess that were never extinguished, for the moment they were on the point of going out they turned into balls of stone (*globos saxeos*). Bladud encouraged necromancy (and was thus a magician, L. *magus*) and had a pair of wings built for himself with which he tried to fly through the upper air; he fell on the temple of Apollo at Trinovantum and was killed (Wright 1985: 18). This detail of Geoffrey's Bladud is a reminiscence of another magus, Simon in the apocryphal Acts of Peter, who also made wings for himself and crashed to his death. In Geoffrey's *Historia,* Bladud is the benevolent father of King Leir. I believe it most likely, however, that Chrétien got both Meleagant and Bademagu from oral rather than Galfridian tradition, as the father appears in *Culhwch and Olwen* under the name "Baeddan," closer to *Bade-* than is the *Blad-* form of Wace and Geoffrey. "Bademagu" derives, then, from *Baeddan* compounded with L. *magus* 'the magician'.

In *Lancelot,* Bademagu's unnamed daughter shares her father's penchant for thwarting Meleagant's evil designs toward Lancelot. She searches out the hero after he has returned to the prison where Meleagant has had him interned, passes him the pickax he uses to break out of captivity, nurses him back to health, and gives him the best horse anyone has ever seen (6700). In fact, she treats Lancelot "as if he were her father" (6667). Chrétien's continuator Godefroy de Lagny has her tell Lancelot that she is helping him in gratitude for a service he rendered to her (6572–78), namely cutting off the head of the knight before the Sword Bridge (2781). She is thus also the fifth of the five damsels whom Lancelot encounters on his travels. The second and the third damsels are one and the same, since the third asks for and obtains the life of the knight who unhorses Lancelot at the ford (892), promising a gift in return. Chrétien also says that Lancelot recognizes her by her words (922), a reference to the second damsel's reminder that both Lancelot and Gauvain owed her recompense (704–7). Including Meleagant's sister, there are six manifestations of damsels in the poem: Lancelot cannot tell from seeing them that the second and third are the same person or that the fifth and Meleagant's sister are identical. The second damsel offers correct information about what Lancelot is seeking, including the name of the queen's abductor and of his father the king, the name of the kingdom, and how to gain entrance to it. A likely possibility, in my opinion, is that all five damsels are Meleagant's sister, a woman shapeshifter who shares in the necromantic skills of her father and both tests and guides Lancelot on his journey.

In counterpoint with the father-son pair Bademagu and Meleagant, Lancelot meets another such couple while he is in the company of the fourth damsel. The son in this case is in love with the damsel and wants to take her off with him, but Lancelot refuses to abandon her. The father, like Bademagu but with greater success, attempts to convince his son to act more prudently (1711–13), a goal reached when father and son hear that Lancelot is the knight destined to free the captives from the land of Gorre. In the case of each father-son pair, the son seeks a sexual relationship with a woman forbidden to him by Lancelot.

A third kin group that Lancelot encounters is that of the hospitable vavasor who gives him shelter. The vavasor and his wife have seven children: two knights, three boys, and two daughters (2045–50). Natives of Logres, they are living as captives in the land of Gorre. The two knights accompany Lancelot to the passage of stones, which leads to the Sword Bridge.

Of the three kin groups that Lancelot meets, one is no obstacle to his quest and two are in the end helpful to him in his search for the queen, even though in two of the groups a hostile young man acts as an impediment.

Lancelot's relationship with Guinevere is marked by only one adulterous act in the romance, although his return to the court at the end, in the absence of any sense of an ending to the relationship, leaves open the possibility that the illicit liaison will continue. A woman's adultery is an offense against the integrity of the kin group, for it potentially allows children to be born of a man's wife who are not his offspring. In medieval Continental law codes, only legitimate descendants were allowed to inherit. Lancelot, the hero without lineage, threatens the purity of King Arthur's potential posterity, a potential that is never realized because Guinevere bears no children.

YVAIN: AVENGING KIN

Yvain, who later hides his name by identifying himself as the Knight of the Lion, is at first simply called *mesire Yvains* ("milord Yvain," 56), but later Lunete, in recognizing him, names his father first:

You are the son of king Urien
And your name is milord Yvain.
[Fil estes le roy Urïen,
Et avés non mesire Yvains.]   (*Yvain* 1016–17; see also 1818)

Laudine is equally taken by his father's royal rank and tells him that one
of the reasons she is prepared to accept him as a husband is that he is a
king's son (2050). Later, to convince her barons of Yvain's worthiness, she
praises him as a man endowed with courtliness, intelligence, and vassalic
qualities, but she precedes the recitation of those attributes by touting his
primary quality as a potential marriage partner, namely his pedigree, that
he is the son of Urien and thus a man of high lineage (*haut parage,* 2125).

Yvain's mother's name is not mentioned in the romance. In *Perceval* Gauvain discusses Yvain and his kin with Ygerne, who asks him:

"And does he [Urien] have any son at the court?"
— "Yes, lady, two sons of great repute.
The one is called my lord Yvain. . . .
And the other one is named Yvain,
Who is not his uterine brother,
On which account he is called the Bastard.
["Et a il a la cort nul fil?"
— "Dame, oïl, deus de grant renon:
Li uns mesire Yvains a non. . . .
Et li autres a non Yvains,
Qui n'est pas ses freres germains;
Por che l'en l'apele l'Avoltre.]   (*Perceval* 8150–52, 8157–59)

Chrétien knew, then, of the Knight of the Lion's half-brother but does not
refer to this brother in *Yvain.*

He does refer to Yvain's half-brother, however, in *Erec et Enide,* in a passage in the list of those who are at King Arthur's court at Caradigan:

And Yvain the son of Urien;
Yvain of Loenel was at the back,
On the other side Yvain the Bastard;
Beside Yvain of Cavaliot
Was Gorsoein of Estrangot.
[Et Yvains li filz Urïein;
Yvains de Löenel fu outre,
D'autre part, Yvains li Avoutre;

Lez Yvain de Cavalïot
Estoit Gorsöein d'Estrangot.]   (*Erec* 1702–6)

According to *Perceval,* the first and third of this superabundance of Yvains
are half-brothers. In his *Lanzelet,* Ulrich von Zatzikhoven mentions Ywan
de Loenel as a knight whom Lanzelet unhorses at a tournament.

The last Yvain, Yvain de Cavaliot, is endowed with the name of a contemporary of Chrétien, the prince of southern Powys Owein Cyfeiliog
(1130–1197). He was the nephew of Madog ap Maredudd, prince of Powys,
who gave him Cyfeiliog in 1149. A much-admired poem, "Owein's Drinking Horn" (W. *Hirlas Owein*), composed in 1156, is ascribed to him in the
Red Book of Hergest (see Bromwich 1955–56; and Gruffydd Aled Williams
1999). Owein Cyfeiliog was an opponent of Henry II of England in 1165, according to the *Chronicle of the Princes* (Thomas Jones 1955: 145), but then
became the king's ally. Gerald of Wales, in his *Journey Through Wales,* tells
an anecdote about Owein and the king:

> [Owein] had frequently opposed the plans of his own leaders and had es-
> poused the cause of Henry II, King of the English, so that he had become
> a close friend of that king. One day when he was sitting at table with the
> king in Shrewsbury, Henry passed to him one of his own loaves, to do him
> honour, as the custom is, and to show a mark of his affection. With the
> king's eyes on him, Owain immediately broke the loaf into portions, as if
> it were communion bread. He spread the pieces out in a row, again as if
> he were at holy communion, picked them up one at a time and went on
> eating until they were all finished. Henry asked him what he thought he
> was doing. "I am imitating you, my lord," answered Owain. In this subtle
> and witty way, he was alluding to the well-known avariciousness of the
> king, who had the habit of keeping church benefices vacant for as long as
> possible so that he could enjoy the revenues. (Thorpe 1974: 202–3)

It may have been the alliance with Henry II that brought Owein Cyfeiliog's
name into Chrétien's ken.

Yvain and his father, Urien, based on the historical Urien of Rheged and
his son Owein, are among the few Celtic figures to pass into Continental
romance as an intact father-son pair (Bromwich 1978: 479).

Calogrenant, mentioned in none of Chrétien's other romances, is Yvain's
first cousin (*cousin germain,* 580) in *Yvain,* but the audience is not informed
as to whether this relationship is through Yvain's father or his mother.

However that may be, Chrétien represents Yvain as feeling an obligation, which we have seen recognized in law codes of a slightly later period, to avenge the shame that his cousin underwent as a result of being defeated in single combat by Esclados li Ros (*Yvain* 579–87), an undertaking that drives the plot in the rest of the romance. Aside from one passing reference, however, Calogrenant is never heard of again and is not even numbered among the knights who accompany Arthur to the magic fountain, although Chrétien takes pains to say that not a single knight was left behind (2176–79). Calogrenant is a cousin invented for the purpose of motivating a kinship duty, Yvain's obligation to avenge the shame of a kinsman, and once this function is set in motion he disappears from view.[15] Likewise Arthur's nap was engendered to allow Yvain to undertake the adventure of the fountain without the king's forbidding him from doing so (Hunt 1974: 95–97).

Yvain's lady Laudine is, of all the ladies sought by knights in Chrétien's romances, the one who most obviously resembles a fairy, living as she does in a castle to which men have access only by means of a magic fountain (pl. 4). The son of a famous father, Yvain contracts marriage with a lady whose kingdom is quite mysterious, although she, too, is endowed with an ancestry in her father, Laudunet, who is, Chrétien tells us, the subject of a lay (2153–55).[16] Like the marriage of Erec and Enide, this ceremony is conducted according to norms: Laudine is given away by her chaplain (2152), and the wedding is witnessed by all her vassals (*voiant touz ses baron,* 2150).

Yvain thus becomes the knight of the fountain, and the cessation of the sixty-year-old *coutume* of the fountain is avoided (2104–6). The only reason the coutume is in danger, however, is that Yvain has himself killed the previous defender, Esclados. He has thus killed a man for the sake of his own determination to avenge the shame incurred by a kinsman, and has in the end inserted himself into that man's place. This would be precisely the source of Laudine's shame if it were to become known, but she manages to convince her barons of Yvain's worth as a husband and defender of the fountain, and to carry off the wedding itself, without revealing to anyone in her court except her confidante Lunete that she is marrying the man who killed her husband. Shame comes only from carrying out a reprehensible act in public. Laudine marries Yvain not out of love but out of the necessity of her people, who need a lord (2047).

Having taken the place of Esclados, Yvain has no choice but to defend the fountain, and is thus placed in a situation analogous to that of Mabonagrain in *Erec,* that is to say that having married Laudine he is in thrall to the custom and must defend the fountain against all challengers. One function of Yvain's madness, however, is that it allows him freely to choose the role of defender of the fountain, as he chooses freely to return to his wife's side.

PERCEVAL: THE QUEST FOR KIN

What has attracted, even obsessed, readers of *Perceval* more than any other aspect of the tale is the Grail itself. What does it signify? Where did it come from? Chrétien claims in lines 66–67 to have gotten a book from Count Philip of Flanders and Alsace:

> This is the Tale of the Grail,
> Of which the count gave him the book.
> [Ce est li Contes del graal,
> Dont li cuens li bailla le livre.]

If *dont* ("of which") refers to the tale, then presumably the book contained a Grail story; if it refers to the Grail, the book transmitted to Chrétien an account of the Grail but not necessarily a story in which it figured. Whether narrative or treatise, did the book really exist, or was it simply a pretext, a way of lending authority to the romance?

Whatever the book contained, preoccupation with the Grail theme has obscured other aspects of *Perceval* to the detriment of appreciation of the whole. However fascinating the Grail may be, in my view the key to Chrétien's romance lies not so much in the Grail as in the relationship between two narrative complexes that dominate the part of the work devoted to the exploits of knights errant. At the core of these two complexes are two kin groups, the lineage of the Fisher King, represented by Perceval, and the lineage of Arthur, represented by Gauvain.

The reader does not learn about the Fisher King's lineage in a straightforward manner but rather has to reconstruct it (fig. 4) according to information that Perceval's close kin—his mother, his cousin, his uncle—reveal to him incrementally in the course of the romance.

Perceval's mother tells him that his father was a knight, the best reputed and the most feared in the Illes de Mer, who was wounded between the legs.[17] She herself is, she says, of knightly lineage. They came to live in the waste forest when Perceval was two years old. Perceval's two brothers went off, on their father's advice, to serve, respectively, the king of Escavalon (463) and King Ban of Gomorret (467). These kings, for different reasons, could both be seen as unfriendly or threatening to Arthur (Ménard 1984;

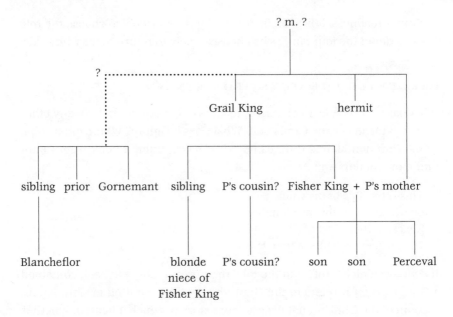

Figure 4. Perceval's lineage

Cazelles 1996: 9–10). The king of Escavalon does not appear to have been
an ally of Arthur because, as transpires later in *Perceval,* he was killed by
Arthur's nephew Gauvain. King Ban, present at the wedding of Erec and
Enide in *Erec,* line 1971, is the father of Lancelot according to both Ulrich
von Zatzikhoven's *Lanzelet* and the prose *Lancelot* (Ban de Benoÿc) and thus
father of the knight who cuckolds Arthur (Blaess 1978). Both of Perceval's
brothers were knighted on the same day but were killed on their way home
and their father consequently died of grief (481).[18] This apparent absence
of other close kin is why Perceval is so precious to his mother (486). He
sets off to be made a knight by King Arthur, but in fact at Arthur's court he
is turned aside from this goal when Keu tells him he can have the arms of
the Red Knight and he sets off to procure them. In the end it is Gornemant
de Gohort who makes him a knight.

After Perceval enters the Fisher King's castle but just before he sees the
Grail procession, the Fisher King gives him a sword that can be broken only
through a peril known to the swordmaker (3140–43). He has made only
three swords and will die before making another. This sword, destined for
Perceval (3168), came through the intermediary of the Fisher King's blond
niece or granddaughter (3145)—see the use of the word *niece* with this second, more archaic meaning by Ygerne in ll. 8065, 8087, 8275, 8278, 9049—

who is not further identified. (The scribe of one manuscript of *Perceval*, London, College of Arms, Arundel XIV, inserts a passage of 428 lines after l. 3926 in which the sword breaks while Perceval is fighting Orgueilleus de la Lande and the Fisher King declares that he will be restored to health by the man who can join its pieces together again. Two other manuscripts also contain interpolations at this point. See Busby 1993b: 395–412.)

The woman whom Perceval encounters just after leaving the Grail castle informs him that they are first cousins (*germaine cousine, cousins germains*, 3600–3601). The relationship between first cousins in Chrétien's day was, as mentioned, considered extremely close. Of what aunt or uncle of Perceval is this cousin the daughter? If we presume that Perceval and the woman are first cousins on his mother's side—and this is likely since the woman asserts that she was present at the interment of Perceval's mother and that she grew up in the mother's house, and is well informed about the mother's kinsman, the Fisher King—Chrétien names only two of the mother's siblings: the hermit and the Grail King (see fig. 3). Without multiplying entities of which Chrétien gives us not the slightest clue in the surviving text of the romance, it appears that, if the relationship is through his father's side of the family, Perceval's unnamed *cousine* may be the Grail King's daughter.[19] Is she also the blond niece (or granddaughter) who sent the sword to the Fisher King? Since she knows not only who made the sword but that it has never drawn blood (3655–59), this identification is not to be ruled out on the grounds of information provided by the narrative, but precisely where she would be placed in the genealogical diagram of Perceval's kin is another matter.

This cousin also tells Perceval that the Fisher King was wounded in battle, pierced between the haunches or thighs by a javelin (3513).[20] No other man in *Perceval* is described in this way except Perceval's father (436), which would lead to the possibility that he is to be identified with the Fisher King.[21] An objection to this thesis is that the hero's mother says that his father is dead. This seeming impediment is not one in actuality, however, since Gauvain's mother and his grandmother Ygerne, though also deceased, appear in the romance. The Grail castle, like Ygerne's castle of the Rock of Champguin, is situated outside the land of the living, in the Otherworld. Just as the Rock of Champguin is associated with white (*guin*),[22] the Grail castle is with black, the color of mourning. The Fisher King is dressed in a black robe and a black hat, both lined in purple (3089–91). Note, however, that the lance and its point are white.

The hermit whom Perceval meets on Good Friday tells him that Perceval's mother was the hermit's own sister, and the person who is served by the Grail, that is to say the Grail King, is the Fisher King's father. Furthermore, the Fisher King's father is the brother of the hermit and of Perceval's mother (6415–19). This makes the Grail King the hero's maternal uncle and the Fisher King his first cousin, however strange this might seem since the Fisher King is said to be gray-haired (3087) and thus qualified to belong to an earlier generation than Perceval's. One would normally expect first cousins to be of roughly the same age.

If the Fisher King is indeed Perceval's father and Perceval's mother is the sister of the Grail King, Perceval and his brothers would have been conceived by acts of incest between nephew and aunt.[23] The Grail King would then be not only Perceval's uncle but his grandfather and the Fisher King would be both his cousin and his father. Such a generative act would, of course, have been highly reprehensible in the late twelfth century. According to canon law, an aunt and her nephew were related in the third degree of kinship, so that marriage between an aunt and her nephew would constitute incest.

The text of *Perceval* is open to this interpretation, for the hero's cousin explains to him[24] why he did not ask the fateful questions:

You should know it happened to you
On account of the sin of/against your mother,
For she died out of grief for you.
[Por lo pechié, ce saches tu,
De ta mere t'est avenu,
Qu'ele [est] morte del doel de toi.]   (*Perceval* 3593–95)

The phrase *lo pechié . . . De ta mere* is ambiguous: it can mean either 'the sin committed against your mother' or 'the sin your mother committed'. The hermit's discussion of sin makes it clear that Perceval committed one, but it could be that his mother also sinned. Likewise *lo rei pescheor* (subject case: *li reis peschierre*) can mean in the phonetics of the period either 'the fisher king' or 'the sinner king', since *pescheor* from L. *piscatorem* 'fisher' and *pecheor* from L. *peccatorem* 'sinner' were homophones (Bourciez 1956: §273b). If both Perceval's mother and the Fisher King are sinners, did they commit the sin of incest with each other? Perceval's mother says that she, like her husband, was of the highest knightly lineage: Could it be one and the same lineage?

Note that the reading for the last line quoted above from the Roach edition of ms. *T* (Roach 1959, Bibliothèque nationale, fonds français 12576, also the base ms. for Busby 1993b) is identical in the Guiot ms. (Poirion 1994c: l. 3595), but ms. *B* (Bern, Bürgerbibliothek, ms. 354) has "who is dead out of grief for you" (Méla 1994b: l. 3533) (*Qui est morte de doel de toi*), which, unlike the reading of *T,* does not make the mother's death the cause of the son's reticence. The reading of ms. *B* is shared by six of the other fourteen manuscripts, *FLMQRS* (Hilka 1932: l. 3595 and variant), so the manuscript tradition is divided between two readings of this crucial line.

That the Fisher King could have been cured if Perceval had not failed to ask the proper questions implies that his wound is susceptible to being healed through other than medical means. If so, it may have been caused by an other than physical wound, a moral fault, namely the sin of living in an incestuous relationship with Perceval's mother.

Chrétien has one of his characters, Arthur's mother, Ygerne, raise the issue of incest during Gauvain's visit to the castle of the Rock of Champguin. Ygerne discusses with her daughter, who is Gauvain's mother—although neither woman realizes his identity—the desirability of Gauvain and Clarissant marrying. Such a union would, of course, constitute brother-sister incest. The younger queen expresses the wish that God should give them affection for each other as brother and sister have for each other, so that they should love each other and become one flesh. In the presence of so many correspondences between the Perceval adventures and the Gauvain episodes, it is difficult to believe that Chrétien is not here signaling by a counterexample the likelihood of incest in Perceval's family.[25]

The Grail King has been confined to a single room and kept alive by eating only a host for twelve years,[26] according to his brother the hermit, but this seems to be calculated back from the time when Perceval saw the Grail. Otherwise one would expect a pluperfect tense in the verb of line 6429:

And he, who is spiritual,
Because for his life he needs nothing more
Than the host that comes in the Grail,
For twelve years has been this way,
Because he has not come out of the chamber
Into which you saw the Grail enter.
[Et il, qui est esperitax
Qu'a sa vie plus ne covient
Fors l'oiste qui el graal vient,
Douze ans i a esté issi
Que fors de la chambre n'issi
Ou le graal veïs entrer.]   (*Perceval* 6426–31)

Whatever caused the Grail King's weakness would, then, have happened twelve years or more before Perceval's arrival at the Grail castle.

Perceval's mother and father, both from noble lineages of the "Isles of the sea" (*Illes de mer*, 419, 425–26),[27] came to the waste forest with his two brothers and him when he was a little more than two years old (458), as stated above. If when Perceval comes to Arthur's court and is knighted by Gornemant he is fifteen,[28] as is likely since it was the age of majority at which knighthood might be conferred, the Grail King's debilitation and Perceval's father's emasculating wound would have occurred in the same year. If the Fisher King is indeed Perceval's father, the Grail King's confinement would have begun at around the same time that the debilitating wound of his son, the Fisher King, was incurred.

The fates of the Grail King and of his son the Fisher King are obviously linked: they live in the same castle, and a question posed about the vessel in which food is being carried to the one would have cured the other. Whether or not the Fisher King is Perceval's father, the Grail King is certainly his uncle.[29] There is, then, nothing strange in the role of potential savior assigned to Perceval for his uncle and the uncle's son, his first cousin on his mother's side, given the prime importance of uncle-nephew and cousin-cousin relationships in this period.

Perceval's initial knowledge about the Fisher King comes from his unnamed first cousin. She is sitting under an oak tree beside the body of her dead lover, a knight whose head has been severed by another knight. She declares her kinship with the hero:

> I know you better than you know me
> And you do not know who I am.
> With you I was brought up
> In your mother's house for a very long time;
> I am your first cousin
> And you are my first cousin.
> [Je te conois mielz que tu moi
> Et tu ne sez pas qui je sui.
> Avoques toi norrie fui
> Chiés ta mere molt lonc termine;
> Je sui ta germaine cosine
> Et tu iés mes cosins germains.]   (*Perceval* 3596–3601)

This cousin is a crucial source of information for Perceval. In answering her question, he comes to know that he is Perceval the Welshman and to

learn the nature of the Fisher King's wound and at least the surface identity of the Fisher King and the Grail King. She tells him that if he had asked
the right questions—why the lance bleeds, where the Grail procession was
heading, what is done with the Grail—the Fisher King would have been
cured of his wound and would have been able to rule his land.

Unlike Perceval's maiden cousin, another woman plays only a bit part in
the romance, never appearing in scene—unless she happens to be identical with Perceval's first cousin—namely, the Fisher King's niece—or granddaughter, since as we have seen the Old French word *niece* can have either
meaning—who sends the king the sword that he immediately presents to
Perceval. This precious weapon, as stated above, was forged by someone
who made just three swords, and only he knows in what unique perilous
situation it will break. Perceval later learns from the cousin that the sword
will fly into pieces during a battle and that the swordmaker, Trebuchet
the Smith (Triböet in the *T* ms. edited by Roach), lives "at the lake under
Cothoatre" (*au lac qui est soz Cothoatre, Perceval* 3675). This form designates
the Middle English hydronym Scottewatre, the River Forth in Scotland, but
the use of the preposition *soz* 'under' seemed to some to imply that Chrétien
thought of it as the name of a castle or town (see Roach's note to this line
in 1959: 282). More likely is that the smith lives in an underwater realm.
In any case, the sword is said to come from the Fisher King's blond niece
(3145–46). If the Fisher King and Perceval's mother had been united in marriage, this blond niece and Perceval's cousin might well be the same person, and the cousin would then know about the sword because she was the
one who sent it as a gift to the Fisher King (see Fowler 1959: 32; and West
1971–72: 57, who make the same conjecture but without the hypothesis of
incest).

Perceval's love, Blancheflor, is the niece or granddaughter (*niece,* 1901)
of Gornemant of Gohort (1892). She also mentions having an uncle who
is a prior (*prieus,* 1911), so perhaps he and Gornemant are brothers. Her
father is dead (2280). The relationship between this kin group and Perceval's is obscure, but it is noteworthy that the Welsh *Peredur* makes Gornemant the brother of the Fisher King. In *Peredur* there is only one king, so
that the roles played by the Fisher King and the Grail King are united in
one person. In that case, Perceval and Blancheflor would have been at least
half-brother and sister and their erotic relationship would have been forbidden. Although Perceval's mother has asked him not to take the *sorplus*
from any maiden he meets (*Perceval* 548), there is no reason why he should
follow her precept with any greater common sense than was reflected in

his conduct with the woman in the tent. Close consanguinity might explain why Chrétien has the two refrain from making love (2058–69), although he has them spend the night together in the same bed. Perceval's lineage would then have a figure analogous to Clarissant in the lineage of Gauvain, namely a female offspring in the third generation with whom the hero, in this case Gauvain, flirts but who is his own unrecognized sister.

After Perceval is trained as a knight, Chrétien's romance is organized around the narratives of two great adventures: the Grail castle and the castle of the Rock of Champguin. The two marvels resemble each other in a number of ways. Access to each is obtained through information conveyed by men in boats: in Perceval's case the Fisher King and the Grail King, who encourage him to look for a castle in which to stay that in the event materializes out of nowhere, in Gauvain's by the boatman who takes the hero across a wide body of water and explains the castle to him. In each castle are two generations of sovereigns, the Grail King and his son the Fisher King, Queen Ygerne and her royal daughter, but while the castle of the Rock of Champguin is a fortress of ladies ruled by women, men are in charge of the Grail castle. Each castle is situated beyond the boundaries of the lands of the living and is ruled by a rich sovereign. The Grail castle looms up when Perceval least expects it, and his cousin tells him immediately after his experience there that she knows of no dwelling for fifty leagues in the direction from which he came. After his response she realizes it was the castle of the rich Fisher King. The two kingdoms are in severe conditions: the Grail castle is in a wasteland that will not be fertile until the Fisher King is cured, and in Champguin the dubbing of knights and the marrying of maidens awaits the arrival of a savior, and the older women have been unjustly deprived of their holdings.

When Gauvain finds out from Guiromelant that the ladies ruling the castle he has just visited are Arthur's mother and his own, his first reaction is to reflect that Arthur has had no mother for a long time and that he, Gauvain, has had none for at least twenty years. The explanation, of course, although Chrétien does not articulate it explicitly, is that the castle of the Rock of Champguin is not a land of the living, even though its fields are teeming with game. It is not a land of the dead either but, rather, an Otherworld kingdom. That the castle gates are made of ivory and ebony is no accident, for they are analogous to the gates of hell in the *Roman d'Enéas* (Petit 1997: ll. 3080–81) and in the *Aeneid,* made of ivory and horn. The Grail castle, too, is an Otherworld kingdom, but one whose fields are barren. The hero of each adventure is linked to Escavalon, Perceval because his brother served its king (463) and died while on a journey home, Gauvain because he is on his way to fight a duel before the king of Escavalon. (Escavalon is an Otherworld kingdom whose status as such is signaled by Gauvain's hunting a white doe—white animals in Celtic lore are enchanted—just before he reaches it [5677–85].) Perceval says several times in his journey that he wishes to return to his mother; he cannot do so, however, because she is dead. As Keith Busby has remarked, Gauvain, in contrast, finds his mother although he is not looking for her, but he finds her because she, too, is dead (1984: 22), or at least no longer a part of the world of the living. At issue in both the Grail castle and the Champguin episode is a series of questions: the ones Perceval does not ask and the ones Gauvain does ask of Guiromelant. The parents of Perceval and the mother of Gauvain all came to their respective dwellings upon the death of King Uther Pendragon (445, 8740).

These parallels are not fortuitous (see Antoinette Saly's studies gathered in Saly 1994). Above all, the two adventures are the narratives of heroes who encounter their own kin unexpectedly in mysterious Otherworldly castles. As in three romances preceding *Perceval,* Chrétien is using the adventures of one knight—Mabonagrain in *Erec,* Gauvain in *Lancelot,* Calogrenant in *Yvain*—as a foil against which those of the hero can be seen to have an enhanced meaning.

But three other kin groups also play roles in the Gauvain section of *Perceval.* One is the royal household of the king of Escavalon, who is "more handsome than Absolom" (4792). This young man has a sister, whom Chrétien does not name. Guingambresil is his tutor (*maistre,* 6072, the same term applied to Lunete in *Yvain,* line 1593, and to Thessala in *Cliges,* lines 3135, 3148). Guingambresil has accused Gauvain of having treacherously killed his lord (4760, 6095), the father of the royal siblings (5863).

The charge of *traïson* 'treachery' is the key here, as one knight could legitimately kill another under many circumstances provided the battle was waged fairly. The accusation of traïson is specified: Gauvain has killed the king without a prior challenge (4761), which would indeed impute to him "shame and reproach and blame" (4762). Gauvain realizes that unless he defends himself against the charge, he will shame not only himself but his entire lineage (5098–5101). Chrétien's audience will learn indirectly that this is a false accusation, since Gauvain's success in the castle of the Rock of Champguin could not have been accomplished, says the boatman who informs Gauvain about the castle, had he been a *traître* 'traitor' (7559). As far as the public within the romance is concerned, the truth or falsehood of the accusation will be decided by a single combat that is supposed to take place between Guingambresil and Gauvain in the young king's presence at Escavalon. Before the king realizes Gauvain's identity, however, he sends an escort to his sister with the message that she should receive Gauvain hospitably, which she does, much to the rage of the burghers of Escavalon, who consider her conduct shameful. The man whom Gauvain has allegedly killed treacherously must have been the same king of Escavalon whom the elder brother of Perceval served before being killed, and Madeleine Blaess (1978) has observed that the lineage of Escavalon must have been hostile to King Arthur, since Arthur's nephew killed its king. (This idea is developed extensively in Cazelles 1996.) If this is true, Perceval's mother's assurance to her son that Arthur will grant him arms ("For he will give them to you, I am quite certain" ["*Qu'il les vos donra, bien le sai*"], *Perceval* 512–15) is puzzling. Gauvain's duel with Guingambresil is put off for a year, and the king of Escavalon sends Gauvain off in quest of the Bleeding Lance, which, says a wise vavasor of Escavalon, will destroy the kingdom of Logres (6168–71), that is to say, Arthur's own kingdom.

The second lineage in question is that of Guiromelant, called in line 9124 "the Guiromelant" (*li Guiromelans*), the most handsome knight in the world (8544–45). Guiromelant, who holds the castle of Orqueneseles as a free-hold, hates Gauvain because Gauvain's father killed his own father (8779) and Gauvain killed his first cousin (8779–83). Guiromelant has killed the lover of the Hateful Damsel, Orgueilleuse de Nogres. The role Guiromelant plays, asking Gauvain about his experiences in the castle of the Rock of Champguin and informing him of the identity of the two queens he met there, is analogous to that played by Perceval's cousin for Perceval, but whereas Perceval failed the test that he encountered in the Grail castle, Gauvain succeeded in surviving the Wondrous Bed (*Lit de Merveille*). Unlike Perceval's cousin, Guiromelant has no link of kinship with the knight whom he is informing, but he does have ambitions to become Gauvain's brother-in-law because he is in love with Gauvain's sister, Clarissant, even though he has never seen her except across the river that runs in front of the castle of the Rock of Champguin (9018–19).[30]

The third kin group that Gauvain encounters is that of Greoreas, a knight whom he finds lying wounded under an oak at the boundary of Galloway. Although Gauvain cures Greoreas with an herb, Greoreas is enraged at him because Gauvain had made him eat with dogs for an entire month with his hands tied behind his back in punishment for having raped a damsel. Greoreas steals Gauvain's horse, Gringalet. An anonymous nephew of Greoreas later comes riding up on the horse (7302) and challenges Gauvain, who defeats him. Shortly afterward, this nephew serves as Gauvain's payment to the boatman who ferries him across the water to the castle of the Rock of Champguin. Greoreas may be the same person as Grigoras, dwarf vassal of the dwarf king Belins, in *Erec* 2001.

Gauvain is in a state of enmity with all three of these kin groups because of past offenses either he or his father has committed. While in the process of encountering his own female ancestors, he is continually challenged by knights who are hostile to him for his having committed what they view as crimes against themselves or their kin.

In addition to natural kinship, other kinds of kinship were also recognized in twelfth-century France: the spiritual kinship that existed between godmothers and godfathers and their godsons and goddaughters, and the legal kinship established by the practice of fosterage. Only this second type is relevant for the study of Chrétien de Troyes. A noble household would sometimes send a son to be raised by another household, and the boy, termed a *nourri,* would then enjoy many of the same privileges as a son related by blood. In *Perceval,* Gauvain hears about a difficult case involving fosterage and vassalage from a passing squire.

Melian de Lis is not merely the lord of Tibaut of Tintagel but his foster son, having been given into Tibaut's care by his father, Tibaut's lord, on his deathbed (4834–45). But Melian undertakes to fight Tibaut because he has been thwarted in his desire to become the lover of Tibaut's eldest daughter. She has turned him down first because she does not agree to love a mere squire (*escuier,* 4852), and then later, after he becomes a knight, she refuses to have him unless he proves himself by fighting in a tournament against her father, for, as she remarks, things that one obtains freely are not nearly as satisfying as those one has to pay for in some way. In the words of the squire who first informs Gauvain about Melian and Tibaut, Melian is undertaking to prove himself in the tournament,

> For love has such great mastery
> Over those who are in her grip
> That they would not dare to oppose anything
> That she should deign to command them to do.
> [Qu'amors a si grant seignorie
> Sor ciax qui sont en sa baillie
> Qu'il n'oseroient rien veer
> Qu'ele lor daignast comander.]   (*Perceval* 4871–74)

Tibaut assembles all his kin to seek advice but can find only one who rec-
ommends that he should do battle against his own lord because the others
are afraid that Melian would destroy them. The squire from whom Gauvain hears this story urges him to take part in the tournament on behalf
of Tibaut and his people, advice he at first rejects, but eventually he is led
to take Tibaut's side as the champion of the Maiden of the Short Sleeves,
younger sister of the haughty woman who inspired the tournament. Gauvain's first act is to knock Melian de Lis to the ground and send his horse
to the little girl.

Nothing more is heard of Melian, and one is left with the impression,
based on the unpleasant characteristics that Chrétien assigns to him and
his intended lover, that the unfaithful foster son has received his just des-
serts. Chrétien has also tacitly conveyed his sense that the duties of kinship, be it only legal and not blood kinship, should not be subordinated to
the claims of a concept of love that resembles Lancelot's. The relations of
Melian and Lancelot to their respective ladies are quite different, but in
each relationship the conflict is between a set of social obligations and an
all-encompassing love. The tale of Tibaut and Melian is like a lay inserted
into the greater narrative of *Perceval,* without consequence for the tale as a
whole but reinforcing the idea that the dominant theme of *Perceval* is the
problematics of kinship.

During Gauvain's adventure in Escavalon, the young king sends him into
the city to his sister, along with the message that, by the great love and faith
that should be between her and him, she is to welcome Gauvain warmly.
This love between the siblings is referred to when the message is delivered
(5798–99), when the sister agrees to welcome Gauvain (5813), and when
she defends Gauvain in spite of the admonishment of a vavasor of Escavalon who tells her that Gauvain killed her father (5964–75). Chrétien's curious insistence on brotherly love is yet another aspect of the many references to the relations between close kin in this romance. It appears to be a
counterpoint to the relationship between Gauvain and the woman whom
he later discovers is his sister, Clarissant; as mentioned above, his grandmother Ygerne, ignorant of Gauvain's identity, thinks that they would make
a desirable couple, like Aeneas and Lavinia, and Gauvain's mother concurs,
formulating the hope that they should love each other as much as a brother
and sister until they are one flesh (9057–64)!

Perceval is about people who offend against the rights and obligations
of kinship (Melian de Lis, Perceval, and, perhaps most egregiously, his
mother) and people who respect kinship (Blancheflor, the hermit, Gauvain,

the king of Escavalon and his sister, and Ygerne). Whatever Perceval knows about his kin group is told to him by the kin, not only by his mother, who omits telling him about the Fisher King and the Grail King, although presumably she was informed about them, but by his cousin and his hermit uncle. Of the two questions that Perceval should have asked in the Grail castle, the one answered by the hermit concerns not some metaphysical or religious enigma but simply an identity: Who is served by the Grail? The answer to that question would be: "Your mother's brother," and perhaps also "Your father." As Perceval says to the hermit, because he and the hermit are uncle and nephew, they should love each other better (6438). This admonition would apply all the more to Perceval and the Grail King.

The parallelism of the two mysterious castles, of the lineages of Perceval and Gauvain, and of the two heroes' exploits leads me to believe that if he had finished *Perceval,* Chrétien would have led the hero back to the Grail castle, where he would have cured the Fisher King and taken his hereditary place as king. Chrétien's careful balancing of the qualities and adventures of the two lineages would otherwise seem incomplete and futile, and I do not believe that was his intention. The insistence with which he has Perceval state that he will return to Blancheflor's castle (2929, 2954, 2960) and hold the land there as his own (2930–31) seems to signal that Beaurepaire would also have played a role in the completed romance.

KINSHIP RELATIONSHIPS IN CHRÉTIEN

In the inheritance system of primogeniture that obtained in twelfth-century northern French society, firstborn sons of noble families were normally assured of inheriting from their parents. Those below the first in birth order could seek to marry heiresses or pursue their fortunes in the church. Georges Duby has commented on the tendency of younger sons to "marry up." Among Chrétien's heroes, Erec and Cliges have no siblings, and Alexandre is firstborn. Yvain, who may or may not be a firstborn son or the only legitimate one, marries a widow who is endowed with a castle, and the possibility of his inheriting from his father is never raised. That Yvain is not "marrying up," however, is obvious from Laudine's estimate when she calls him "a higher lord than is fitting for me" (*plus haut segnour qu'a moy n'afiert, Yvain* 2132). Perceval is the only surviving son of his widowed mother and does not marry. Neither does Gauvain, who is the eldest son of Lot. There is no "marrying up," then, among these characters, and none save perhaps Yvain belongs to the category of younger sons. As Jacques Le Goff has remarked, everything happens as if all Chrétien's heroes were sons who had no brothers (Le Goff 1979: 183).

Erec and Enide are married with full benefit of clergy, as are Alexandre and Soredamor, and Yvain and Laudine. Even Enide's forced marriage to Count Oringle of Limors is carried out in the presence of a chaplain (*Erec* 4756–65). Of Cliges and Fenice it is said simply that the Greeks give her to him as his wife and that they are both crowned (*Cliges* 6869–70). Mabona-grain and his lady have not been married either before their families or in a church ceremony.

Erec, Alexandre, Cliges, and Yvain all marry women from outside their social contexts, and Perceval meets Blancheflor on his travels. Exogamy is the rule. The only woman who is sought within the knight's social circle is Guinevere, and her relationship with the seeker, Lancelot, is adulterous.

Actions motivated by the desire to avenge others are normally under-taken on behalf of kin: a father (Guiromelant), a first cousin (Calogrenant, and Guiromelant here, too), but once on behalf of a lord (Guingambresil). Engygeron, Clamadeu's evil seneschal, was present at the death of Blanche-flor's father (*Perceval* 2280) and also killed one of Gornemant's brothers (2308–9), who was perhaps also Blancheflor's father, because she describes herself as Gornemant's niece. Were Perceval to have returned to the Grail and asked the right questions, this would have benefited his first cousin, the Fisher King, and perhaps also his uncle, the Grail King. Perceval's cousin informs him of the identity of the Fisher King, as do the Hideous Damsel and Perceval's uncle the hermit. Enide's cousin is a counterexample of her own conduct. Cliges measures himself successfully against his maternal uncle Gauvain. Alis's marriage to Fenice and Melian de Lis's tournament challenge of Tibaut de Tintagel are hostile acts committed against one's own blood kin or legal kin.

To be without one's kin, to have betrayed one's kin, or to act out of keep-ing with the dignity of one's ancestors are actions that render the twelfth-century noble despised and vulnerable. When Lancelot has been freed from prison, the strongest term he can find to apply to Meleagant is *li forsligniez* 'he who has abandoned the conduct of his lineage' (*Lancelot* 6716), which is every bit as damning an epithet as the other one he uses in the same line, *li traïtres* 'the traitor'.

Patrilineality tends to be slightly privileged over matrilineality in Chré-tien's narratives. When heroes identify themselves through their family ties, it is in relation to their fathers: Erec, son of Lac, Yvain, son of Urien, Ydier, son of Nut. On the other hand, the link between Arthur and his sister's relations is blurred by the absence of a name for the sister, Gauvain's and Soredamor's mother. The woman who raised Lancelot is likewise anonymous, although in Lancelot's case genealogy is obscured. Nothing is said about the kin of Guinevere or of the empress Tantalis of Constantinople.

Exceptions to the emphasis on patrilineality are found in Chrétien, especially in his first and last romances but also in *Cliges*. In *Erec et Enide,* Enide's cousin and the count of Lalut are both related to her through her mother, Tarsenefide. In *Cliges,* Chrétien invents a sister for Gauvain in order to link Arthur's kin group with that of the emperors of Constantinople. A striking feature of *Perceval* in the context of late twelfth-century French society is its focus on relatives on the mother's side. An important role is given to Gauvain's kin in the poem, but only to his female ancestors and his sister. The males in his family, with the exception of Agrevain, who appears but briefly, are only mentioned. Perceval's lineage is conceived through his mother, sister of the Grail King and the hermit. If the Fisher King is Perceval's father, this relationship has to be deduced on the basis of subtle clues and is never articulated. Perceval would then be invested gradually with knowledge of his mother's kin and the mysteries he is called upon to resolve would be those relating to his father's identity. Genealogical concepts among twelfth-century French nobles, however, are evolving away from the female side and toward the male line. Either Chrétien had reasons to go against the prevailing spirit of his age in *Perceval,* or he was depending in this regard on narratives coming to him from another society, archaic in this respect, whose genealogical ideology differed from what was developing around him.

Is kinship ever "too close"? Are any of the love relationships that Chrétien recounts between kin who are so close that their unions would be considered consanguinous? In only one of Chrétien's works, *Philomena,* is incest between persons related through marriage the focus of the narrative.

In *Philomena,* Progné, daughter of the king of Athens, is married to Tereus, tyrant of Thrace. Tereus rapes Progné's sister Philomena. Even if she had been Tereus's sister, says Chrétien, this forced relationship would not have been considered wrong because a god told the pagans they could do whatever they wanted without it being a crime. The implication is that what Tereus did was wrong, but only because it was an act of "disloyalty and madness" (*desleauté et forsenage,* 484) toward a woman to whom he was related by marriage. After the rape, Tereus cuts out part of Philomena's tongue so that she cannot speak, and tells Progné that her sister is dead.

Progné believes her husband and makes a sacrifice to Pluto, lord of devils. Tereus in the meantime continues to rape the captive Philomena daily. She sews the story into an embroidery and has it delivered to Progné, who resolves to avenge herself by killing her five-year-old son, Ithis, and feeding him to Tereus. Progné kills the child at the prompting of devils. When Tereus realizes that he has been tricked into eating his own son's flesh, he feels shame and wants to take vengeance on his wife and sister-in-law. But the Fates (*Destinees*, 1442) change him into a hoopoe, Progné into a swallow, and Philomena into a nightingale. One can hear Philomena singing in the woodlands in springtime: *"Oci! Oci!"* ("Kill! Kill!").

In spite of a number of violent scenes in Chrétien's other works, there is nothing there to match *Philomena* for sheer brutality. What is interesting is that the only translation we have from his hands should be a tale of incest. I believe that *Perceval* is also such a tale, and we do know that Chrétien was interested enough in the topic to have chosen *Philomena* from among many stories available in the *Metamorphoses*. Also significant is that he takes pains to separate the moral values of the ancient world from those of his own time, which are the subject of the next chapter.

Chapter 3

Values

Although the kinship relations that are implicated in every facet of twelfth-century French social relations play essential roles in Chrétien's romances, they provide only a map of the conduits through which values flow, of the intensity of values, and of the limits to which they extend. The values themselves provide the moral armature for the romances, and the progress of knights and ladies through the adventures of their lives is measured accordingly. Chrétien had little way of knowing, of course, what values obtained in the distant past when, he appears to have believed, Arthur lived, nor would it necessarily have occurred to him to think that those values differed from the ones he was accustomed to. What is at play, then, is a set of values derived from the society of northern France in the second half of the twelfth century.

THE RANGE OF VALUE TERMS

Knighthood, and concomitantly the ideals that accrued to it, was in full development by the period in which Chrétien was composing his romances. Knights were "a group which . . . was on the verge of becoming a caste" (Hunt 1981: 96). The primary set of values of the knights and ladies whose deeds are the principal subject of the five romances involve the praise and fame that accrue to those performing laudable actions and the blame incurred by those whose actions are viewed as ignoble. Chrétien's works do not consist merely of sequences of encounters, adventures, and marvels: how men and women deal with those events are his primary subject. The most direct way to examine the moral universe of Chrétien's characters is to look at the terms he uses to express values and how he works out the relation between actions and values.

When a character performs a good action, this results in the acquisition of honor (*honor*). As a result, the character receives praise (*los*); the corresponding verb is *löer* 'to praise'. Thus early in *Erec et Enide* the reader is told that no knight at Arthur's court has acquired more praise than Erec (*Erec* 84). He is consequently said to have a good reputation (*pris*). Enide's father acknowledges immediately upon learning Erec's name and that of his father that he would be a prestigious son-in-law:

> "We have certainly heard
> Speak of you in this land.
> Now I love and esteem you much more,
> For you are worthy and brave.
> Never will you be put off by me:
> I present my beautiful daughter to you
> To be entirely at your command."
> ["Bien avommes oï
> De vos parler en cest païs.
> Or vos ain plus assez et pris,
> Car mout estes prouz et hardiz.
> Ja de moi n'iroiz escondiz:
> Tot a vostre commandement
> Ma fille bele vos present."]   (*Erec* 670–76)

Good repute is here represented as such a powerful quality that a virtuous vavasor would give his daughter away in marriage to a newcomer who has just arrived, basing the decision on the stranger's reputation alone.

At issue are public qualities: the reward for doing good or for fighting well is not expressed in Chrétien and contemporaneous writers of romance as a feeling of fulfillment or satisfaction, an interior recompense, but rather as approbation by the community. Guiromelant says it well in *Perceval*, anticipating his battle with Gauvain:

> For a battle between such worthy men
> As we two are thought to be
> Should not be done in hiding,
> But it is, rather, quite right that there should be
> Many ladies and knights there;
> For when one of us is defeated
> and everyone knows it,
> The winner will have a thousand times
> More honor than he would have
> If no one but he were to know it.
> [Que bataille de si preudomes

Com l'en quide que nos doi somes
Ne doit on pas faire en agait,
Ainz est bien drois que il i ait
Dames et chevaliers assez;
Que quant li uns en ert matez
Et toz li mondes le savra,
Mil tanz plus d'enor i avra
Li venquieres que il n'aroit
Se nus fors il ne le savoit.]   (*Perceval* 8861–70)

Honor and praise, correspondingly, are acquired by performing well in
public view. The distinction between public and private was also important in other areas of society, and nowhere more than in the law. Crimes
tended to be classified according to whether they occurred in public or
in private. Thus murder was taking another's life under cover of night or
killing and then hiding the body, whereas homicide was killing during a
public confrontation (Gonthier 1998: 21). Rapine was stealing violently in
public, whereas theft (L. *furtum,* O. F. *larrecin*) was taking another's goods
stealthily (Gonthier 1998: 26). Punishment for crimes routinely included a
public demonstration that entailed the shaming of convicts, often dressed
in their best clothes to accentuate the difference between their ordinary
state and the misery of their punishment (Gonthier 1998: 89, 91, 127).

Shame is an apprehension of external sanctions for one's conduct or
state of being in the form of disapproval coming from others whom one respects and whose approval one seeks. Thus the functioning of shame itself
constitutes a system of external sanction. Its primary area of operation is
the public arena, before witnesses. The judgment of the people who can
generate shame may inform a social ideal to which the subject wishes to
conform and which he or she therefore espouses. Falling short of this ideal
leads to shame. Shame can, of course, become internalized when the character is depicted as imagining, by anticipation or retrospection, the possibility of being regarded as shameful. Acceptance of the ideals of society
allows the subject to be "ashamed of" himself or herself. Shame may result
from being in a certain state that is beyond one's control: thus a person may
be ashamed of having been born illegitimately, a state that has nothing to
do with the personal responsibilities of the illegitimately born individual.
To take a historical example, King Louis VII of France is said to have been
advised not to divorce Eleanor of Aquitaine, and thereby lose control over
vast territories in southwest France, because he would be shamed by the
fact that her kin had engineered the rift between them (Duby 1983: 194–

95). Once a person is shamed, the principal remedy is to seek to regain the respect of others, and a secondary expedient is to take vengeance on the shaming party.

Guilt, by contrast, is an internal mechanism that requires interior movements of remorse, repentance, and atonement. The guilty person disapproves of his or her own conduct, not because it will be subject to the gaze of others, but because it is morally wrong. Guilt, then, is obviously possible only if the subject has internalized a set of moral precepts. One does not normally fall into guilt without having taken some action for which one is responsible, so for guilt it is necessary to have behaved as an agent. Original sin, incurred through acts of Adam and Eve, is an exception. The remedy for guilt is to repent and be moved to return any goods that the guilty party has acquired by improper means or to restore the injured party to the state that obtained before the offensive act.

The ideals that need to be pursued if a knight is to protect himself from shame are clear enough in Chrétien's works. Knights like Erec possess a number of positive qualities, the chivalric virtues.[1] Erec is *preu,* he has prowess (*pröesce*), which means that he is excellent at the physical feats a knight needs to perform. Yvain declares openly that he is pursuing adventure to test his prowess and courage (*Yvain* 360–61). *Pröesce* also, however, entails having the intelligence (*sen*) and the knowledge (*savoir*) to know when to exercise those skills, so Erec has wisdom (*sagesce*). He is faithful (*leal*) to his lord and ready, not just to be brave (*vaillant*) and to fight for him with boldness (*hardement*), but to give him sound advice in time of need, which is to say that he does what a good vassal should and so is endowed with *vasselage.* Thus Enide, distraught because she thinks she has caused Erec's death, praises him:

> "How unfortunate you were,
> Lord, you who had no equal.
> In you Beauty was reflected,
> Prowess had tested itself in you,
> Wisdom had given you his heart,
> Largess had crowned you,
> She without whom no one has great repute."
> ["Con mar i fus,
> Sire, cui pareilz n'estoit nus!
> En toi s'estoit Beautez miree,
> Pröece s'i iere esprovee,
> Savoirs t'avoit son cuer doné,

Largece t'avoit coroné,
Cele sanz cui nuns n'a grant pris."]   (*Erec* 4631–37)

Here the knightly virtues have been cast as allegorical figures measuring Erec's qualities and finding them worthy.

The term *vasselage* does not seem to be applied to women in a society in which primogeniture guaranteed male prerogatives and few women were actually vassals, but women as well as men are said to have *pröesce* and to acquire honor because of their reputation (*pris*). Women in particular should ideally be lovely (*gent*), as are most women in Chrétien's romances who are noble (*gentil*), and at times they are also called upon to be bold (*hardi*). Both men and women should demonstrate courtliness (*cortoisie*), which consists of the qualities that are appropriate for life at a sophisticated contemporary court such as those of Champagne and Flanders and the royal courts of France and England. These included not just politeness but devotion to friends—see *Lancelot* 6488–89, where the hero reproaches Gauvain for lacking courtliness in not having rescued him. One of these courtly characteristics is an innate nobility that is signaled by an open, truthful way of speaking and acting (*franchise*). Another is open-handedness (*largesce*), a willingness to give gifts, especially to those of a lower social status,[2] but *largesce* also signifies moral generosity. Knights and ladies should be capable of love (*amor,* a noun that could be feminine in medieval French and is thus often portrayed allegorically as a woman) and should know how to carry out her commands. Such behavior comes naturally to those who are of good stock, *de bon aire,* which came to be taken as one word, the adjective *debonaire.*

The ideal king, in relation to whom Chrétien measured Arthur's actions, should uphold the right (*droiture*) and justice (*justise*), law (*loi*), reason (*raison*), and truth (*verité*), as well as fidelity (*foi*) in accord with the principles that guided his ancestors. The king is thus the ultimate judge, a role that Arthur is seen playing in mediating the conflict between the heiresses of Noire Espine (*Yvain* 6304–6436). Arthur describes his basic and extremely conservative ideals to his court in *Erec:*

"I am king, I must not lie
Or consent to meanness
Or falsehood or immoderation:
I must preserve reason and legality.
This is the quality of a loyal king,
That he must uphold the law,

Truth and faith and justice.
I would not want in any way
To commit a wrong or disloyal act,
Toward the weak any more than toward the strong;
It isn't right that anyone should complain about me.
Nor do I want to abolish
The custom or the usage
That my lineage is in the habit of upholding.
It ought really to bother you
If I now wanted to establish
Other customs, other laws,
Than those my father the king upheld."
["Je suis roi, ne dois pas mentir,
Ne vilenie consentir,
Ne fauseté, ne desmesure:
Raison doi garder et droiture.
Ce apartient a leal roi,
Que il doit maintenir la loi,
Verité et foi et justise.
Je ne voudroie en nule guise
Faire deslëauté ne tort,
Ne plus au foible que au fort;
N'est droiz que nuns de moi se plaigne.
Ne je ne vuil pas que remaigne
La costume ne li usages
Que suet maintenir mes lignages.
De ce vos devroit il peser,
Se je or voloie eslever
Autres costumes, autres lois,
Que ne tint mes pere li rois."]   (*Erec* 1789–1810)

The sovereign must also be careful, however, to guard against flattery and the currying of favor (*losenge*). In troubadour and trouvère poetry, the flatterers (*lauzengers*, O. F. *losengiers*) are among the most vilified of courtiers, typically attempting to gain favor with a lord by revealing to him that his wife has bestowed her affections on another man. In *Lancelot*, where such a situation of complicity might be expected to arise, Chrétien has no such manipulating characters approach Arthur even though the relationship between Lancelot and the queen is known to at least one courtier (see *Lancelot* 213). The juridical situation that arises in *Yvain* when the younger daughter of the lord of Noire Espine pleads with Arthur to restore to her the lands from which her sister has excluded her shows clearly, however, that even when he is inclined toward a suppliant whose cause is just (*Yvain* 5905–7, 5924–26), Arthur cannot impose his will but can only attempt to persuade (*Yvain* 4782). He must, in the end, give the opportunity for judicial combat to decide the issue, although he takes a more interventionist stand when the champions recognize each other and refuse to fight to a conclusion. Neither here nor elsewhere in Chrétien's works is Arthur depicted as an absolute ruler; he is, except in *Cliges,* at best an ineffective figurehead, high though his reputation might be. This quality bears importantly on the plots of *Lancelot,* where Arthur allows Keu to lead the queen away as the prize in his duel with Meleagant, and of *Perceval,* where the king fails to react to the Red Knight's theft of his cup.

Few characters in Chrétien's romances are portrayed as motivated to behave in ambivalent ways. By far the vast majority belong either to those who attempt to act in accord with right principles of conduct—Arthur, Erec, Enide, Liconal, Tarsenefide, Guivret, King Evrain, Alexandre, Soredamor, Cliges, Jehan, Bademagu, Gauvain, Calogrenant, Lunete, the lady of Norison, Perceval, Blancheflor, Gornemant of Gohort, Ygerne, Clarissant, Guiromelant, any vavasor (see Woledge 1969)—or to the forces of destruction and evil—the robber knights in *Erec,* Count Galoain, Count Oringle of Limors, Angres of Windsor, the anonymous duke of Saxony and his nephew, Meleagant, Esclados, Count Alier, Harpin de la Montagne, the *luitons* in the castle of Pesme Avanture, any dwarf the hero or heroine happens to encounter, and almost any seneschal.

But there are some characters whose moral principles do not quite place them in either of these camps: Keu, Alis, Bertran of Thrace, Lancelot, Guinevere, and Orgueilleuse de Nogres, all of whom are the subjects of discussion later in this chapter. Fenice's conduct is presented as praiseworthy but can be accepted as such only if one understands the overriding role of shame in Chrétien's system of values. Other characters start out as threatening figures but are defeated and join the Arthurian court or have enchantments lifted from them: Ydier, son of Nut, Mabonagrain, Clamadeu, Engygeron. Still others are shadowy: Morgan, Thessala, the hideous herdsman whom Calogrenant and Yvain meet.

Among the evil qualities that one finds attributed to the dark characters in Chrétien's romances are a readiness to commit treachery and betrayal (*traïson*), wrongs (*torts*), misdeeds (*mesfaits*), outrages (*outrages*) and ugly actions (*laidures*), injuries (*forfaits*) and mean acts (*viltés*), to tell lies (*mençonges*), and to promote faithlessness (*deslealté*), falseness (*fauseté*), and evil (*mauvaistié*). Often the hostile characters act in this way because they are of filthy stock (*de put' aire,* often treated as an adjective, *deputaire,* the opposite of *debonaire*) or because of their inherent excessive pride (*outrecui-dance* or *orgoil*) and haughtiness (*estultie*). These last qualities are extreme compared to the good characters' justifiable pride—*fierté,* sometimes meaning, in regard to men, 'fierceness', considered a virtue in a martial context. The bad kind of pride leads evildoers to issue threats (*menaces*). At times they are compared to thieves (*larrons*) or they may even live by their evil ways, like the robbers (*robeors*) who threaten Erec and Enide. In the end, however, dishonor (*deshonor*) befalls them.

Virtuous men and women may, of course, exhibit or be accused of undesirable traits from time to time, and without this Chrétien's characterization would not be interesting. In many cases characters are said to act according to folly (*folie*), the most frequently found negative value-word in the five romances. The encyclopedic *Livre de Sidrac* (late thirteenth century), after describing the folly that is madness, distinguishes a different type of folly:

> But there is another kind of folly that is very bad for those affected and for other people. That is to say those who live badly and who take from others and who steal and who kill people and swear false oaths and who sin in many ways . . . and one should be on one's guard against them. For by their folly evil happens to them and to other people.
>
> [Mais il i a autre maniere de folie que est mult malvaise por aus et por l'autre gent. Ce est a savoir ceaus qui mal vivent et qui tollent d'autrui et qui emblent et qui tuent la gent et fausement jurent et qui pechent par mult de manierez . . . et s'en doit on mult garder. Car por lor folie sont maus a aus et as autrez gens.] (Ms. Bibliothèque nationale, fonds français 12444, cited in Fritz 1992a: 6)

Folly thus encompasses a wide range of negative activity, including, in Chrétien's romances, indiscretion, outrageous behavior, madness, and sins such as adultery. Fools are sometimes said to behave as if they are out of their senses (*forsenez*).

Gauvain is accused, albeit falsely, of treason (*traïson*) for having allegedly killed the king of Escavalon without first publicly challenging him (*Perceval* 4759–65), which would be a violation of the chivalric code except under the most extreme circumstances (see, for example, *Erec* 4858–62). Folly and treachery expose characters to the blame (*blasme*) brought on by shame (*honte*) and trouble or annoyance (*enui*), because then they would be acting as do the uncouth or uncourtly (*vilains*) and might be accused of being evil or lawbreakers (*felons*). Others might then treat them with disdain (*despit*), or think they are *recreant*—unwilling to uphold justice, cowardly, or, for knights, simply negligent in maintaining their skills. Sometimes, however, they have merely transgressed (*trespassé*) against a prohibition. Shame can also be a force for good, when it inspires someone to praiseworthy conduct:

> Unhappiness passes and shame lasts
> In a vigorous and upright man,
> But in the bad man it dies and grows cold.
> [Dolors trespasse et hontes dure
> En homne viguerreus et roide,
> Mais el malvais muert et refroide.]   (*Perceval* 2904–6)

Honte derives from a Frankish root, **haunitha*,[3] and thus entered Gallo-Romance sometime after the victory of the Franks in the late fifth century but before there was a consciousness of French as a language distinct from Latin. In this sense *honte* is somewhat unusual, as most medieval French words for basic emotions derive from the lexicon handed down in spoken Latin: *amor, colpe* (guilt), *humilité, joie, merci, peor* (fear), and *vergogne* (shame). From Frankish also derive, however, *orgoil* (< **urgoli*), *haïr* (to hate) (< **hatjan*), and *hardir* (to become brave) (< **hardjan*), whence *hardi*.

Such are the principal value terms in Chrétien's romances. How does the set of values that they articulate differ from what might be considered the ideal? What virtues and vices are not included?

A seemingly praiseworthy quality is to show pity (*pitié*) toward the downtrodden, as Yvain does repeatedly, and also to take pity on or extend mercy (*merci, grace*) toward a defeated enemy. Thus one of the instructions that Gornemant of Gohort gives Perceval is to spare defeated knights who ask for mercy. In another context, just before his judicial combat with Meleagant over whether Keu has made love to Guinevere, Lancelot goes out of his way to swear that if he gets the upper hand he will show Meleagant no mercy (4984), although he is never given the chance to make good on this oath since he acquiesces when the queen asks that the combat be ended. In the same romance, however, the hero fails to grant mercy to a defeated enemy. Lancelot is accosted by a knight who mocks his desire to cross the Sword Bridge and recalls to him the shame of the cart episode; the knight then offers to ferry Lancelot across the river in exchange for the right then to cut off Lancelot's head or retain him at his whim. Lancelot refuses and they do battle. When Lancelot wins the combat, he offers to accede to the knight's request for mercy (*Lancelot* 2750), but only if the knight agrees to incur shame by himself climbing into a cart. The knight demurs, offering to do anything but that, and begs again for mercy (2770). At that point Meleagant's sister rides up and asks and receives an unspecified favor of Lancelot, which turns out to be the head of the defeated knight, whom she calls the most disloyal person who ever lived, maintaining that to kill him would be no sin (2812). The knight asks a third time for mercy, now in the name of God and the Virgin Mary. After some pressure from the allegorical figures Largess and Pity (2830–65), Lancelot decides for the first time in his life not to take pity completely on a vanquished foe but rather to limit his mercy to allowing the knight to rearm and fight on while he, Lancelot, pledges not to move from the spot where he is standing. When Lancelot triumphs once again, however, he cuts off the knight's head despite the knight's reiterated requests for mercy (2903, 2911) and his insistence that killing him would in fact be a sinful act (2915). Lancelot gives the severed head to Meleagant's sister. This might not seem to be the most magnanimous course of action, but Chrétien gives no overt sign of his disapproval.

Routine respect for the dignity of those who are not of noble rank seems not to have been one of the values shared by knights in this period or in Chrétien's romances. The scene in which Gauvain has to defend himself with Excalibor against the townspeople of Escavalon plays up the cowardice of the burghers, who are shown exhibiting much unseemly fear (5992–99).

The lack of regard for religious values reflected in this set of value terms is remarkable. *Pechié* 'sin' does occur in Chrétien's corpus (see below the discussion of *Perceval*), but not nearly as often as *folie, honte, traïson,* and allied words such as *traïtre* 'betrayer', or *tort.*

A still more remarkable omission is any overt allusion to the concept of the feeling of guilt. Not that *corpe* or *colpe* 'guilt' does not occur in Chrétien; but it is found only eight times in the five romances and always refers metaphorically to juridical guilt rather than actually to sentiments. Enide assigns to herself the guilt for what she thinks is Erec's death (*Erec* 4644). In *Lancelot,* Keu wishes to show he has no guilt by disculpating himself in combat of the accusation that he has made love to the queen (*colpe,* 4899; *ancolpe,* 4900). Yvain admits that he is guilty for having stayed away from Laudine for longer than he had promised (*Yvain* 6775).[4] The three references to guilt in *Cliges* are all in the context of love casuistry (*Cliges* 503, 559, 561). Finally, Engygeron invokes a proverbial expression: often one who has no guilt pays for what others do (*Perceval* 2196–97). These eight occurrences, with only two characters declaring themselves guilty, are a meager harvest of clear references to guilt in more than thirty-six thousand lines of narrative. *Honte,* by contrast, occurs more than 180 times.

In every society there are sanctions that impel men and women to act in ways that benefit the collectivity. Just as the ultimate benefit of good behavior in the society Chrétien depicts in his romances is not an internal feeling of satisfaction but rather the external reward of praise and honor conferred by the surrounding society, so the principal sanction of evil, or of the suspicion of inadequacy, or even of inconsiderate actions is not a sentiment of guilt but rather general condemnation by the community, designated as shame. Chrétien uses honte constantly as the ultimate threat to the reputations not only of knights but of ladies.[5] Honte can be generated only in a public setting: someone has to know that the character has either done wrong or been humiliated by a hostile agent, and news of the opprobrious act has to spread so that the community realizes that it has taken place. The means by which this news travels is not always apparent, especially when the character who is branded by honte is traveling through an alien land. Thus many of the people whom Lancelot meets while traveling toward and within the land of Gorre after he has been shamed by sitting in the cart already know of that shame. Once shame has been incurred, it appears to be internalized: that is to say, the character is then viewed as feeling the shame even when others are not present as witnesses (for a subtle analysis of the internalization of honte in Chrétien, see Hult 1988–89). Honte can be dispelled only by some act of vengeance that takes place in a public forum, allowing one to "save face," or by an act of reparation.

Let us see how this set of values is exemplified in Chrétien's tales.

EREC ET ENIDE: THE SHAME OF RUMOR

A key scene for the problematics of *Erec et Enide* is the conversation between the hero and his bride that takes place just after their wedding in Carnant. Enide has heard that people are talking about Erec's having relinquished the practice of arms in favor of spending copious amounts of time with her, the wife whom he has made his lover (*Erec* 2434–35).[6] Not that he has abandoned largess (2446–48), but the time he passes in loving her crowds out his desire to go to tournaments (2430–33), a propensity that greatly troubles his male companions. Chrétien had here the opportunity of appealing to the concept, propounded by several theologians of the eleventh and twelfth centuries, such as Peter Damian (d. 1072) and Hugh of St. Victor (d. 1141), that taking excessive pleasure in the sexual act, even within the bonds of marriage, is sinful (Brundage 1987: 197–98). Instead he invokes a purely secular concern. As a result, knights and their squires blame him as a *recreant* in matters of armed combat and chivalry (2459–62). Recreancy (*recreantise*) is the quality of those who give up fighting out of fear or lassitude and here, by extension, those who, although knights, do not keep themselves in proper fighting trim. This public reprimand disturbs Enide so much that one morning, after they have made love, she expresses aloud the thought that is worrying her, believing that Erec is asleep.

> "The earth should swallow me up,
> Since the very best knight,
> The bravest and the most fierce,
> The most handsome and the most courtly
> Of all those who were ever count or king,
> Has entirely abandoned
> All chivalry on my account.
> Thus I have truly brought shame upon him.
> I would not have wanted this for anything."
> ["Bien me devroit sorbir la terre,
> Quant toz li mieudres chevaliers,
> Li plus hardiz et li plus fiers,
> Li plus beax et li plus cortois,
> Qui onques fust ne cuens ne rois,
> A de tout en tout relenquie
> Por moi tote chevalerie.
> Donques l'ai je honi por voir.
> Nel vousisse por nul avoir."]   (*Erec* 2494–2501)

The central conflict in *Erec*, then, is between the imperatives of love and the demands of chivalric readiness, and Enide blames herself for her lover's obsessiveness in loving her. The question of who is to blame is, in fact, never resolved in *Erec*, perhaps because Chrétien did not think it so important. If Erec has indeed neglected chivalric practices, there is no reason for the reader to believe that Chrétien conceived of his course of conduct as an act of the will or a deliberate decision. What is of capital importance, however, is not so much what Erec has done but that his doing it has become an open matter, the subject of rumor and discussion. It has thus caused *honte* to be imposed on him.

This is the worst consequence of all for one imbued with the set of values prevalent in twelfth-century French courtly milieus, so Enide takes pity on her husband and lover, exclaiming: *"Con mar i fus!"* (2503). *Mar* is an adverb that derives from L. *mala hora,* ablative case, meaning 'in a bad hour'. It confers on whatever verb it is attached to a sense of the unfortunate, the unlucky, the bad break, the fatal: "How unfortunate that you were there." "Too bad for you that you were there!" This is apparently a reference to Erec's presence in the kingdom of Lalut, where he met his future bride and won the Test of the Sparrow-Hawk. The subsequent events and the very love that Erec feels for her have, against all expectation, resulted in shame.

To dispel the shame that Erec's peers have ascribed to him, Erec places himself and his wife in the most perilous situations, riding without escort in forests populated by robber horsemen and nobles without honor who attempt to exploit the couple's vulnerability. By overcoming them all—first three, then five hostile knights, Count Galoain, two giants, Count Oringle of Limors, and, in addition, Keu and Guivret le Petit—and making the enchantment of the Joy of the Court dissipate by worsting Mabonagrain, Erec proves that the charge of recreancy brought against him was wrong. By her conduct in resisting what might have been tempting offers to become the lover of Count Galoain and mistress of all his holdings, and to marry Count Oringle and receive half his land in dowry, Enide has also proven her devotion, leading Erec to exclaim that he has tested her and is now certain of her love.

Immediately after seeing Erec's reaction to her bedroom utterance Enide regrets her action, engaging in self-analysis. She realizes that what caused the best man in the world, who wanted nothing but her, to turn against her was her *orgoil,* which led her to say such a great *outrage* (2602–4). The excessive pride she is thinking of is her worrying over Erec's reputation and consequently revealing to him what people were thinking of his conduct, with the implication that she should have left well enough alone and allowed him to discover the change by himself. Chrétien leaves unresolved the issue of whether this analysis is correct, by the hypothetical wording that ends Erec's conciliatory admission in the reconciliation scene, while he is riding with Enide in his arms in the moonlight:

> He hugs her and says, "My sweet sister,
> I have tested you in everything.
> Do not be at all dismayed,
> For now I love you more than I ever did before,
> And I for my part am certain and sure

That you love me completely. . . .
And if you have misspoken anything in my regard,
I pardon you and hold you harmless
For both the offense and the words."
[L'estraint et dit: "Ma douce suer,
Bien vos ai dou tot essaïe.
Ne soiez de rien esmaïe,
Q'or vos ain plus que ainz ne fis,
Et je resui certains et fis
Que vos m'amez parfaitement. . . .
Et se vos m'avez rien mesdite,
Je le vos pardoing et claim quite
Et le forfait et la parole."]   (*Erec* 4914–19, 4923–25)

A few days after the reconciliation, in the castle of Penuris, the two find
the privacy to make love day and night (5232), coming together for the first
time since they left Carnant. Enide has incurred shame in the eyes of her
husband, but not in view of anyone but him. Just as her shame was confined within the couple, so is her reconciliation.

Erec's *honte*, by contrast, as a public phenomenon, is removed publicly
by three events. The first is his encounter with Arthur's itinerant court
toward the middle of the journey. Erec refuses to be turned aside despite his
wounds. On this occasion, Gauvain, paragon of knighthood, without recognizing Erec, pronounces him "Truly the best knight / That I ever thought I
would see" (*Le meillor chevalier por voir / Que je cuidasse onques veoir*, 4117–
18). The second event is that Erec has sent back to Arthur's court Cadoc of
Tabriol, the knight whom he rescued from the two giants, with the request
that Cadoc inquire of Arthur who Erec is and thereby honor Erec (4521).
The third is that Erec himself recounts to Arthur and his courtiers the tale
of his adventures (6467–87) in the presence of Guivret le Petit, witness to
his victory over Mabonagrain. No one can henceforth impute to him the
debilitating vice of recreancy.

The sequence of events that follows the wedding reaffirms what has
already been proven in what Chrétien calls the first section (*premerains
vers,* 1840), namely that Erec has sufficient prowess to avenge shame, in
this case the shame caused by an outrage (*outrage,* 989, 1022), namely that
Ydier's dwarf retainer struck him and Guinevere's lady-in-waiting with a
whip. The main section, then, concerns not primarily the testing of prowess but a testing of the relative weights that should ideally be given to love
and chivalry.

CLIGES: HONOR AND SHAME WITHIN THE KIN GROUP

Erec was falsely accused of recreancy, but in *Cliges* there is a scene in which this moral defect is portrayed vividly. The shameful party is decidedly not, however, a character for whom Chrétien is attempting to arouse sympathy but rather one who, although genealogically well endowed, remains unnamed: the duke of Saxony. The duke first encounters shame by proxy. He sends his likewise anonymous nephew as a messenger to inform the German emperor that the emperor will have no peace unless he complies with a previous promise and sends his daughter Fenice to be the duke's bride. The nephew, in the company of three hundred Saxons, challenges Cliges, the nephew of Fenice's fiancé, the emperor Alis of Constantinople, to battle. Cliges unhorses the duke's nephew, causing him to attempt to avenge this shame; but, says Chrétien, "One who wishes to avenge his shame / Sometimes only makes it grow" (*Tex cuide, se il li loist, / Venchier sa honte qui l'acroist, Cliges* 2885–86). Cliges again unhorses the duke's nephew, doubling his shame (2891). The Saxons flee to a ford, where Cliges causes the nephew still greater shame and annoyance (2908) by unhorsing him yet a third time.

Later, the Saxons and their duke accost the Greek cortege on its journey back to Constantinople, on the banks of the Danube. In the first encounter, after Cliges kills the duke's hapless nephew, he sees another Saxon knight charging toward him who does not wish to be counted among the *recreant* (3433). Cliges kills this man as well. He then places the enemy's head on the point of his lance and, mounted on the dead man's horse, charges boldly into the Saxon ranks. In the course of this battle, Cliges and the duke meet and Cliges unhorses his opponent. Then, inspired to acquire *los* (3618), he rescues Fenice, who has been abducted, allowing only one of her captors to escape so that he can report Cliges's name to the duke (3765).

This amounts to a challenge in guise of a report and it leads to a crucial scene. The duke of Saxony challenges Cliges to single combat, but in the midst of their encounter the duke decides that he does not wish to see it through. He takes refuge in the values of chivalric society, alleging that were he to win against such a young man, it would bring him neither praise (*los*) nor repute (*pris,* 4105), and even to admit that the two had fought would bring the duke shame and Cliges honor (4109). This, however, is unacceptable to the young knight, who wants his victory to be seen and not just known about. So Cliges asks the duke to admit publicly (*oianz touz,* 'within earshot of everyone', 4118, 4125) that in stopping the battle he is not showing mercy to Cliges, to which the duke consents. Cliges thus acquires honor and *pris* (4128), while the Saxons fall to the ultimate moral depths:

> The duke returns to Saxony,
> Unhappy and checkmated and embarrassed,
> For among his men there are not two
> Who don't consider him wretched,
> Failed and cowardly.
> The Saxons, in all their embarrassment,
> Went back into Saxony.
> [Li dus en Sesoigne repaire,
> Dolenz et maz et vergondeus,
> Car de ses homes n'i a deus
> Qui nel tieignent por mescheant,
> Por failli et por recreant.
> Li Saine o toute lor vergoigne
> S'en sont reperié en Sessoigne.]   (*Cliges* 4138–44)

In spite of this resounding triumph, however, Cliges decides, as did his father before him, that in order to win honor he must associate with the *preudomes* 'worthy men' at Arthur's court.

This extraordinarily denigrating treatment of a high-ranking noble figure, the duke of Saxony, has led a number of scholars to believe that Chrétien is adumbrating here the fall from imperial grace and the eventual disgrace of Duke Henry the Lion of Saxony, which occurred in the period 1176–1180 (see pp. 13–14, above).

Cliges has long been recognized as an anti-*Tristan* or counter-*Tristan* (see the treatment in Fourrier 1960: 124–54). Interestingly, it is in the text of *Cliges* that Chrétien tells his audience that he himself wrote about King Mark and Ysolt the Blonde, which is commonly understood as a reference to a lost narrative of Tristan and Ysolt. From Chrétien's use of a pun on *l'amer* ('loving', but also 'the bitter' and, written as *la mer*, 'the sea'), it appears likely that his narrative was in the tradition associated with the *Roman de Tristan et Ysolt* of Thomas d'Angleterre, which has survived only in fragments, rather than with Béroul's romance.

In any case, Chrétien has his characters refer several times in *Cliges* to the Tristan tradition. When Fenice reveals to her tutor, Thessala, that although she will marry the emperor Alis, she is in love with his nephew Cliges, she immediately declares her wish that they not emulate the love of

Tristan and Ysolt "of whom one tells so many follies / That it shames me to recount them" (*Dont tantes folies dist l'en / Que hontes m'est a raconter,* 3102–3). Indeed folly (*folie*) is a word that is often applied to adulterous love. In Béroul's *Roman de Tristan,* for example, after it has been discovered that Tristan has leapt from his bed into Ysolt's, he offers to do judicial battle with anyone who claims that he has loved the queen "in folly" (*par folie*) (Ewert 1939–71: l. 802). Discovering the lovers sleeping in their forest bower, King Mark renounces killing them because, seeing that they are clothed and that a sword lies between them, he does not believe that their intent was "foolish love" (*fole amor*) (Ewert 1939–71: 2013). The follies that Fenice says are ascribed to Tristan and Ysolt are, in fact, accusations of adultery and, more than this, of adultery between the king's wife and his nephew, a relationship that falls well within the bounds of incest as conceptualized in this period in the Christian world.

Fenice and Cliges are potentially in precisely this situation, and if even telling about Tristan and Ysolt would cause Fenice shame, acting like Ysolt would cause a shame that is infinitely greater. For in Ysolt, love lost its nobility and became vile (*Amors en lui trop vilena, Cliges* 3106).

Later, when Cliges has returned from Arthur's court and he and Fenice have revealed their love to each other, she declares that no one will learn baseness (*vilanie*) from her example, for never will Cliges be called "Tristan" nor she "Ysolt." If the contrary were to occur, then their love would not be worthy (*preuz*). In that kind of love there would be blame and vice, Fenice declares, and one might well expect her to continue on to the effect that she and Cliges would never be able to make love. She does not, however. Rather, she places a condition on their coming together as lovers. Cliges must first separate her from his uncle so that Alis can never find her again. In that way, no one will blame them (5204–6). They separate and consider this notion, and the next day Cliges proposes that the two of them go to Britain, where Arthur will welcome them more joyfully than Helen was welcomed in Troy when Paris led her there. This is an unfortunate comparison with yet another adulterous woman, however, and Fenice returns to her own simile: in that case people, ignorant of the potion administered to Alis that preserved Fenice's virginity—consummation was, after all, a necessary condition of the marital bond—would speak of them as of Ysolt and Tristan and would blame their pleasure (5250).

Fenice then invokes a counsel of St. Paul that has the inconvenience of not being found in any scriptural text: whoever does not wish to remain chaste should act so wisely as to avoid touching off scandal, blame, or reproach (5261–63). She then proposes to have herself buried alive but as if dead, to be disinterred later by Cliges. After that, if Cliges can find a place where no one will take note of them, they can live together:

> If the thing is done cleverly,
> Never will ill be spoken of it
> Nor will anyone criticize it,
> For in the whole empire it will be thought
> That I have rotted in the ground.
> [Et se la chose est par sen faite,
> Ja en mal ne sera retraite
> Ne ja nus n'en porra mesdire,
> C'on cuidera par tot l'empire
> Que je soie en terre porrie.]   (*Cliges* 5295–99)

What makes this arrangement acceptable is not that Fenice's marriage with Alis remains unconsummated—for even if this were not generally known, the two lovers would know it in their hearts—but that adultery that becomes public leads normally to blame, detraction, and shame. Thus Lancelot's adultery is never said to cause him shame, but when he and Guinevere meet after he returns to court from the tower in which Meleagant had him imprisoned, Lancelot avoids doing all that his heart desires, for if he were to do so within sight of everyone (*veant toz, Lancelot* 6840), it would be the height of folly. The false death that Fenice undergoes, the central plot device of *Cliges,* has as its sole stated justification to avoid the public humiliation of shame.

The couple does in fact avoid shame, but only for a time. Cliges's slave Jehan, a master craftsman, constructs a tower in the woods where the two lovers can make love endlessly without anyone else knowing about their hideaway. One day a young knight, Bertran, catches sight of the lovers sleeping naked side by side in the walled orchard beside the tower. Cliges pursues Bertran and cuts off his leg below the knee. Bertran manages to reach Constantinople, however, and the shame is upon Alis (6457), whose wife is now known to have been living with another man. This shame is intensified (6558) when Alis learns from Jehan, who has been captured, that the enjoyment he thought he had had from making love to his wife was only the effect of the potion. Nor does it please Alis to be reprimanded and challenged in public by Jehan over his having married despite his promise to Cliges's dead father that he would remain celibate. Alis is so unhappy at not being able to find the lovers, who have gone to Britain to seek Arthur's help, that he goes out of his mind (6245), ceases eating and drinking, and dies a madman.

Whether Alis's fate is justified by the events of Chrétien's tale is another matter. Is the reader obliged to condemn a man who becomes emperor only because he is led to believe by a mendacious partisan that the rightful emperor, his brother, is dead, who agrees to share the power with that brother when he turns up alive, who wants to remain faithful to a promise not to marry (2592) but finally marries because of pressure from his vassals, who is tricked by a potion into thinking he makes love to his wife, who is cuckolded and tricked by her and his own nephew, and who, finally, is then shamed publicly with mortal consequences when the illicit love is discovered? Just as it is difficult for the reader of the romances of Tristan not to feel some sympathy for King Mark, so the reader of *Cliges* may well find it difficult to condemn Alis's actions. Perhaps Chrétien also felt this way, which would account for the romance's curious ending in which he explains that it is because of Fenice that the Byzantine emperors confine their wives to the bedroom and place them under the guard of eunuchs.

The punishment inflicted on Bertran is curiously out of keeping with his offense, which is simply that, with no evil intent, he happened upon Cliges and Fenice in a compromising situation. Such a fate makes moral sense only if one views Bertran as the means by which the public eye falls upon a hitherto private relationship. The distinction between public acts, for which one takes responsibility, and private acts, which seem to have no moral consequences, is a key to understanding Chrétien's moral universe. In his literary world, adultery is apparently not morally problematic as long as it takes place out of sight, shielded from the sanction of shame.[7]

What of Paul's saying that Chrétien has Fenice invoke before she conceives the stratagem of the False Death? Chrétien has taken an utterance ascribed to Paul in the Bible and modified it for the values of his society. Rather than "better to marry than to be tortured in hell" (1 Cor. 7.9), he has Paul advise, "If you are going to sin, do it out of sight." This modification fits perfectly a milieu in which shame is the ultimate sanction for misconduct. A Latin proverb appears to be at the source of this counsel: if you are not chaste, then at least be careful (*Si non caste, tamen caute,* see Walter 1994: 1163–64). Ironically, Paul is invoked at the onset of a process that could not be more out of keeping with Christian moral orthodoxy, whether of the twelfth century or any other period. Moreover, the Pauline reference to hell is effaced. The contrast between the alleged source and the proverb's cynical advice underscores the secular nature of moral decision-making in Chrétien's romances.

LANCELOT: SHAME AND LOVE SERVICE

Lancelot is also about shame, but a paradoxical shame inflicted in seemingly arbitrary fashion on Lancelot by Queen Guinevere. The scene of Lancelot in the cart, after which Chrétien named his romance (*Lancelot* 24), and by which Godefroy de Lagny calls it (7103), is one of shaming.

Lancelot is searching for the queen and meets a dwarf who is driving a cart and holding a long stick in his hand (347–49). The dwarf tells Lancelot that if he climbs into the vehicle, he will soon know the queen's whereabouts. Understandably Lancelot is reluctant to ride in this nefarious conveyance in which felons are often transported. His hesitation is occasioned by his receiving contradictory interior advice from Reason and Love. Reason tells him not to do anything that will bring him shame or reproach. Reason, says Chrétien, is not in the heart but only in the mouth (*N'est pas el cuer mes an la boche, Lancelot* 370)—the word *raison* in Old French commonly means 'speech' in addition to 'reason'. Love, however, which does dwell in the heart, advises him to jump into the cart, which he does, dismissing his misgivings about shame (376). This is precisely Lancelot's problem and the core problematic of Chrétien's romance: under the impulsion of love, Lancelot decides to do things that lead not to his honor but to his shame. In pursuit of his passion, he follows a trajectory that is just the opposite of that pursued by Erec, Alexandre, Cliges, Yvain, and Perceval, that is to say of all Chrétien's other heroes. Even Gauvain, riding with Lancelot in this scene, believes that climbing into the cart would be *molt grant folie* 'an extremely foolish thing' (389). Guinevere, however, implies later to Lancelot that he should not have felt shame at the prospect of getting into the cart, a sentiment that made him hesitate for two steps[8] before he climbed in (4484–87) and caused her to become cold toward him. Indeed, the queen's opinion does not seem far from the view that Lancelot expresses a few lines before she reproaches him for his hesitancy, when he states to himself that everything he did for her seems to him to be an honor, even stepping into the cart (4369–71). But her expectations are absolute: even a slight hesitation in conforming to them is enough to make her reject Lancelot. He can reach his goal if he agrees to make shame into honor, honor into shame.

As Lancelot progresses toward his goal of finding and liberating the queen, those he meets along the way remind him of the cloud of shame that hangs over him: the populace in the castle of the Perilous Bed (405–19, 439–40), the First Damsel (581), the knight guarding the passage of stones (2214–19), the knight who offers to ferry him across the waters into Gorre (2596–2600). This impending shame sometimes angers Lancelot, as, for example, when he defeats the second of these knights and offers to free him only if he climbs into a cart himself. Yet he cannot undo his shameful act, nor would he want to if it has furthered his progress toward the queen, so with that one exception he simply submits to public opprobrium.

Whenever it is a question of actions that do not directly involve love, however, Chrétien has Lancelot slip back into the normal set of values for a knight living in his society: to avoid shame and seek honor. Thus in contemplating whether he should rescue the Fourth Damsel from what he believes is the threat of rape, Lancelot formulates the chivalric code perfectly: "I would prefer by far to die / With honor than to live in shame" (*Asez mialz morir . . . vuel / A enor que a honte vivre,* 1114–15). Likewise Lancelot fights vigorously to prevent being shamed by losing his first battle with Meleagant. Shame, then, is desirable only when it furthers Lancelot's love relationship with the queen. Lancelot thus submits to it voluntarily a second time at the tournament of Noauz, when he fights his worst at the queen's whim to prove to her that he is entirely in her service (5669–71). Matilda Bruckner points out that the tournament of Noauz occupies a key place in *Lancelot* analogous to that of the castle of Pesme Avanture in *Yvain* and the Joy of the Court in *Erec,* all three of these crucial episodes constituting a high point of the second series of the respective heroes' exploits (Bruckner 1993: 62).

Relationships like the one between Lancelot and the queen, however, were considered highly shameful in medieval society. Adultery was punishable by the most severe penalties, which included being paraded naked in public, the payment of heavy fines, public castration, being burned alive, and other forms of execution, depending on local law and custom (Benton 1968: 105–9; Gonthier 1998: 129–31). Adultery with the wife of one's lord was considered a heinous crime, as a treasonous abuse of the feudal tie. The horrible death of the knight Gautier de Fontaines at the hands of Count Philip of Flanders, who suspected the knight of cuckolding him (see above, pp. 50–51), was warning enough for those tempted to convert the literary relationship between aspiring lover and lady into a real-life affair.

Wace does not hesitate in the *Roman de Brut* to make his sentiments on this point known in treating Guinevere's adultery with Arthur's nephew Mordred:

> After this great felony
> Mordred committed another base act,
> For, against Christian religion,
> He took to his bed the king's wife,
> The wife of his uncle and his lord
> He took, like a traitor.
> [Emprés ceste grant felunie
> Fist Modred altre vilainie,
> Kar, cuntre crestïene lei,
> Prist a sun lit femme lu rei,
> Femme sun uncle e sun seignur
> Prist a guise de traïtur.]   (Arnold 1938–40: ll. 13025–30)

No such condemnation is found in Chrétien's *Lancelot*.

In order to be shameful, the adultery would have to be known to the public or at least to the offended husband, of course, but Chrétien goes out of his way to create a witness to Guinevere's faith in someone other than her husband as her savior. As Keu is taking the queen to his assigned combat with Meleagant, Count Guinable overhears the queen address an absent man (*amis* in ms. Chantilly, Musée Condé 472, meaning 'friend' or 'lover') under her breath to the effect that if he knew, he would not let her be led off without trying to prevent it (209–11). This Count Guinable is not mentioned again in the romance, although he might well have been, had Chrétien rather than Godefroy of Lagny completed it. It is possible that Chrétien meant to imply that Guinable then informed Lancelot of the queen's predicament, but if so for some reason Chrétien left the matter unexplicated (see Foulet 1977). Another indication that Lancelot's passion is notorious comes from the wife of Meleagant's seneschal, who is skeptical about the knight's conditional profession of devotion—he promises to give her "all he has" of his love—since, she says, she has heard that he has already given it away (5476–88).

In *Lancelot*, then, Chrétien departs from his presentation of knightly values in a radical way, turning them on their head inasmuch as the central theme, the illicit love between Lancelot and Guinevere, is concerned. What is remarkable is not merely that he portrays without the slightest overt condemnation an adulterous affair that would be unacceptable under both feudal law and Christian moral teaching but that he reverses for the knight who is in love the roles of shame and honor. In this respect, *Lancelot* is a revolutionary work, unique among the romances composed in medieval French.

YVAIN: SELF-SHAMING

The theme of *Yvain* as expressed in its prologue is prowess (*pröesce*), the excellence that comes from performing well the activities of one's station in life. For a monk, prowess signifies learning and piety, for a woman faithfulness and chastity (whence the English *prude,* from the feminine form of *preu* 'endowed with excellence'), for the knight skill at fighting on horseback and effectively supporting his lord with all that this entails. King Arthur's prowess, Chrétien states in the opening lines of the prologue, teaches one how to be preu and courtly. Chrétien is presenting Arthur's period as a golden age, one in which people knew how to love well because they were preu and generous and full of honor (23). Since Yvain is the central male figure of the romance, his prowess comes as no surprise, but it threatens to fade in the course of the tale and has to be reinvigorated. Knights like Yvain who possess prowess that they are willing to use in the service of others are called *preudomes* 'men of excellence'.

Shame makes its appearance in *Yvain* at the very onset of the narrative proper, when Chrétien comments that Calogrenant told a tale to five of the other knights of Arthur's court, as well as to the queen, not about his honor but about his shame (60). The upshot of the story is, in fact, that Calogrenant is shamed by having been defeated in single combat by Esclados (540)—although one might well wonder what Chrétien conceived to be Calogrenant's motivation in telling the story, an act that compounds the shame by making his defeat public in Arthur's court. The mysterious Esclados has attacked Calogrenant at the fountain because Calogrenant has shamed him by inflicting damage on his forest without having proffered a formal challenge (489–94). Yvain in turn, calling Calogrenant a fool for having hidden the tale of his adventure for so long, undertakes to avenge the shame done to his cousin (582–87, 746). The first movement of the plot, then, concerns a series of shamings: Esclados is shamed by Calogrenant, then shames Calogrenant, and Yvain consequently feels tainted by his cousin's shame through kinship solidarity and promises publicly to avenge that shame.

The seneschal Keu imposes a refinement on Yvain's shame by implying that the project of avenging Calogrenant's defeat owes a lot to the quantity of wine drunk at the recent meal celebrating the feast of Pentecost. This taunt later compels Yvain, when he is victorious over Esclados and in fact has killed him, to want to bring back some token that will end Keu's defamation and confirm Yvain's success (1345–57, 1535–37). The external sanction of shame is here internalized as the anticipation or fear of being shamed. But in the meantime Yvain falls in love with the dead man's wife, so that both Love and Shame are obstacles to his departure from Laudine's castle (1533). Yvain's concern about proof is overtaken by events, however, when Arthur and his knights arrive at the fountain, giving Yvain, now married to Laudine and consequently himself charged with defending the fountain—itself a proof of his success against Esclados—the opportunity to unhorse Keu and inflict shame upon *him* (2282). Although this may not appear to be a great feat of arms, it is important symbolically, since Keu, as the prime agent of ridicule in Chrétien's romances, spewing vilification at every opportunity, plays the role of a spokesman for shame. This is no doubt why Keu is a catalyst for many a plot development in medieval French romance. In *Perceval,* he is made to pay for his cruelty in slapping the Laughing Girl, who predicts Perceval's greatness.

Laudine herself runs the risk of incurring shame, so she consents to marry Yvain only if it is done in such a way that no one but she and Lunete can ever say that she is the woman who married her husband's killer (1807–10).

The second movement, Yvain's absence from Laudine, is motivated by a similar polarity between honor and shame. After the marriage celebrations, Yvain asks a rash boon of Laudine, for his honor, he says, and for hers (2553). She grants his request. The gift turns out to be permission for Yvain to take leave of her so that he might prove himself in tournaments, for Gauvain has convinced him not to let his wedded state interfere with his knightly prowess, expressing the sentiment in quasi-proverbial style: "May he be shamed by Saint Mary / Who marries only to become worse!" (*"Honnis soit de Sainte Marie / Qui pour empirier se marie!"* 2487–88). Yvain wishes to avoid the accusation of recreancy (2561), a reprise of the motivating theme of Erec and Enide's adventures in the forest.

Yvain's madness is provoked by an anonymous maiden's visit to the tent that he and Gauvain share, where Arthur and many knights have joined them. This woman reproaches Yvain for having acted like a faithless dissembler and demands back from him the ring of invulnerability that Laudine had given him. Yvain is speechless because he has lost his wits (*sens,*

2775). He is in great anguish (*ennui*). Having been shamed, he wants to take vengeance on the person who caused his shame, but the difficulty is that that person is himself:

> He hates nothing so much as himself,
> Nor does he know in whom to take comfort
> Concerning himself, whom he has killed.
> He would rather go crazy
> Than not to be able to take vengeance
> On him who has taken joy away from himself.
> [Ne het tant riens com li meïsmes,
> Ne ne set a qui se confort
> De lui meïsmes qu'il a mort.
> Mix ameroit vis erragier
> Que il ne s'en peüst vengier
> De lui qui joie s'est tolue.]   (*Yvain* 2790–95)

Although Chrétien does not use the word *honte* in this scene, it is obviously Yvain's shame, as well as his inability to avenge it, because of its very nature, that leads him to go mad.

After Yvain is rehabilitated by the lady of Norison, who has an unguent concocted by Morgan the Fay applied to his body, he undergoes a series of tests. Each time he meets an adversary, it is a question of shame or honor, beginning with the honor he achieves in capturing Count Alier through his prowess (3252, 3295). Under the sobriquet Knight of the Lion (*Chevalier au lion*), he avenges the shame done to the family of his friend Gauvain's sister (4148), who trust in his prowess because he is accompanied by his lion (4004–6). He then shames Lunete's three accusers (see the hope expressed in 3758, later carried out), overcomes shame to free the captive girls from the castle of Pesme Avanture (5113, 5584), and is honored by fighting Gauvain to a stalemate over the inheritance of the heiresses of Noire Espine in spite of the desire to shame each other that each of the combatants feels when neither knows the other's identity (6012–16).

Yvain's success in these increasingly selfless tests leads to his rehabilitation: from the nadir of his fortunes—his madness and nakedness during the time when he lives as a wild man without reputation (*pris*) in the forest—he is restored to dignity as the Knight of the Lion, then reveals his true identity (6274; see Duggan 1969). From the shamed figure who runs away from Arthur and his fellow knights so that he will not go mad in public, Yvain reacquires his fame: the younger sister of Noire Espine seeks him out as a champion because of "the great renown of your reputation" (*li grans renons de vostre pris,* 5056).

All of Chrétien's romances are tales of shame and honor, but in *Yvain* this set of values is more prominent than in the other four, its interest arising from the fact that the most intense shame is inflicted by the hero on himself after he is publicly accused. Chrétien seems to have set up Yvain as a counter to Lancelot. Each has incurred shame as a result of his own actions, but Yvain takes steps to free himself of the burden of shame, whereas Lancelot achieves his goal, Guinevere's love, only by corroborating his willingness to be shamed at her command in the tournament of Noauz. Paradoxically, Yvain's shame is consequent upon an act of omission, his forgetting to return to Laudine by the time he promised, not a course of action that is deliberately conceived but nevertheless an offense against the loyalty he owed her as his wife. That shame cannot be avenged, so Yvain undergoes a series of adventures in each of which a threatened shame is overcome, resulting in honor and the reestablishment of a good reputation for him as the Knight of the Lion and then finally under his own name. James Laidlaw, who analyzes thoroughly the role of shame and pity in *Yvain,* notes twelve occurrences of *honte* in the episode of the castle of Pesme Avanture alone (1984: 198).

The ending of *Yvain* is, however, less than fully satisfying. The hero has regained his reputation, but that is not what persuades his wife to accept him again. Wishing to get back into Laudine's good graces, Yvain decides to return to the fountain and set off the storm repeatedly so that she will have to make peace with him (6513). This has the intended effect on Laudine, but she does not realize the identity of the offending party. Lunete suggests finding the knight who killed her three accusers and the giant, and Laudine swears on relics to help that knight return to his lady's favor, a variation on the theme of the rash boon. "In the game of truth Lunete has captured her in a quite courteous manner" (*Au jeu de verité l'a prinse / Lunete molt cortoisement,* 6624–25). Lunete then fetches Yvain from beside the fountain, leads him into her lady's presence, and reveals to her his name. The reconciliation takes place, but only because Laudine does not wish to renege on her oath (6758, 6781). Remarkably Chrétien declares that Yvain is happier now than he has ever been, *for he is loved and cherished by his lady* and she by him (6790–95). The notion that one can be constrained to love is as bizarre in a twelfth-century context as it would be today. Similarly, Chrétien gives no plausible reason why Yvain did not remember his promise to return to his wife within a year, and in the end has him confess only that he was led by foolishness (*folie,* 6774). Chrétien generally follows the idealizing tendency of twelfth-century romance in ascribing high motives to characters for whom he wishes to create sympathies, but in *Yvain* his portrayal of motivation has come up a bit short.

PERCEVAL: SIN AND SHAME

The ideals and values of knighthood are highlighted in *Perceval* by the hero's unformed state at the outset of the romance. Perceval is lacking in experience and naive (*nice,* 681, 701, 1012, 1299, 1365) and consequently, whatever his native gifts, becomes worthy only through training and adjustment to the values and expectations of his society. An important factor in his naïveté is the lack of shame. Not until line 3786, when he speaks with the lover of Orgueilleus de la Lande, long after he has endured Keu's taunting and been formed at the hands of Gornemant of Gohort and after he has heard that he was responsible for his mother's death, is Perceval said to feel shame. Even then the shame he feels is a passing sentiment that only makes him blush rather than a reaction with longer-lasting consequences. As far as his prowess is concerned, he is not termed *preu* until he rides out against Clamadeu's knights, more than two thousand lines into the poem, and it is only in line 4595 that prowess is ascribed to him by a figure of the court, when the queen welcomes him to Arthur's encampment.

The preudome who instructs Perceval, Gornemant, turns out to be Blancheflor's uncle. Before the young man leaves his mother, however, she also gives him a set of instructions—she terms it a *sens* (527), a bit of intelligence—in proper behavior, anticipating that he will soon become a knight. To what extent are Perceval's actions governed by the instruction received from his mother and from Gornemant?

Perceval should help women and maidens who ask for aid, his mother tells him, for whoever does not honor women slays his own honor. If he loves a woman, he is to do nothing with her that is against her will. Kissing is fine, but not making love (*le sorplus* 'the remainder, going all the way'), from which he should refrain on his mother's account. He may accept a ring or an alms-purse as a love token. He should not accompany any man without knowing his name and surname, for by the surname one knows the man. He should frequent the company of preudomes and converse with them; they always give their companions good counsel. He should pray to God in church that he might obtain honor and live his life so as to come to a good end. When Perceval asks what a church is, his mother gives a very brief and theologically thin summary of some Christian beliefs (573–94), characterizing Christ merely as a prophet rather than as God (on which see Olschki 1966: 64–65). Perceval promises his mother to go to church; she calls God's blessings down on him and sees him off.

This maternal account of Christian doctrine includes Christ's death, but not the incarnation or the resurrection, the indispensable events of Christian history from which the church derives its authority and that are commemorated in the principal feasts of the liturgical calendar. Chrétien was perhaps consciously having Perceval's mother give an incomplete summary of her religious beliefs, in the context of the state of isolation in which she keeps herself and her son. Jean-Charles Payen wondered whether, in fact, the typical Christian living in a rural milieu in this period would have had any firmer grasp of Christian doctrine than Perceval's (Payen 1984: 122). Chrétien may, however, have wished to portray Perceval's mother as assenting to heretical tenets, perhaps in the manner of a sect like the Passagini of northern Italy, who followed both Jewish and Christian practices but did not believe in Christ's divinity (see Fichtenau 1998: 66; Manselli 1963). If one accepts this second alternative, Perceval would progress from ignorance of Christianity, through a state of belief in articles of heretical faith, to orthodox Christian belief attained when he hears about the essential mysteries of faith from the pilgrims whom he meets on Good Friday. Unfortunately, the text provides us with no more than evidence for surmise.

Gornemant's training, imparted in only a two-day period, begins with practical instruction in the skills of combat: how to hold shield and lance, how to handle a horse, maneuvers there is no shame in not knowing if one has never been taught (1469–72). Perceval learns quickly and well because he is being instructed by Nature (1480–84)—in this context, the propensities he has by reason of his noble birth. He is taught how to fight with a sword if attacked or as a second means of defense if his lance shatters. Gornemant has Perceval discard the homespun garb that his mother made for him in favor of fine clothing. He receives Perceval formally into the order of knighthood (1632–38) by strapping on his spur and sword and giving him a symbolic kiss. Moral instruction follows. Perceval is not to kill any knight whom he reduces to asking for mercy. He is not to speak too much, for those who are too free with their speech often say things that redound to their detriment (1649–56). Perceval is to comfort women who are in need of counsel and he should go to church to pray. He is to cease repeating that his mother told him how to act, lest this be taken as a sign of foolishness. Perceval receives a third set of precepts from his uncle the hermit, but so late in the romance that the reader never has occasion to see whether he obeys them.

Soon after leaving home, and with his mother's instructions still in mind, Perceval mistakes the tent of Orgueilleus de la Lande for a church and enters it to pray for food; he kisses Orgueilleus's lover and takes her emerald ring, mistaking his mother's permission to do such things as an injunction. When he first sees Gornemant, Perceval tells the vavasor that what has led him there is his mother's advice that he frequent preudomes and believe what they tell him (1402–6). Likewise he learns Gornemant's name by following his mother's advice and asking to know it (1541–46). Later in his career, and despite Gornemant's reinforcing of his mother's advice to pray in church, Perceval does not enter a church for five years. His mother's exhortation that he should help women may be considered to play a role in his determination to defend Blancheflor against Engygeron, although he is already in love with her by that point. Because Gornemant taught him not to speak too much, he is reticent when he first arrives in the castle of Beaurepaire (1857). The calamitous occurrence of Perceval's life, however, neglecting to ask the questions in the Grail castle despite his impulse to do so, results directly from this same instruction of Gornemant, at least inasfar as its motivation is to be accounted for on the material level (3244–53). Surely this is a sign that, for the first time in Chrétien's production, a knight cannot reach the highest levels of achievement while basing himself on worldly wisdom alone. Furthermore, the disaster that ensues from Perceval's failure to ask the questions falls, not just on the knight himself, but on the Fisher King and his entire kingdom.

And yet, the episode in which Gauvain champions the interests of the Maiden of the Short Sleeves (*la Pucelle as manches petites*) in Tintagel against her sister involves a young person who is also naive (*nice,* 5358) and also in a position to receive instruction from one of her elders, in this case her father, Tibaut of Tintagel. She not only takes this teaching to heart but succeeds in her immediate goals specifically because of what her father tells her. Because she has asked Gauvain to fight on her behalf in the tournament, Tibaut counsels her to send Gauvain a love token (*drüerie*), a sleeve— detachable in those days—or a wimple, for the hero to wear, and when she replies that her sleeves are too small, he has a sleeve made for the purpose. He also instructs her to go by herself and present the sleeve to Gauvain, which she does. When Gauvain worsts Melian de Lis, the sister's favorite, he sends Melian's horse to the Maiden of the Short Sleeves as a gift. This captivating scene between the experienced knight and a girl young enough to be carried in her father's arms shows that education in the ways of the world can be effective, but toward worldly ends. The Maiden of the Short Sleeves, unlike Perceval, is not laboring under the spiritual weight of any flaw that would lead her to follow aimlessly and in an excessively literal way the instructions she receives.

The uniqueness of *Perceval* is clear on the moral level if one considers the status in this romance of the concept of sin. Perceval is the only one of Chrétien's heroes whose conduct is explained through sin, and this difference is all the more striking when one considers that not even Lancelot's adultery is ever referred to as sinful. The cousin Perceval meets in the forest tells him he failed to ask the proper questions in the Grail castle because he sinned against his mother, who died of grief because of his departure. This act is referred to as a sin seven times in the romance (3593, 6393, 6399, 6409, 6433, 6471, 6496). A knight among the thirteen penitents whom Perceval meets in the forest rebukes him for bearing arms on Good Friday, which would have been contrary to the truce of God, which forbade war on specified days. The knight imparts to him an impromptu and rudimentary summary of Christian doctrine, including the crucifixion, the salvation of humankind, the divine nature of Jesus, the virgin birth, the incarnation, the necessity of faith for salvation, the harrowing of hell, the resurrection, and the responsibility of the Jews. In confessing to the hermit on Good Friday, Perceval says he forgot God and failed to believe in him for five years out of grief and despair at not asking about the Bleeding Lance or whom the Grail served, and for the second time he then learns that this failure derives from the sin of having left his mother. Says the hermit, "Sin cut out your tongue" (*Pechiez la langue te trencha,* 6409). In teaching Perceval, Gornemant had invoked a proverb: "And the wise man says and recounts: / He who speaks too much commits a sin" (*Et li saiges dit et retrait: / Qui trop parole pechié fait,* Méla ed., 1611–12),[9] but the proverb closest to this wording among those extant from medieval France, *Trop parler nuist* (Morawski 1925: no. 2428), "It's harmful to speak too much," differs in an essential way. Chrétien has taken a nontheological proverb and transformed it into a statement that sin results from speaking too much, which is a key to his intentions. This transformation cannot be ascribed to the requirements of rhyme or meter, because the proverb is only four syllables long and could easily have been incorporated into an octosyllabic rhyming couplet had Chrétien not wanted to modify it to incorporate the concept of sin.

In absolving Perceval, the hermit frees him from the consequences of the sin of having occasioned his mother's death. Perceval thus reaches

through the sacrament of penance and sorrow for his sins a stage of rehabilitation that Erec, Yvain, and Lancelot only attained by undergoing successfully a series of knightly tests.

The hermit answers one of the two questions that Perceval should have
asked in the Grail castle, informing him that the person whom the Grail
serves is the Fisher King's father (whom the critical tradition refers to as
the Grail King), but he does not say anything about the Bleeding Lance.
For Perceval's sin, the hermit assigns penance: the knight is to go to mass
every morning, believe in God, honor and love him, honor good men and
women, stand up out of humility when a priest approaches, help widows
and orphan girls. If he does these things, he will be restored to his rightful state of grace. The hermit also teaches his charge a prayer based on
the names of God, which he is only to say at a time of very great peril.[10]
Perceval adores the holy cross and receives communion on Easter Sunday,
sharing the hermit's frugal and meatless meals. The hermit links knightly
values with Perceval's dedication in going to mass: "You can still grow in
repute, / And you will have honor and paradise" (*Encor porras monter en
pris, / S'avras honor et paradis,* 6457–58). This is an unusual passage in Chrétien's romances in that it makes the association between religious practices
and the profane goals of knighthood, to which it adds the goal of salvation.

The contrast with the other four romances in this respect is remarkable.
In fact, the word *pechié* 'sin' occurs more frequently in *Perceval* than in the
entire remainder of Chrétien's corpus. Only two other characters, both un-
alloyed villains, the traitor Angres of Windsor in *Cliges* (1697) and Meleagant in *Lancelot* (3444), are accused by others of having committed a sin.
In *Lancelot* (4185, 4221), Guinevere seeks forgiveness for the "sin" of having
rejected Lancelot because he hesitated in climbing into the cart, surely an
ironic gesture on Chrétien's part, because her atonement for what is at most
a sin in the context of the "religion" of *fin'amor,* will lead her to commit
adultery with Lancelot. Finally, in Perceval's encounter with the knights at
the beginning of *Perceval,* that is to say in his period of naïveté, he remarks
that he has sinned in calling the knights devils because they are really God
himself and his angels (*Perceval* 138–54). One of the women accompanying
the lady of Norison in *Yvain* says she does not know through what pechié
the hero has come to live naked in the forest, but the word has there the
sense of 'misfortune'.

That Perceval had no knowledge of the sin he has committed against his
mother is confirmed by the hermit (6393), which leads to an interesting
theological point. It was Christian belief that all humans bear the stain of

original sin, even children, although many of them have no knowledge of it and certainly committed no act of the will allied to it. But can one commit a personal sin without knowing about it? (For a review of critical opinion on Perceval's sin, see Rutledge 1980–81.) Alan of Lille, a contemporary of Chrétien who was probably born in the 1120s and died in 1203, writes in his *Liber Poenitentialis,* which seems to have been composed in the 1180s, that a confessor should inquire about whether a given sin is committed knowingly or in ignorance (*Praeterea inquirendum est utrum peccatum factum sit scienter vel ignoranter,* Longère 1965, 2:33 [book 1, ch. 23]). Alan thus admits of sins committed without knowing that one has sinned and goes on to say that knowledge increases the guilt whereas ignorance alleviates it. In the twelfth-century *Sententiae Atrebatenses* of the school of Laon, sentence 87 discusses the issue of a sin committed without knowing it (*ignoranter,* Blomme 1958: 60; see also Payen 1967: 393) and like Alan assigns to this type a lesser degree of culpability. Thomas Aquinas, writing some eighty years later in his *De Malo,* question 3, article 86, holds that ignorance can be the cause of sin (Oesterle 1995: 124–25). It is not as if Perceval did not have the necessary knowledge to act benevolently toward his mother. After all, she informed him plainly:

> "You were all the comfort
> That I had and all the good,
> For none of my own people survived."
> ["Vos estïez toz li confors
> Que jou avoie et toz li biens,
> Car il n'i avoit plus des miens."]   (*Perceval* 484–86)

Perceval nonetheless decided to leave her to seek his fortune at Arthur's court. His ignorance of having sinned applies, then, to the fact that she died, because the sin consists of his having caused his mother's death. It is, nonetheless, a sin according to some medieval theologians. For those thinkers influenced by the ethical writings of Peter Abelard, however, sin consists in the intention of doing evil, not in the act itself (Chenu 1969: 18). Chrétien knows this principle, for it allows Laudine to rationalize marrying Yvain under the guise of his having killed her husband, Esclados, in self-defense, because killing without the intention of killing is not murder. But from *Yvain,* Chrétien seems to have regressed to a less progressive theological tradition in *Perceval.*

Leonardo Olschki (1966) pointed up the curious nature of the religious beliefs exposed in *Perceval.* Until late in his adventures, the hero's knowledge of religious doctrine of any kind is severely limited. From his mother he knows not that Christ was divine but that he was "a prophet," not that God created the world (although when he first meets Arthur he does swear "by the faith that he owes the Creator," *Perceval* 994) but merely that he is the most beautiful of things, not that devils are the agents of evil but merely that they are ugly, not that angels are God's messengers but merely that they are beautiful. Chrétien's intention does not appear to have been to lay out the principles of a radically new kind of knighthood of which Perceval is the embodiment but, rather, only to highlight the superiority of a religiously aware and contrite knight, Perceval, over one who is wholly motivated by a concern for worldly achievement and rewards (see, for similar views on the presentation of religion in *Perceval,* Imbs 1956 and Payen 1984).

Another of Perceval's actions is ascribed to the influence of sin, his encounter in the tent with the lover of Orgueilleus de la Lande. Having been kissed by Perceval and had her ring taken by him, she is justified in conjecturing that sin motivated his visit (3810), but in this case the analysis appears to be inaccurate because Perceval's conduct, despite its seemingly sexual overtones, results simply from his naïveté.

With the hermit's revelation of Perceval's kinship ties with the Fisher King and the Grail King, the central chain of motivation of the romance becomes clear. Perceval's mother is afflicted when she hears that he wants to become a knight because, she says, her kin are all dead and he is all she has. In leaving her, Perceval commits a sin. A consequence of this sin is his inappropriate silence in the Grail castle. If he had not been silent, the Fisher King would have been cured and been able to rule in peace (3586–90, 4670–74). There is thus a clear line leading from the death of Perceval's mother's kin to Perceval's silence and the continued barrenness of the Fisher's kingdom. Only one thing is wrong with this scenario: if the Fisher King is Perceval's first cousin and the Grail King is his uncle, then Perceval's mother does not lack kin at all—would not lack kin, that is, unless both the Grail King and the Fisher King were dead or at least departed from the world of the living into an other world. In the preceding chapter I stressed the castle of the Rock of Champguin as an Otherworld kingdom, as well as the Grail castle's parallels with it. The Grail castle, like the Rock of Champguin, belongs to the Otherworld. Consequently, to the parallel between the Fisher King and Perceval's father, both wounded "between the thighs," is added another parallel: both of these men are dead, as is the Grail King, who is properly referred to as having the quality of a spirit (*espiritax,* 6426). And yet the Grail King—and this is presumably true also of the Fisher King—is also alive in some sense, because it is said that the single host served to him in the Grail has sustained his life for twelve years (6422–31). Living and at the same time not living, bathed in the atmosphere that Anthime Fourrier called *le réalisme magique* 'magic realism' (Fourrier 1960: 111). This is not the only paradox of the Grail King, for the hermit says he has not left for the last twelve years the room in which he dwells (6430), but when Perceval first saw the Fisher King fishing, he was accompanied in his boat by a second man who must have been the Grail King.

Both of these castles inhabited by those who are dead but still living are earthly paradises, Otherworlds inspired by Celtic legend, analogous to the Isle of Avalon, where, the Bretons believed, Arthur lived after suffering "mortal" wounds at the battle of Camlann, and where he was ministered to by his sister, Morgan the Fay.

In *Perceval* there are two types of good repute open to men, the renown of knighthood and the renown of holiness. The pilgrims whom Perceval meets in the forest and who explain to him that God became man for the salvation of humanity tell him that the hermit is a preudome and a holy man, so holy that his life depends only on God's glory (6303–6). *Yvain* also depicts a hermit, who feeds the hero moldy bread and cooks his venison for him—the eating of raw meat was forbidden in Christian homilies (Salisbury 1994: 64)—but although this hermit is called a *preudome* (2839) and a good man (2861, 2873, 2882), he is never called saintly. The Grail is termed a holy thing (6425),[11] and presumably the Grail King is also holy by association because the host served in the Grail sustains him.

Of the two knights whose adventures Chrétien has the reader follow, Gauvain is definitely not a holy man, but he enjoys the renown of knighthood. No knight can rule in Champguin unless he is handsome and wise, bold, noble of heart, loyal, and free of greed, villainy, and evil (7593–96), so Gauvain must have those qualities. He has modesty—a characteristic that Chrétien prized, as his practice of calling villainous characters Orgueilleus or Orgueilleuse shows—because he tells Ygerne that he is neither among the best nor among the worst of the knights of the Round Table (8129–30). Perceval, also a renowned knight in the scene in which he meets the hermit, appears to be advancing toward spiritual values in that scene.

Gauvain is subjected to a series of tests by Orgueilleuse de Logres, the Hateful Damsel, whose name means 'the haughty one of Logres'[12] and who is the instrument of shame in the Gauvain adventures just as Keu is the instrument of ridicule in *Yvain* and earlier in *Perceval*. Gauvain meets

Orgueilleuse in a sumptuous castle located just inside the limits of Galloway. This is a kingdom, like Gorre, from which it is said that no knight
ever returns (6603–4) but that Gauvain insists on entering because to do
otherwise would expose him to the accusation of recreancy (6619). Orgueilleuse makes no secret of her role, promising Gauvain that, if he recovers
her horse for her, she will accompany him to ill adventure, trouble, sorrow, shame, and misfortune (6717–18, 6863–65) unless he demonstrates his
courage (*hardement,* 6721).

The sequence of shamings begins when Greoreas steals Gauvain's horse,
Gringalet, in revenge for his once having punished Greoreas for raping a
women by making him eat with dogs for a month, his hands tied behind
his back. In retaliation for this act of severe shaming, Greoreas now has put
the shame on Gauvain (7117). Orgueilleuse then leads Gauvain to a stream
across which is situated the castle of the Rock of Champguin, which he insists on visiting because otherwise he would be thought a coward (7623).
After Gauvain enters the castle and passes the test of the Wondrous Bed
(plate 5), he meets the Hateful Damsel again, this time in the company
of a knight, Orgueilleus del Passage a l'Estroite Voie (named in 8646–48),
whose task it is to guard the passage into Galloway and whom Gauvain defeats. For this victory, he is said to have acquired the *pris* and *los* of the
whole world (8586). One more task awaits Gauvain, crossing a perilous ford
to pick flowers for Orgueilleuse, a feat that has been achieved by no man
before him but that he accomplishes nonetheless.

Guiromelant, the most handsome knight in the world and king of Orqueneseles, who has sworn only to speak the truth to Gauvain, praises him as
one who has had an honor that no knight ever attained by surviving the
Wondrous Bed (8725). But Guiromelant also wishes shame on Gauvain, in
revenge for Gauvain's having killed his first cousin and for Gauvain's father
having killed his father (8778–83). Is one of these the same man whom
Guingambresil has accused Gauvain of killing without a prior challenge,
the king of Esclavon (see Le Rider 1978a: 294)? In any case, single combat
between the two is set for seven days later, to give Arthur time to arrive
so that the battle will be public rather than hidden (8858–60), but Chrétien's readers never see the outcome because the romance breaks off before
Arthur's arrival.

Gauvain then rejoins Orgueilleuse, who, now that her attempts to shame
Gauvain have all come to naught, tells him the story of how she became
so haughty (*estolte,* 8928) and uncourtly (*vilaine,* 8951). Because the knight
whom she loved was killed, she had resolved to act in such an exasper-

ating manner toward knights that one of them would finally kill her. She asks Gauvain to fulfill this goal so that no woman will ever speak shameful things to any knight (8963), but he refuses. Paradoxically, this malignant creature is depicted as a woman of principle, one whose inner self was transformed by her harsh experience and who herself does not undergo shame.

Perceval never reaches the height of worldly reputation attained by Gauvain. Unlike Chrétien's other characters, Perceval does appear to feel guilt in the sense of experiencing an interiorized and private sense of responsibility, not for having caused his mother's death, but for having broken one of her instructions, namely having neglected to worship God in church (593–94). When he meets the penitents in the forest on Good Friday (plate 6), hears the mysteries of the Christian faith recited, and learns that they have just confessed, he sighs deeply and begins to weep because he feels he has committed a misdeed toward God and repents of it (6316–37). This idea is repeated with slight variation a little farther on in the text when Perceval asks advice of the hermit because he fears that he has offended God (*dotoit / Avoir vers Damedieu mespris* (6354–55). This channeling of the consciousness of a misdeed inward to produce an emotion is guilt. Perceval goes on to say that he has acted badly for five years, wishing he were dead and forgetting God, because of the grief he had of not having asked the questions in the Grail castle (6372–86). The hermit assigns the penance to him for his sin (6433, presumably the sin of having caused his mother's death). If he carries out his atonement, he will grow in reputation (*pris,* 6457) and he will have honor in heaven. Afterward Perceval adores the cross and weeps over his sins (6496). On Easter day, he takes communion. This is the last we hear of Perceval from Chrétien de Troyes.

In distinction from Chrétien's other praiseworthy heroes, Erec, Cliges, or Yvain, then, Perceval does not participate fully in the ethical give-and-take of shame and renown. The only emotion that responsibility for his own conduct elicits in him is not shame but remorse, and in fact he is never said to undergo any particular feeling about his mother's death, even though he expresses several times the intention of going back to see what happened to her when she fell at the bridge (2917–21, 2956–57, 3621–24).

THE ROLES OF SHAME AND GUILT IN CHRÉTIEN

In cultures in which responsibility is collectively shared according to societal conventions such as the solidarity of the kin group, shame often plays a dominant role in the sanctioning of good and evil. Twelfth-century French society is just such a culture. Guilt is present in Chrétien's romances, but it plays a peripheral role compared to shame. It is a question, not of opposing the concepts "guilt culture" and "shame culture," but of which of the two, shame or guilt, is the most common and important sanction in a given society or depiction of society. For the Arthurian world as Chrétien depicts it, shame is by far the most forceful and most frequent sanction.

Unlike shame, guilt is the internal sanction for infractions against cultural norms, implying a mechanism of judgment, a conscience. The increase in the number of penitentials—handbooks for confessors—in this period bears witness to the growing practice of the examination of conscience. Guilt is felt as an emotion, and is thus internal to the psyche, although it derives from the incorporation of cultural norms that are public, and it often manifests itself publicly just as public shame is at times internalized. Guilt derives from the self-reflective gaze.

Is there a progression or evolution in values through the five romances viewed chronologically? Each of Chrétien's five Arthurian tales tells a story of adventures against a background of societal judgment, but in each case the problematics of honor and shame are different. From the fear of rumor in *Erec,* in which the knight's wife is the conduit through which news of potential shame reaches him, Chrétien takes us through the shaming of a blood relative in *Cliges,* voluntary submission to shame in *Lancelot,* the knight's self-shaming in *Yvain,* and the eclipse of shame in favor of guilt as the ultimate sanction in *Perceval.*

The set of values shown in *Lancelot* contrasts sharply with what is found in the three romances that precede that work or are contemporary with it, *Erec, Cliges, Yvain.* Although it is impossible to prove for lack of positive evidence, it seems to me that this difference can be ascribed to the interpretation *(sen)* that Marie de Champagne gave to Chrétien along with the narration of Guinevere's abduction (*Lancelot* 26). In addition to the humiliation that Lancelot undergoes in being at first rejected by Guinevere and in fighting his worst at the tournament of Noauz, his actions are constantly undercut by treatments that make him look ridiculous. At the outset of his quest for the queen, he does not care which of Gauvain's horses he accepts (290–98). He nearly commits suicide by falling from a window of the castle of the Perilous Bed (550–74). He promises to do all the second damsel wants if only she will tell him where the queen is (633–34), while, as Chrétien emphasizes, Gauvain promises only to do all that is in his power (627–634). Lancelot forgets his own name, whether he is armed, and where he is going and coming from, and he loses himself at the ford (745), recovering his senses only when he has been knocked into the water. He nearly faints at the sight of Guinevere's comb. He adores the queen's hairs that are caught in its teeth and places them between his shirt and his body, believing them to be a talisman against sickness that is more efficacious than the intervention of St. Martin or St. James, two of the great miracle-working saints of the Middle Ages (1424–94). He fights Meleagant backward so that he can keep looking at Guinevere. He adores her as if she were a holy relic just before they make love (4652–53), and on leaving her he bows to the room as if it were an altar (4716–18), an implicit comparison of the queen's body with the communion host, the body of Christ. Leaving Guinevere is said to be martyrdom for Lancelot (4689–91). He attempts suicide by tying himself to the neck of his horse—surely a highly ineffectual method. Through these depictions, unlike those of his other knightly heroes even when their fortunes are at the worst, Chrétien undermines a character in whose conduct he has no faith. *Lancelot* is, then, an anomaly among Chrétien's romances in its portrayal of the principal hero and his values.

Did Marie de Champagne, seeing through this stance, terminate her patronage of Chrétien in favor of Godefroy de Lagny? In his last romance, Chrétien has Perceval greet the queen in a way that would not lead one to believe she was the adulterous wife of the *Lancelot:*

> "May God give joy and honor
> To the most beautiful, to the best
> Of all ladies who exist,
> As witness all those who see her
> And all who have seen her."
> ["Diex doinst joie et honor
> A la plus bele, a la meillor,
> De totes les dames qui soient,
> Tesmoinz toz icels qui le voient
> Et toz ciaus qui veüe l'ont."]   (*Perceval* 4587–91)

Although one might dismiss this praise as flattery spoken in Guinevere's presence, toward the end of the same romance Gauvain praises her in even more lavish terms in her absence:

> "She is so courtly
> And so beautiful and so wise
> That never did God make law or language community
> In which one could find such a beautiful woman.

From the time when God formed
The first woman from Adam's rib,
There never was a lady so renowned.
And well should she be:
Just as the wise teacher
Instructs little children,
So my lady the queen
Teaches and instructs everyone;
For from her all good descends
And it comes and flows from her.
No one can go
From her disconsolate.
She knows well what each is worth
And what she should do for each
In order to please him.
No man has accomplished a good or honorable deed
Without informing my lady of it;
No man was ever so downcast
As to leave my lady's presence chagrined."
["Ele est tant cortoise
Et tant est bele et tant est sage
C'ainc Diex ne fist loi ne langage
Ou l'en trovast si bele dame.
Des que Diex la premiere fame
Ot de la coste Adan formee,
Ne fu dame si renomee.
Et ele le doit molt bien estre:
Tot ausi com li sages mestre
Les petis enfans endoctrine,
Ausi ma dame la roïne
Tot le mont ensaigne et aprent;
Que de li toz li biens descent
Et de li vient et de li muet.
De ma dame partir ne puet
Nus qui desconseilliez s'an aut.
Ele set bien que chascuns vaut
Et qu'ele doit por chascun faire
Por coi qu'ele li doie plaire.
Nus hom bien ne honor ne fait
Qui a ma dame apris ne l'ait;
Ja nus hom n'ert si deshaitiez
Qui de ma dame parte iriez."]

(*Perceval* 8176–98)

This portrait of the paragon of all female virtues and values hardly applies to the woman who submitted to Lancelot's suit. Furthermore, in *Yvain,* which may have been composed in the same period as *Lancelot* but seems to have been finished later, Chrétien portrays a knight who is anything but subservient to his lady—one whose fault, in fact, is quite the opposite of subservience (see Nitze 1955: 178). These sharp differences in the treatment of the queen and in the concept of love signal a movement in *Yvain* away from Marie de Champagne's preferences and back to Chrétien's own proclivities.

Like *Lancelot, Perceval* stands out from the other romances as concerns the sanctioning of conduct. In contrast to the other romances in which Gauvain, although important, does not quite match the protagonist in accomplishment, the sequence of Gauvain's adventures in *Perceval,* more than 2,700 lines in length, places him potentially on the same narrative footing as the principal male character. Each has launched himself on a quest, Gauvain to bring back to the king of Escavalon the Bleeding Lance that, it is said, will destroy the kingdom of Logres, Perceval to find out whom the Grail serves and why the lance bleeds (4727–40). The difference in the way the quests are phrased is, however, of prime significance. Perceval's quest, half of which he achieves when his uncle tells him about the Grail King, is a search for meaning, whereas Gauvain's is a hunt for a physical object that he promises to take back with him. Similarly, the sequence of adventures that Perceval has leads him to the spiritual realization that he has sinned, after which he repents. Gauvain's adventures place him in the same category as Erec, Yvain, Cliges, and Lancelot: various adversaries attempt to shame him and he in turn shames them. Gauvain succeeds splendidly in a worldly way, achieving greater repute and higher honor than any knight alive, while Perceval, in the truncated text that we have, appears well on his way to achieving salvation. The set of profane values on which the other four romances are centered[13] has been displaced by the polarity of sin and salvation.

This trajectory Chrétien navigates not only by focusing on the adventures, tests, and marvels coming to him from the Celtic tradition but by incorporating the ethical stance of courtliness and the nascent consciousness of interiority, which are the subjects of the next chapter.

Chapter 4

Interiority and Responsibility

Chrétien was a writer with stories to tell. Part of his storytelling is to portray his characters as making decisions about choices they face. He depicts them not merely on the basis of external manifestations, such as their physical appearance and their words, but as creatures who think and who have an interior life. How he accomplished this is the subject of this chapter.

The sense of the interior life, highly developed in St. Augustine, was not so much appreciated amid the strife and instability of the ninth, tenth, and eleventh centuries, but in the twelfth century there was a reawakening of interest in what we would call the processes of the psyche. The primacy of self-examination in matters of moral conduct goes back to the twelfth century. As Alan of Lille, author of one of the first confessor's manuals, put it in a sermon: "Whoever seeks himself above himself becomes a devil; whoever seeks himself beside himself becomes a Pharisee; whoever seeks himself beneath himself makes of man a herd; whoever seeks himself within himself makes of man a spirit" (*Qui querit se supra se fit diabolus, qui querit se iuxta se phariseus, qui querit se infra se fit homo pecus; qui querit se intra se fit homo spiritus,* D'Alverny 1965: 272). Alan was a contemporary of Chrétien.

At issue in this topic as in so many others considered in this study is the degree to which medieval and modern mind-sets differ. Can readers who conceive of mental and emotional processes in the light of contemporary psychology adequately appreciate the characterizations that medieval authors of romance attempted in their works? I believe that they can and that the vaunted "strangeness" of the Middle Ages is not so alien to us that we cannot with effort strip away the layers of mental structure that come between us and that period sufficiently to be able to see how Chrétien viewed the psychology of his characters. One has to span the distance between medieval and modern mind-sets, and in doing so the most press-

ing task is allowing Chrétien's characterizations to be seen as he understood them.

Given that we know so little about authors of this period who composed
romances, this is not an easy undertaking. The very names of the authors of
the *Roman de Thèbes* and the *Roman d'Enéas* are unknown. We do not know
all the processes and texts on which education was based in the mid-twelfth
century, although it is clear that the *Roman de Thèbes* draws on Statius's
Thebaid and *Enéas* is based on the *Aeneid.* For both of these works, readers
seem to have been attracted to the love themes, although the legends and
myths that they transmit would also have been of great interest, particularly for their dynastic aspects in the context of Henry II's assumption of
the throne of England. How the authors' educations might have prepared
them for writing these adaptations is difficult to ascertain, and about their
life experiences we know nothing. We do know, however, that they lived
in one of the most fertile periods of human creativity, a period that saw
the rise of Gothic architecture and art, the rise of cathedral schools, the re-
newal of interest in Roman law, the slow but inexorable exposure to ancient
Greek philosophy sometimes mediated by thinkers in the Arab world, the
development of enlarged self-reflection in religious practices, especially
in confession and penance, the efflorescence of the influential corpus of
courtly poetry expressed in the first person among the troubadours, and an
increased emphasis on the role of intention in moral matters pioneered by
the great philosopher Peter Abelard.

One manifestation of the greater emphasis on interiority and the subject is Andreas the Chaplain's *Art of Loving with Dignity* (*De arte honeste
amandi*), called in its English translation *The Art of Courtly Love* [Parry
1964]). This book is thought to have been composed after 1174 but before
August 1186 and thus is contemporaneous with Chrétien. Influence between Andreas and Chrétien is not readily visible, but they were writing
in the same courtly milieu. Andreas was a chaplain at the court of King
Louis VII of France, Marie de Champagne's father, and in his work he refers
to Marie as rendering seven judgments in cases of love casuistry. Andreas
treats love in ways analogous to the manner of nascent scholasticism. The
work is divided into three books, the first two on what love is and how to
keep it, the last a palinode on rejecting love. Andreas presents twenty-one
judgments on love rendered by Eleanor of Aquitaine, her daughter Aalais
of Blois, Elisabeth of Vermandois (wife of Philip of Flanders), and Hermen-
garde, vicountess of Narbonne, in addition to Marie. In one of Marie's judgments, set forth in a letter that is incorporated into the text and is dated

May 1, 1174, Andreas has the countess declare that love cannot exist between a husband and wife because they are obligated to cede to each other's desires whereas love is a free gift. He also sets out typical dialogues for lovers on three levels of the social hierarchy—commoners, nobles, and high nobles—and formulates a series of rules of love. The very fact that such a subjective phenomenon as love should be treated in this way is yet another manifestation of a new interest in interiority, although modern interpreters are not agreed on the quality of Andreas's treatment—serious, ironic, humorous, playful, cynical, perhaps politically charged, and, in the third book, misogynistic. The treatise was condemned as heretical by the bishop of Paris, Etienne Tempier, in 1277.

MEDIEVAL IDEAS OF INTERIORITY

When a person living in the late twelfth century in northern France succeeded in "looking inside," what would the view be like? Theories built on Freudian notions such as the subconscious, repression, the psychological significance of dreams, and the Oedipus complex are of little use in a society that differs from those of western Europe today in such fundamental ways as the functioning of shame and guilt and the sense of kinship responsibilities. Concepts of the person are just as time-bound as concepts of justice and liberty. In the twelfth century, dreams were frequently thought to derive not from the psyche itself but from angels or devils, exterior entities, and visions were correspondingly taken to be a positive manifestations of sainthood or negative signs of demonic possession. Dreams and visions, then, were not conceived as symptoms of inner turmoil, as they were by nineteenth-century psychological theorists and their successors. In order to explore medieval interiority, it is important at least to attempt an approach to medieval concepts of the mind.

A number of aspects of interiority make their appearance or become increasingly visible in the course of the twelfth century. One difficulty is to decide whether certain phenomena are contributing to interiority in a causal way or, rather, result from an increased awareness of mental processes. Among these phenomena are the growing practice of private confession and private penance, the examination of conscience and the concomitant popularity among clergy of penitentials, the adaptation of the exercise of examining one's conscience to different states of life and professions—thereby increasing attention to the particular conditions of the subject—the expanding emphasis on guilt, and the invention of techniques of inquiry for ferreting out heresy. Self-reflective literary works appear, such as Guibert de Nogent's *Monodiae* (ca. 1115), Abelard's *Historia calamitatum* (from the 1130s), Guy de Bazoche's apologia dedicated to his mother— Guy was associated with the court of Troyes in Chrétien's time—and the *De rebus a se gestis* of Gerald of Wales (d. 1223). But these nascent stirrings toward a full-fledged consciousness of interiority were just that: beginnings. There was as yet no word for what we term "personality" (Benton 1991: 345).

DESIRE AND THOUGHT, THE HEART AND THE EYES

In Chrétien de Troyes's romances, the heart is "the seat of all consciousness and all dispositions of the spirit" (Brault 1972: 143). Metaphors involving the heart are found in all his works beginning with *Erec* in which, stressing the equal moral and physical qualities of Erec and Enide, Chrétien says that each has stolen the other's heart (*Erec* 1510). The metaphor of the heart's susceptibility to being displaced, imprisoned, or stolen is found in all of the first four romances (see Brault 1972: 145). In particular, Cliges tells Fenice that while he was away in Britain, his heart was left behind with her and his heart-less body was like the bark of a tree without its trunk; now that he has come back, the heart has no desire to return to him (*Cliges* 5114–27). On the other hand, Fenice's heart, she says, has been off in Britain, and *she* was nothing but bark. They then agree, however, that their hearts have come together (5138–70).

Chrétien realizes full well that the images of the heart are metaphors, and he playfully tells his audience this in an earlier passage of *Cliges* in which he discusses the impossibility of two hearts existing in the same body, stating that this is just a way of saying that two people share the same desire (2774–2808). The immediate source of the metaphors of the heart's portability appears to have been the *Roman d'Enéas,* composed around 1160 and referred to by Chrétien (*Erec* 5329–38).

Defects of character are also reflected in the heart. Meleagant would have been a good knight, but he has "a heart of wood, / Completely hard and pitiless" (*un cuer de fust / Tot sanz dolçor et sanz pitié, Lancelot* 3166–67). Here apparently wood has a negative connotation, unlike the metaphor of the bark and the trunk in *Cliges.* Even when Meleagant is about to die, his heart advises him against asking for quarter (7083–85).

That the heart is also the center of ideas, intentions, and desires other than those motivated by love is seen in many passages. The heart is the locus of thought. As Calogrenant remarks in *Yvain,* the ears are the conduit by which the voice enters the body, but words that the ears hear are lost if the heart is not disposed to understand them, and in that case they are not taken into the bosom but immediately go off again (*Yvain* 150–68). This necessity for ears and heart to be in tune with each other is based on the Gospel of Matthew (13.15). Enide formulates the proverb "the heart thinks something other than what the mouth is saying" (*el pense cuer que ne dit boche, Erec* 3380). In *Perceval,* when Gauvain sees Ygerne approaching, his heart tells him that she is the queen, and Chrétien remarks that the heart often engages in guessing (8103). When in *Cliges* the duke of Saxony sees that he has nothing to gain and much to lose in fighting Cliges, the way he expresses it is that "heart and desire" (*Cliges* 4114) have come to him such that he wants to give up the quarrel. Pity resides in the heart (*Erec* 3810), as does courage: Guivret le Petit is said to be small but "courageous . . . with great heart" (*Erec* 3676). The knight who unhorses Lancelot at the ford swears by "the heart in his bosom" (*Lancelot* 751).

The heart, then, in addition to figuring in metaphors that are familiar in many languages and cultures, perhaps because they have survived from an earlier time, appears in Chrétien to be the locus of interior movements that in modern civilization would be considered as originating or at least being processed in the brain, whether they be classed as mental or emotional.

Chrétien adds other physiological details. The eyes, which prepare the way for love, send their message to the heart, and kisses may give the heart a drink of sweetness. The eyes of the newlyweds Erec and Enide exercise power by communicating with their hearts (*Erec* 2087–96). In *Cliges,* where the association of eye and heart figures most prominently, the metaphor of love shooting an arrow into the lover's heart occurs in regard to Soredamor's feelings for Alexandre; she accuses her eyes of having betrayed her and rendered her heart unfaithful to her. Soredamor concludes, however, that one cannot love with the eyes alone, and thus these organs have no fault because the heart is telling them what to look at (*Cliges* 460–510). Alexandre in turn conceives an extended metaphor involving eye and heart, wondering why, if Love has shot an arrow through his eye into his heart, the eye escapes feeling pain. But the eye is, after all, only the mirror of the heart, and the sentiment that passes through it into the heart makes the heart burst into flames. The image then shifts and the heart is compared to a candle burning in a lantern. The heart sees light through the eyes, but what it sees may deceive it. Now both his heart and his eyes have become Alexandre's enemies (*Cliges* 702–55). Love's arrow comes in for the same lengthy treatment as the relationship between heart and eye, and Alexandre's thought that he would be happy if he could only have the feathers and notch of the arrow (*Cliges* 793–96, 842–53) has erotic overtones that seem to anticipate the description of the rose at the end of Jean de Meun's *Roman de la Rose.* On the amorous exchanges in Chrétien's romances, Erich Auerbach has observed that "the grace and attractiveness of this style— whose charm is freshness and whose danger is silly coquetry, trifling, and coldness—can hardly be found in such purity anywhere in the literature of antiquity. Chrétien did not learn it from Ovid; it is a creation of the French Middle Ages" (Auerbach 1957: 115).

Yvain and Laudine engage in a rapid exchange of questions and answers in which the knight tells how he came to want to put himself at her mercy:

"Lady, he says, the force comes
From my heart, which has attached itself to you;
My heart created this desire in me."
"And who put it in your heart, fair sweet friend?"
"Lady, my eyes." "And the eyes who?"
"The great beauty I saw in you."
"And the beauty, what's its responsibility in this?"
"Lady, such that it makes me love."
"Love? And whom?" "You, dear lady."
"Me?" "Truly, truly!" "In what way?"
"In such a way that it cannot be any greater,
In such a way that my heart
Does not leave you, nor do I find it anywhere else;
In such a way that I can think of nothing else."
["Dame, fet il, la force vient
De mon cuer, qui a vous se tient;
En cest voloir m'a mon cuer mis.
—Et qui le cuer, biaus dous amis?
—Dame, mi oil. —Et les oilz, qui?
—La grant biautés que en vous vi.
—Et la biautez, qu'i a forfayt?
—Dame, tant que amer me fait.
—Amer? Et qui? —Vous, dame chiere.
—Moy? —Voire voir! —En quel maniere?
—En tel que graindre estre ne puet;

En tel que de vos ne se muet
Mon cuer n'onques alleurs nel truiz;
En tel qu'ailleurs pensser ne puis."]   (*Yvain* 2017–30)

This scene is a catechism lesson in love, spelling out its immediate cause and effects in the lover Yvain, as well as the process that led from cause to effect, Laudine's beauty transmitted through his eyes to his heart, where love arises.

The physics of the eye was a topic of concern in twelfth-century science, discussed by Averroes and other thinkers influenced by Aristotelian scientific theory, and the theme of the heart and the eye may have its ultimate source in Plato's *Phaedrus.* These metaphors, then, are very much in line with contemporary speculation about the functioning of vision. Ruth Cline traced them in a number of Latin works but found them primarily in Hebrew, Greek, and Arabic literary and philosophical texts. Chrétien's primary immediate inspiration appears to be, in this case again, the *Roman d'Enéas,* and in particular the episodes that depict the love between Eneas and Lavine (Cline 1971–72: 264–67, 292–93, 296).

Chrétien was known for his skillful use of this complex of images of heart and eye, as is shown by the testimony of the poet Huon de Méry, who writes in his *Tournoiement Antechrist* (composed between 1234 and 1240), just after himself mentioning that Love's arrow wounds the heart without harming the eyes:

But if one wanted to speak the truth,
Chrétien de Troyes spoke better
Of the wounded heart, the arrow, the eyes,
Than I could tell you.
[Mes qui le voir dire en vodroit,
Crestïens de Troies dist miex
Du cuer navré, du dart, des ex,
Que je ne vos porroie dire.]   (Wimmer 1888: ll. 2599–2603)

The eyes take on a disproportionately large role in the communication of love in Chrétien's works, and he gives little attention to the other senses: the sound of the lover's voice or footsteps, the feel of soft skin or hair, the scent of perfume. Just as shame, which depends for its existence on acting within view of others, is the dominant sanction for conduct in twelfth-century French society, so love is governed almost exclusively by the visual apprehension of the lover's image and is conceptualized as operating through the sense of sight.

SPEAKING TO ONESELF

On the streets of Troyes and the other market towns of Champagne in this period, as well as in towns throughout France and in the castles of the nobility, one of the most popular forms of entertainment consisted of epic poems that were presented by itinerant performers, called jongleurs. These poems, chansons de geste ("songs of lineage"), were abundant, and more than a hundred have survived in manuscripts copied in the medieval period. The most popular chanson de geste was the *Chanson de Roland,* but in the genre are a number of other masterworks including the *Chanson de Guillaume, Raoul de Cambrai, Garin le Loherain, Le Pèlerinage de Charlemagne à Jérusalem et à Constantinople,* and *Girart de Roussillon.* The depiction of the mental life of characters is carried out by indirect means in the chansons de geste. The poets tell how characters decide to act, but this portrayal of motivation is typically presented in the speech of characters, and occasionally in the jongleur's commentary. Indirect discourse is rare, and even rarer are sentences that begin with the equivalent of such phrases as "she thought that . . ." or "it seemed to him that . . . ."

In the decade of the 1150s, writers composing French romances based on models from the ancient world begin to express characters' motivations not just in dialogue but by presenting their thoughts and feelings. Monologues are rare in the various branches of the *Roman d'Alexandre,* and all are spoken by men. They are more frequent in the *Roman de Thèbes* and at times are placed in the mouths of female characters. In all the romances of antiquity, monologues tend to follow the model of the chansons de geste, that is to say they are mostly speeches of regret for a character who has just died. The *Roman d'Enéas,* however, includes among its twenty-one monologues a dozen that are devoted to the theme of love. Of these, ten are spoken by females (two by Dido and eight by Lavine), totaling 633 lines, and only two are pronounced by a male, Eneas himself, for 310 lines. Almost a tenth of the work is given over to monologues about love. Fully a third of the episode of Lavine consists of such monologues. In contrast, the *Roman de Troie,* ca. 1165, contains only 440 lines of monologue on amorous themes, divided among four monologues by women (two by Medea, two by Briseïda) and four by Achilles, despite its greater length at 30,316 lines. (See the treatment of monologue in the romances of antiquity in Petit 1985: 553–60.) The anonymous author of the *Roman d'Enéas* was not only highly skilled at exploring the anxieties of nascent passion in his adaptation into the vernacular of Virgil's *Aeneid,* but the monologue was his principal instrument in this exploration. In representing lovers' emotions in his romances, Chrétien takes his cue from the *Enéas*.

Monologue is not, however, a technique applied to just any character. Chrétien reserves it for the exposition of amorous relationships, and generally for the conflicts that young people undergo when they feel the first stirrings of love.

The first two monologues in Chrétien's extant romances are by Enide, beginning with her short lament over Erec's having given up chivalry, which ends with the troublesome exclamation "*Con mar i fus!*" (2492–2503). After Erec's disturbed reaction and his command that Enide should dress in her best robe and mount on her best palfrey, she speaks to herself again, engaging this time in self-analysis. Enide asks herself why she spoke such craziness and, suspecting that her husband is about to send her off alone, regrets that she will no longer be able to see him. This second soliloquy is framed by proverbs, first the narrator's "the goat scratches until it can't lie down comfortably" (*tant grate chievre que mal gist,* 2584), then, as the last line of her speech, Enide's remorseful "one doesn't know what good is unless one has tried evil" (*ne set qu'est bien qui mal n'essaie,* 2606). Proverbs provide in romances of this period a body of "tried and true," albeit sometimes inconsistent, principles, said to originate among the peasantry, that can be applied to life situations (see Schulze-Busacker 1985). Enide's self-criticism is akin to the religious examination of conscience that is gaining popularity in this period. Given that Chrétien never pronounces a judgment on the question of whether Enide's conduct and Erec's reaction to it are in keeping with right conduct, one might expect him to have Erec likewise engage in self-examination, but this does not occur.

In a third monologue, likewise spoken out loud, Enide evokes Fortune, an allegorical figure common in medieval literature and art (Patch 1927), who, she says, once held out its hand to her but has now retracted it, with the result that Enide is now no longer to speak to her husband (2778–90). Speak she must, however, despite the prohibition, when she sees that Erec is in danger from two successive groups of hostile knights, and each infraction is preceded by a monologue in which Enide convinces herself to break silence (2829–39, 2962–78). While Erec sleeps that night, she stays awake in watch, blaming her own pride that has now led to her shame (3104–14).

Erec et Enide is a psychological romance. It is Enide's apparent complicity in the accusation of recreancy that weighs upon Erec rather than any concrete action he has taken, and the series of tests that he imposes on Enide results in her proving that her loyalty toward him is genuine.

After Enide tells him that Count Galoain is plotting to betray him, Erec realizes that she is indeed being faithful to him (*Erec* 3482–83). Nonetheless he again imposes silence on her, and when she breaks it to advise that they flee before Count Galoain's hundred knights, he declares himself offended and threatens punishment. Yet again Enide breaks silence to warn that Guivret le Petit is charging toward Erec, but she does so only after taking counsel with herself and undergoing an interior struggle. This struggle is again represented as a spoken monologue (3735–60). When Enide does speak, Chrétien tells us that although Erec threatens her, he realizes that she loves him more than anyone and that he loves her as much as one can love (3763–65). In fact, Erec never imposes a punishment on Enide for violating his orders not to speak. The process of Erec's successive prohibitions results not simply in his reestablishing a trusting relationship with Enide but in his arriving at a point of self-knowledge. On Enide's part, her conduct shows that she is a "faithful lady" (*loial dame, Erec* 3808).

One further ordeal awaits Enide in the forest, as Erec refuses to stay with King Arthur's itinerant court. Seeing her husband faint from his wounds, in a further monologue interrupted by narration she asks Death to kill her because her imprudent words have caused Erec's death, for which she alone bears the guilt (4612–14, 4617–27, 4631–45, 4649–63). "Guilt" (*corpes*, 4644) is here used in the juridical sense of the state of the person who has committed an offense rather than as a feeling of remorse. In the last bit of monologue, Enide resolves to kill herself. She draws Erec's sword from its sheath, but God makes her hesitate, and the arrival of Count Oringle distracts her with yet another set of problems as the count takes her to his castle of Limors and forces her to marry him. The resolution of this dangerous episode through Erec's revival leads to the final reconciliation in the scene in which the two ride the same horse in the moonlight. Erec then finally admits out loud to Enide their mutual love and affection and pardons her having misspoken, "if she ever did so" (4924–25).

All eight of these soliloquies are, to judge by the verbs that introduce them, spoken out loud, and all except the end of the first bedroom speech pass unheard by other characters. What is quite striking, however, is that all the monologues are Enide's. The audience is not given the privilege of hearing the words of any other character lamenting or engaging in decision-making or in self-analysis. That Chrétien chooses to concentrate in this way on his female protagonist may point toward a female patron for *Erec et Enide* (see pp. 11–12, above; cf. p. 69).

Cliges marks a break from the techniques of soliloquy found in *Erec* in that, in addition to monologues spoken by the female characters Soredamor and Fenice, one is also assigned to a male protagonist, Alexandre. Greater emphasis is accorded to female psychology, however, in that women deliver four monologues (Soredamor three and Fenice one), whereas only one is spoken by a male.

Soredamor is the first to speak to herself during the sea passage between the island of Britain and Brittany, wondering whether Alexandre is in love with her. She addresses her eyes as a lord would address a vassal and accuses them of betraying her, then asks herself a series of rhetorical questions about the respective responsibilities of eye and heart, the paradox of desiring what makes her suffer, and the role of Love as a master with whom she does not wish to consort (*Cliges* 475–523). "Thus she debates with herself" (*Einsint a lui meïsmes tence,* 524).

That night, after the ship has docked, Chrétien gives each of the lovers a long monologue, 242 lines for Alexandre, 149 for Soredamor. Alexandre asks himself (626–868) if he is not a fool and answers in the affirmative. He invokes the metaphor of love as a sickness but rejects the notion that he can find relief in an herb, a root, or a drink (a reminiscence of the potion that Tristan and Ysolt drank). He could search out a doctor—Soredamor—but the doctor would not pay him any heed. Does he know the nature of the illness? Yes, it is caused by Love. Should he retreat? Yes, but how? Should he reject Love's teaching? It could be useful some day. There follows a series of considerations of Love's arrows, replete with rhetorical questions, paradoxes, metaphors of the eyes and heart as unfaithful servants, and a long and sexually suggestive disquisition on the charming physical qualities of the arrows that merges imperceptibly into contemplation of Soredamor's face and body. In the end, Alexandre decides not to declare war on Love but rather to submit; better to suffer through the sickness than to be cured by something other than its source. Soredamor, in the meantime, cannot sleep and engages in a disputation (*plait,* 892) in the form of a spoken monologue (893–1042) concerning Alexandre's moral and physical attributes, her love for him, the confusion her obsession with him is causing her, the demands of Love as a tutor, the resonances of her own name—Soredamor, which she interprets as *sororee d'Amor* "gilded by Love" (976)—and how she should reveal her love to him.

The queen gives Alexandre a shirt into which has been woven a strand of hair from Soredamor's head. After he has distinguished himself for prowess in the battle against the forces of Angres of Windsor and presented his prisoners to Guinevere, Soredamor sees that he is wearing the shirt and debates whether to approach him (1384–1410). Again a verb of speaking is used, which would normally indicate that the words are spoken out loud, but in such a context that they are not overheard, and the line following the speech begins "in this thought" (*en cesti pensé*), showing that Chrétien conceives of this soliloquy, and presumably others like it, as an interior monologue. The monologue is once more in the form of questions and answers, and thus really a self-questioning similar in form to the examination of conscience, as Soredamor struggles over whether to call Alexandre *ami* or to address him by his name, which seems to her to have too many letters. If only his name were "fair sweet friend" (*biaus douz amis*)!

The second generation of lovers in *Cliges* is assigned only one monologue. Chrétien narrates in the third person the process by which Cliges and Fenice fall in love, using the soliloquy only for Fenice (4352–4510), after Cliges leaves for Britain without having declared his love openly. She debates aloud—"She objects and responds to herself / And makes the following disputation" (*A lui sole oppose et respont / Et fait tele opposition*)—the nature of words he has spoken to her, that he is "entirely hers." How can she make herself his suzerain lady? As in the case of Enide's second monologue, this one ends in a proverb, endowing the monologue with a finished quality:

> For the peasant says in his proverb:
> If you give yourself into the hands of a worthy man,
> It's bad if you don't improve in his company.
> [Que li vileins dit en sa verve:
> Qui a preudome se comande,
> Mauvais est s'entor lui n'amende.]   (*Cliges* 4508–10)

Fenice is willing to take a chance on confiding in the man she loves. The two come to declare their love for each other by discussing where their respective hearts have been during Cliges's absence, as discussed above. Once love has been declared, there is no further need for self-analysis, and the technique of the private or internal monologue is not employed in the rest of the romance.

Although in *Lancelot*, as in *Cliges*, the monologue is not limited to female speech, this romance sponsored by Marie de Champagne ushers in a different use of the device. Here it is a question no longer of innocent young people falling in love or engaging in self-criticism but of the vicissitudes of an adulterous liaison.

The attribute by which Lancelot comes to be identified, the cart, causes a crisis in the hero's resolve. Upon hearing from the dwarf that, to learn of Guinevere's whereabouts, he has to climb into the cart, Lancelot continues to walk for two steps (Hult 1994: variants following l. 360). He hesitates because Reason is advising him not to mount the cart, an ignominious conveyance, whereas Love is taking the opposite side of the argument. Because Love commands him to, he jumps into the vehicle, not caring about shame. What is striking about this scene is that one would expect it to include a debate in the form of a soliloquy like the one Fenice speaks in *Cligès*, or like the interior conversation in which Love and Reason take part in the *Roman de Thèbes* (ms. P, ll. 9355–75, cited in Petit 1985: 595–96), but Chrétien chooses simply to describe the conflict between Love and Reason rather than to dramatize it. This means of development is all the more unexpected in that Chrétien's model for the conflict appears to be a passage from Ovid's *Metamorphoses* (book 7, 19–20), in which Medea, in a soliloquy, speaks of an inner struggle between desire (*cupido*) and mind or reason (*mens*). Similarly, when the fifth damsel, Meleagant's sister, asks Lancelot to cut off the head of the knight who has shamed him by reminding him of the cart episode, the hero hesitates in thought (2831) while the conflicting interests of Largess (here "Moral Generosity") and Pity pull him in opposite directions. He finally decides, but without the benefit of a monologue, to allow the knight to take a new weapon and fight on, eventually decapitating him.

Lancelot does engage in an analytic monologue, however, when the Fourth Maiden stages the feigned rape scene and asks for his help (1097–1125). The hero is torn between the courage he should feel in rescuing the maiden from her attacker and his misgivings about facing six adversaries at once. He is ashamed even to be hesitating. Nowhere else in Chrétien does a male protagonist hesitate or debate in exercising his courage. Lancelot here has to decide to do what Chrétien's other heroes do without having to engage in a reasoning process.

Guinevere, by contrast, hearing the rumor that Lancelot is dead, says to herself quietly, so that no one can hear, that she will not eat or drink if the news is true. She rises from table and laments, once again so that no one hears her, then, wishing to die, puts her hands around her own throat. Finally, however, she does something quite bizarre when she confesses to herself, repenting of the sin of having rejected her lover (4182–86). This reversal of the sacrament of penance, confessing and repenting of what in terms of Christian morality would be viewed as a laudable refusal to see the man who is pursuing her, a married woman, must be ironic on Chrétien's part. Guinevere goes on to speak again to herself, but this time the speech is couched in direct discourse (4197–4244), rehearsing all her misdeeds toward Lancelot: it was she who delivered the mortal blow to him in refusing to see or speak to him; this sin of murder can never be redeemed; if only she could have held him once naked in her arms; better to live and suffer for him than to die and find peace.

Chrétien then sets up a parallel scene for Lancelot. Rumor flows in the other direction, as Guinevere's refusal to eat or drink for two days gives rise to news that she has passed away. Lancelot is determined to commit suicide and speaks, addressing Death (4263–83): he is hurt to the quick, but if God does not consent to his death, may he allow Lancelot to hang himself from his horse, forcing Death to let him die. Lancelot then ties himself by the neck to his horse's saddle to be dragged to death. Asking God to consent to a suicide is, theologically, no less ironic than Guinevere's confessing to herself the "sin" of rejecting her lover, than Lancelot's adoring the queen as if she is a relic (4652–53) or bowing down before her as if before an altar (4718). The suicidal stratagem fails, however, and Lancelot once again speaks to Death, this time reproachfully (4318–96), and he muses about the identity of the crime that led to the queen's rejection. Was it because he climbed into the cart? Lancelot echoes Soredamor's thoughts (see *Cliges* 1406–10) in wondering whether to call the queen his *amie* and to consider him her *ami*, deeming himself deserving of the title since he incurred shame for her in the cart. Those who are ignorant of Love do not realize that anything done for her is pardonable. The rumor of Guinevere's death is now corrected, leading to the interview in Bademagu's castle at which Lancelot learns that his fault was not having climbed into the cart but rather having hesitated for two steps before doing so. Lancelot immediately consents to the queen's analysis, offers reparation, and receives her pardon.

A final monologue, lines 6468–6529, is found in the section of *Lancelot* composed by Godefroy de Lagny. Lancelot speaks it while he is imprisoned in the tower, and this time the soliloquy is really spoken out loud, because it is overheard by Meleagant's sister. Lancelot addresses first Fortune, whose turning wheel has now placed him at its lowest point, then the Holy Cross, the Holy Spirit, and finally Gauvain, who should be coming to his rescue. He calls down the power of God and St. Silvester upon Meleagant for shaming him.

There are in all five soliloquies in *Lancelot,* one by Guinevere and four by Lancelot. With the exception of Lancelot's final lament, they serve to prepare the lovers for the act of adultery.

Yvain contains one of the best-known monologues in Chrétien's works, the debate in which Laudine decides whether to marry Yvain. But before that scene, Laudine engages in self-debate over the whereabouts of the man who has killed her husband, Esclados, for the corpse's wounds are bleeding, a sign that the perpetrator is present:

> Thus the lady debates with herself,
> Thus all by herself she struggles with herself,
> Thus she torments and upsets herself. . . .
> [Ainsi la dame se debat,
> Ainsi tout par li se combat,
> Ainsi se tourmente et confont. . . .]   (*Yvain* 1243–45)

The nature of this first monologue is public, however, as it is introduced by the phrase "The lady cried out as if out of her senses" (*La dame . . . crioit comme hors de sens,* 1204–5). Laudine blames the killer's invisibility on God, although the audience knows that it is caused by the ring of invisibility that Lunete has given Yvain. Laudine thinks that he must be a demon of some kind and that she has been enchanted.

Yvain, meanwhile, is touched by the sight of Laudine's mourning. His first brief monologue (1351–57), however, introduced without a verb of speaking and without anyone else present, is a reflection on the disparagement he will continue to suffer from Keu if he returns to Arthur's court without physical proof that he has conquered Esclados. Like Soredamor and Alexandre, he is struck by Love's arrow, shot into his heart through the eyes, and Love has come to dwell in him. He monologizes again, this time at length (1432–1510), on the paradox of loving and consequently being at the mercy of a woman who hates him; he refuses to commit treachery toward Love, which would be a felony, and will love her whose friend and enemy he is at the same time; he discourses on the beauty of Laudine's hair, eyes, and throat, which Nature outdid herself in forming; no, rather God made her, to astonish Nature.

Lunete undertakes to convince her lady to marry Yvain under the threat of Arthur's imminent arrival, so that he can defend the fountain. Laudine then engages in a remarkably short internal debate (1760–72), not with herself as the imagined interlocutor but with Yvain, conceiving that she is interrogating him "through speech and legal procedure" (*par raison et par droit de plait,* 1755). On the basis of this internal trial, Yvain is proclaimed innocent, and the next morning Laudine tells Lunete that she is ready to accord sovereignty over her land and herself to the man who killed her husband. The key step in this internalized process is that Laudine recognizes that Yvain acted only in self-defense and without malice, a verdict Yvain later echoes when kneeling in her presence. Such a realization takes advantage of a moral development still recent in Chrétien's time, the substitution of a concept of responsibility based on intention—what motivated the act in question—for one based merely on the result of the act (theft, perjury, killing). This development was chiefly the work of Peter Abelard (1079–1142), especially in his *Ethics* (late 1130s), for whom the essence of sin is consent to an evil act and not the act itself (Luscombe 1971: 4 and passim; Chenu 1969: 18).

After his episode of madness and in the lion's company, Yvain returns to the fountain, where he speaks to himself about suicide, because he hates himself for having alienated joy through his own misdeed (3527–58).

In Chrétien's final romance, four short monologues are spoken by the young Perceval himself, musing first that the wonderful creatures he sees in the forest are devils (113–24), then that they are rather God himself and his angels (137–54), then that the tent of Orgueilleus de la Lande must be a church (655–66), and finally that Arthur cannot make knights if he cannot speak (927–30). All these speeches are designed to show Perceval's naïveté. Only one other monologue is found in this, the longest of Chrétien's romances, and it is spoken by Perceval's cousin, whom he comes upon in the forest, lamenting out loud her lover's demise and asking to die (3434–52). The love monologue plays no role in *Perceval,* not even in the scenes between the knight and his amie, Blancheflor.

In his early romances, *Erec* and *Cliges,* Chrétien assigns monologues to his female characters almost exclusively—eight to Enide, three to Soredamor, one to Fenice—and has only one male character—Alexandre—speak in monologue. In the last three romances, this propensity is reversed: eleven monologues are given to male characters and only four to females. The development from female to male monologues corresponds to a thematic movement from stories of adolescent love to tales involving more mature lovers or, in the case of *Perceval,* the eclipse of the theme of worldly love by the theme of spiritual progress. The monologue is a device that allows the reader to identify with the character in question; nowhere does Chrétien have an unsympathetic character engage in monologue.

All of the monologues but two are introduced by verbs of speaking. Except for those two passages—Yvain's concern with physical proof of his victory over Esclados and Laudine's imagined interrogation of her prospective husband—the distinction between speaking out loud (although often out of earshot of other characters) and true internal monologues is blurred. Chrétien is representing the thinking process of his characters but is presenting it as spoken words.

In addition to dialogue, monologue, and internal speech, Chrétien and other writers of romance often simply comment, of course, that a character is having a reaction or is thinking a thought. The passage in which Chrétien describes Yvain coming upon the lion and the serpent in combat is typical of the way he represents thinking without direct speech.

> He takes counsel with himself
> About which of the two to help.
> Then he says that he will help the lion
> Because one should only inflict damage on
> A harmful and felonious creature.
> And the serpent is harmful. . . .
> [A lui meïsmes se conseille
> Auquel des deuz il aidera.
> Lors dist c'au lyon secorra
> Qu'a enuious et a felon
> Ne doit on faire se mal non.
> Et li serpens est enuious. . . .]   (*Yvain* 3354–59)

Chrétien here tells what thought process follows upon the protagonist's sighting of the two beasts, namely his spoken—although solitary—decision about which of the animals to help. Then follows the justification for that decision. All this is expressed as a monologue in indirect discourse even though no other person is present to hear him. Chrétien conceives elsewhere of this solitary kind of speech as "speaking in one's heart": thus when Gornemant of Gohort sees how well Perceval handles himself when armed on horseback, he says in his heart that if the young man had spent his whole life practicing he could not have done better (*Perceval* 1487–90). Similar expressions are found in the *Roman d'Enéas* to introduce internal monologue: to say "between one's teeth" (*antre ses danz,* Salverda de Grave 1929–31: ll. 8425, 9928) or to speak "in one's heart" (*an son corage,* 8939).

Because Chrétien represents thought in quoted speech as well as in indirect discourse, the monologues are obviously a way of foregrounding the main characters, who are represented in their interiority by external

means. Although he followed the author of the *Roman d'Enéas* in his preference for this device, Chrétien's status as the classic author of Arthurian
romances ensured that his characters became the principal models for subsequent writers of French romance.

FORGETTING ONESELF

Chrétien conceives of his characters as having an awareness of the world
that it is possible to suspend by falling into deep thought. Thus Enide believes that Erec is engaged so deeply in thought that he "forgets himself"
(*soi meïsmes oblie, Erec* 3758–59) and does not realize that a knight is about
to attack him. Yvain never forgets himself, but he does forget to return to
his wife at the proper time, which is a form of forgetfulness that, for many
a modern reader, stretches the limits of plausibility.

In the case of Lancelot, forgetting oneself almost leads to disaster. Having chosen to cross into Gorre over the Sword Bridge, Lancelot is thinking
of the cart like one who has no force or defense against Love, which has so
taken charge of him that he forgets himself. Here Chrétien goes into some
detail: Lancelot forgets where he is, what his name is, whether he is armed,
where he has come from and where he is going. He remembers nothing
(*Lancelot* 716–21). He thinks of only one thing, and this thought effaces his
sight and his hearing until, when his horse carries him to a ford, the knight
guarding it unhorses him into the stream. When his quest for the queen
finally results in his entering her bedroom by bending open the bars on the
window, Lancelot does not realize that he has cut two of his fingers (*Lancelot*
4645–46), so intent is he on approaching Guinevere. The blood oozing from
those cuts gives rise to Meleagant's false accusation that Keu has made love
to the queen, leading to an indecisive judicial combat between Lancelot
and Meleagant. Although Chrétien does not say that Lancelot forgets himself in the bedroom scene, the hero does indeed ignore his wound because
his mind is on something else.

Perceval, too, becomes lost in thought, at the sight of the color of three
drops of blood shed by a goose on the snow, one of the most popular
scenes in the romance (plate 7). He is reminded of the colors in the face
of his beloved Blancheflor and thinks about this so long that he forgets
himself for an entire morning (*Perceval* 4202). This event happens near
Arthur's encampment, and when Sagremor invites the young knight to
the camp, Perceval hears the invitation but pretends not to. The angry
Sagremor charges at him, but Perceval sees him coming and unhorses him.

A similar scene ensues with Keu, whom Perceval hears challenging him. Perceval breaks Keu's arm and dislocates his collarbone in the encounter, thereby avenging the Laughing Girl. Now it is Gauvain's turn to bring Perceval into the encampment, and he accomplishes the task with courtesy. So often do knights in the imaginary Arthurian world fall into reverie that the king is said to have formulated the courtly advice that one should never startle a knight from his thought, whatever it might be (4352–56).

At the beginning of the romance, Perceval does not know his own name, but when his cousin asks him what it is, he guesses it is "Perceval the Welsh-man" (*Perchevax li Galois*). The authorial voice says that Perceval is guessing right (3572–77), so either Chrétien thought there was some level below or beyond consciousness at which a character could plausibly be aware of his name without having articulated it before, or Perceval's ignorance of his name is implausibly corrected as an aspect of the fate that has been imposed on him, like his responsibility for his mother's death.

Perceval never consciously knew his name, but Lancelot in his pensiveness forgets his name and unlike Perceval does not have the excuse of being young and naive. This is but one of several details contributing to the notion that Chrétien's portrayal of Lancelot is ironic.

KILLING ONESELF

The impulse to kill oneself, a defining possibility for the self-reflective creature, occurs among Chrétien's characters in all five romances, with increasing importance (see the thorough treatment in Lefay-Toury 1979).

Thinking that her husband has died of his wounds, Enide is inspired to commit suicide, to the point of preparing to use Erec's sword for the purpose (*Erec* 4664), but God takes pity on her so that, in the time it takes her to rehearse her unhappiness, Count Oringle rides up and presents her with a new set of problems. When Fenice is buried, Cliges postpones killing himself until he can see whether she will survive the entombment (*Cliges* 6063–67). Yvain also contemplates suicide, but does not move further toward the act, although his lion does. Thinking him dead of an accidental wound, the beast removes the knight's sword from its sheath with his teeth, props it up, and is hurtling toward it when Yvain revives (*Yvain* 3502–21). Chrétien depicts the lion as capable of human sentiments and of interiority, and animals are so represented routinely in medieval bestiaries as well as, of course, in such beast epics as the *Roman de Renart*.

Both Lancelot and Guinevere are tempted to commit suicide, Lancelot not once but twice, from anguish over love. When Lancelot, looking out from the castle of the Perilous Bed, sees the queen's cortege disappear in the distance, he leans out the window and wants to hurl himself down to the ground, but Gauvain restrains him and reproaches him for hating his own life (*Lancelot* 574). Actually there is no reason for Lancelot to commit suicide at this point, as he has just seen the queen for the first time since her abduction, albeit from afar, but his foolish impulse is one more indication that Chrétien is undercutting his characterization. Lancelot has greater justification the second time, after he has lent credence to the false rumor of Guinevere's death, but his chosen method, tying himself by the neck to his horse's saddle (4288–89), seems ignominious. When Guinevere thinks Lancelot has been captured and killed, she abstains from food and drink, a more dignified path toward death—although because of a turn in the plot she does so for only two days (4246).

During the chaste night that Blancheflor spends in bed with Perceval, she tells him that she will stab herself to death the following day because she expects her enemy, Engygeron, to capture her castle (*Perceval* 1998, 2032–34). Perceval himself later says he wishes he had died after leaving the Grail castle and forgetting God (6382), but he never attempts suicide.

Finally, one character who acts reprehensibly, Orgueilleuse de Logres, tries to engineer her own death by provoking Gauvain to kill her. She does so out of chagrin at the death of a lover killed by Guiromelant (8947–63), or at least that is what she tells Gauvain: one cannot be sure that she is a reliable narrator of her own thoughts, however, because she shows herself elsewhere to be deceptive.

The idea of killing oneself arises surprisingly frequently in Chrétien's romances, considering that, for a Christian, suicide was a mortal sin for which one could not, ipso facto, subsequently atone and seek expiation. It was condemned as a sinful act, a violation of the commandment not to kill. Legally, the punishment for killing oneself was similar to that imposed for killing someone else. The bodies of those who committed suicide were sometimes dragged through the streets and hanged on a gibbet, and they could be denied Christian burial unless the suicide was thought to result from insanity (Gonthier 1998: 106, 175). That Chrétien never refers to suicide as a sinful or reprehensible act is a remarkable token that his primary values are profane, despite the enhanced role of Christian values in *Perceval*.

In the chansons de geste of this period, in which character analysis is carried out through the poet's commentary or in dialogue, not even characters who wish for death move to the momentous step of attempting to kill themselves. In the renowned Oxford version of the *Chanson de Roland,* for example, Aude has no desire to live after Roland's demise, but the poet has her drop dead rather than end her own life. That suicide is even presented as a possibility for Chrétien's characters is an indicator of interiority.

ALLEGORY AND INSIGHT

Without a set of original metaphors for talking about movements and impulses of the psyche and the forces external to the person that influence them, Chrétien turns to the allegorical personification of abstract emotions and qualities. The use of such personifications goes back to Roman and Greek antiquity. Their popularity in Chrétien's period is ascribable to the influence of three works: Martianus Capella's *Marriage of Philology and Mercury (De Nuptiis Mercurii et Philologiae),* an encyclopedic allegory on the seven liberal arts written in the first half of the fifth century and influential in the Middle Ages; the *Psychomachia* of the early Christian writer Prudentius, which contains personifications of mental states; and Boethius's *Consolation of Philosophy.* Personification is widely found in the works of some twelfth-century authors writing in Latin, the most important of whom are Bernard Silvestris of the school of Chartres,[1] author of the *Cosmographia* (see Whitman 1987), and Alan of Lille, author of the *Anticlaudianus* and the *Complaint of Nature,* whose influence on Chrétien has been explored by Claude Luttrell (1974).

Chrétien uses personifications for emotions: *Amors* (Love), *Esperance* (Hope), *Haine* (Hate), *Hardemens* (Bravery), *Honte* (Shame); for virtuous qualities: *Reisons* (Reason), *Largece* (Generosity, Largess), *Proesce* (Prowess); and for vices: *Malvestiez,* signifying evil in general but here, in a knightly context, Cravenness or Cowardice, *Pechiez* (Sin), and *Peresce* (Indolence). The external forces that are personified, in addition to the Divine Will, are *Drois* (Justice), *Fortune* (Fortune), *Mort* (Death), and *Nature* (Nature). Reason plays an important role in Martianus Capella's work, as does Nature in Alan of Lille. These figures are assigned the sex that their grammatical gender requires, *Drois, Hardemens,* and *Pechiez* as male entities and the rest as female, including *Amors,* which can have feminine gender in Old French.

Chrétien may have used other allegorical entities, for it is not always clear whether a given abstraction is to be read as a true personification or is simply the subject of a verb of action in a transitory metaphor. One of the tasks of the editor as intermediary between the medieval text and the modern reader is to signal allegorical figures through capitalization, but this practice is not always applied consistently.

Chrétien's first romance is remarkably devoid of personifications of internal qualities, although the external forces Fortune, Death, and Nature are all brought into play. In *Cliges,* by contrast, in addition to this trio, Largesce is invoked several times in the speech in which the emperor Alexandre advises his son Alexandre to be openhanded with the wealth that his father is supplying him. There Largesce is extolled as the queen of all the virtues, capable of making one a "worthy man" (*preudome*), which the qualities of courtesy, knowledge, nobility, wealth, force, chivalry, bravery, lordship, and beauty cannot accomplish by themselves even if in concert. Largesce is said to surpass the other virtues as the rose surpasses other flowers (*Cliges* 208–12). This overblown praise of openhandedness in a text composed by a writer in need of patronage seems not only to be self-serving but to reveal some anxiety over compensation for a romance that mentions no patron by name. Although Laudine praises the dead Esclados by declaring that Largesce was his friend and Hardemens his companion (*Yvain* 1296–97), nowhere but in *Cliges,* not even in the Bildungsroman *Perceval,* does Chrétien have a character so highly recommend the generosity of nobles.

In *Lancelot,* in addition to the personifications of Reason and Love, treated above in the discussion of monologue, Chrétien cites the abstract qualities Prowess (*Proesce*), Cowardice (*Malvestiez*), and Indolence (*Peresce*) (*Lancelot* 3175–78), having King Bademagu of Gorre observe that Lancelot is a consummate knight, because no one in whom Marvestiez lodged could have succeeded in crossing the Sword Bridge. Malvestiez, Bademagu thinks, has a greater capacity to produce shame in her adherents than does Proesce to generate honor, for with the help of Malvestiez and Peresce more evil is done in the world than good. It is precisely in terms of the values of Malvestiez and Peresce, however, that Lancelot is vilified in the tournament at Noauz, when he fights his worst at the queen's behest. The crowd seeks him out in vain the evening of the first day, commenting that Malvestiez has put him to flight, for she has taken him over completely and no one makes for an easier life than she. Proesce does not deign to sit beside him, continues the crowd, but Malvestiez has found the right dwelling place, in a man who is willing to do her honor by losing his own (*Lancelot* 5740–56). When Lancelot appears at the tournament the next day, the crowd hoots at him and repeats that Malvestiez has him so much in her control that he is defenseless against her (5866). Chrétien has the young Alexandre invoke the same opposition between Malvestiez and Proesce in *Cliges* (161–63).

When Yvain leaves Laudine, he leaves his heart behind, and his body lives in the hope of returning to his heart; and so in a bizarre way, says Chrétien, Yvain makes a heart out of Esperance, who often betrays and breaks her oaths. Yvain will never know just when Esperance will have betrayed him, however, since he violates the agreement to return to Laudine in one year (*Yvain* 2651–62). Esperance plays no role in Chrétien's other romances.

In an earlier passage, Yvain is said to have no desire to leave Laudine's castle because Love and Shame, approaching him from different directions, are keeping him there, Love because of the beautiful widow and Shame because he does not want to return to Arthur's court without proof of his successful exploit at the fountain (*Yvain* 1533–41). When Yvain is about to fight a duel with Gauvain over the inheritance of the two daughters of the lord of Noire Espine, neither knows the other's identity, which presents Chrétien with the opportunity for one of the longest narrative pauses in his romances, in which he discourses on the paradox of Love and Hate existing simultaneously in the two knights (5995–6101). Don't these men still love each other? Yes and no, Chrétien responds in a rare first-person statement, and he will prove it to his audience in such a way as to find reason (*raison,* 6000) in his proposition. The two knights would celebrate seeing each other if their identities were revealed, and would even be ready to sacrifice themselves for each other should the occasion arise, but since neither recognizes the other—an improbability rendered plausible by the fact that they are dressed in armor and their faces are thus not visible—each is filled with hatred for his opponent and a desire to shame him. Love and Hate can only exist in one dwelling because in the body there are several members, so perhaps Love was in a secluded bedchamber and Hate was installed in a gallery with an exterior view. Now Hate is ready to fight and spurs toward Love, who is hidden away but should come out and see the enemies of its friends, those enemies being people who love each other with a holy love. So Love is blind, not recognizing the two friends, and Hate is unable to say why they hate each other, which makes each wish the other's death. But if Yvain gets the worst of it, can he justifiably complain about being harmed by a friend, or can Gauvain rightly complain if injured? No, because he will not know the enemy's identity. The insights of characters are obviously heavily circumscribed by forces external to them.

Love is the sentiment most frequently allegorized in Chrétien, which is not surprising given his constant preoccupation with lovers and the strong classical tradition of personified Love to which he was exposed in Ovid. In the *Ars amatoria,* a work that Chrétien says he translated and that he refers to as the *Art d'amors* (*Cliges* 3), the personified Amor appears several times, most notably in the first thirty lines of book 1, where he is depicted as a boy who shoots arrows and wields a torch. Ovid's *Remedia amoris,* which Chrétien appears also to have translated and which he refers to as the *Comandemenz d'Ovide,* introduces Amor in its first line, and the first forty lines consist of a dialogue with him. Amor also appears in the *Amores* and the *Metamorphoses.* An additional influence may have been the troubadours, as Amors is the dominant figure in both of Chrétien's lyric poems, "D'Amors qui m'a tolu a moi" and "Amors tençon et bataille," composed in the troubadour style. As is the case with the love monologue, however, Chrétien's use of Amors as an allegorical figure was probably also influenced by the *Roman d'Enéas* (see, for example, Petit 1997: ll. 8165–8294) and perhaps, too, in this case the *Roman de Troie* (20703–74).

Amors figures in Chrétien's three middle romances, always as a feminine figure, as is the case in the lyric poems. That she does not make an appearance in *Erec et Enide,* in which the two protagonists do not engage in monologue or dialogue about their feelings for each other until after they have been married, is an argument in favor of dating sometime after *Erec* the Ovidiana that Chrétien mentions in the prologue to *Cliges.* Amors is absent from *Perceval* despite moments at which Chrétien might have found it appropriate to introduce her, such as the night that Blancheflor spends in Perceval's bed and the scene in which he contemplates the drops of blood on the snow. Perceval, as Chrétien tells us in passing, was ignorant of love just as he was of everything else (*Perceval* 1941–42), which may account for this lack. More likely, however, is that, by the time of his last romance, Chrétien's concerns have turned from secular love to the charity that he highlights in the prologue (*Perceval* 43–50).

Slightly over half of the appearances of Amors in personified form in Chrétien's romances are in *Cliges,* in which she is mentioned more than forty times. This is in keeping with the importance in that romance of self-analytical monologues on love. Chrétien introduces Soredamor by saying that she disdains Amors (445–46), who then takes vengeance on her by shooting an arrow into her heart, unleashing the flood of sentiments that will result in her marriage to Alexandre and the birth of Cliges. When the adolescent Cliges places himself in Amors's service, he thereby exposes himself to fear, since

Love without dread and without fear
Is fire without warmth and without heat,
Day without sun, hive without honey,
Summer without flowers, winter without frost,
Sky without moon, book without letter.
[Amors sanz crieme et sanz poor
Est feus sanz chaut et sanz chalor,
Jorz sanz soleil, ree sanz miel,
Estez sanz fleurs, ivers sanz giel,
Ciel sanz lune, livre sanz letre.]   (*Cliges* 3841–45)

And so Cliges comes to fear Fenice as he comes to love her, just as a servant fears a master. Fenice, by contrast, meditates on the phrasing Cliges used when he took leave of her to travel to Britain, in which he referred to her as "her to whom I belong entirely" (*cele qui je sui touz,* 4269). She conjectures that Amors must have captured him in her grasp (4370). In addition to the more expected functions of Amors in the monologues, Soredamor comments on her role in the makeup of her own name, which, as noted above, she analyzes as *sororee d'Amor* 'gilded by Love' (976).

Amors appears in *Lancelot* and *Yvain* approximately an equal number of times. In *Yvain* most of these occurrences are clustered in the passages in which the knight falls in love with Laudine and in the scene that precedes his combat with Gauvain. This last, touching on the love between knightly companions, shows that the semantic range of *Amors* is not limited to sexual attraction. In *Lancelot,* Amors plays a key role in the cart scene and elsewhere in the sequence of actions leading up to the episode in which *Lancelot* and the queen make love, but surprisingly makes no appearance after that, which is to say in the last third of the poem.

The personification of these abstract qualities, which Chrétien tends to invoke in contrasting or complementary pairs, places him in the category of writers influenced by a tendency to view universal qualities as having a real existence outside their material manifestations, an aspect of the general climate of philosophical Platonism that was still prevalent in some circles in twelfth-century France. Whether he was aware of the implications of his method or was simply incorporating an established literary convention is impossible to say. Whatever the case may be, he chose to use the personification of abstract categories to express psychological and moral nuances in an allegorical language familiar to his audiences. Allegory has its own difficulties, of course, that are shared with metaphorical language of any type, because the figurative creatures that it evokes have only a few qualities that are useful in the literary situation and cannot be employed consistently or extensively in a work whose essence is narrative. Thus Amors shoots an arrow that wounds the lovers, or acts as a master toward servants, or binds the lovers in her ties, but once their love is consummated in marriage the wound, the hegemony, and the chains are forgotten and the plot reverts to a predominantly literal level of discourse as the author deals with the long-term consequences of love or with conflicts between marriage and knighthood.

Some forty years after Chrétien, in Guillaume de Lorris's *Romance of the Rose,* allegorical figures for abstract qualities will be depicted on the wall of the garden of pleasance and some will become the armature of the plot. Among the psychic and moral qualities so treated are Hate (*Haine*), Felony (*Felonie*), Desire (*Covoitise*), Avarice (*Avarice*), Envy (*Anvie*), Sadness (*Tristesse*), Hypocrisy (*Papelardie*), Amusement (*Deduiz*), Happiness (*Leesce*), Indolence (*Oiseuse*), and Courtliness (*Cortoisie*). Chrétien and writers contemporary with him are the forerunners in French of this use of allegorical registers to explore the psyche, which will become the dominant mode in the fourteenth and fifteenth centuries in works in which narrative is subordinated to metaphor. That Love creates an impulse in the heart that is opposed to the counsels of Reason (*Lancelot*) or of Hate (*Yvain*) and that Largess and Pity can pull the knight in different directions (*Lancelot*) are depictions that imply already a concept of psychology in Chrétien.

MADNESS

The archetypal depiction of madness in Chrétien's romances is that of the knight Yvain. Having killed Laudine's husband and fallen in love with her at first sight, Yvain wins her hand in marriage by placing himself entirely at her mercy, denying guilt under a plea of self-defense, declaring that he loves her and thinks of nothing else but her, and promising to defend her fountain. She accepts him out of political need and because he is a good knight and the son of a king, although her vassals and Amors also counsel her to do so. But no sooner is the weeklong marriage feast concluded than Yvain asks her to grant an unspecified request. She does so, and what she has consented to turns out to be leave for Yvain to go fight in tournaments so that he will not be accused of recreancy (2561). She declares that her love will turn to hate unless he returns within a year, that is by the eighth day after the feast of St. John the Baptist, July 1 in the modern calendar. In exchange for his promise to return, she gives him a ring of invulnerability that will protect him from bloodshed, imprisonment, and all other harm if he thinks only of her.

Although Yvain leaves his heart behind with Laudine, thinking of her is precisely what he does not do. Six weeks after the deadline, while Arthur is visiting the encampment of Yvain and Gauvain near Chester, the realization suddenly takes hold of Yvain that he has failed to keep his promise. He wants to weep, but shame prevents him. The thought of what he has done continues until a young woman comes riding in on a palfrey to denounce him before the king as disloyal and treacherous: he has stolen her lady's heart and has not returned it to her. Laudine was so taken with him that it troubled her sleep and she had a depiction of the days and seasons painted on her bedroom walls. Laudine does not ask for restitution, only that Yvain should not return and that he should give the ring back to her.

With this encounter in the presence of Arthur and his court, Yvain is publicly shamed. He is dumbstruck, and everything he sees is painful to him. He wants to be alone, in a place where no one would know about him. He hates himself more than anything in the world and wants to take vengeance on himself for having stolen away his own joy.[2] He slips away from the camp. Into his head rises a vortex (*troubeillons*, 2804) so powerful that he loses his mind (*il forsenne*, 2805). He tears off his clothes and runs into the forest, leaving his friends wondering where he is.

While in the forest, Yvain lives like an animal, naked and eating raw meat. Chrétien does not have him speak during this episode. He still has enough presence of mind, however, to steal a bow and arrows from a boy. He forgets everything that happens to him during the time of his madness (2822–23), his crisis over forgetting to return to Laudine having led to a hiatus in his own memory. A hermit who is making a clearing in the forest sees the naked Yvain one day and flees from him, but charity moves him to put bread and clean water out on the windowsill of his hut for Yvain. When Yvain deposits a deer he has killed at the hermit's door, the hermit skins and cooks it, leaving it out for the wild man. The lady of Norison and two of her companions pass by some days later, and one of them recognizes the sleeping Yvain by a scar on his face. She sees that he has lost his senses and remarks that "if God were to give him good fortune by putting him back into his senses" (*Se Dix si boine destinee / Li donnoit qu'il le remeïst / En son sens*, 2942–44), he could be of use to the lady of Norison in her struggle against a certain Count Alier. The lady of Norison then gives her companion a box of unguent that has come from Morgan the Fay, so that the madness (*rage*) and the storm (*tempeste*) can be removed from Yvain's head (2950). In spite of her lady's admonition to be sparing, the woman spreads the unguent over Yvain's entire body, and the madness and black bile (*melancolie*) leave his brain (3004–5). Yvain recovers his sense and his memory and, ashamed of his nakedness, dresses himself in clothing that the woman has deposited by his side. She then pretends to come upon him by accident and leads him to the castle of the lady of Norison, where he is given a bath, a shampoo, a shave, and a haircut.

During his period of madness, Yvain encounters three helpers: one is unwilling, the boy from whom he steals the weapons with which he hunts; one is at first fearful but then willing, the hermit; and the third is quite willing, the companion of the lady of Norison. The hermit not only gives Yvain nourishment but out of Christian sentiments maintains the knight's link with human culture by transforming raw meat into cooked for him. After the initial encounter, the hermit is able to provide for Yvain by skinning the deer that he leaves at his door and selling the skins in order to buy barley, straw, and whole grain with which to make bread. Thus despite his madness, Yvain engages in human exchange, even if at the lowest economic level. The woman cures Yvain's folly with the help of God and Morgan the Fay's unguent: Chrétien apparently saw no difficulty in associating God with a pagan sorceress, and indeed God effects Yvain's return to sanity through Morgan's medicine, which the lady of Norison later calls her most precious possession (3124–25).

This unguent has the effect of driving the melancholy from Yvain's brain: "For from his brain there issued forth / The madness and the melancholy" (*Que du chervel l'en issi hors / Le rage et le melancolie,* 3004–5). Melancholy was, in medieval physiology, one of the humors, fluids that were viewed as the origin of vital functions (see Stanley Jackson 1986 for a history of the concept of melancholy). Neo-Platonic physical science, popular in the Middle Ages and deriving in this instance from the tradition of Hippocrates and Galen, sees the world as made up of four categories, heat, cold, moistness, and dryness, that combine to give rise to the four substances of which everything else in the macrocosm is composed: fire, air, water, and earth. When the substances enter the microcosm or "small world" of the human body through food and drink, the fluids resulting from a double digestion in the stomach and the liver are transformed by the liver into four humors, the "offspring" of the elements: fiery substance becomes yellow bile (L. *cholera rubea*), air becomes blood (L. *sanguis*), water becomes phlegm (L. *phlegma*), and earth becomes melancholy (L. *melancolia* 'black bile', also termed *atra-*

bilis and *cholera nigra*). The liver then distributes these humors among the various organs of the body. In this way, man, the microcosm, is made of the same substances as the macrocosm. The prime locus of melancholy in the body is the spleen. A local source that was available in Chrétien's time, setting forth with great authority this theory received from previous authors, was Guillaume de Saint-Thierry's *Nature of Body and Soul* (*De natura corporis et animae*), probably composed before 1145 (Lemoine 1988: see esp. 71–93). Guillaume was a Cistercian monk in the abbey of Saint-Nicaise in Rheims, and later in the abbey of Signy, where he died in 1148.

If the body's humors are in balance, a healthy complexion results. The dominance of a particular humor causes a corresponding temperament: yellow bile an excitable (choleric) disposition, blood an easygoing (sanguine) character devoid of sadness and bitterness, phlegm a sluggish, unemotional (phlegmatic) nature, and black bile a sad (melancholic) temper. According to the Dominican philosopher Albertus Magnus, who died in 1280, sanguine people enjoy good health, the choleric are tall and thin, the phlegmatic are small and fat, and the melancholy are slight, short, and dark. Disorders of the humors, with the exception of blood, give rise to particular types of insanity. Excess of yellow bile produces frenzy (L. *phrenesis*), a mixture of yellow and black bile results in mania (L. *mania*), and phlegm affected by fever leads to lethargy (L. *lethargia*).

According to Chrétien, however, Yvain has in his brain the fourth type of imbalance, *melancolie* (3005). One of the main conduits through which the humoral theory of madness came to medieval European thinkers, including Guillaume de Saint-Thierry, was Constantine the African (d. ca. 1087). Constantine was a Muslim converted to Christianity who taught in the Benedictine school at Montecassino, had access to Arabic treatises, and wrote an influential translation of Ishaq ibn Imran's *On Melancholy*. Constantine describes the physical mechanism of the onset of melancholy as follows: "The smoke of black bile, when it rises to the brain and comes to the locus of the mind, darkens, disturbs, and obscures its light, preventing it from understanding what it used to, but showing it what it should understand" (*Fumus . . . colere nigre cum ad cerebrum saliat et ad locum mentis veniat, lumen eius obscurat, turbat, et perfundat, prohibens nequid comprehendere solebat sed quod opertet et comprehendat*, Malato and Martini 1959: 49–50). The vortex—*troubeillon*, a form of *tourbillon* with metathesis—that Chrétien shows rising into Yvain's brain and causing him to go mad (2804) corresponds to this smoke. French *tourbillon* derives either from L. **turbi-*

nionem or L. **turbiculonem,* developments based on the noun *turbo, turbi-nem* 'vortex' linked to L. *turbare* 'to disturb', one of the verbs that Constantine uses to describe the effect of the smoke of melancholy.

The principal symptom of melancholic madness is a combination of fear and sadness. Yvain's fear manifests itself in his desire to run away from Arthur and from his companions. Constantine the African defines sadness as "the loss of a very beloved thing" (*rei multum amatae amissio,* Malato and Martini 1959: 49) and specifies that the loss of "one's loved ones" (*amata sua*) and "a precious thing that cannot be recovered" (*rem pretiosam quam restaurare non possunt,* Malato and Martini 1959: 55) leads to melancholy. In Yvain's case this would be the loss of his wife, Laudine, that has just been announced to him.

Melancholy, according to Constantine, makes the sufferer want to leave his familiars and seek solitude. Another effect of the type of melancholy that affects the brain is that the melancholic can become taciturn (Malato and Martini 1959: 52, 57). Silence characterizes Yvain's madness as, despite the hermit's essential role in preserving his life with bread and water and in cooking his venison, Yvain never speaks with him or, for that matter, with anyone until the madness is cured. From the time he hears the messenger's condemnation, "he lacks speech" (*parole li faut,* 2775).[3] Constantine points to yet another effect, namely that the fumes that rise to the brain make one sleep excessively: "Those who are excessively sleepy have their sensible faculty bathed in melancholic smoke" (*Nimium habentes somnum virtutem sensibilem in fumum melancolicum immersam habent,* Malato and Martini 1959: 63). The lady of Norison and her companions consequently find Yvain asleep in the forest in broad daylight. Finally, according to another source, the twelfth-century Hugh of Fouilloy's *Medicine of the Soul* (*De medicina animae;* 1880: col. 1190), melancholy leads to a desire for death, an effect that Yvain experiences after he almost goes mad a second time when he comes upon the storm-producing fountain (3488, 3527–49). These diagnostic signs found in the writings of medieval thinkers earlier than or contemporary with Chrétien accord with the label of melancholy that he assigns to Yvain's madness.[4]

Constantine the African cites certain foods as harmful to the melancholic because they generate black bile. Although there is an error in the manuscript tradition of Constantine's *On Melancholy,* a comparison with a parallel passage in Ishaq ibn Imran's treatise leads to the information that one of these inadvisable foods is game (see Malato and Martini 1959: 51, n. 3). It seems, then, that in having the hermit prepare venison for Yvain,

Chrétien is maintaining his hero in a melancholic state until he can finally be cured by Morgan the Fay's unguent.

The theory of humors was not applied only to human beings among God's creatures. Guillaume de Saint-Thierry explains in the first book of his *Philosophy of the World* (*De philosophia mundi*) that the differentiation of animals into species also results from the dominance of one or another substance, and consequently one or another humor:

> But as the earth was muddy from the water placed on top of it, boiling with heat, it created from itself diverse types of animals: and if in one fire predominated, choleric animals were born such as the lion; if earth, melancholy ones, such as the cow and the ass; but if water, phlegmatic ones such as pigs. From that part, however, in which equal elements come together equally, the human body was made.
>
> [Sed cum terra ex superposita aqua esset lutosa, ex calore bulliens, creavit ex se diversa genera animalium: et si in aliqua plus abundaverit ignis, cholerica nata sunt animalia ut leo; si terra, melancholica, ut bos et asinus; si vero aqua, phlegmatici, ut porci. Ex quadam parte vero, æqua elementa æqualiter conveniunt, humanum corpus factum est.] (Guillaume de Saint-Thierry 1895: col. 55)

The lion, then, is a complementary companion for Yvain, as both of them are affected by an imbalance of bile, for the animal yellow bile and for the man black bile.

What would have been the active ingredient of this unguent that cures Yvain? Chrétien's contemporary Hildegard of Bingen (1098–1179), an authority on medicines, advises that an unguent of crushed fennel be used to cure melancholy.[5] The lady of Norison tells her companion to apply the remedy sparingly to the sleeping Yvain, specifically to spread it only on his forehead and his temples since only his brain is in need of medicine (*Yvain* 2968–73). The companion, however, in her enthusiasm to effect a cure, uses up the whole box of unguent, applying it over the entire body of the naked knight, right down to the toes (3000–3001). She later throws the empty box into a stream but tells her lady that it fell from her grasp when her horse tripped. Hildegard of Bingen directs that her fennel ungent be spread not only on the forehead and the temples but on the breast and the stomach as well.[6] Chrétien comments that the prodigality of the woman who uses up all the unguent on Yvain is folly, but the notion of using it liberally may have come to him from Hildegard's treatise or an analogous medical source.

Another character who goes mad in Chrétien's romances is the emperor Alis in *Cliges,* whose few symptoms differ from Yvain's. The Thracian knight Bertran sees Fenice and Cliges sleeping together naked and manages to reach Constantinople with this news, where he announces to Alis what he has seen. Alis has Cliges's freedman Jehan taken prisoner, but Jehan reproaches the emperor publicly for breaking his promise not to marry and brazenly tells him that if he, Jehan, should die, Cliges will avenge his death by killing Alis. Furthermore, he reveals that the potion kept Alis's marriage with Fenice from being consummated and that Fenice's death was feigned. Alis swears to take vengeance on Cliges for this shame and vilification. Chrétien does not show Alis undergoing his mental crisis, but the report that the Greek messengers give Cliges is that he was so unhappy at not being able to find Cliges that he lost his senses (*le sen chainga*), ceased eating and drinking, and died as a madman (*forsenez,* 6647). This is the opposite of Yvain, who during his madness was famished to the point of eating moldy bread, and Chrétien does not speak of self-hatred in Alis's case. The symptoms given are so few, however, that it is impossible to say if Chrétien conceived of Alis's death as having been caused by mania, by frenzy, or by melancholy.

As is the case with the mechanism of perceptions and sentiments, with characters' solitary thoughts, and with temptations of self-destruction, insanity does not figure in the thematics of contemporary chansons de geste except incidentally, in such formulaic phrases as "he almost went out of his head" (*a pou n'enrage vis*) that characterize the knights' reactions when they are angry or provoked. The mechanisms of madness only interest audiences of vernacular works with the awakening of sensitivity to the interior life in intellectual and courtly circles.

MOTIVATION AND THE UNITY AND DEVELOPMENT OF CHARACTERS

In medieval romances, as in any coherent narrative, the motivation by which characters act is an essential component of plot. Chrétien usually lets his audiences know the reasoning involved in the sequence of motives that leads the principal characters from one action to another, also an aspect of interiority.

Chrétien's concept of the custom (*costume*) provides a framework for many of these motives. In a fundamental study, Erich Köhler (1960) analyzed the use of this concept in Chrétien's works, defining the custom as an institutionalized right. Köhler interpreted the custom as a means of controlling the unexpended and thus dangerous energy of knights as well as, following the nineteenth-century philologist Gustave Gröber, the point of departure for the idealization of the concept of adventure. The custom is for Köhler at one and the same time the foundation of Arthur's power as a king who rules according to custom and the source of his weakness as he must constantly keep his young knights occupied with new undertakings. Chrétien has Arthur comment on his relationship to custom:

> ". . . I do not want to abolish
> The custom or the usage
> That my lineage is in the habit of upholding.
> It ought really to bother you
> If I now wanted to establish
> Other customs, other laws,
> Than those my father the king upheld."
> [". . . Je ne vuil pas que remaigne
> La costume ne li usages
> Que suet maintenir mes lignages.
> De ce vos devroit il peser,
> Se je or voloie eslever
> Autres costumes, autres lois,
> Que ne tint mes pere li rois."]   (*Erec* 1804–10)

Köhler distinguishes among three kinds of customs in Chrétien's romances. The first is made up of obligations: those that King Arthur is obliged to observe, such as the Hunt for the White Stag in *Erec* and the obligations of vanquished knights to render themselves prisoners at the direction of the victor, normally at Arthur's court. Defeated knights are eventually integrated into the court in *Erec* (Ydier) and *Perceval* (Clamadeu, Orgueilleus de la Lande, the sixty knights whom Perceval sends there during his five years of wandering), and the lady of Norison receives Count Alier as her prisoner in *Yvain*. The second type comprises customs that produce discordant effects, which are then set right by a knight of Arthur's court, such as the Test of the Sparrow-Hawk in *Erec* (see 579) and the storm-producing fountain in *Yvain*, said to have been established over sixty years before (*Yvain* 2106). These customs are formidable obstacles only as long as their champions are not knights of Arthur's court. The third sort is composed of evil customs that Arthur's knights abolish forever, such as the Joy of the Court in *Erec* that has resulted in many deaths because of a woman's selfish behavior, the castle of Pesme Avanture in which preternatural creatures keep three hundred maidens in what we would term sweatshop conditions, and the customs of the kingdom of Gorre, evil because their very establishment was wrong. That the test of the Grail in a finished *Perceval* might have been classified in this last category is possible, but it is equally likely that it would have belonged in the second type.

A crucial custom, according to Köhler, is that Arthur and others in positions of power must acquiesce in unspecified requests made of them, including consent that a knight be permitted to undertake an adventure: this is the motif of the rash gift or rash boon, in French *le don contraignant,* that is never refused,[7] however extraordinary the consequences (treated comprehensively in Frappier 1969a; see also Ménard 1981). Among the most consequential of Arthur's rash gifts is his consent that Keu should do battle with Meleagant over the queen. Lancelot grants a rash gift to Meleagant's sister that requires him to do battle for a second time with the knight at the ford when she specifies that the gift she wants is that knight's head (*Lancelot* 2566–2941). In *Erec,* Mabonagrain rashly consents to his lady's requirement that he defend the Joy of the Court (6048–49).

Köhler contrasts this mechanism of the ideal king in Chrétien's romances, bound by custom, with the historical situation in which the Capetian monarch can only strengthen his position in society by violating customal rights that guarantee the privileges of the feudal nobility. In the romances, disturbances caused by customs are quelled not by the king but by the individual knight, who either abolishes the custom or rectifies it so that it serves the community instead of those whose conduct is marked by outrage, folly, and pride. The hero leaves Arthur's court, the harmony of which has been disturbed in some way, undertakes a quest for adventure while insisting that he remain apart from the court (witness the initial refusals of Erec and Perceval, despite the entreaties of other knights, to be reunited with the court), and returns to the court in a joyful scene of reintegration. The adventure itself results in harmony between the knight's ideal self and the imperfect reality of his exploits.

This is a fruitful idea, but I would modify it to say that it is not the knight as an individual but the knight as a representative of his actual or metaphorical kin group who sets things right.[8]

In asking whether the motives given to justify characters' actions in Chrétien's romances meet the test of plausibility, the modern reader must tread carefully: what was plausible in the late twelfth century or within the conventions of the romance may not appear so in other times and circumstances. But readers experiencing the world created by a consummately skilled tale-teller have a right to expect at least internal consistency and logic in the decisions that the narrator has his characters make. The custom and the rash gift are important institutions of that created world, designed by Chrétien and consequently essential to the issue of motivation.

At Arthur's court in the castle of Caradigan on Easter, Erec is accompanying Guinevere while the king and the other knights are engaged in the Hunt for the White Stag (plate 8), a custom that Arthur is determined to enact, when Ydier's dwarf strikes both Guinevere's maiden and Erec himself with a whip. The hero's decision simply to follow Ydier is well taken: Erec, armed only with a sword, would have been foolhardy to attempt to avenge his shame immediately because Ydier is fully armed with lance and shield. Chrétien praises his character's prudence: "Folly is not the quality of a vassal; / In this regard Erec acted very wisely" (*Folie n'est pas vasalages; / De tant fist mout Erec que sages, Erec* 231–32). Pursuing Ydier leads Erec to the town of Lalut, where he meets Enide and receives her father's permission to marry her. By challenging Ydier in the custom of the sparrow-hawk with arms borrowed from Enide's father, and defeating him in a struggle that has the hallmarks of a judicial combat (Le Rider 1998: 385–89), Erec is able to avenge the shame while at the same time showing his admiration for the beautiful and wise Enide.

The young couple is married at Caradigan, and after Erec's triumphal performance at a tournament held on the plain before Edinburgh (*Danebroc*, 2133), the two travel to Carnant, capital of Lac's kingdom. Erec passes all his time in amorous dalliance (*dosnoier*) with Enide, often not rising from bed until after noon, to the extent that he no longer cares about the pursuit of knightly practices and ceases frequenting tournaments. His companions begin to talk of recreancy, the defect of knights who abandon chivalric pursuits. Enide does not wish to tell Erec this for fear of his reaction, but one day in bed he emerges from slumber to hear her speaking words of regret over him. When Erec demands to know the meaning of the words, Enide first feigns not to know what he is asking about, then claims he must have been dreaming, before finally telling him that his conduct with her has caused his reputation to suffer. Erec orders her to prepare to leave Carnant and tells her not to speak to him, unless he first addresses her, on the solitary journey that they are about to undertake.

Chrétien never discusses in his narrator's voice Erec's motives for these extraordinary orders, an omission that, I think, was deliberate and that has given rise to much discussion (see Press 1969). The reader who wants to

make sense of the tale is forced to conjecture about the motives that Chrétien had in mind for Erec or, in a reception mode, to supply motives ab-
stracting from those of the author. A key element in either case is Enide's attempt to deny that she spoke the fateful words. It is perfectly plausible that
Chrétien was thinking that this lack of *franchise* would inspire his readers
to think that Erec also suspected Enide of hiding from him a disdain that
would be shameful for him. It would also be desirable for Erec to perform
a series of acts of prowess in Enide's presence so as to convince her that
his amorous attentions have not made him a *recreant*. That he is testing
her faithfulness emerges later when he mentions having done so ("I have
well tested you in all things," *Bien vos ai dou tot essaïe*, 4915). He may be
punishing her. Erec has certainly lost confidence in her love, because when
the series of adventures in the forest is over, he says: "And I am once again
sure and certain that you love me completely" (*Et je resui certains et fis /
Que vos m'amez parfaitement*, 4918–19). But whatever conclusions readers
have drawn, that Chrétien does not in his own voice comment on Erec's
motives from the journey's beginning may be viewed as a mark of the subtlety of his art. He draws the readers into the tale by holding something
back, leading them to speculate on motivation for the sequence of events
that encompasses most of the rest of the romance and providing clues only
in the form of Erec's declarations when the journey is over. In this case,
Chrétien's ambiguity is a positive aspect of his storytelling skills, leading
his audience to engage itself in the narrative (see Duggan 1977).

In the series of adventures that takes place before the journey's end,
Enide warns Erec repeatedly: about the band of three robber knights, then
the group of five, the perfidy of Count Galoain, and the approach of King
Guivret. Just before Erec's combat with Guivret, he comes to the realization
that Enide still loves him and that he still loves her (3763–65), thus clearing
away doubt and arriving at full knowledge of his own sentiments. Enide de-
spairs to the point of attempting suicide when she mistakenly thinks Erec
has died from his wounds, and she resists Count Oringle's approaches but
cannot prevent him from marrying her forcibly. Oringle strikes her for refusing to eat, and the commotion wakes Erec, who kills Oringle. When the
two ride off on one horse, Erec's words to Enide,

> ". . . if you have misspoken anything in my regard,
> I pardon you and hold you harmless
> For both the offense and the words"
> [". . . Se vos m'avez rien mesdite,

Je le vos pardoing et claim quite
Et le forfait et la parole"] (*Erec* 4923–25)

signal their reconciliation. The Joy of the Court episode and the coronation scene only serve to confirm that their renewed love is superior to constrained love service and worthy of the highest level of nobility.

Erec is a well-constructed romance in that a careful reading leads to
the conclusion that its main characters' apparent motives are consistent
and plausible. It is probably, in fact, the best constructed of Chrétien's five
major works, considering that *Perceval* is unfinished. Erec's character develops in the sense that he achieves a fuller appreciation of his love for
Enide after the crisis of the bedroom scene, but he cannot be said to have
undergone an internal transformation, only to have arrived back at the
state he was in before he became obsessed with making love to his wife.

Cliges stands out from Chrétien's other romances in that an Arthurian
custom plays no part in its narrative. In fact, Donald Maddox goes so far as
to term the four remaining works Chrétien's "customal romances" (Maddox
1991: 6). The figure of the knight errant who goes in search of adventure (*chevalier errant / Qui aventure alast querant, Yvain,* 259–60), traveling
through the land with no particular destination in mind, dealing with whatever adversary he comes upon (see Chênerie 1986), is also absent, as it is
from *Lancelot. Cliges* is also the only one of Chrétien's five romances that
does not begin at Arthur's court, although that court is viewed by both
its heroes, Alexandre and Cliges, as the prime locus of chivalry. It is also
the only romance in which Arthur is depicted as a forceful figure, in the
manner of his representation in Wace and Geoffrey of Monmouth. Finally,
Cliges tells the stories of two generations of protagonists, Alexandre and
Soredamor, and Cliges and Fenice. Some of these features no doubt derive
from the mysterious source book that Chrétien says he saw in the cathedral of St. Peter in Beauvais, but others, such as the narration of the hero's
birth and the story of his parents, come from the author's desire to compose
a counter-*Tristan,* reflected in references to characters who figure in the
courtly *Tristan* tradition as counterexamples (see the thorough treatment
in Fourrier 1960: 124–54).

Although Alexandre is the elder son of one of the most powerful sovereigns in Christendom, the emperor of Constantinople, he wants to be
knighted by King Arthur, which requires him to journey to Britain. The
motive for this desire is Arthur's renown for courtesy and prowess (*Cliges*
152–53, 347–51), and Arthur agrees to knight him. While accompanying the

king on a journey from England to Brittany, Alexandre falls in love with
Soredamor and she with him, both suffering from the attacks of the allegorical figure Amors. When they marry with the queen's help, Cliges is born,
who will repeat the trajectory of his father in journeying to Britain, with
somewhat similar motivation but aided by advice received from his father.

During Alexandre's absence, the situation in Constantinople has become
complicated. The emperor is about to die and recalls Alexandre from Britain, but an embassy sent to fetch him results in the false news that he has
been killed in a shipwreck. As a result, Alexandre's younger brother, Alis,
is crowned emperor. Hearing news of this development, Alexandre returns
to Greece, where Alis agrees to cede the power to his brother on condition
that he, Alis, retain the crown and title of emperor. Alexandre also extracts
from Alis the promise, central to the motivation in the rest of the romance,
that he will not marry, so that Cliges will succeed him as emperor (2527–
38). Alis survives both Alexandre and Soredamor, becoming, in fact, the
sole ruler.

Evil counselors soon persuade Alis to marry, however. The chosen bride
is Fenice, daughter of the other powerful European emperor, the ruler of
Germany, even though she had been promised to the duke of Saxony. Complicating matters, Cliges and Fenice fall in love. Fenice's governess, Thessala, concocts a potion that makes Alis think he is making love to his wife
while he is actually sleeping and that blocks his desire during his waking
hours.

Alis offers to share the power with Cliges (4177–78), as he did with the
young man's father, but Cliges, although already a knight, maintains that
he is too young and inexperienced to rule alongside his uncle. He insists
on traveling to Arthur's court, where he gains renown in a tournament at
Oxenfort (Oxford) in which he bests successively Sagremor, Lancelot, and
Perceval and fights Gauvain to a draw. When he returns to Greece, he and
Fenice come to the understanding that she will be his lover only if she can
avoid the public shame visited upon Tristan's lover, Ysolt. With the help
of Thessala and the artisan Jehan, Fenice undergoes a false death, is en-
tombed, and is exhumed and taken by Cliges to a tower built by Jehan,
where they live as lovers for over a year until discovered by a hunter,
Bertran, who tells the emperor what he has found. When Jehan is taken
captive, he defies the emperor, recalling publicly the oath Alis had taken
that he would not marry so that Cliges would succeed him as emperor
(6489–99) and informing Alis of the marriage potion. Having fled to Britain, Cliges is on the point of returning with a fleet to take power by force

when news reaches him that Alis has gone out of his mind with frustration and died. Cliges and Fenice then rule as emperor and empress.

The weak link in this sequence of motives is that, although Alis took bad advice and married against his oath, he offered to share the power with Cliges, who insisted that he was too young to accept such a responsibility. One might then expect Cliges to mention the idea of co-regency again when he returns from Britain to Greece, but he never does so. Furthermore, Chrétien does not have Cliges himself bring up the issue of Alis's promise of celibacy, and it is only the discovery of the lovers that precipitates Cliges's rightful accession to the throne. Finally, in a romance in which the author has God make the moon rise earlier than it usually does so as to place traitors at a tactical disadvantage (1694–1700), it is more than a bit incongruous that the adulterous liaison between Cliges and Fenice should receive no negative comment, whatever the failings of the offended husband.

The main characters in *Cliges* cannot be said to have undergone development or change with the exception of Soredamor. She is represented as disdainful of love and as having found no man worthy of her affection, an outlook that changes radically when Love takes vengeance on her. Her character does not really change, however: rather she realizes that not only is she capable of love but in fact she loves Alexandre. Fenice and Cliges fall in love at first glance, but this is not presented as a change in the character of either. In fact, it is Fenice's steadfast refusal to become another Ysolt that drives the plot in the second half of the romance. Alis goes back on his word, but this is not a change of character either. The sympathetic characters in *Cliges* all come into possession of what they most desire, but psychological transformation simply does not figure in the romance.

Chrétien does not portray the initial motives of the lovers in *Lancelot*, leaving his readers in the dark as to the sentiments of Lancelot and the queen or conversations that he as author might imagine to have taken place between them before Meleagant's challenge. That we are to understand that there was some amorous communication between them is implied by Guinevere's murmured but overheard comment to the effect that an absent "friend" would not allow her to be led off without a challenge if he knew what was happening (*Lancelot* 209–11). This friend can only be Lancelot.

The situation that places Guinevere in danger of being led away is caused by Arthur's rash consent to Keu's request for a favor in return for his threat to leave the court, which is in turn motivated by Keu's character as a boasting and overconfident boor.[9] Meleagant's challenge also arises from an extreme character, treacherous, haughty, and in fact thoroughly evil. More puzzling, however, is Arthur's weakness of character as reflected in his initial reaction to the declaration of Meleagant, in the king's own hall, that he is holding captives from Logres who will never be released:

> The king replies that he will have to
> Put up with this, if he cannot help it,
> But that it bothers him deeply.
> [Li rois respont qu'il li estuet
> Sofrir, s'amander ne le puet,
> Mes molt l'an poise duremant.]   (*Lancelot* 61–63)

Meleagant then walks back to the door of the hall with impunity. This is not the Arthur of *Culhwch and Olwen* or of the *History of the Kings of Britain* or the *Roman de Brut,* or even the Arthur of *Cliges* who puts down the rebellion of Angres with great ferocity; this is a pusillanimous king who is not only unmotivated to protect his subjects but willing to be humiliated in his own court by an overbearing intruder. The source for the tale of Guinevere's abduction may have suggested this new Arthur to Chrétien, but in most versions of the abduction of Guinevere, in contrast to *Lancelot,* Arthur at least takes part in the queen's rescue (see Webster 1951b). Arthur is also depicted as docile in *Perceval* when he takes no vengeance on the Red Knight for pouring a cup of wine over Guinevere. The radical departure from all previous tradition does, however, pose a problem: Arthur's world is interesting precisely because, as depicted by Geoffrey, Wace, and the Welsh tradition, he was an energetic and powerful leader, so the description of a do-nothing king appears to undercut the reason for evoking Arthur at all. Here it is a question not of the internal consistency of *Lancelot* but of the consistency with which Chrétien depicts Arthur throughout his œuvre and in relation to prior tradition.

Lancelot himself is motivated by his love for Guinevere, succeeding in a series of tests along his path of pursuit while rejecting distractions that might hinder him. He hesitates for the space of two steps to climb into the cart because of the shameful nature of the vehicle. That Guinevere rejects him only makes sense in the context of absolute love-service, a motif found not only in the scene in which Lancelot accepts without objection the queen's explanation for her chagrin but in the episode of the tournament at Noauz in which he declares himself to be "entirely hers" (*suens antiers,* 5656) and acquiesces in her commands that he twice fight his worst and then that he fight his best. This total obedience to the lady's command, often seen in troubadour poetry in the form of a promise made by the poet to his lady as a rhetorical strategy, is articulated elsewhere in Chrétien's works just twice. The first instance is in *Erec,* in the relationship between Mabonagrain and Enide's cousin, which results in Mabonagrain's being held in thrall through the custom of the Joy of the Court. The second is when Cliges tells Fenice that he is taking leave of her to go to Britain "as from her whose I am completely" (*come a cele qui je sui touz, Cliges* 4269), in the context of a relationship that is, like that between Lancelot and the queen, adulterous, at least technically.

While Lancelot is imprisoned through Meleagant's treachery in the tower belonging to Meleagant's seneschal, he laments that Gauvain does not search him out (*Lancelot* 6484–6522). Why did Chrétien not have Lancelot inform Gauvain during the tournament of Noauz, however, that he had promised to go back to prison afterward? Why did he not have him tell Gauvain the location of the prison? Lancelot had promised the seneschal's wife that he would return to prison after the tournament, a promise that he keeps, but nothing in the oath he swore to her (5495–97) prevents him from revealing where he was imprisoned. This is a flaw in the motivation of *Lancelot,* although a minor one since the lamentation occurs just in time to be overheard by Meleagant's sister, who has come to free Lancelot. Another surprising development is that, although the romance centers on the relationship between Lancelot and Guinevere, the queen seems to have passed from Lancelot's consciousness after his imprisonment in the tower, as he never thinks of her or mentions her again (Hult 1989b: 86). These problems result from a lack of coordination between the tale as Chrétien left it and Godefroy de Lagny's ending section.

Although the queen seems to change her mind unduly about Lancelot, first acknowledging that he would not have allowed her to be taken off as a prize for the combat between Keu and Meleagant, then refusing to see him in Gorre, and finally consenting to see him, these vicissitudes do not result from developments in his character but only from her analysis of signs that Lancelot is or is not completely devoted to her. She admits him to a private interview only after realizing that he would gladly kill himself for her (see 4430–32). Guinevere's character does not change any more than Lancelot's in the course of the romance.

The ending of *Lancelot* is weak. Lancelot returns just in time to keep the rendezvous for the battle against Meleagant in which Gauvain was prepared to take his place. Guinevere is restrained by Reason from making any public display of affection for the hero, so she puts off greeting her lover until they are in a better and more secure situation (6850–53). Lancelot then kills Meleagant, whom no one pities. The king and the others disarm Lancelot in an atmosphere of rejoicing. The narrator concludes: "Lords, if I were to speak further, it would exceed my material" (*Seignor, si j'avant an disoie, / Ce seroit oltre la matire*, 7098–99). There is no resolution to the story, no happy ending such as is provided by the coronation of Erec and Enide or Cliges and Fenice, or by Laudine's final acceptance of Yvain. Matters are left at loose ends. Whether there could possibly have been a felicitous resolution to *Lancelot,* given the continuation of the adulterous relationship between the two principal characters, is an apt question. I do not believe a more stable ending would have been possible, given the contradictions between love and social responsibility that are inherent in the plot of this romance.

This weakness as well as the previous two discussed can always be ascribed to Godefroy de Lagny, who tells us that he has taken up the composition of Chrétien's romance from the point at which Lancelot was immured (7109), that is to say from somewhere in the vicinity of line 6133. But in fact it is probable that Chrétien passed on to Godefroy the major outline of his tale, if one believes that his continuation was carried out with Chrétien's "willingness" (*boen gré,* 7106).

Chrétien was constrained by Marie de Champagne to write *Lancelot.* The phrase he uses to express Lancelot's absolute love-service to the queen, that he was "hers entirely" (*suens antiers,* 5656), is the one that he uses to express his own relation as a poet to Marie in the prologue (4). Many details of the romance show that he was unsatisfied with the assignment, chief among which are the various scenes in which the character of Lancelot is undercut (see above, pp. 129–30). In no other romance does Chrétien clothe love in the trappings of religion or have a knight commit adultery with a woman who is in a properly consummated marriage, a set of circumstances that led Gaston Paris to coin the term "courtly love" (*amour courtois,* Paris 1881, 1883; see also Hult 1996).

That Chrétien did not finish *Lancelot* accords with the theory that some personal factor, either his own reluctance or Marie de Champagne's discontent with his work, prevented him from carrying the project through to completion. I believe that Chrétien accepted the assignment, proceeded with it, but was unable to treat his main character with the seriousness of *san* that Marie de Champagne required, and either gave the romance over willingly to Godefroy de Lagny or was constrained to do so.

The sequence of motives in *Yvain* is complicated. Yvain is inspired to undertake the test of the fountain because he wants to avenge the shame experienced by his first cousin Calogrenant, but once he is exposed to Laudine's beauty, desire intervenes, and he becomes fixed on fulfilling his amorous inclinations when New Love steals his heart (*Yvain* 1364–65). Laudine, by contrast, appears to be moved not by love but rather by a need that Lunete brings to her attention, namely that she must find a capable defender for the custom of the fountain. She believes that Yvain must have killed her husband, Esclados, through treachery, but later convinces herself that he acted in self-defense (1768–72) and consents to marry him, she says, to fulfill her people's need (2047). Lunete is motivated to act as a go-between out of gratitude for Yvain's having once been kind to her at Arthur's court (999–1013), but also to enhance the honor of her lady (1596, 3655). As Rosemarie Deist has observed (1995: 51), Lunete's appearances punctuate key intervals in the development of Yvain's character.

The wedding of Yvain and Laudine is only an interlude for the hero, however, as he soon gives in to the argument that he should accompany Gauvain to a series of tournaments so as not to allow marriage to lessen his worth. After all, says Gauvain, love that is acquired after a delay is all the more enjoyable, an idea that Chrétien may have picked up from the troubadour Raimbaut d'Aurenga (Roncaglia 1958; see above, pp. 5–6). Yvain's request to Laudine for permission to leave rests on the avoidance of recreancy (2561), an argument that recalls the thematics of *Erec*. That Yvain forgets his promise to return to Laudine a year later strains credulity, even in a society in which accounting for time was not, as it is in the modern world, an obsession (Lock 1983, Duggan 1986a). Yvain is, after all, protected by the ring of invulnerability that his wife has given him, which should have served as a reminder of his duty to her. One might plausibly think, too, that, as the knight charged with defending the fountain, Yvain would from time to time ask himself what has become of the custom during his absence. The time limit is also tied to a significant moment in the Christian calendar, as it occurs a week after the feast of St. John. In spite of all this, however, Chrétien does have Yvain forget and, after the messenger confronts him before Arthur's court and takes back the magic ring, has the knight go mad from the desire to take vengeance on himself for his shame.

Before he isolates himself in the woods as a madman, however, Yvain strips off all his clothing. In an age in which gesture often signaled transcendent meaning, the act of putting off one's clothes is highly significant, reminiscent of Paul's metaphorical exhortation to "put away the old man and put on the new" (Eph. 4.22–24). Chrétien's understanding of melancholy has been discussed above, but on a spiritual level Yvain puts off his old, imperfect self, loses his character entirely in going mad, and then puts on a more perfect self. This rehabilitation is signaled by three gestures: accepting the clothing set out for him by the lady of Norison's companion, taking on the lion as his companion, and hiding his old name by substituting for it the sobriquet Knight of the Lion, under which he acquires a new reputation (see Duggan 1969).

Yvain's motivations in the series of tests that follow the curing of his madness are not clearly articulated. It seems that the purpose of the tests is to reestablish his renown in society by having him engage in increasingly selfless actions, helping people toward whom he is less and less obligated. Chrétien nowhere states, nor do his characters mention, the rationale behind the sequence of adventures as a set, although the discrete episodes have clear motivational underpinnings.

Yvain's combat against Count Alier is inspired by his desire to help someone in need (3079) who has already helped him. He kills the fire-breathing serpent out of pity for the lion, symbol of courage, and the beast humbles himself before the knight and makes it clear that he is grateful (3403).[10] The lion protects Yvain, hunts for him, and guards his horse at night. When Yvain meets Lunete at the fountain, he recalls that he promised to defend her in combat against her three accusers so that she should suffer no harm on account of his not returning to his wife at the proper time (3717–23). In the meanwhile, he takes pity (3938) on Gauvain's nieces and nephew and saves them, with the lion's assistance, from the giant Harpin de la Montagne (plate 9). He then defeats Lunete's accusers, killing the seneschal and reducing the seneschal's two brothers to asking for mercy, again with the help of the lion, which he carries away, wounded, on his shield. The two prisoners are burned at the stake according to the principle that those who accuse someone falsely should suffer the fate that would have been visited upon the accused (4566–69).

Because he wishes to acquire repute (*los,* root of the verb *aloser,* 5092), Yvain consents to defend the younger heiress of the lord of Noire Espine, who has sent a messenger to seek out the Knight of the Lion on account of his renown (5056). In the castle of Pesme Avanture, he encounters three hundred women working in a *genicia,* a workshop commonly found in manor houses where women would manufacture cloth (Goetz 1993: 112), but here they are prisoners kept in enforced poverty. In fighting the two demons, Yvain agrees, against his better judgment (5502–08), to remove the lion from his side because of the terms of the custom, and he wins only when the beast escapes and comes to his aid. Yvain refuses the reward due to the person who vanquishes the demons, the hand of the castellan's daughter, because of his prior obligations (5717, 5742), which is to say that he is already married. Fulfilling his obligation to the younger heiress of Noire Espine, he fights Gauvain to a draw, neither one recognizing the other initially.

Yvain now wishes to return to Laudine, but the manner in which he obtains her consent raises issues that reveal a weakness in the motivation of the romance. Yvain goes to the fountain and unleashes the storm, which allows Lunete once again to advise her lady that she needs a capable man to defend the fountain or she will lose her reputation (6560). Lunete counsels Laudine to seek out the Knight of the Lion. She then has Laudine swear on relics (6622) to do all she can to reconcile this knight with his lady, an oath whose seriousness is out of keeping with the ostensible obligation that is incurred. Chrétien does not, after all, have Yvain swear on relics that he will help the younger heiress of Noire Espine. The oath Lunete proposes is also misleading, one might even say treacherous, because Laudine does not know that the Knight of the Lion is Yvain himself, with the result that when he does reveal his identity to her and confess his folly in not returning to her in time, she is constrained to take him back. Erich Köhler sees this expedient as a "refined ruse" necessary to reconcile Yvain, rendered vulnerable by loss of the joy of love, with the anonymous and impenetrable forces behind the figure of Laudine (1974: 199). Nevertheless, that this forced reconciliation, brought about by the defender of the fountain becoming himself its challenger and by a deceptive oath, should lead to renewed love between Laudine and Yvain (6793–95) leaves something to be desired on the level of motivation. It also raises other issues. If no one was there to defend the fountain during Yvain's absence of more than fifteen months, how did the custom survive? Are we to think that Laudine took no steps to safeguard her subjects in all that time? Or is the fountain located in such an isolated (Otherworldly?) place that it can be found only through the hideous herdsman?

Certainly one could argue that the modern reader is not justified in expecting polished realism from a twelfth-century author, but what is at issue here is a standard no higher than Chrétien sets in his other romances. He has the difficult problem of balancing a number of considerations, but he shows himself capable of doing so elsewhere. He must tell an exemplary courtly tale, incorporate narrative elements of Celtic myth, and justify the motivation of his characters' actions. Yet he simply does not provide cogent reasons for Yvain's forgetfulness or a cogent explanation for Laudine's custodianship of the fountain and its custom. He succeeds much better at synthesizing the mythic tradition, the needs of narrative interest, and the consistency of characterization in *Erec* and *Perceval* than he does in *Yvain,* which I see as highly entertaining and even edifying, but not as a convincing story on the level of motivation. And yet, in *Yvain,* for the first time, Chrétien tells the story of a knight who does change his character and become a better person in the course of the romance. Yvain's final exploit, championing the cause of the younger heiress of Noire Espine, is undertaken purely out of charity—*par pitié et par franchise* (*Yvain* 5983)—toward a woman whose identity he does not even know (Maranini 1970: 748).

Motivation in *Perceval* cannot be grasped fully, because the romance's unfinished state does not allow the reader to see the final results of the principal characters' actions. In addition, some episodes are explained only after the fact, and it is entirely possible that Chrétien planned to provide certain rationales in the part of the romance that he did not live to complete.

The young Perceval, dazzled by the knights whom he meets while practicing javelin throws, wishes to become one himself and so is determined to seek out the king who makes knights (*Perceval* 493–94). He receives instructions on how to conduct himself first from his mother, then from the man who confers knighthood on him, Gornemant of Gohort, and follows both sets of advice in the straightforward way that might be expected from a boy brought up in seclusion, away from sophisticated society. He also learns extremely quickly the techniques of fighting on horseback, an expression of the medieval belief that the effects of noble ancestry would surface when a person is put to the test. He embroils Orgueilleus de la Lande with his lover by taking her ring, in naive conformity to his mother's counsel, harming the woman and leading himself later in the romance to fight and defeat Orgueilleus. In keeping with this character, Perceval takes seriously Keu's jibe to the effect that he should go seize the Red Knight's arms, with the result that he kills the knight and puts on his armor. Perceval promises to avenge himself on Keu for slapping the Laughing Girl, who predicted greatness for him, a promise he keeps later in the romance when he breaks Keu's arm. These actions are all motivated directly or peripherally by Perceval's determination to become a knight.

A second sequence of motives drives Perceval, however, once he has achieved knighthood: a desire to rejoin his mother, whom he saw falling to the ground as he was leaving home. This desire cannot be fulfilled, for his mother has died.

With the death of Perceval's mother one enters a thematic field in which motivation is eclipsed by another force whose nature is unclear. The young man is told by both his cousin and his uncle that he has sinned because his mother died of grief at his having left her (plate 10), but she instructed him in preparation for the journey, made new clothes for him, and, although she was unhappy that he was leaving, even wished him joy upon his departure (618–19). In fact she never forbade him to leave her. The sin in question is one of which he had no knowledge (6393), and without knowledge there can be no motivation in the ordinary sense of the term. Yet as a result of the sin, Perceval failed to ask the right questions in the Grail castle, the action on which the entire romance centers. In *Perceval,* therefore, the main character's motives have been eclipsed by a force that is beyond his comprehension and beyond the power of his will. That Perceval undergoes a spiritual conversion just before the last scene in which he figures in the romance leaves little doubt that this force is an effect of divine providence.

Although the trajectory of his life does not depend entirely on him, or perhaps *because* of that, Perceval changes in the course of the romance from a naive boy (*nice*) who demonstrates no regret at all to one who leaves his lover because he wants to return to his mother and who shows deep remorse in the hermit scene. He is the only one of Chrétien's characters for whom the author writes specifically of change. When Arthur sees Perceval for the second time, he comments:

> I had great sorrow for you
> When I first saw you,
> For I did not know the improvement
> That God had destined for you.
> [Molt ai eü de vos grant doel,
> Quant ge vos vi premierement,
> Que ge ne soi l'amendemant
> Que Diex vos avoit destiné.]   (*Perceval* 4566–69)

This remark refers simply to Perceval's knightly reputation and the improvement he has made from the time Arthur last saw him as a rude and untutored boy arriving from the Gaste Forest and acquiring arms by killing a man, to this moment after both Clamadeu and Orgueilleus de la Lande have presented themselves at court as knights defeated by Perceval, and after he has in addition bested Sagremor and injured Keu. How Chrétien has Arthur express the change, however, as destined by God, is no mere formula and signals that divine grace plays a strong role in Perceval's development. Shortly after Arthur's remark, Gauvain, Gifflez, and Kaadin vow to undertake quests in response to the challenge of the Hideous Maiden, but Perceval "says something entirely different" (*redit tot el,* 4727), pledging not to sleep two nights in the same dwelling or to fail to enter any strange land or fight any superior knight until he has found out whom the Grail serves and discovered the Bleeding Lance and why it bleeds. This self-imposed prohibition (see Reinhard 1933: 318–19) is the vow of a man who has not merely lost his naïveté but found a goal that—unlike the quests of the other three knights—transcends the immediate values of knighthood and that promises to repair the results of his failure at the Grail castle. Although Perceval's spiritual progress suffers a setback when he passes five years without thinking of God or entering a church, he is brought back onto the right path by confessing his sins.

Gauvain's actions, by contrast, appear all to be motivated by the search for knightly glory.[11] He engages himself to save the maiden at Mont Esclaire and acquire the sword with the strange baldric while Perceval sets off in quest of the Grail and the lance. Under the accusation of having treacherously killed Guingambresil's lord, Gauvain must journey to Escavalon to defend himself in judicial combat or else incur shame and reproach (4762). Gauvain's adventures in Galloway, as interesting as they are, reveal no change in his character. Even the interlude of the Maiden of the Short Sleeves, charming and unusual as it is within the context of Chrétien's works, concerns worldly values. Unlike Perceval, Gauvain does not appear to develop inwardly in the course of the romance as it has come down to us.

INTERIORITY AND VALUES IN CHRÉTIEN

Chrétien is a writer of psychological romances in the sense that his principal characters are assigned motivations that they follow with fair consistency. They each adhere to a set of values, and those values appear to be quite similar for Erec, Alexandre, Cliges, and Yvain on the male side, and again similar for Enide, Soredamor, and Fenice. Laudine, Lunete, and Blancheflor are less fully sketched, as female characters who do not engage in self-analysis or amatory monologue or dialogue. The treatment of these female characters is closely conditioned by their unmarried—in the case of Fenice irregularly married—state. Lancelot and Guinevere are motivated by a set of values dependent on the concept of the male lover's total subservience to his lady, in this case a lady married to Lancelot's king. The youthful naïveté of Perceval gives way to a set of primarily secular values that are transmuted into spiritual ones, but his development is truncated by the author's death. The motives of Yvain and Lancelot are inconsistent relative to the behavior of Chrétien's other main characters. Alexandre, Cliges, Enide, Erec, Fenice, Guinevere, Lancelot, Laudine, Lunete, and Soredamor all appear to move according to their natures, which evolve little or not at all. Yvain and Perceval are depicted as evolving and developing toward inner betterment, although not in the pronounced and thoroughly analyzed ways that modern authors of narrative will show their characters changing.

Writing about Hartmann von Aue's *Erec,* James Schultz notes that "the creation of an Arthurian *character* is the work of the reader, for only when the reader has discovered some single viewpoint from which the various contradictions can be explained and reconciled can the name and the behaviour ascribed to it be understood as a coherent character. The creation of an Arthurian character, then, is not an act of composition but an act of interpretation" (Schultz 1983: 60–61). This may well be true for Hartmann's *Erec* and for other German Arthurian romances that Schultz studies, but it is not true for Chrétien de Troyes's *Erec, Cliges,* or *Perceval,* in which coherence of character is strongly maintained. In *Lancelot* and *Yvain* character is not primary, but neither is it merely a function of plot. Schultz also writes (1983: 59), this time of Hartmann's *Iwein:* "Let us for the moment simply note that all Laudine's distinguishing traits are external. Arthurian characters, that is, are not Jamesian but Aristotelian. They do not exist as coherent psyches of which the plot is a consequent revelation; they are born, rather, out of the needs of the plot, and we know them only by the actions to which they owe their existence. In Arthurian romance plot comes first, character second." I could subscribe to such a view, but I do not believe that Chrétien has generally painted his characters as possessed of inconsistent motives and intentions. The balance between plot and character in his romances is finely maintained, with considerations of plot dominating only in *Yvain* and in the final part of *Lancelot,* written by Godefroy de Lagny.

Chrétien de Troyes viewed interiority and responsibility in keeping with the ideas of his age. The heart was the seat of all human thought and emotion and could best be conceptualized for him and his contemporaries through allegorical figures. Thinking was a kind of internal speech and was effectively represented as overheard monologue. Characters could become so absorbed in their activities as to forget themselves and so deeply fallen into despair as to kill themselves. The body and the mind were healthy if the humors were in balance, but a shock could result in madness. Chrétien's protagonists usually act in ways consistent with their depicted outlooks, which is to say that they are possessed of unity of character.

Chrétien participates in the progression toward examining the inner workings of the human psyche that is visible in certain developments in Christian theology and philosophy, such as the examination of conscience, which necessitated a movement of self-reflexivity and the growing emphasis on the subject, and on intention as the key element in the theology of sin and penance. His own point of view does not, however, seem to be deeply Christian in his first three romances. It is, of course, clothed in a veneer of Christianity such as would have necessarily been imposed on it by the author's presence in the Christian environment of northern France in the twelfth century. For example, he depicts the larger causes of the events of the world as forces beyond the visible, namely God and the devil. Thus when the moon rises earlier than expected on the evening on which Arthur's forces are fighting those of the rebel Angres of Windsor, this is a sign of God's favor because God hates traitors more than anything (*Cliges* 1694). Chrétien does not, however, openly condemn suicide or criticize either his principal characters' successful attempts to circumvent the responsibilities of marriage and kinship in *Cliges* or outright adultery that is a violation of feudal ties in *Lancelot*. In *Cliges* he invokes a cynically distorted saying of Paul, making it into a counsel that if one has to sin, it should at least not be in public. References to religion in the form of religious exclamations increase in *Yvain*, although the moral impetus for the characters' actions is not particularly Christian.

From this type of pious expression, still incidental, Chrétien moves on to doctrinal exposition in *Perceval* in the words addressed to the hero by his mother and especially in the accounts provided to him by the knightly pilgrim and by his uncle. Nevertheless, even though *Perceval* is in the last analysis imbued with a religious spirit, still there Chrétien depends heavily on material that is ultimately of pagan origin, namely the Celtic myths and folk beliefs that are the subject of the next chapter.

Plate 1. Historiated initial that opens Lancelot *in the Guiot manuscript: Marie de Champagne. Paris, Bibliothèque nationale, fonds français 794, f. 27, detail.*

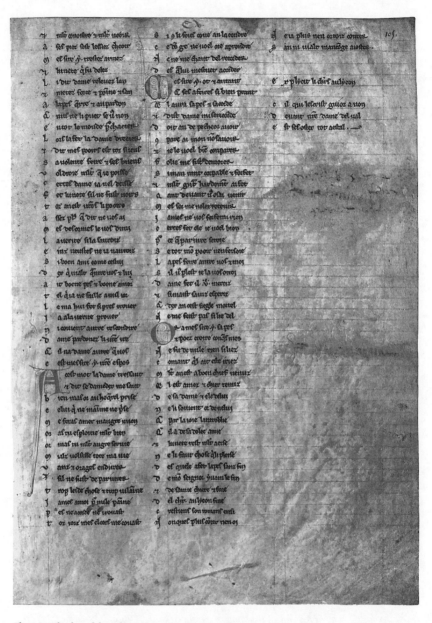

Plate 2. The last folio of Yvain *in the Guiot manuscript, followed by the scribe's colophon. Paris, Bibliothèque nationale, fonds français 794, f. 105r.*

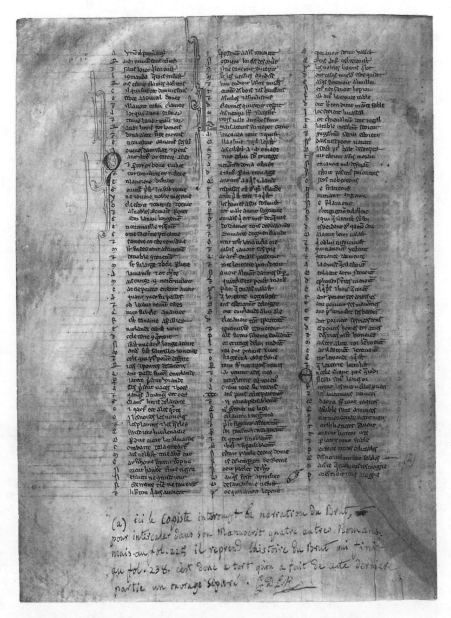

Plate 3. The last two lines of this folio, indicated by the manicule, signal the insertion of Chrétien's romances and the First Continuation of Perceval in Wace's Roman de Brut. Paris, Bibliothèque nationale, fonds français 1450, f. 139v.

Plate 4. *Yvain pours water on the stone beside the fountain and fights Esclados. Paris, Bibliothèque nationale, fonds français 1433, f. 65r.*

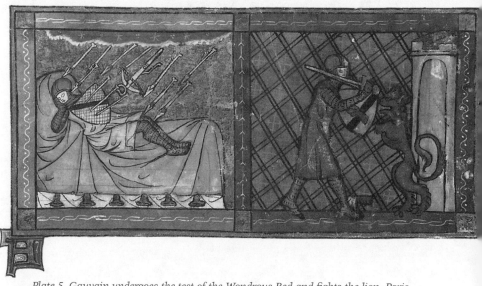

Plate 5. *Gauvain undergoes the test of the Wondrous Bed and fights the lion. Paris, Bibliothèque nationale, fonds français 12577, f. 45r, detail.*

Plate 6. Perceval meets the penitents on Good Friday and visits his hermit uncle. Paris, Bibliothèque nationale, fonds français 12577, f. 36r, detail.

Plate 7. Perceval's reverie before the drops of blood on the snow. Montpellier, Bibliothèque interuniversitaire, Section Médecine H249, f. 27v, detail.

Plate 8. Arthur hunts the White Stag. Paris, Bibliothèque nationale, fonds français 24403, f. 119r, detail.

Plate 9. With the help of his lion, Yvain kills the giant Harpin de la
Montagne. Princeton, Princeton University Library, Manuscripts
Division, ms. 125 of the Garrett Collection of Medieval and Renaissance
Manuscripts, f. 56r, detail.

Plate 10. Perceval, carrying three javelins, says goodbye to his mother; he kneels in front of the knights he meets in the forest; Perceval's mother falls as he leaves; Perceval battles with the Red Knight and seizes Arthur's cup. Paris, Bibliothèque nationale, fonds français 12577, f. 1r.

Chapter 5

Celtic Myth, Folklore, and Historical Tradition

hrétien draws extensively upon myth, that is to say on narratives that have as their function to explain events of fundamental import such as natural phenomena or the foundation of social customs and entities. His works also contain mythic elements that he has refined on the basis of what he has received or even that he is himself elaborating. At the same time, Chrétien takes pains to present characters who have obviously played a mythic role in ways that integrate them into the everyday fabric of the world he has created, so that the distinction between their ordinary movements and their mythic nature is perceived only with difficulty. This mode of presentation has the effect of enhancing the atmosphere of strangeness and mystery as the reader moves from quotidian events to the realm of inexplicably powerful forces without perceiving where the boundary between the two lies.

THE TRADITION OF CELTIC MYTH

As discussed in Chapter 1, Chrétien was intimately familiar with Ovid, having translated not only his *Ars amatoria* and *Remedia amoris* but also two narratives from book 6 of the *Metamorphoses*. One of these, which Chrétien refers to as "The Shoulder Bite" ("Le Mors de l'espaule," *Cliges* 4), was the story of King Pelops, and the other, "The Metamorphosis of the Hoopoe, the Swallow, and the Nightingale" ("De la hupe et de l'aronde et dou rousignol la muance," *Cliges* 6–7), was a tale of betrayal, incest, and child murder involving Philomena, Procne, and Tereus (*Metamorphoses* 6.426–674). Only the second of these adaptations has survived the Middle Ages, as *Philomena* in the fourteenth-century collection known as the *Ovide moralisé*.

In spite of his knowledge of Ovid's work, however, which served as a repository for Greek myths of transformation, Chrétien turns to ancient learned sources in his five romances only through incidental references. In contrast, he draws extensively upon the tales and beliefs of the Celtic peoples who inhabited Brittany, the British Isles, and Ireland. The languages of those peoples are divided into two groups, Goidelic or Q-Celtic, which comprises Irish, Manx, and Scottish Gaelic, and Brythonic or P-Celtic, consisting of Welsh, Breton, Cornish, and Gaulish.

Although the territory of what had come to be known as France was once inhabited by the Celtic Gauls, their Gaulish language had died out in the late Roman Empire and is only extant through inscriptions and citations by ancient authors (available in Savignac 1994; see also Lambert 1997).

The Bretons were not Gauls. Their ancestors had migrated from Britain onto the continent of Europe from the fifth into the eighth centuries A.D. Nonetheless, according to the *Description of Wales* (*Descriptio Cambriae*) by Gerald of Wales (Geraldus Cambrensis, d. 1223), in his time "in both Cornwall and Brittany they speak almost the same language as in Wales. It comes from the same root and is intelligible to the Welsh in many instances, and almost in all" (translation in Thorpe 1978: 231; see also J. E. Caerwyn Williams 1991: 253–54). Stories were thus easily transportable among speakers of the three languages in Chrétien's day, and the Breton aristocracy, like their Welsh and Irish counterparts, were patrons of poets and storytellers. Patronage of Breton poets and storytellers by Bretons lords apparently began when these nobles, fighting against the Normans from the ninth century on, expanded their territory to include French-speaking subjects and began themselves to take on characteristics of the French nobility. But the proper name Bard, meaning in P-Celtic 'bard, poet', occurs as late as 1131 (J. E. Caerwyn Williams 1991: 255–56). Stories, lore, and mythological tales were carried by the immigrants to Brittany, as is always the case with large migrations of peoples. Just what those stories were, however, is a matter of conjecture because there are no extant substantial Breton literary texts from before the fifteenth century (Fleuriot 1987a: 21) and no literary manuscripts from before the sixteenth.[1]

The body of Welsh lore (W. *cyfarwyddyd*) was passed on in tradition by various means, including mnemonic triads, or groupings of three elements, such as the Three Noble Retinues of the Island of Britain or the Three Chief Officers of the Island of Britain. The collected triads as annotated by Rachel Bromwich (1978) are an extraordinarily rich store of knowledge about Celtic mythic and folkloric materials.

The account of a journey undertaken by nine canons of the cathedral of Laon in 1113 testifies to a lively Breton tradition about Arthur in the early twelfth century. These canons embarked on a trip to raise funds for rebuilding their cathedral, burned the previous year. While in Cornwall they heard one of the local inhabitants defending the notion that Arthur had not died, "just as the Bretons are in the habit of quarreling with the French about King Arthur" (*sicut Britones solent jurgari cum Francis de rege Arturo*). This is an allusion to the "Breton hope," that is to say, the belief that Arthur had not died but was recovering from his wounds and would return to assume leadership once again. The account of the canons' journey is recorded by Herman of Tourney in his work on the miracles of the virgin of Laon, written around 1145 (Tatlock 1933; see also Tatlock 1950: 204–5). The belief that Arthur would some day again lead the British and the Bretons against their oppressors was the subject of references in the Middle Ages by other writers, including William of Malmesbury, writing around 1125 (Mynors 1998, 1: §287), Henry of Huntingdon in 1138, Wace, at the end of the Arthurian section of his *Roman de Brut* around 1155, and William of Newburgh around 1200 (Arnold and Pelan 1962: ll. 4705–23; on the Breton hope, see Loomis 1959b and the summary in Fleuriot 1987b: 112–15).

In addition to the traditions that would have survived in Brittany proper, many Breton fighting men had accompanied William the Conqueror to Great Britain and had kept up their contacts with the home country. Numerous paths existed, then, for continued exchanges between insular and Continental Brythonic traditions.

Another set of paths was provided by interpreters, termed in Latin *latinarii*, in English *latimers*, and in French *latiniers* or *latimers*, who translated in the multilingual milieus of Norman Britain and Ireland and of France in the eleventh and twelfth centuries. Constance Bullock-Davies cites an interesting passage from the *Song of Dermot and the Earl*, an account of the Norman conquest of Ireland in the form of a chanson de geste. The author discusses his source, a latimer

Who told me his story
Of which I compose here a record.
He was Maurice Regan.
He who composed this work
Spoke with him person to person.
He explained to me his story.
This Maurice was an interpreter
For King Dermot, who held him most dear.
[Que moi conta de lui l'estorie
Dunt faz ici la memorie.

Morice Regan iert celui.
Buche a buche parla a lui
Ki cest jest endita.
L'estorie de lui me mostra.
Ici Morice iert latimer
Al rei Dermot ki mult l'out cher.]   (Bullock-Davies 1966: 23)

Alas, we have no account of this type of transmission from Breton into French for Chrétien's benefit, but he is likely to have drawn similarly on Celtic oral sources.

The name most commonly cited in connection with the transmission of insular Celtic lore to the Continent is Breri (Bleheri, Bleri, Bledhericus). The earliest citation is found in Thomas d'Angleterre, who in his *Roman de Tristan* invokes as a source Breri,

Who knew the deeds and the tales
Of all the kings, of all the counts,
Who had been in Britain.
[Ky solt les gestes e les cuntes
De tuz les reis, de tuz les cuntes
Ki orent esté en Bretaingne.]   (Wind 1960: Douce fragment, ll. 848–51)

Thomas's citation is in the context of divergent sources for the tales about Tristan; he takes Breri's transmission as an index of authenticity. In lines 6549–50 of ms. *A* of the *First Continuation* of *Perceval,* Breri is cited as an authority:

Never did the king conquer so much,
As Breri has told us.
[Ainz mes li rois tant ne conquist,
si come Bleheris nos dist.]   (Roach 1949–83, 3, part 1: 423)

The *Second Continuation of Perceval,* composed in the late twelfth or early thirteenth century, bears in one of its manuscripts, London, British Library, Additional 36614 (*L*), a reference to

   Breri
Who was born and engendered
In Wales, whose tale I tell,
And who told it thus to the count
Of Poitiers who loved the story.
[Bleheris
Qui fu nes et engenuïs

En Gales, dont je cont le conte,
Et qui si le contoit au conte
De Poitiers qui amoit l'estoire.]   (Roach 1949–83, 4: 539)[2]

Pierre Gallais has proposed, with arguments bolstered by a study of Arthurian names occurring in Continental charters as evidence for the spread of Arthurian tales, that this count of Poitiers was William IX, the earliest troubadour whose poems are extant (Gallais 1967; see also Mary Williams 1937: 224). The *Elucidation,* a prologue to Chrétien's *Perceval* written at the very end of the twelfth century or the beginning of the thirteenth, mentions that master Blihis said that no one should reveal the secrets of the Grail (Thompson 1931: ll. 12–13); in the same text, a knight named Blihos Bliheris is said to have been the first to tell the tales of the kingdom of Logres at Arthur's court (Thompson 1931: ll. 116–72). Gerald of Wales mentions in his *Description of Wales* a "famous Breri the storyteller" (*famosus . . . Bledhericus fabulator*) who lived a little before his time. A historical Breri, called "Latimer," made a gift to the priory of St. John at Carmarthen and appears in sources dating to the period 1113–1135. He is Bledri ap Cadivor, a Welsh ally of the Normans (Gruffydd 1912, Mary Williams 1937), whose father, Cadivor ap Gollwyn, died in 1091. Whether or not these are all reminiscences of the same person, it was obviously traditional to ascribe great knowledge of tales to Breri.

Chrétien appears to mention Breri under the form Bleobleheris (*Erec* 1710) as a knight of Arthur's entourage, but because he adds no information as to this character's knowledge or storytelling talents, it is unlikely that he was aware of him as a transmitter of tales. The historical Bledri ap Cadivor is the rare interpreter for whom we have a name and possibly a social milieu. Interpreters as well as poets certainly contributed to the transmission of Celtic lore into French.

As posited in Chapter 1 and later in this chapter, the influence of Geoffrey of Monmouth and of Wace's *Roman de Brut* on Chrétien is at best fragmentary and uncertain. Chrétien had access to substantial Celtic material from other sources, however, including the books that he mentions in *Cliges* and *Perceval* and the professional storytellers whom he criticizes in *Erec* and whom he calls "those who wish to live by storytelling" (*Erec* 22). These appear to have been bilingual speakers of French and Breton or speakers of French who were knowledgeable about Celtic tradition. Wace himself bears witness to their activities in speaking of the Round Table "about which the Bretons tell many a tale" (*dont Breton dïent mainte fable,* Arnold and Pelan

1962: l. 1212). A little farther along in his work, in speaking of the period of twelve years of peace that Arthur established, Wace writes:

> During this great peace that I recount—
> I do not know if you have heard this—
> The marvelous exploits were undertaken
> And the adventures encountered
> Which are told so often about Arthur
> That they are turned into fictions:
> Neither entirely falsehood nor entirely truth,
> Nor entirely folly nor entirely wisdom.
> The story-tellers have told so much
> And the tale-tellers made up so much,
> In order to embellish their stories,
> That they have made everything seem fiction.
> [En cele grant pes que je di,
> Ne sai se vos l'avez oï,
> Furent les mervoilles provees,
> Et les avantures trovees
> Qui d'Artur sont tant recontees
> Que a fables sont atornees:
> Ne tot mançonge ne tot voir,
> Ne tot folor ne tot savoir.
> Tant ont li contëor conté
> Et li fablëor tant fablé
> Por lor contes anbeleter,
> Que tot ont fet fable sanbler.]   (Arnold and Pelan 1962: ll. 1247–58)

It is these tale-tellers who were the main source for Chrétien's knowledge of what Jean Bodel, in a passage of his *Song of the Saxons* (*Chanson des Saisnes*) that is of fundamental importance for our view of how poets of this period categorized their subjects, calls the "matter of Britain" (*matiere de Bretagne*):

> For any one who understands, there are only three matters:
> Of France, of Britain, and of Rome the great;
> And among these three matters there is no resemblance.
> The tales of Britain thus are insubstantial and pleasant,
> Those of Rome are wise and instructive,
> Those of France are true, as is every day apparent.
> [N'en sont que trois materes a nul home vivant:
> De France et de Bretaigne et de Ronme la grant;
> Ne de ces trois materes n'i a nule samblant.

Li conte de Bretaigne sont si vain et plaisant,
Et cil de Ronme sage et de sens aprendant,   (Brasseur 1989:
Cil de France sont voir chascun jour aparant.]   ms. *A*, ll. 6–11)

Jean Bodel is here attempting to bolster the value of his own poem, which belongs to the matter of France. Chrétien's attitude toward the storytellers seems to have resembled Wace's more closely than Jean's: that what they told was partly truth and partly fiction.

THE WELSH ROMANCES

A question that is still under active discussion and that is of prime importance for any discussion of Celtic myth in Chrétien's works is the relation between Chrétien's *Erec, Yvain,* and *Perceval* and the three Welsh prose romances that deal with the same material, respectively *Gereint Son of Erbin* (*Gereint ab Erbin*), *Owein,* also known as *The Tale of the Lady of the Fountain* (*Chwedyl Iarlles y Ffynnawn*), and *The Story of Peredur Son of Efrawg* (*Historia Peredur ab Efrawg*). These romances are included in the collection of eleven medieval Welsh tales known as the *Mabinogion,*[3] which also contains two Arthurian texts that have no non-Welsh counterparts, *The Dream of Rhonabwy* (*Breuddwyd Rhonabwy*) and *Culhwch and Olwen* (*Culhwch ac Olwen*).

Gereint parallels the plot of *Erec* in many respects, but although its heroine's name is Enid, the eponymous hero's name is that of a sixth-century king of Dumnonia, Geraint. Various elements of Welsh lore that are not in *Erec* are incorporated into *Gereint:* characters from Welsh tradition appear, such as the porter Glewlwyd Mighty Grasp and Arthur's physician Morgan Tud, whose name appears in place of that of Morgan the Fay, and others found in *Culhwch and Olwen.* From that text also comes Arthur's dog, Cafall. The name of the Ydier figure's father, Nut in Chrétien, is given as Nudd, a Celtic mythological figure, showing that the Welsh storyteller understood this equivalence. The kingdom of Enid's uncle is Cardiff rather than Lalut, and the court of Arthur, who is entitled "emperor," is at Caerleon on Usk rather than at Caradigan. In *Gereint,* the prize given to Enid in Arthur's court—but without mention of her status as the most beautiful— is the severed head of the white stag, which is decidedly out of keeping with the courtly refinements of *Erec.* Between the marriage of Gereint and Enid and the coronation scene three years pass, and Gereint is crowned in the middle of the tale rather than at the end. A catalogue of nobles is presented, analogous to the catalogues in the wedding and coronation episodes of *Erec,* but it is a recital of those accompanying the couple on their journey to the court of Gereint's father. When Gereint overhears his wife's lament in bed, he thinks she is meditating love for another man, and Gereint has her put on her worst dress rather than her best for the journey of adventures. Other details separate the two texts, but these are among the most significant. *Gereint* may have been composed in the first half of the thirteenth century, although a late twelfth-century date is not to be excluded (see Middleton 1991: 148–50).

The Lady of the Fountain has as its hero Owein, whose name is that of a late sixth-century king of Rheged, which was situated in the old British north, around the Solway estuary and perhaps extending south into Yorkshire. Most of the tale is devoted to the adventures at the fountain, including its initial testing by Cynon, son of Clydno, also a figure of the sixth century, who plays the role assigned to Calogrenant in *Yvain.* Arthur does not conceive his project to visit the fountain until three years after he has first heard Cynon's story. When he does arrive there, Owein and Cei (= Keu) do battle immediately, and although Owein is victorious, the battle is repeated the second day when Cei complains that he had been defeated unfairly the first time. The battle with Gwalchmei (= Gauvain) takes place during Arthur's search for Owein at the fountain rather than as a culminating event toward the end of the story. Owein returns to Arthur's court for three more years before realizing that he has not kept his promise to the lady of the fountain. His solitary time in the wilderness occupies only a brief stretch of narrative, and there is no hermit to help him. Owein defends Luned (= Lunette) without revealing his identity to her. After this, without the battle over the inheritances of the heiresses of Noire Espine — which, as Diverres points out (1981–82: 155–57), would make no sense in this period under Welsh law, which did not admit the possibility of women inheriting land — the reader is told abruptly that Owein and Luned went to the lady of the fountain's kingdom and then he took her to Arthur's court. In the last episode, which follows this reuniting of the couple, Owein defeats the Black Oppressor and frees twenty-four ladies whom this villain had held captive after having killed their husbands. A number of features of *Owein* can plausibly be explained if one assumes derivation from Chrétien's *Yvain* (Hunt 1974). *Owein,* by contrast, like *Gereint,* contains elements of Welsh lore not present in its French counterpart.

R. L. Thomson has dated *Owein* as far back as the late twelfth century on the basis of syntactic and orthographic features (R. L. Thomson 1991:

159). The presence of rowel-spurs, not attested in Europe until the mid-thirteenth century (Hunt 1974: 109–11), in the Red Book of Hergest version of *Owein*, the only complete text, casts doubt on this early dating, which could only apply, then, to an earlier hypothetical version of the text.

The name of the eponymous hero of *Peredur* corresponds, like Owein's, to a historical sixth-century personage of the old British north, Peredur, son of Eliffer. In the romance, he is said to be the son of Efrawg, which, curiously, is in Welsh the toponym "York." It is possible that *Peredur vab Efrawg,* the most obvious meaning of which is "Peredur son of Efrawg," does not actually contain a patronymic but rather derives from a misunderstood Latin *praetor ab Eburaco* 'official or magistrate from York' (Pokorny 1950–51: 39), the preposition *ab* 'from' being mistaken for the Welsh *(m)ab* 'son of' commonly used to designate male descent. The narrative and the relationships among characters in *Peredur* differ substantially from what is found in *Perceval.* Peredur, for example, is the sister's son of the Gornemant figure, who himself has two sons. At the beginning of the romance, Peredur meets the three knights while in his mother's company. Among the items of advice she gives her son is that if he sees a fair woman, he should make love to her, even if it is against her will. In the following analysis, I follow Thurneysen's useful division of the text into four parts according to divisions found in the Red Book of Hergest, labeled I(a), I(b), II, and III (1910–12).

The equivalent of Chrétien's Grail King is another maternal uncle, a lame king who instructs Peredur to rejoin the pieces of his broken sword three times. Peredur succeeds in doing so only twice. When the Grail procession with the bleeding spear enters the hall, shrieking and lamentations break out. On the Grail (called merely a *dysgl* 'platter'), carried by two maidens, is not a host but a severed human head resting in a pool of blood. Peredur does not ask the king about what he sees. The next morning, Peredur leaves the castle, but there is no mention of its being deserted. The woman he meets in the forest is not his cousin but his foster-sister, and he immediately takes vengeance on the knight who has killed her husband. Peredur falls in love with a maiden in a castle (equivalent to Chrétien's Blancheflor), who comes to his bed during the night on the advice of her men to offer herself to him. Peredur sends her away that night but stays with her for three weeks, defeating her enemies. Her name is not given in the text, and Peredur only tells her his name when he is leaving. Peredur then comes to a castle where a mother and her son are being held by the nine witches of Caer Loyw (that is, Gloucester). One of the witches leads him to their court, where he is instructed in how to ride a horse and handle weapons. The incident of the blood on the snow takes place outside a hermit's cell, where Peredur unhorses twenty-four knights before defeating Cei and breaking his arm and shoulder blade. He soon learns from Gwalchmei that he has thus avenged two dwarves, a male and a female, whom Cei had struck when they praised Peredur in Arthur's court. This section of the romance, which Thurneysen (1910–12) labeled I(a), corresponds roughly to the plot of *Perceval.*

Arthur takes Peredur back to his court at Caerleon (Carlisle), where the knight falls in love with Angharad Golden Hand and vows not to speak to any Christian until she returns his love, which leads to his later being termed the "Mute Knight" or "Mute Lad." Following this episode, Peredur leaves the court and comes to the edge of a round valley, where he encounters a chained lion in front of a pit filled with human and animal bones. He strikes at the beast, first leaving it hanging from its chain over the pit, then severing the chain. At a castle in the center of the valley, Peredur then encounters and kills a host of giants whose leader he forces to convert to Christianity. He also kills a serpent lying on a ring of gold. Returning to Arthur's court, Peredur once again meets Cei, who wounds him in the thigh because Peredur, in accord with his oath, refuses to speak with him, Cei being a Christian. Cei does not recognize Peredur, who, maintaining his silence, does not offer his name. Peredur then defeats a knight who has approached Arthur's court and whom the king is about to engage in combat, and from then on he is called the "Mute Knight" (see Rejhon 1985–86: 116). When Angharad, not recognizing Peredur, says she would love him if he were not mute, he begins to speak again and the two are reunited. In this sequence of episodes, which Thurneysen labeled I(b), the plot of *Peredur* has strayed away from all relation to Chrétien's *Perceval.*

Peredur now experiences a series of adventures: he kills the one-eyed Black Oppressor, meets the sons of the King of Suffering, kills a monster called the Addanc with the help of a magic stone given to him by the empress of Constantinople, meets the Lady of the Feats, and kills the Black Worm of the Dolorous Mound. He rules with the empress of Constantinople for fourteen years. At this point manuscript Peniarth 7 of *Peredur* notes: "Here ends the youth [*kynnyd*] of Peredur son of Efrawg." This series of adventures constitutes Thurneysen's section II.

Abruptly the text then says that Peredur is at Arthur's court at Caerleon on Usk, and *Peredur* begins once again, in Thurneysen's section III, to parallel the plot of *Perceval.* A hideous woman tells the hero that in failing to ask the proper question about the Bleeding Lance, he failed to heal the king and restore the realm to prosperity. Peredur swears not to sleep until he finds out the story of the bleeding spear and its meaning. Upon this follow the adventures of Gwalchmei, with an episode analogous to Gauvain's adventure in Escavalon, after which the focus is on Peredur. The Good Friday scene results in Peredur's meeting a priest who, unlike the hermit in *Perceval,* does not hear his confession, speak of his mother, or identify himself as the hero's uncle but, rather, merely directs Peredur to the castle of Wonders. After an intermediary adventure with a king and his daughter, Peredur reaches the castle of Wonders, where he watches a set of chessmen move themselves in a game of chess and hurls a gaming board into a lake. To recover the gaming board, he undertakes a series of feats. A resolution of sorts is prepared when Peredur encounters two figures sitting together in a castle, Gwalchmei and a lame, gray-haired man. A young blond man goes down on his knee before Peredur and tells him that he is his cousin, a shape-shifter, and that he appeared to the hero in various shapes: as the hideous woman at Arthur's court, as the maiden carrying the bloody head on the platter, and as the young man bearing the bleeding spear. The head belonged to Peredur's cousin, he is told, who was killed by the witches of Caer Loyw. Peredur and his companions send for Arthur's war band, and the tale ends when they kill all the witches of Caer Loyw.

The narrative of *Peredur,* of which only section I(a) and section III up to the Good Friday episode correspond to *Perceval,* is replete with gratuitous adventures and contains many internal contradictions (Lovecy 1991: 176–80). Although there is no indication that the text is incomplete, Peredur does not in fact discover anything about the bleeding spear, and his oath not to sleep until he did make such a discovery is quickly forgotten. The manuscript tradition of *Peredur* is complicated, and in one version the text ends with the hero's fourteen-year sojourn at the side of the empress of Constantinople.

Did Chrétien get his Celtic material for *Erec, Yvain,* and *Perceval* from the Welsh romances? Do the Welsh texts derive from the French poems? If so, are the French poems their only sources? Or do the Welsh and the French works derive from common sources now lost? These questions make up what was termed the *Mabinogionfrage* in the nineteenth century and the early twentieth, the heyday of German scholarship. The answer one adopts must depend on internal analysis, as we have no external evidence that would help us decide among the various possibilities.

An ingenious theory of Rachel Bromwich (discussed below) posits that the names of Erec and Enide derive together from Breton tradition, which would make it appear that the Welsh hero's name Gereint represents a change made to a previously existing tale. In addition, the character known in Chrétien as Guivret le Petit is called in *Gereint* Gwiffret Petit, an epithet that corresponds to, and must come from, the French *petit* 'small'. *Gereint* appears, then, to be dependent on *Erec* and not vice versa. Its anonymous author, however, incorporates elements of Welsh life and lore, giving the tale a thoroughly Welsh aspect that is shared by *Owein* and *Peredur.*

The abrupt ending of *Owein* makes it very likely that this romance also derives from its French counterpart. The position of Brynley F. Roberts (1977: 143) cited by Rejhon (1985–86: 119) seems right on the mark: that the text of *Owein* is just what one would expect from the attempt of a literary Welshman to adapt a French romance into the Welsh prose tradition.

In *Peredur,* the recourse to the hero's vow not to speak to any Christian as an explanation for his refusal to speak with Cei is a crude rationalization compared with Perceval's reverie on the colors of his lady friend's face. But most telling is the resemblance of certain episodes of *Peredur* to plot elements that occur not in Chrétien's *Perceval* but in his *Yvain:* the encounter with a lion in each work, the incognito activity of the two heroes under the respective titles of the Mute Knight and the Knight of the Lion, and the reconciliation of each with his beloved because he remains incognito, all in sections of *Peredur* that have no parallel with the plot of *Perceval* (Rejhon 1985–86). Furthermore, the resemblances between *Peredur* and *Yvain* cannot be mediated by *Owein,* which does not contain the details in question. In contrast with Chrétien's unfinished but coherent *Perceval, Peredur* is an amalgam of episodes of seemingly disparate provenance.

The three Welsh romances share a common style (see Roberts 1984: 225) and are transmitted together. *Gereint* is preserved in three medieval manuscripts, *Owein* in three, and *Peredur* in four. Two renowned manuscripts contain all three texts: the White Book of Rhydderch (Aberystwyth, National Library of Wales, Peniarth 4 and 5), in which the three tales are not copied contiguously, and the Red Book of Hergest (Oxford, Bodleian Library, Jesus College CXI), in which *Owein* and *Peredur* are contiguous. The hypothesis of a single author for *Owein* and *Peredur* is rendered probable by the knowledge of the plot of *Yvain* shown in *Peredur* on one hand, and on the other the striking resemblances between *Owein* and *Peredur* (analyzed in Rejhon 1985–86: 118), including the appearance in both texts of the Black Oppressor and of a game that consists of shooting arrows at the hilts of knives, found nowhere else in the literature of medieval Wales.

Another resemblance is noteworthy. After the Good Friday scene that is the last part of *Peredur* with a counterpart in *Perceval,* while Peredur is on his way to the castle of Wonders, the hero encounters a king who sends him to his court to meet his daughter. Peredur and the daughter take dinner together, and the daughter's laughter attracts the attention of an attendant who advises the king to prevent the two from becoming lovers. The king has Peredur imprisoned. Hearing that a hostile earl is coming to challenge the king, Peredur asks the princess to arrange for him to leave his prison and also requests that she provide him with a horse and armor. She does so, and Peredur, dressed in a red surcoat and carrying a yellow shield, takes part in a series of encounters between the king's army and the earl's men in which he is victorious for three days running. At the end of each day he returns to prison. On the fourth day Peredur kills the hostile earl and returns again to captivity. When the king learns who has disposed of his enemy, he frees Peredur out of gratitude and offers him his daughter's hand in marriage, which Peredur declines to accept.

In spite of many differences of detail, this episode, which replicates the commonplace of the three-day combat (Thurneysen 1910–12: 187; Delcourt-Angélique 1981), shares important motifs with Chrétien's *Lancelot,* in which the hero is imprisoned by Meleagant's seneschal but manages to talk the seneschal's wife, who is enamored of him, into allowing him to leave the prison under a promise to return after he takes part in the tournament of Noauz. Lancelot promises to accord her all the love he has available to give, and the woman recognizes, laughing, that this means no love at all (*Lancelot* 5482–85). Lancelot dresses in the seneschal's red arms (*Lancelot* 5499), goes to Noauz, and fights for three days in the tournament. After winning, he returns to his prison, much to the chagrin of the ladies who organized the tournament to vet out potential mates (Bruckner 1993: 68–69). In the two texts a knight is temporarily freed from prison by a laughing woman who is in love with him but whose love he does not reciprocate, on a pledge to return to captivity, which he keeps; in both texts he dresses for his combat in red clothing that is provided by the woman, and in the end he is victorious after several days of battles. The place and dramatis personae of the episode of *Peredur* in which this motif of "combat while freed on parole" takes place are curiously vague: all the characters whom Peredur encounters, including the king and his daughter, are anonymous, and the town where the court is located is likewise unnamed. It seems that the episode was inserted for the sole purpose of exploiting the motif. There is no evidence for the existence of a Welsh version of *Lancelot,* and the hero's name is not of Welsh origin. I think it likely that the Welsh author of *Peredur* had heard a reading of Chrétien's *Lancelot* in Old French, as well as readings of *Perceval* and *Yvain.*

That *Gereint, Owein,* and *Peredur* each has a different relationship with the corresponding romance of Chrétien is unlikely. The hypothesis that accounts for the various pieces of evidence in the most straightforward manner is that all three result from a single bilingual Welsh storyteller hearing Chrétien's three romances plus at least part of a fourth, *Lancelot,* read out loud or performed from memory (see Duggan 1989), either in France or in the Norman milieu of England or Wales,[4] and then retelling them from memory (see Foster 1959: 204–5) in a manner typical of Welsh narrative art and incorporating elements of native lore and perhaps other sources. The practice of having French romances read out loud in this period, in which literacy was not widespread, is known not only from the scene in *Yvain* in which a girl of seventeen reads to her parents (*Yvain* 5358–70) but also from the episode of the romance *Hunbaut* in which a girl is reading to an audience of sixteen knights and ladies (Winters 1984: 3048–53; both passages are cited in Chapter 1). The details of Welsh lore that the storyteller would have added in retelling the tales may or may not have corresponded to what was in Chrétien's own sources. The choice of generating Welsh versions of *Erec, Yvain,* and *Perceval,* and not of *Lancelot* and *Cliges*—if indeed this last was available to the Welsh storyteller—seems to have been based on the familiarity of their heroes to a Welsh audience (Roberts 1983: 182).

The Welsh romances, then, are not only valuable in their own right as manifestations of the art of storytelling in medieval Wales but also of interest to the student of Chrétien as indices for probing what Chrétien might have seen as useful in the world of Celtic myth for conveying his cultural agenda.

NAMES FROM CELTIC TRADITION IN CHRÉTIEN'S ROMANCES

The mythic material in Chrétien can profitably be discussed under two broad headings: the names and characters in his works that go back to Celtic antecedents, and the plots and motifs of his romances that owe something to Celtic tales. Names that are shared with Celtic analogues are likely to derive, if not from the analogue itself, then from a common source; it is a question, then, of cognate forms, in some cases of forms with which elements of narrative were associated. In the case of plots and motifs, there is also the possibility that story elements belong to a general fund of folk-loric material (see Guerreau-Jalabert 1983, 1992) or that it is a question of polygenesis. In each case, a judgment must be made on the basis of the evidence.

We will have occasion in this chapter to consider the nature and origin of many names occurring in Chrétien's romances. In discussing possible sources of names in the Brythonic branch of the Celtic languages, a branch that includes Welsh, Cornish, and Breton, scholars have recourse above all to Middle Welsh evidence, since no Breton or Cornish texts have survived from the twelfth or thirteenth centuries.

Chrétien is likely to have called upon a variety of sources for Celtic materials in the course of his career, as there is some inconsistency in his transmission of Brythonic names. To cite only one example, he calls Arthur's kingdom Logres consistently in *Lancelot,* but only once in all the rest of his Arthurian romances, namely in *Perceval,* lines 6169–70, where he assigns it by popular etymology the meaning of "land once inhabited by ogres" (*qui jadis fu la terre as ogres*).

Names of characters who appear in more than one text or who are mentioned in the two catalogues in *Erec* — the list of those at Arthur's court and the list of guests invited to the wedding — are treated first. An analysis of Arthurian place-names in Chrétien follows. The discussion then turns to elements of plot.

Names of Characters

Although Geoffrey of Monmouth's *History of the Kings of Britain* and its vernacular translations brought Arthur to the attention of non-British audiences, he was already long renowned in Welsh and Breton tradition. Arthur's name corresponds to the Latin *Artorius,* which is attested as a personal name of four men living in Britain in the sixth and seventh centuries, perhaps reflecting the practice of naming children after a famous figure (Chadwick and Chadwick 1932: 161–62).[5] It may be related to L. *Arcturus* with its connotations of 'northern' but also 'bear-like'. A gloss on the *History of the Britons* (*Historia Brittonum,* see below) renders Arthur as L. *ursus horribilis* 'fearsome bear' (see Bromwich 1978: 544–45).

References to Arthur are largely positive in heroic poems and tales, but the Welsh saints' lives — the *Life of St. Padarn,* the *Life of St. Cadog,* the *Life of Gildas* — tend to depict him as a tyrant (see Chambers 1966: 80–85, 243–49).

The dates of the earliest heroic references in Welsh are controversial. What were once accepted as sixth- or seventh-century texts have come to be considered by some as the work of poets and transmitters who lived in the ninth, tenth, and eleventh centuries, but still preceding any sign of Arthur in French. Although the ultimate sources may be much older, it is safe to assert that in the ninth century Arthur was already a famous figure in Britain.

In a poem found in the *Gododdin,* a collection of elegies preserved in the thirteenth-century Book of Aneirin about the battle of Catterick (W. Catraeth) that took place about A.D. 600, it is said of a warrior, Gwawddur, that he "used to bring black crows down in front of the wall of the fortified town—though he was not Arthur" (Koch 1997: 23). Attracting crows was a metaphor for killing men in battle, so the poet is referring to Arthur as the model of a skilled warrior. In this earliest allusion to Arthur, which John Koch thinks belonged to the earliest layer of the *Gododdin,* dating to before A.D. 638, there is as yet no reference to his kingship and he is evoked in a northern British ambiance. Arthur may originally have been a figure who lived toward the year A.D. 600 in the old British North (see the balanced views in Kenneth Jackson 1959; also Koch 1997: 147–48), an area that comprised Strathclyde, Rheged, Gododdin, and Galloway.

The *History of the Britons,* dated to the ninth century and ascribed falsely to Nennius in an eleventh-century prologue, is the earliest text to assign to Arthur the leadership role in the struggle of the Britons against the Angles and Saxons who invaded Britain in the fifth and sixth centuries. It calls him a "leader in battle" or "general" (*dux bellorum*) and enumerates twelve battles that he won against the Saxons at various places, most of which are not easily identified: the Rivers Glein, Dubglas, and Bassas, Celidon Wood—in the phrase "the Battle of Celidon Wood" (*Cat Coit Celidon*)—the fortress of Guinnion, the City of the Legion (Caerleon, that is, Chester), the River Tribruit, Mount Agned, and Mount Badon. At Guinnion, Arthur is said to have carried the image of the Virgin Mary on his shoulders, which probably means painted on his shield, and to have led a slaughter of the Saxons. At the last, the battle of Mount Badon, the *History of the Britons* says that Arthur killed by his own hand 960 of the enemy. The alliteration found in *Cat Coit Celidon* and the fact that some of the place-names of battles rhyme together in their Welsh forms may point to a poem about Arthur in Welsh verse, analogous to battle-listing poems about other early British heroes (Chadwick and Chadwick 1932: 155; Thomas Jones 1964; Bromwich 1975–76: 168–70).

Only one of the twelve battles ascribed to Arthur in the *History of the Britons* is referred to in an independent early source—namely, the battle on the River Tribruit to which an important poem from the Black Book of Car-marthen, "What man is the gatekeeper?" ("Pa gur yw y porthaur?") alludes (translations in Sims-Williams 1991: 40–45; and Bromwich and Evans 1992: xxxv–xxxvi). "Pa gur," which dates from the eleventh century at the latest, is a dialogue between the gatekeeper Glewlwyd and Arthur, who in order to gain entrance to the fortress of the giant Wrnach Gawr enumerates those who accompany him. They include Cei, Bedwyr, Mabon, son of Modron, and Llacheu, who appear in Chrétien's romances as, respectively, Keu the seneschal (passim), Bedoier the constable (*Erec* 1731), Mabonagrain (*Erec* 6124), and Arthur's son Loholt (*Erec* 1728). Another poem, "The Spoils of the Otherworld" ("Preiddeu Annwn") from before the twelfth century, tells of an expedition undertaken by Arthur and three shiploads of his companions to free Mabon from an Otherworld stronghold where he is kept a prisoner (Haycock 1983–84: 58).

The *History of the Britons,* in addition to listing Arthur's twelve victories, associates with him two marvels: a cairn whose top stone bears the foot-print of Arthur's dog, Cafall, and the tomb of Arthur's son Amr, killed by his father. The tomb is said to vary in length each time it is measured. The mar-vels show that in the ninth century Arthur was already a figure of legend in Britain, and their juxtaposition with a supposedly historical account may point to a legendary source for the *History of the Britons*'s account of Arthur as a whole (Padel 1994). It is also possible, however, that the *History*'s nar-rative of Arthur is based on Welsh historical verse, which for the very early period tends always to be based on historical events rather than on legend (Jarman 1981).

Another early source is the *Annals of Wales* (*Annales Cambriae*), from the middle of the tenth century, two of whose entries concern Arthur. For the year A.D. 516, the *Annals* record "the Battle of Badon in which Arthur carried the cross of Our Lord Jesus Christ on his shoulders for three days and three nights, and the Britons were victorious" (*Bellum Badonis in quo Arthur portavit crucem domini nostri Jhesu Christi tribus diebus et tribus nocti-bus in humeros suos, et Brittones victores fuerunt*). For the year 537, the entry is "the Battle of Camlann in which Arthur and Medraut fell" (*Gueith Cam-lann in qua Arthur et Medraut corruerunt*). This last entry is the earliest men-tion of the personage known as Mordred and later identified as Arthur's nephew, as well as the earliest reference to the battle of Camlan, to which Geoffrey of Monmouth refers as the cataclysmic end of Arthur's reign.

The lives of Welsh saints, written in Latin, tend to set Arthur up as a foil against which to illustrate the influence and powers of the saints, which implies that authority and power is ascribed to him. In the *Life of St. Cadog,* from around 1100, Arthur is called "most illustrious king of Britain" (*rex illustrissimus Britannie*) and is accompanied by Cei and Bedwyr.

The earliest Arthurian literary narrative is the eleventh-century *Culhwch and Olwen* (translated in Jones and Jones 1974 and Ford 1977). In this extremely important Welsh prose tale, Arthur's first cousin Culhwch can only marry Olwen if he accomplishes a series of feats set by her father, Ysbaddaden Chief-giant, including freeing Mabon from prison and hunting the great boar Twrch Trwyth. Culhwch receives Arthur's assistance and eventually achieves his goal. Among the dramatis personae are Gwenhwyfar (Chrétien's Guinevere), Cei (Keu), Bedwyr (Bedoier), Arthur's sister's son Gwalchmei (Gauvain), Maelwys, son of Baeddan (Meleagant, son of Bademagu), Edern, son of Nudd (Ydier, son of Nut), Don (Do, father of Gifflez), Mabon, son of Modron (Mabonagrain), Drwst (Tristan), and Urien Rheged (Urien, father of Yvain). Allusions are made to the battle of Camlan. Unlike Chrétien's romances, in which magical occurrences intrude rarely—although with great effect—*Culhwch and Olwen* has an aura of constant magic and the preternatural about it, and its characters have fantastically exaggerated qualities. An example is the description of Cei's attributes:

> Cei had these gifts: he could hold his breath under water for nine nights and nine days; a wound inflicted by Cei no doctor could heal; victorious was Cei; he could be as tall as the tallest tree in the forest when it pleased him. He had another peculiarity: when it would be raining hardest, whatever he held in his hand would be dry for a fist-length all around because of the greatness of his passion; and when his companions were coldest he would be fuel to kindle their fire. (Ford 1977: 132)

This is a different universe from Chrétien's fictional world, in which the actions of the seneschal Keu are plausible on a purely human level.

All these Welsh texts predate Geoffrey of Monmouth's *History of the Kings of Britain,* ca. 1138, which places Arthur in the context of a legendary genealogy that goes back to Aeneas.

The name Arthur begins to appear in Continental documents in the ninth century in Brittany and from around the middle of the eleventh century in Maine and Anjou (Gallais 1967). These attestations of the name are taken as a sign that parents are naming their sons after a famous Arthur, presumably the Arthur of Celtic legend, first in Breton-speaking areas, but then also in adjoining regions to which his fame would have spread.

About many of Arthur's associations and feats as recorded by Welsh tradition and by Wace and Geoffrey of Monmouth, Chrétien is silent. He never mentions Arthur's battles against the insular Saxons or the battle of Camlan, nor does he mention the instigator of this final struggle, Mordred. Of the Isle of Avallon he says only that Guilemer ruled there, who was the lover of Morgan the Fay (*Erec* 1950–54). He only once alludes to Merlin in passing, in *Erec,* lines 6684–86, but merely to date from Merlin's time the sterling's prevalence as a currency in Britain. This is not entirely surprising, however, as the Galfridian tradition associates Merlin with Arthur's father, Uther, rather than with Arthur himself with the exception of one passage toward the end of the *History of the Kings of Britain* in which Geoffrey refers to Merlin as having prophesied to Arthur (Wright 1985: 146; see Thorpe 1966: 282n). Chrétien does not borrow Wace's or Geoffrey's names for Arthur's shield Pridwen (in Wace, Priven, the name in Welsh tradition not of a shield but of Arthur's ship), or for his spear Ron (Roit in Wace and Rhongomiant in Welsh tradition), and he assigns the sword Escalibor (Caliburnus in Geoffrey, Calibore in Wace, Caledfwlch in Welsh) to Gauvain in *Perceval,* line 5902, without ever associating it with Arthur himself. Only in *Cliges* is Arthur depicted as the dominant king and warrior that one encounters in Wace's *Roman de Brut* and in Geoffrey. Arnold reports (1938–40: xcvi–xcvii) that of the approximately four hundred Celtic names in the *Roman de Brut,* only a dozen are found in *Erec,* and only one more of the four hundred appears in the rest of Chrétien's works. This lack of dependence on Wace's *Brut* and on Geoffrey supports the hypothesis that Chrétien drew largely on Celtic sources and that the few names he happens to share with Geoffrey and Wace were not taken from them.

Arthur's father, Uther Pendragon (*Perceval* 455, 8740, simply called Pandragon in *Erec* 1807), and his mother, Ygerne (*Perceval* 8742), are characters in Geoffrey and Wace. Uther is not identified as Arthur's father before Geoffrey. Unlike Chrétien, Wace and Geoffrey depict the Kings Lot, father of Gauvain, and Urien, father of Yvain, as brothers. Yvain (in Welsh, Owein ab Urien) is in Wace and Geoffrey a king of Scotland through his uncle, a detail that is not in Chrétien.

Morgan the Fay, whom Chrétien mentions as Arthur's sister Morgue (*Erec* 4214, 4216), skilled at concocting healing unguents (*Erec* 4213, *Yvain* 2953) and the lover of Guilemer (*Morgain la fée, Erec* 1950–54), lord of the Isle of Avalon, is not mentioned in Wace or in Geoffrey's history, which calls Arthur's sister Anna (Wright 1985: 98–99); she is "Enna" in the *Roman de Brut* (Arnold and Pelan 1962: 1. 279). In Geoffrey's *Life of Merlin* (*Vita*

Merlini), however, the leader of the nine sisters ruling over the Island of Apples, also called the Fortunate Island, is Morgen (Clarke 1973: ll. 908, 920; see also pp. 203–6 for conjectures on the origin of the name and its etymology, most probably the same as the Irish name Muirgein 'sea born'). An author of the first century A.D., Pomponius Mela, records the Gaulish belief that on the island of Sena off the coast of Brittany dwelled nine virgins who controlled the winds and the sea with their incantations, healed those who could not be healed elsewhere, knew the future, and could turn themselves into whatever animals they wished (text cited in Loomis 1941: 908). In the *History,* Geoffrey mentions the "isle of Avallon," *insula Avallonis* (in Wace, Avalon), as the place to which Arthur was carried for his wounds to be healed. The Isle of Avallon is the Welsh *Ynys Afallau* 'Isle of Apples'. No text before Chrétien's *Erec* assigns a brother to Morgan, however. Chrétien is likely to have picked up this feature of the Arthurian biography also from oral tradition, perhaps Breton tradition.

The name of Arthur's wife, Guinevere, whom Geoffrey calls Guenhuuara (variant forms Guenhuuera, Guanhumara, Gwenwara) and Wace Gahunmare (variant Genoivre), derives from W. Gwenhwyfar 'white enchantress, white fairy'. Geoffrey asserts that she was of noble Roman stock and that Cador, duke of Cornwall, was responsible for her upbringing, but Chrétien mentions neither of these details. Guinevere is also mentioned in *Culhwch and Olwen* under the form Gwenhuyfar and in Caradog of Llancarfan's *Life of Gildas* as Guennuvar (see Bromwich 1978: 380–85). The form Guenievre first appears in *Erec,* line 125.

The antecedents of Keu and Bedoier are the most ancient of Arthur's warrior companions. Although Bedoier is mentioned in *Erec,* line 1731, as Arthur's constable, one of the highest offices in a court, he nowhere again appears in Chrétien's romances. Keu, by contrast, plays significant roles in every romance except *Cliges,* from which he is absent altogether. His Welsh counterpart, Cei or Cai, is represented as a hero of many exploits, on which the poem "Pa Gur" focuses, including killing the monstrous Cat of Palug. Cei's father, Cynyr, destined him, according to *Culhwch and Olwen,* to have a cold heart and hands, to be stubborn, and to stand water and fire better than any man; when he carries a burden, it will become invisible (Bromwich 1978: 304–5; Ford 1977: 128–29), and we have just seen that *Culhwch and Olwen* enumerates other marvelous qualities of Cei. Only one of the attributes attributed to him in the Welsh tale seems to have passed through to the French Keu: Cei is said to be an unparalleled officer, which appears to correspond to Arthur's opinion of him in *Lancelot* in which the king grants

Keu a rash promise to keep him from leaving his service (82–179). In *Erec* (1736), Keu is said to have a son, Gronosis, "who knew much about evil" (*qui mout sot de mal*), and Roger Middleton has traced this name back through readings in various manuscripts of *Erec* to "Garanwyn," the name of Cei's son in *Culhwch and Olwen* (see Gowans 1988: 49). Keu is Arthur's seneschal, one of the highest officials in a twelfth-century court, a designation that he first acquired in Geoffrey's *History* and the *Roman de Brut* (Arnold and Pelan 1962: l. 2771). According to Geoffrey and Wace, Keu is also the count of Anjou, an assignment that Chrétien does not give him but that would have been a significant precedent for the Plantagenets, lords of England and Anjou. Keu comes to be associated with the kitchen, perhaps through popular etymology, the medieval French form Keu being homophonous with *queu, keu* 'cook'. Thus immediately before the scene in *Lancelot* just referred to, Keu is eating with the servants of Arthur's household while Meleagant is issuing his challenge to the king. In Chrétien's works, Keu seems to be in a continuous state of irritability, ready to fly into a rage when he encounters those who do not follow his lead or share his opinions. In any case, in Chrétien an exemplary hero he is not, constantly acting in a boastful manner but failing to back up his words with capable chivalric deeds (see Gowans 1988; Merceron 1998).

The hero who consistently acts in an exemplary manner, Gauvain (Eng. Gawain), is the sister's son of Arthur in Chrétien's romances as well as in Geoffrey, who calls his mother Anna, and Wace, who names her Enna. All sources give his father as Loth of Lodonesia, which is the region of Lothian in Scotland. The earliest mention of Gauvain (see Busby 1980: 30–49) is under the form *Walwen* in the *History of the English Kings* of William of Malmesbury (*Gesta Regum Anglorum,* Mynors 1998, 1: §287), ca. 1125, who also knows him as Arthur's nephew. William speaks of the discovery of the tomb of Gawain—fourteen feet long!—who ruled in Galloway. Gauvain's antecedent may thus, like Arthur, be a personage of the Old North, and in *Perceval* he becomes the lord of the castle of the Rock of Champguin in Galloway. Indeed the form *Walwen* found in William of Malmesbury appears to be related to *Walweitha* 'Galloway'. Gauvain corresponds to the hero of Welsh lore Gwalchmei, also sister's son of Arthur. His mother according to *Culhwch and Olwen* is Gwyar. Pierre Gallais found that the name Gauvain, alien to the body of saints' names from which Christian names were traditionally chosen, began to be used around the beginning of the twelfth century in Poitou and Anjou (Gallais 1967: 75–79). Gallais believed that stories about Gauvain were circulating as early as 1085 both in Great Britain and in Brittany (Gallais 1967: 48–49; see also Busby 1980: 46). Although Gauvain is not the principal hero of any of Chrétien's romances, he figures large in all of them as a paragon of chivalry and a knight whose attraction to women is reciprocated. In *Perceval,* the series of his adventures is the topic of a section of more than four thousand lines. Gauvain is represented in the famous Arthurian scene on the archivolt of the porta della Pescheria in the cathedral of Modena under the name Galvaginus, which like *Gauvain* derives from an Old Breton form *Walcmoei* influenced by analogy with other personal names ending in *-ain, -ein,* and *-en* such as *Yvain* (see Bromwich 1978: 369–75). The Breton form of the etymon indicates that Chrétien got the character Gauvain from Breton lore.

Chrétien calls Gauvain's horse *le Guingalet* (*Erec* 3951, *Perceval* 6209, 7136), derived from the Welsh, or equivalent Breton, epithet *y kein caled* 'the fair hardy' or 'the hard backed'. This is the name of Gwalchmei's horse in the Welsh triads (Bromwich 1978: 270–71, 1991: 280; see also Bromwich 1997: 113–14).

The figures most obviously coming from Breton lore, however, are Erec and Enide. Erec is the French form of the Breton Guerec, a name borne by several rulers of the ancient Breton kingdom of Vannes, including its sixth-century founder. The kingdom was called *Bro Weroc(h),* later *Bro Werec* and, in French orthography, *Broerec,* 'land of Waroch', displacing an early name, *Bro Wened,* French orthography *Broenid,* 'land of the Veneti' (Bromwich 1961: 164–65, 1978: 347–48, 1991: 279, 284). Waroch II (r. 577–594) was the historical king under whom Vannes became Breton in 579. Waroch also invaded the region of Nantes and plundered its vineyards (Guadet and Taranne, book 9, ch. 18; Chédeville and Guillotel 1984: 62–64, 72, 159, 175). Gregory of Tours recounts these and other battles in his *History of the Franks* (Guadet and Taranne, book 5, ch. 26, and book 10, ch. 9). Neither Geoffrey nor Wace mentions Erec or his father, King Lac.

The knight Yvain, son of Urien, who is first mentioned in *Erec,* line 1702, is based on the historical Owein, son of Urien. Urien Rheged ruled the northern British kingdom of Rheged in the late sixth century (see Bromwich 1978: 516–20). Both Owein and Urien fought the English and were celebrated by the bard Taliesin. Owein is in the Welsh triads one of the three fair princes of the Island of Britain (Bromwich 1978: 7), and his mother is said to be Modron (Bromwich 1978: 185), the Great Mother goddess. A tale survives in a sixteenth-century manuscript that tells of a ford where dogs used to bark without anyone daring to find out what they were barking at. Urien went to the ford, found a woman washing, and made love to her. She then informed him that she was the daughter of the king of Annwfn, the Other-world, and had been fated to wait there until she should conceive a son by a Christian. Returning at the end of a year, Urien received from her Owein and his sister Morfudd (Bromwich 1978: 459). The motif of the hero meeting a goddess bathing at a ford is found elsewhere in Celtic lore (see Mac Cana 1983: 66, 86). Yvain passes into French along with his patronymic, an unusual phenomenon. The form *Ivain* is also found in the manuscripts of Chrétien's *Yvain*. The Middle Breton form of the name is *Ivan,* the Old Breton *Ewen* or *Euuen* (Bromwich 1978: 480). The name Ivanus occurs in a Breton charter of 1083 (Morice 1968, 1: cols. 457, 469).

The form of the name Perceval, first attested in Chrétien's *Erec,* line 1522, as *Percevaux li Galois,* is certainly influenced by popular etymology: *percer* 'to pierce' and *val* 'valley' (compare the name of another hero of romance, Perceforest). A corresponding figure in Celtic lore, Peredur, may be at the root of the name Perceval. In *Peredur,* the hero is called Peredur ap Efrawc, and he is also found under that name in the *Dream of Rhonabwy* and in *Gereint* (Bromwich 1978: 491). Peredur plays a role in Geoffrey of Monmouth's *Life of Merlin* (Clarke 1973: ll. 26, 31, 68), where Merlin is his ally, and there he is associated not with Wales but with the north of Britain. Another Peredur, son of Morvidus, appears as a king first of Northumbria and Scotland, then of all of Britain, in Geoffrey's *History* (Wright 1985: 33–34).

In *Erec,* Ydier, son of Nut, is the hero's adversary in the Test of the Sparrow-Hawk; he names himself in line 1046 and is sent in defeat to Arthur's court, into which he is integrated. He later attends Erec's coronation at Nantes. Nut is the Romano-British god Nodons or Nodens (W. *Nydd, Llydd;* Ir. *Nuadu Argatlám* 'of the Silver Arm'), a sea god who needs the help of Lug (W. *Lleu Llaw Gyffes,* Lleu 'Skillful-hand', Ir. *Lugh Samildánach* 'Skilled in many arts together') to rule because he is blemished by the loss of his arm. At Lydney Park in Gloucestershire a temple was dedicated to Nodons in which he was depicted with tridents and fish. King Nuz is mentioned in Robert Biket's *Lai du cor,* which may predate *Erec.* Ydier, son of Nut, corresponds to the Hiderus filius Nucii mentioned once in the *History of the Kings of Britain* and the Edern fab Nud of *Culhwch and Olwen.* The figure Isdernus in the Arthurian scene depicted on the cathedral of Modena, from before Chrétien's time, is undoubtedly this same character. Ydier is also the hero of the early thirteenth-century *Roman d'Yder* (Adams 1983), in which he is the son of Nuc. It is likely that Chrétien got Ydier li fiz Nut from Breton tradition rather than through Geoffrey. A charter from the year 1128 preserved in the cartulary of the monastery of Quimperlé in Brittany mentions a certain Yder, son of Nud (*Hedern filius Nud,* Maître and de Bertou 1896: 171–72), a name that reflects Breton awareness of the personage whom Chrétien calls Ydier, son of Nut.

The two catalogues in *Erec,* one consisting of those present at Arthur's court when Enide arrives there and the other of those invited to the wedding of Erec and Enide, serve as an index to the Celtic heroes and avatars available to Chrétien early in his career. The first of these catalogues contains the names of knights who will figure as characters in his later romances as well—Gauvain, Lancelot, Yvain, son of Urien, Perceval, Gornemant, Tristan, Ydier, Sagremor—but also those of a number of figures who are attested in Celtic lore but who do not turn up again in Chrétien or who are not associated with particular narrative motifs. Not all the names mentioned are attested outside of Chrétien. The forms in question sometimes differ from manuscript to manuscript, as scribes were called upon to copy names of characters with whom they were unfamiliar. In addition, in these passages some manuscripts contain lines that are absent from other manuscripts.

Gifflez li filz Do is mentioned twice in *Erec* as a knight of Arthur's entourage (1725, 2226) but is not present in the *History of the Kings of Britain* or in the *Roman de Brut.* He is Gilfaethwy fab Don, an important character in *Math, Son of Mathonwy,* one of the Four Branches of the *Mabinogi,* all tales with mythological underpinnings (Jones and Jones 1974: 55–75; see also Bartrum 1966: 90). Gifflez, son of Do, Ydier, son of Nut, and Yvain, son of Urien, are among the rare father-and-son pairs—in the case of Gifflez, mother and son—in Welsh (or perhaps Breton) lore to survive intact in the passage into French Arthurian literature (Bromwich 1983: 43, 1991: 278). Don in Welsh tradition is the counterpart of the goddess Danu, mother of the gods in Irish; the River Danube appears to take its name from her (but see Lambert 1997: 37).

Karadoc Briesbraz, a knight of Arthur's court in *Erec,* line 1715, is Caradawc Breichfras, whose epithet means 'strong arm' in Welsh (literally *breich* 'arm' and *fras,* a lenited form of 'strong') but was understood as *brie(f)s bras* 'short arm' in French by popular etymology. This reconstrual of the epithet motivated a story to explain how Karadoc's arm came to be shortened (told in the First Continuation of the *Perceval,* Roach 1949–1983, 1: ll. 6221–8004). Karadoc was associated with Vannes (Bromwich 1978: 299–300) and probably came into Chrétien through the intermediary Breton form Karadués Briebras (Bromwich 1983: 43, citing Piette 1965: 187; Bromwich 1991: 293, n. 28). In Robert Biket's *Lai du cor,* Garaduc is the hero, but he does not bear an epithet. Garaduc probably reflects a Welsh lenited form.

The name of Belin, a guest at the wedding of Erec and Enide, corresponds to that of one of the greatest kings of Britain according to Geoffrey and Wace, Belinus, said to have attacked Rome itself. Chrétien, however, makes Belin the dwarf king of the Antipodes (*Erec* 1989–2000). Belin's brother in *Erec* is the giant Brien (1994–96), whose onomastic counterpart in the *History of the Kings of Britain* is Belinus's brother Brennius, in Wace Brenne.[6] But Chrétien here depends on a source other than Geoffrey or Wace, neither of which makes Belinus a dwarf or Brennius a giant. Furthermore, in Wace the form of the giant's name is Brenne rather than Brien. Neither author associates Beli with the Antipodes or represents him as a contemporary of Arthur. In Welsh tradition, Brennius is Bran the Blessed, who is indeed a giant in *Branwen, Daughter of Llyr,* the second branch of the *Mabinogi,* so once again it appears that Chrétien is drawing on a source other than Geoffrey or Wace, one closer than either of them to Brythonic myth. Bran also appears in Irish tradition as the hero of a saga, the *Voyage of Bran.* Bran, son of Llyr, that is, 'Sea', is a prime candidate for the Celtic antecedent to the Fisher King, who is said in *Perceval* to have been wounded between the thighs, because Bran is said in *Branwen* to have been wounded in the foot by a poisoned spear and is referred to there as Morddwyd Tyllion 'the thigh with holes' (Derick Thomson 1976: 37; Jones and Jones 1974: 37). Moreover, Robert de Boron calls the Fisher King Bron.

Graislemier de Fine Posterne and his brother Guilemer, said to be lord of the Isle of Avalon and lover of Morgan the Fay (*Erec* 1948–54), correspond to historical figures associated with two kingdoms in Brittany, respectively Grallon Mor, sixth-century founder of Cornouailles, and Guiamar or Guigemar, the name of several rulers of Léon in the eleventh and twelfth centuries (Bromwich 1961: 462–63, 1991: 279). In Marie de France's lay *Guigemar,* the eponymous hero is said to be the son of the lord of Léon.

In *Erec,* Chrétien assigns a son to Arthur, Loholt (1728), mentioned by neither Geoffrey nor Wace. In fact, Wace writes that Arthur and Guinevere had no offspring, a detail not mentioned explicitly by Geoffrey (Arnold 1938–40: 9657–58). In Welsh, Llacheu, son of Arthur, is part of the earliest tradition, mentioned in the Welsh Arthurian tale *The Dream of Rhonabwy,* in a poem found in the Black Book of Carmarthen (see Bromwich 1978: 416–18), and in two of the Welsh triads (Bromwich 1978, triads 4 and 91).

The early thirteenth-century French romance *Perlesvaus* tells how Loholt, son of Arthur, died at the hands of Keu and how his head was buried in Avalon, and the Welsh equivalent of *Perlesvaus,* part 2 of *Y Seint Greal,* identifies Loholt with Llacheu (see the note in Nitze et al. 1932–37, 2: 297–99). In the German *Lanzelet,* which gives a form of the legend of Lancelot that is independent of Chrétien's, Ulrich von Zatzikhoven identifies Guinevere (Ginover) as the mother of Loholt (Lôût) (Spiewok 1997: l. 6889; Webster 1951a: 119 and n. 205; see also Busby 1981), but the *Lancelot* of the Vulgate Cycle says his mother was Lisanor of Quimper, to whom, it claims, Arthur was wed before he married Guinevere. The Vulgate Cycle also knows Loholt as Arthur's son, and various sources allude to his death at the hands of Keu. Because Geoffrey of Monmouth and Wace mention neither Llacheu nor Loholt, Loholt must have come to Chrétien from some other source, a Breton source because the form of the name Loholt points to a Breton origin (Bromwich 1978: 418).

Tristan "who never laughed" (*qui onques ne rist*) is also mentioned as a knight of Arthur's court (*Erec* 1709) and was presumably the nephew of Marc in Chrétien's lost romance about King Marc and Ysolt (*Cliges* 5). Tristan's counterpart in Welsh tradition is "Drystan," a name of Pictish origin borne by a British king in southwest Scotland in the early sixth century. A sixth-century inscription at Castle Dore in Cornwall also bears the name *Drustanus.*

Rachel Bromwich has suggested that the prominence of certain figures of Brythonic origin in French romance, coupled with a paucity of tales about them in Welsh, argues for their having been transmitted to Brittany at an early time, perhaps before the twelfth century (Bromwich 1991: 280). Some would have made this passage in written sources, others orally. The fact that the Welsh materials provide only occasional and often isolated confirmation of the Brythonic nature of names in Chrétien leads to the conjecture that other names in the lists of knights at Arthur's court and in attendance at the wedding of Erec and Enide may also be derived from Celtic lore. Not that transmission of Celtic materials to Chrétien and other French romancers was exclusively through Brittany. There was constant travel back and forth between the island of Britain and the continental lands of Brittany, Normandy, and Anjou, and various conduits, in both written and oral forms, were open for Celtic names, story-patterns, motifs, and the remnants of myths to move across the English Channel, as well as from Ireland to the Continent and from Brittany into neighboring French provinces.

Geography: The Arthurian Decor

In *Erec, Yvain, Lancelot,* and *Perceval,* the setting of actions is in places that were occupied by Celtic-speaking peoples in Chrétien's time or were quite close to Celtic-speaking lands. Arthur's court is located at various times in Caradigan (Cardigan [Mary Williams 1937: 219], *Erec*), Roais (*Erec*), possibly Camaalot (reading in four manuscripts of *Lancelot:* see Méla 1994b, variants to 29), Carlion (Caerleon-on-Usk in southwest Wales, *Perceval*), Cardoil (Carlisle, in *Erec, Yvain, Perceval*), Dinasdaron in Wales (*Perceval*), and Chester (*Yvain*). Dinasdaron is an unidentified location in *Perceval,* the name a compound formed with W. *dinas* 'fortress' (see Nitze and Williams 1955: 271–72). The itinerant nature of Arthur's court corresponds to the twelfth-century practice of the king traveling from place to place to take care of the affairs of his kingdom. In *Erec,* a tournament takes place at Edinburgh (Danebroc). In *Perceval,* the action late in the romance takes place in Galloway in southwest Scotland (Galvoie). Yvain's fountain, and thus also Laudine's castle, is in Brocéliande, now the forest of Paimpont in Brittany, although no passage over water is mentioned in the three-day journeys of Calogrenant, Yvain, or Arthur and his companions from Carlisle (Carduel) to Brocéliande. Chrétien either did not realize the geographical difficulties or they did not matter to him in this case or for *Erec,* in which the journey from Wales to Nantes is made on horseback with no mention of crossing the sea (*Erec* 6572–75).

In *Cliges,* by contrast, Arthur's court is at Winchester in England (as would have been fitting, for example, for Chrétien's contemporary Henry II) and the romance presents many other venues: Constantinople, Athens, Regensburg, Cologne, the banks of the Danube, and, in England, Southampton, Dover, Canterbury, London, Windsor, the River Thames, Shoreham, Wallingford, and Oxford. Except for Arthur's journey to Brittany, in which no towns are mentioned, the entire romance takes place outside Celtic-speaking areas of Chrétien's period. When, toward the end of the romance, Cliges calls on Arthur for help, the king assembles his men from Flanders, England, Normandy, Brittany, and France down to the passes of Spain; these lands, with the exception of Flanders, were all under the suzerainty of the Angevin Henry II of England (Bullock-Davies 1981: 30). *Cliges* is thus geographically anomalous among Chrétien's romances. The precision with which Chrétien depicts the geography of southern England and the siege of Windsor in *Cliges*—in contrast with the imprecision of the passages from Wales to Brittany in *Erec* and *Yvain*—may mean that he crossed to Great Britain himself (Bullock-Davies 1981) or that the patron of *Cliges* was in the Plantagenet sphere of influence or that the English toponyms were in his source—or any combination of these three possibilities.

The action of *Lancelot* is divided between Logres, which is Arthur's kingdom, and Gorre. *Logres* has its origin in a Brythonic root, as exemplified by the Welsh *Lloegr* 'England,' which Eric Hamp (1982) derives from an etymon signifying 'having a nearby border, being from near the border'. Geoffrey of Monmouth uses the Latinized form *Logria.* The kingdom of Bademagu is called Gorre, a form close to Old French *voirre* 'glass'. Chrétien himself calls Maheloas "lord of the Isle of Glass" (*li sires de l'Île de Voirre, Erec* 1943). The likely identification of Gorre is Glastonbury, referred to in Welsh as *Ynys Wydrin,* 'the Isle of Glass'. Geoffrey of Monmouth's Isle of Avalon was identified as Glastonbury, not by Geoffrey himself but by others before the end of the twelfth century (Lloyd-Morgan 1991). The most striking occurrence in this connection was the "discovery" in 1190 or 1191 of the tomb of Arthur and Guinevere, recounted in Gerald of Wales's *Education of the Prince* (*De principis instructione*) and *Mirror of the Church* (*Speculum ecclesiae*), among other texts. Gerald reports that Arthur's exhumed skull bore the traces of more than ten wounds. The story of this alleged finding, which may have been inspired by the desire of the Plantagenet dynasty to put an end to the belief in Arthur's eventual return and may be based on an Irish analogue (Carey 1999), was told too late to have influenced Chrétien.

As Jean Frappier remarked (1969b: 89), Chrétien's geography is, with the exception of *Cliges,* poetic rather than realistic.

In the course of their adventures, and sometimes as the most important adventure, Chrétien's knights enter a realm resembling the Celtic Otherworld and accomplish great deeds there. One of these locations is Brandigan in *Erec,* a castle situated on an island, from which, it is said, no one ever returns (*Erec* 5428–29). The first element of Brandigan is the name of the mythological figure Bran. The second element of the place-name is based on analogy with toponyms such as Caradigan (Newstead 1939: 109). The Joy of the Court just outside the fortifications of the castle of Brandigan is enclosed by a wall of air within which flowers blossom, herbs grow, and trees bear fruit throughout the year that can be eaten but not taken out of the enclosure. The qualities and attributes of the Otherworld castle are also found in various ways in Lalut, where Erec meets Enide, in the castle of Laudine and the castle of Pesme Avanture in *Yvain,* in Gorre "from which none return" in *Lancelot,* and in the Grail castle, Escavalon, and the castle of the Rock of Champguin, whose lord is never to leave it, in *Perceval.*

PLOTS AND MOTIFS

The milieu in which Chrétien lived was one in which folkloric motifs circulated widely and relatively few people could read, perhaps even fewer write (Clanchy 1993: 12, 15). Elements of stories deriving from various sources were available to him, and he used many of them in his works. But were these plot elements transmitted along with the names that come from Celtic antecedents? Rachel Bromwich has invoked in this context the example of the beheading game in which a challenger allows an opponent to behead him after securing the opponent's promise to submit to the same ordeal at some future time. This motif is familiar to readers of *Sir Gawain and the Green Knight,* but it is also present in stories in which Cúchulainn, Caradoc, or Lancelot play the opponent's role (Bromwich 1961: 439). In this and other instances, such as narratives of the hero's youthful exploits, motifs migrate from character to character, or perhaps one should say names migrate from motif to motif (see Bromwich 1983: 42). In a few cases, however, motif and name travel together, providing evidence of their provenance.

A motif universally associated with Arthur in both medieval and post-medieval versions of his legend is the Round Table, first mentioned by Wace:

> For the noble barons that [Arthur] had,
> Each of whom thought he was better—
> Each considered himself the best
> And no one knew who was the worst—
> Arthur made the Round Table
> About which the Bretons tell many a tale.
> There the vassals were seated,
> All first and all equal.
> [Por les nobles barons qu'il ot,
> Don chascuns miaudre estre cuidot,
> Chascuns se tenoit au meillor,
> Ne nus ne savoit le peior,
> Fist Artus la Reonde Table,
> Dont Breton dïent mainte fable.
> Iluec seoient li vasal,   (Arnold and Pelan 1962: ll. 1207–13;
> Tuit chevelmant et tuit igal.]   Baumgartner and Short 1993: ll. 1019–26)

This innovation must be understood in the context of medieval court life, in which a person's place at the table was a closely observed reflection of status and dignity and not infrequently gave rise to quarrels. Chrétien evokes the Round Table in *Erec* (83, 1685) and *Perceval* (8125), as if it needed no explanation except that it drew together the most accomplished of knights. He could have learned of it from Wace, but a more likely scenario is that he derived it from the oral tradition of stories that Wace mentions as his own source. Surprisingly, the Round Table passes unmentioned in *Cliges, Yvain,* and *Lancelot,* a state of affairs that calls into question, at least for Chrétien, Erich Köhler's interpretation of the table as a sign of the limits of royal power (Köhler 1974: 23).

Erec

The form of the names Erec and Enide depend on their having arisen in connection with a sovereignty myth. Rachel Bromwich (1961: 164–65, 1978: 347–48, 1991: 279, 284) has proposed that someone unfamiliar with the rules of lenition (a type of mutation of initial consonants occurring in Welsh and Breton) construed Bro Wened, meaning 'land of the Veneti', a Gaulish tribe, as "land of Ened," with "Ened" understood as the name of a sovereignty goddess (see above). The theme of the marriage between a king and a woman representing the sovereignty of the land is found in early Irish tales in which the sovereignty of Ireland is conferred upon a man: Niall in the "Adventure of the Sons of Eochaid Mugmedon" and Lugaid in the episode that explains how this hero acquired his epithet, Laigde, which means 'of the fawn'. In these tales, a hunt—for a boar in the first instance, a fawn in the second—leads the hero to an old woman who demands that he make love to her. When the hero consents, she turns into a beautiful young woman and reveals to him that she is the sovereignty of the land, the goddess Eriu, and that he will be its ruler. Both of these are myths of origin, the first for the Ui Neill, the ruling dynasty of Ireland for a period of five centuries, the second for the Erainn people of the south of Ireland. In the case of the Ui Neill origin myth, the story is told by the chief poet of Maelsechlainn II, the last high king of Ireland in Niall's dynasty, who had a political interest in putting forward the story of how his line first became established in the kingship. In the tale that lies behind *Erec,* the aspiring king, here the founder of the kingdom of Vannes, would have been understood as deriving kingship from marrying the sovereignty goddess. The couple Erec (< Werec < Waroch) and Enide (< Ened < Wened) would have thus been constituted.

In *Erec,* the Hunt for the White Stag—white is the color of enchanted animals in Celtic folklore—precedes Enid's arrival at Arthur's court, at which point she receives from the king the kiss that goes to the fairest. Erec's command that Enide come to Arthur's court dressed in her tattered robe may be a remnant of her original role as an ugly creature to be transformed by a kiss into a beautiful young woman. It may be that, in an earlier stage of the tale, the white stag was sent as a lure to bring the hero into the Otherworld, where he would encounter and win a fairy, counterpart of Enide. Another possible remnant is the postponement of Enide's naming until the marriage ceremony, some sixteen hundred lines after her first appearance in the romance. Two lays that are analogues of the sovereignty tale, the anonymous *Graelant* and Marie de France's *Lanval,* contain the motif of prohibition against the hero revealing a fairy figure's name. Enide is represented in Chrétien's romance as a woman who is not merely of high lineage but, in the words of the count of Limors, so endowed with beauty and *franchise* that she is worthy of a kingdom or an empire, a woman that he could only better himself by marrying (*Erec* 4751–55), and thus a sovereignty figure.

The Test of the Sparrow-Hawk has a curious counterpart in a tale that Andreas the Chaplain, who moved in the courtly milieu of Champagne (see above), incorporated into his *Art of Courtly Love* (ed. Parry 1964, ch. 8). A British knight traveling to the court of King Arthur meets a beautiful young woman in the forest who informs him that he can achieve the object of his journey only with her help. She already knows that his quest is to seek a hawk that is standing on a golden perch in Arthur's court; he will first have to defeat two knights to obtain the hawk's gauntlet; and once in the court he will have to defeat another knight, proving thereby that he loves a lady more beautiful than any in Arthur's entourage. This feat will enable him to win his lady's love. The knight accepts the beautiful woman's assistance and defeats an opponent who is defending a golden bridge and who has been shaking the bridge so violently that for some time it is hidden under water. The knight eventually achieves his goal, winning the final duel and taking the hawk from its perch. Attached to the post on which the bird is located is a piece of parchment inscribed with thirty-one rules of love. Andreas appears to be combining elements of the Hunt for the White Stag, after which the successful hunter kisses the most beautiful woman at court, and the Test of the Sparrow-Hawk, both of which are carried out without the help of any "beautiful woman met on the road," obviously a fairy. The submerged golden bridge in Andreas's story recalls the Underwater Bridge of *Lancelot,* and indeed when Chrétien himself refers in that romance to the Underwater Bridge and the Sword Bridge, he suggests the existence of other tales about them: "But there are between the two (bridges) / Adventures about which I remain silent" (*Mais il a assez antre deus / Avantures don je me tes,* Méla 1992: ll. 666–67). What is unclear is whether Andreas got these story elements from Chrétien, whose *Lancelot* was composed either in the period 1177–1181, according to Fourrier, or in 1186–89, according to Luttrell, or whether both Chrétien and Andreas were drawing on analogous sources. Andreas is thought, according to Parry (1964), to have finished his work sometime in the period 1184–1186.

Other analogues to the Test of the Sparrow-Hawk are found in later works: Renaut de Bâgé's *Le Bel Inconnu,* Raoul de Houdenc's *Méraugis de Portlesguez,* and *Durmart le Gallois.* Paule le Rider (1998) believes that Chrétien may have been inspired by the court of Le Puy, held annually at the Feast of the Assumption and known only by indirect testimony, at which prizes for poetry were distributed. There apparently a sparrow-hawk was placed on a perch and the person who felt himself rich enough and generous enough to furnish the costs of the court that year would take the hawk onto his fist. Whereas the Hunt for the White Stag has obvious Celtic overtones, the Test of the Sparrow-Hawk through which Erec both punishes Ydier for his insolence and proves Enide's surpassing beauty may well have occurred to Chrétien through cultural currents flowing from the southeast rather than the northwest.

A curious aspect in *Erec* is the association of Enide with horses. Her first activity in the romance is to take care of Erec's horse when he arrives at her father's house in Lalut. When she leaves with Erec for Arthur's court, her cousin, hearing that Erec wants her to make the trip dressed in tattered clothing, gives her a sumptuous gift of three palfreys, one chestnut, one mottled, and one dappled. The dappled horse is described at some length, and Enide rides off on it (*Erec* 1381–1418). As Erec achieves successive victories over groups of three and five hostile knights, he gives their war horses to her to lead. Later, when Erec orders her to ride with him dressed in her best clothing, she mounts the same dappled horse (2619), which contributes to her attraction as prey for the robber knights. When the reconciliation between husband and wife finally comes, it takes place while they are both riding a single horse (4898–4902). Finally, Guivret, the dwarf king of the Irish, presents Enide with a horse that has the appearance of an Otherworld animal, no less valuable than the dappled horse that she had to leave behind when she and Erec fled Limors. A stripe "greener than a grape leaf" runs down the center of the new gift horse's head, separating the two sides, which are white and black. The horse is accoutered sumptuously in purple cloth, gold, and emeralds, and on its ivory saddlebows are scenes from the

Roman d'Enéas, said to have been carved over a seven-year period by a Breton artisan (5308–51).

Horses are an attribute of Rhiannon (< *Rigantona* 'Great Queen'), who is a manifestation of the goddess Epona 'Great Horse' (Ross 1967: 227, 267), the first element of whose name is cognate with Greek *hippos* 'horse'. One of Epona's epithets was *regina* 'queen' (Ford 1981–82: 118–19). In *Pwyll, Prince of Dyfed,* the first branch of the *Mabinogi* (translated in Jones and Jones 1974: 3–24 and Ford 1977: 35–56), Pwyll sees Rhiannon riding a pale horse on three consecutive days, but on each he is unable to catch up with her even though she appears not to be riding at a great pace while he rides the swiftest horse he can find in her pursuit. Eventually they come together. One night she bears him a son, but the boy is missing before morning. Rhiannon is punished for what is mistakenly thought to be infanticide by being required to tell her story at a mounting-block for seven years and to offer to bear visitors on her back to Pwyll's court. The son appears when another lord, Teyrnon (< *Tigernonos* 'Great Lord'), is protecting a new-born colt from a monstrous claw. Recognizing the boy's resemblance to Pwyll, Teyrnon restores him to his father and mother. Upon hearing that her son has been recovered, Rhiannon declares that her anxiety (W. *pryder*) will be lifted from her, so the boy, whom Teyrnon had called Gwri Golden-hair, is renamed Pryderi (see R. L. Thomson 1957: note to l. 616). Pwyll dies and Pryderi comes to rule over Dyfed. Rhiannon's magic horse-riding and the association of her son with the colt are among the features that reveal her identity as a reflex of Epona, herself in turn a reflex of Matrona, the 'Great Mother' who in Celtic tradition loses her son, Mabon, 'Great Son,' until he can be restored to her.

In the third branch of the *Mabinogi, Manawydan, son of Llyr,* Pryderi gives his mother Rhiannon in marriage to Manawydan (= Ir. *Manannán mac Lir,* god of the sea) so that the two can rule over Dyfed. Pryderi, his wife, Cigfa, Rhiannon, and Manawydan travel together to Hereford in Lloegr, where they take up saddlery. Their craftsmanship is so good that the other saddlers of Hereford conspire to kill Manawydan and Pryderi. So they move to another town and yet another, taking up shield-making, then shoemaking with horse leather, but with the same socially disastrous results. They return from Lloegr to Dyfed, where an enchantment falls upon them. Led by a white boar to a fortress that rises out of nowhere, Pryderi approaches a fountain with a marble slab upon which is a golden bowl fastened to chains that rise beyond sight into the air. When he puts his hands on the bowl, they stick to it, his feet stick fast to the slab, and he cannot speak. The same happens to Rhiannon when she goes in search of him. Both are spirited away by a magician named Llwyd and punished for offenses committed against him. Rhiannon's punishment is to wear ass-collars on her neck. Both are in the end delivered.

Enide's association with horses is not what one would expect of a noble woman living in the society that Chrétien is describing. She is given four horses as gifts and takes care of nine more in the course of the romance. One of the horses is marked with an unnatural green stripe, and unnatural coloring is typical of enchanted or Otherworld animals in Celtic lore (Ross 1967: 327), whose role is frequently to lead characters into an Otherworld setting. That Enide, Erec, and Guivret go to Brandigan immediately after she receives the horse is, then, no coincidence. Both her dappled horse and the one with the tricolored head are described as magnificent animals. Enide's consistent association with horses resembles that of Rhiannon. In addition, both women are punished in ways involving horses, Rhiannon wearing horse-collars and forced to carry guests like a horse, Enide forced to ride a horse while dressed in her best clothing as a temptation to potential robbers. Finally, the gift that Guivret gives Enide, a lavishly worked and decorated saddle, recalls the skill of saddlery practiced by the two male characters of *Manawydan*. The Breton tale or tales that informed Chrétien about Erec and Enide incorporated a foundation myth in which an aspiring king married a woman representing sovereignty, and that woman was, like Rhiannon, associated with horses and with leathercraft.[7]

Bromwich's theory also accords with the placing of Erec's coronation at Nantes in southeast Brittany, as King Waroch's activity included incursions into southern Brittany. In Chapter 1, the possibility was discussed that the composition of *Erec,* with its coronation scene held at Nantes for no reason necessitated by the plot (and in fact it is held at Carnant in Hartmann von Aue's *Erec;* see Resler 1987), had some relation to King Henry II's court held at Nantes at Christmas 1169 at which Henry had the nobles and prelates of Brittany pay homage to his son Geoffrey. The twelve-year-old boy had been engaged in 1166 to marry Constance, heir to Count Conon IV of Brittany. This union, which was not consummated until 1181, consolidated the power of the Plantagenets in Brittany. As the legitimate heir to Brittany, Constance represented the sovereignty of Brittany that Henry sought through his son. *Erec,* with its adumbrations of succession in the sovereignty of Brittany, would have made an appropriate offering to the young couple.

Mabon, the first component of the name of Mabonagrain, Erec's opponent in the Joy of the Court episode, corresponds to the name of the "Great Son" of the "Great Mother" Modron, whose name in Gaulish, Matrona, is the etymon of the river-name "Marne." Mabon is mentioned neither by Geoffrey nor by Wace but is a well-known figure of Celtic mythology whom the Gauls called Maponos and the Romans associated with Apollo (Mac Cana 1983: 31). Mabon is also called in Welsh texts "Gwair" and "Pryderi." In the pre-twelfth-century poem "The Spoils of the Otherworld" ("Preiddeu Annwn"), the first stanza includes the following lines:

> Gwair's prison in Caer Siddi was in order
> Throughout the course of the story concerning Pwyll and Pryderi.
> No-one before him went into it—
> Into the heavy grey chain which was restraining the loyal youth.
> And on account of the spoils of Annwfn he was singing bitterly.
>   (Haycock 1983–84: 58)

Caer Siddi is the "fairies' fortress." In the eleventh-century *Culhwch and Olwen,* Mabon is a captive who was taken away from his mother when he was three nights old and who is sought by Arthur and his men. When Cei and the interpreter Gwrhyr come upon his prison, they hear him lamenting: "Mabon son of Modron is here in prison; and none was ever so cruelly imprisoned in a prison house as I" (Jones and Jones 1974: 126). In the Welsh triads, Mabon is characterized by his quality as a prisoner:

> Three Exalted Prisoners of the Island of Britain:
> Llyr Half-Speech, who was imprisoned by Euroswydd,
> and the second, Mabon son of Modron,
> and third, Gwair son of Geirioedd.   (Bromwich 1978: triad 52)

Similarly, Mabonagrain in the Joy of the Court scene of *Erec* is a prisoner of his lady, albeit initially a willing one. It is important to note that although Mabonagrain has killed previous challengers of the custom of the Joy of the Court, he does not lose his own life in losing to the challenger Erec, which is in keeping with his immortality in the myth from which Chrétien derived him.

The second component of the name Mabonagrain is an enigma. Some link it to the name of Evrain, Mabonagrain's uncle and the keeper of the castle of Brandigan, where Erec and Enide are treated to a feast of all that they desire (*Erec* 5576–77). Brandigan serves as entrance to the custom of the Joy of the Court. (On Brandigan, see Newstead 1939: 106–20.) Intriguingly, Mabon and Evrain also appear in the early thirteenth-century

Arthurian romance *Le Bel Inconnu* of Renaut de Bâgé (fl. 1165–1230), where Mabon is the dominant brother of Evrain and both are magicians (Frescoe 1992: ll. 3347, 3368). *Le Bel Inconnu* is strongly influenced by *Erec* (see, for example, Tyssens 1970; Frescoe 1992: xv–xviii; Ferlampin-Acher 1996: xxiii), and it contains elements analogous to several in Chrétien's work, including the Test of the Sparrow-Hawk, the combat against two giants, and the motif of severed heads impaled on poles. The element *-agrain* does seem to be a development from "Evrain," which in turn appears to be connected with the mythological figure Bran, the initial sound of whose name would be lenited to *v-*, but the precise mechanism of this agglutination of names, if indeed that is what it is, is not clear. On the mythic level, Mabonagrain appears to be a complement to Evrain. The probability of Bran's presence is reinforced by the role of Guivret, the dwarf king, in leading Erec to Brandigan, and thus to Evrain and Mabonagrain, for there is a traditional association between a dwarf king and his giant brother (Harward 1958: 51–61). Mabonagrain is indeed a giant:

> . . . He was quite marvelously tall,
> And if he had not been annoyingly tall,
> There would not have been a more handsome man
>   than he under heaven.
> [. . . Mout par ert granz a merveille,
> Et s'il ne fust granz a ennui,
> Soz ciel n'eüst plus bel de lui.]   (*Erec* 5892–94)

Chrétien himself has Belin, dwarf king of the Antipodes, and his giant brother Brïen, corresponding to Beli and Bran, attend the wedding of Erec and Enide (*Erec* 1989–2000). In *Branwen,* Bran is so gigantic that no house can contain him; he can carry an army on his back, and to get from Britain to Ireland he simply wades across the Irish Sea. That Bran should play a role in a tale of Breton origin is not surprising, as the personal name Bran occurs thirteen times in the period 859–869 in the cartulary of the abbey of Redon, diocese of Vannes (Pütz 1892: 172).

The name "Joy of the Court" (*Joie de la Cort*) has occasioned much comment. Chrétien has Mabonagrain explain that there will be great joy at his liberation from the obligation to defend the custom (*Erec* 6110–16). But why is it the joy "of the court"? When Erec is successful at the contest, he sounds a horn, producing joy among the populace. Noting Bran's association with a horn in Celtic myth, Helaine Newstead suggested that "Joie de la Cort" is a misunderstanding of *Joie del Cor* 'Joy of the Horn' (Newstead 1939: 115).

Rachel Bromwich has taken this line of reasoning one step further to conjecture an original *Jeu del Cor* 'Game of the Horn' (reported in Foster 1959: 196). After Erec's victory and his horn-blast Chrétien says of him, curiously: "Erec was well fed with joy / and well served to his desire" (*Bien fu de joie Erec peüz / Et bien serviz a son creante,* 6182–83). This is perhaps a reminiscence of one of Bran's attributes, a horn of plenty that feeds guests to their entire satisfaction (Newstead 1939: 111).

Ydier, Erec's first opponent in the romance, is the son of Nut, that is to say Nuadu. Mabonagrain, his last opponent, is the son of Modron, or Matrona. Erec's trajectory toward kingship begins and ends, then, with two mythologically charged victories that show him capable of reaching the highest levels of knightly capability. Chrétien gives no sign of realizing the status of these opponents, but in the distant formation of the tales about Erec of which Chrétien speaks depreciatingly, these mythic considerations probably played a significant role.

The historical Waroch's father was Macliav, count of the territory of Vannes. Macliav made a pact with a neighboring count, Bodic, that should either die the survivor would defend the other's son. When Bodic died, leaving his son Theodoric to succeed him, Macliav not only failed to protect him but took possession of his land. Theodoric wrested back from Macliav and his son Jacob the part of their territory that had been Bodic's. Macliav's other son, Waroch, held the balance of the land. (See Koch 1987: 43–44; Guadet and Taranne 1836, 1: 301–2; Thorpe 1974: 273–74.) The historical prototype of Erec, then, was part of a dynasty that had usurped power by betrayal.

What is behind *Erec* on the mythic level? Chrétien calls the initial section of the romance "the first verse," *li premerains vers* (*Erec* 1840), ending with the reception of Erec and Enide at Arthur's court. The visit to the castle of Brandigan and the Joy of the Court make up a section of equivalent length toward the end of the romance, before the final visit to Arthur's court and the coronation scene. Each of these sections is dominated by a mythic theme: the struggle with Ydier, the struggle with Mabonagrain, and the acquisition of sovereignty. The myth is the tale of the heir to a kingdom, Erec, who becomes king only after mating with an Otherworld woman, Enide. She represents sovereignty and he acquires her by defeating an Otherworld king, Ydier, son of Nuadu. Because she is unhappy with the legitimacy of his lineage's claim to the kingship (see the story of Macliav and Bodic, above), he punishes her but at the same time undertakes a testing journey. In the middle of this journey he meets and defeats a second

Otherworld sovereign, Guivret of Penuris,[8] who has all the attributes of a fairy king, including dwarf stature, great wealth and power, great physical strength, generosity, and high-minded conduct (Harward 1958: 62–73). Guivret assists him in recovering the approbation of the sovereignty figure. At the end of his journey, he defeats yet again an Otherworld king, Mabon. Having proved himself to the sovereignty figure through victories over mortal and immortal alike, he is crowned as king of the land of mortals. This foundation myth would have concerned the kingdom of which Nantes is the principal city, that is to say, Brittany.

Erec incorporates the foundation myth of a hero who moves between two worlds and is victorious in both. Chrétien has placed this mythic material in the courtly Arthurian setting and woven into it the social drama of the conflict of values and the psychological drama of trust between husband and wife.

Cliges

Chrétien's romances are characterized by the wonders that the poet weaves into his narratives. In *Cliges* alone, however, the wonders are not Celtic. Alexandre and Cliges encounter no mysterious "customs," nor are they called upon to face creatures behind which one can easily perceive the presence of a fairy woman or a Celtic god. For this and other reasons, including the evocation of a geographically accurate southern England and reflections of twelfth-century European political situations, Anthime Fourrier (1960) placed *Cliges* in the category of "realistic romances" along with Thomas's *Roman de Tristan,* Gautier d'Arras's *Eracle* and *Ille et Galeron,* the anonymous *Partonopeus de Blois,* and Aimon de Varenne's *Florimont,* in which wonders are absent or play only a subsidiary role. And yet *Cliges* is dependent on another influential tale from the matter of Britain, the story of Tristan, Ysolt, and King Mark.

The magic upon which the plot of *Cliges* depends has its source in ancient Mediterranean traditions. The knowledge that Fenice's governess Thessala has of potions and medicines comes from her native country, Thessaly, whence her name. Thessaly, named for one of the sons of Medea, Thessalos, was well known in antiquity as a land in which the black arts flourished. Chrétien has Thessala boast that she has more knowledge of charms and enchantment than ever had Medea (*Cliges* 2982–85), whom he would have known from Ovid's *Metamorphoses,* book 7.

Thessala concocts two potions. The first makes Alis dream that he has made love to Fenice in reality, thereby protecting her from following in the footsteps of Ysolt, who shared her body with two men (*Cliges* 3104–14). The other casts Fenice into a seemingly lifeless state so that she can be buried, then dug up again by Cliges to escape from the court and live with him in a secluded tower built by his slave, Jehan. The first of these potions is Chrétien's substitution for the sacrifice of Brangien, Ysolt's servant who takes her mistress's place in the marriage bed so as to hide the fact that Ysolt is no longer a virgin. The second potion, however, seems to combine motifs from several sources. One is the apocryphal story of Solomon's wife. The doctors of Salerno who suspect Fenice of feigning death recall this example:

> Then they remembered Solomon
> Whom his wife so hated
> That she betrayed him by acting as if she were dead.
> Perhaps this woman has done the same.
> [Lors lor sovint de Salemon
> Cui sa femme tant enhaï
> Qu'an guise de mort le traï.
> Espoir autel a ceste fait.] (*Cliges* 5796–99)

Elie de Saint-Gille, a chanson de geste, also refers to this legend:

> Solomon took a wife whom I remember often.
> For four days she feigned death in her own palace,
> So that she never moved fist or foot or member;
> Then a vassal had his complete will of her.
> [Salemons si prist feme dont souvent me remenbre.
> Quatre jors se fist morte en son palais meesme,
> Que onques ne crola ne puing ne pié ne menbre;
> Puis en fist uns vasaus toute sa consienche.] (Raynaud 1879: ll. 1793–96)

The version of the legend from which Chrétien derived his knowledge of Solomon's wife is lost. Neither *Elie de Saint-Gille* nor *Cliges* itself, however, mentions that she was buried alive. This aspect of the stratagem may have come from Breton lore. In his *History of the Franks,* Gregory of Tours tells how the Breton Macliav, father of Waroch, was pursued by his brother Chanao, who wanted to kill him. Macliav took refuge with a Breton count, Chonomor, who hid him in a hole in the ground and constructed a barrow on top. This trick allowed Macliav to escape, and he later took over the county of Brittany for himself (Guadet and Taranne 1836: book 4, chapter 4).

The story of Alexandre and Soredamor is modeled on that of Tristan's father, Rivalen, and his mother, Blancheflor, as told in the Tristan tales of the "courtly" tradition that includes the romances of Thomas d'Angleterre and Godfried von Strassburg and the Norse *Tristram's Saga.* Many aspects of *Cliges* spring from Chrétien's desire to write a counter-*Tristan*, or perhaps even a neo-*Tristan* (Frappier 1959: 172): the love between a woman and her husband's nephew, the birth of love between Alexandre and Soredamor during a sea voyage, with its play on the words *la mer* 'the sea' and *l'amer* meaning 'to love' but also 'bitterness', the insistence of the barons that the uncle marry, the role of the governess and the servant, the discovery of the lovers in their retreat, and the extensive discussions of nuances of falling in love.

Lancelot

Chrétien tells his audience in the prologue to *Lancelot* that he has received from Marie de Champagne not just the "matter" (*matiere,* 26) of his romance but also the *san* ("interpretation"), to which he applies his own "thought" (*panser,* 28), "effort" (*paine*), and "intention" (*antancion,* 29). Of what did the matter and the interpretation consist?

Chrétien refers only obliquely to the story of Lancelot's upbringing. Trapped between two closed doors in a castle, Lancelot looks at a ring he is wearing and appeals to the fairy, the Lady of the Lake, who gave it to him when he was a child. The ring then reveals to him that his captivity is not an enchantment (*Lancelot* 2353). He later has recourse to the same ring to learn that two fierce lions that seem to threaten him on the other side of the Sword Bridge are only an illusion (3125–27).

The *Lanzelet* of the Swiss priest Ulrich von Zatzikhoven (translated in Webster 1951a), while it was composed twenty to thirty years after Chrétien's *Lancelot,* is an excellent source for early traditions about Lancelot, as it is based on a book brought from England to the Continent by a certain Hugh of Morville, a hostage for Richard Lion-Heart when he was freed from captivity by Emperor Henry VI in 1194. Forms of Old French words that subsist in *Lanzelet* show that Hugh's book was written in the Anglo-Norman dialect. In Ulrich's romance, Lanzelet is the son of King Pant of Genewis and his wife, Clarine. When Lanzelet was a year old, Pant's vassals rebelled, forcing him to leave his castle with his wife and son. Pant soon died and Clarine fled with the boy, but a sea-fairy came in a mist and abducted him. Ulrich never names the fairy, but she has a son named Mabuz and resembles strongly the goddess Modron. She rules over a land of ten thousand women surrounded by the sea, where flowers bloom all year long and the inhabitants live in perpetual joy. The ladies teach Lanzelet good manners and how to act in the company of women, when to keep silence, and how to sing and play the harp and fiddle. The fairy queen has mermen teach Lanzelet how to use the sword and shield. She refuses to tell him his name, however, out of shame, presumably her shame at having abducted him from his mother.

When Lanzelet is fifteen, the fairy gives him a horse, a surcoat, white armor, and weapons, and he sets off into the world. His first experience is shameful: a dwarf from the castle of Pluris strikes first Lanzelet's horse, then Lanzelet himself. Lanzelet is angry but does not take vengeance because he deems the dwarf a creature of too low a status for such action. He returns to Pluris later in the romance, however. A falconer, Johfrit de Liez, instructs him in horsemanship. He soon overcomes and succeeds the king of Moreiz—which appears to be the forest of Moray in northeastern Scotland—after making love to the king's daughter. One day Lanzelet rides off and approaches the castle of Limors, whose lord, Linier, imprisons him. Linier sets a series of tests for Lanzelet, the last of which is a joust against Linier himself, whom Lanzelet, though wounded, manages to kill. The lord's niece Ade nurses him back to health. Lanzelet's repute reaches Arthur's court where the queen, Ginover, wishes to meet him. Arthur's sister's son Walwein (= Gauvain) consequently journeys to meet Lanzelet, who challenges him to combat, but this sequence is interrupted by the arrival of a page who invites the two knights to a tournament in which the forces of King Lot of Lohenis will oppose those of Gurnemans. Dressed in different-colored arms each day, Lanzelet defeats, among others, Keein (= Keu) and Ywan (Yvain), and jousts to a draw with Erec. At Shatel le Mort, he meets Mabuz, who keeps a hundred knights captive and puts them to death at his whim. Mabuz defeats Lanzelet and strips him of his armor. Sent by Mabuz to fight the powerful Iweret of Dodone, Lanzelet encounters him in the wood of Beforet. He finds him under a linden tree that is always green, beside a spring next to which hangs a bronze cymbal that the challenger is to strike three times when he wishes to fight Iweret. In Beforet are magic plants of every type, as well as animals including lions and elephants. Lanzelet kills Iweret and becomes the lover of his daughter Yblis. A maiden then arrives mounted on a white mule to tell Lanzelet his name and the identity of his father and mother. She also informs him that King Arthur is his uncle through his mother.

The romance now turns to Arthur's court at Kardigan. King Valerin of the Tangled Wood is seeking Queen Ginover, for he claims that she was betrothed to him before she reached marriageable age. Valerin offers a challenge: he will do combat with any champion and relinquish Ginover if he is defeated but carry her off if he wins. Arthur agrees to this proposition. Valerin lives in a castle that shines like the sun, surrounded by a thicket populated by serpents who obey him. Below the castle is mist. Lanzelet leaves Yblis with his father's aunt and rides to Kardigan, where he finds Walwein sitting on the stone of honor, which will not endure a man who is guilty of falseness or malice. Walwein is preparing to fight Valerin, but Lanzelet persuades Arthur's court that he should have the honor of championing Ginover. He defeats Valerin, who promises to cause the queen no more sorrow. Lanzelet sends for Yblis, who stays with Ginover, and he is received as a knight of the Round Table.

Lanzelet now sets off for Pluris to avenge the dwarf's insult. He passes the test of defeating a hundred knights in succession, which allows him to marry the queen of Pluris. She manages to make him stay with her for a year by having forty knights keep him under surveillance. Meanwhile at Arthur's court Yblis is the only woman who passes the test of the ill-fitting mantle as one who harbors no adulterous thoughts. Walwein, Karyet, Tristant, and Erec undertake an expedition to Pluris and Lanzelet is freed. Hearing that Arthur is about to hunt the white stag, they return to Kardigan but find that the hunt is called off because Valerin has abducted Ginover. Valerin has promised Ginover that he will not rape her but will only implore her to love him. Valerin's castle cannot be taken by assault, so Arthur sends for Malduc, the wizard of the Misty Lake, who agrees to help if Erec and Walwen, who had killed Malduc's father and brother, are delivered to him after the adventure. Malduc casts an enchantment that allows Arthur and his men to take the castle; Malduc rides off with Erec and Walwein in tow, and Ginover is returned to Kardigan. With the help of Esealt, the tallest giant who ever lived, Lanzelet, Karyet, and Tristant rescue Walwen and Erec and kill Malduc.

Lanzelet then undertakes to kiss a dragon that speaks with a woman's voice; when he does so, the dragon flies to a stream, washes itself, and turns into the most beautiful of women, Clidra the Fair. She had been transformed from her human state for having deceived the man who loved her. Clidra is installed in Arthur's court and put in charge of etiquette.

Lanzelet now returns to his father's kingdom, Genewis, where an uncle who had been guarding his mother, Clarine, leads the other lords in ceding the throne to Lanzelet, who is then crowned king of Genewis. Messengers arrive from the kingdom of the deceased Iweret, Dodone, asking Lanzelet to come and rule over them. Accompanied by Arthur and his court, Lanzelet goes to Dodone and assumes the crown with Yblis by his side. Clarine joins them in Dodone. Lanzelet and Yblis have a daughter and three sons to whom they leave their kingdoms when, grown old, they die on the same day.

Ulrich's *Lanzelet* is a grab-bag of the stock motifs of Arthurian romance, and my summary has even omitted some episodes. Beside the tale of Lancelot as provided by Hugh of Morville, which was in turn informed by Celtic sources, it owes much to other literary works, including Hartmann von Aue's *Erec,* which is a translation of Chrétien's *Erec.* Nonetheless, it provides valuable clues to Lancelot's legend independent of Chrétien, because it is unlikely that anyone who was familiar with the French poet's *Lancelot* would have written a romance about this hero without presenting or at least alluding to his adultery with Arthur's queen. Indeed, Lanzelet appears to make love to almost every available woman in the German romance *except* Ginover.

From a comparison of the plot elements shared by *Lanzelet* and *Lancelot,* it seems probable that the tradition Chrétien knew was of a Lancelot who had been raised by the fairy queen, the Lady of the Lake, and who had attained the status of a knight of Arthur's court. This Lancelot had participated, along with Gauvain, in the rescue of Guinevere from her abductor, whom he had defeated in single combat, but he had not committed adultery with the queen. Because Marie de Champagne gave Chrétien the material for his romance, he must have received from her the story of the abduction of Guinevere and her rescue by Lancelot, with whom she did not have an adulterous relationship, and it is quite probable that the interpretation Marie provided to him was to make the relationship into an adulterous one.

The abduction of Guinevere, the myth underlying both *Lancelot* and *Lanzelet,* is not recounted by Geoffrey or Wace. Chrétien calls his villain Meleagant, but in Welsh tradition he is Melwas, lord of the Isle of Glass. Chrétien knew both the name and the identity of Melwas from some source, however, as he includes in the guest list at the wedding of Erec and Enide Maheloas, lord of the Isle de Voirre ("Isle of Glass"), a temperate land free of toads and serpents (*Erec* 1941–47). Both Melwas and his father, Bademagu, appear in *Culhwch and Olwen,* where they are also father and son, under the forms *Maelwys* and *Baeddan* (Ford 1977: 126).

Marie de Champagne's source did not invent the story of Guinevere's abduction. This is evident from a number of analogues and references to this legendary event (Webster 1951b, Cross in Cross and Nitze 1930: 20–32). Caradog of Llancarfan tells an early version of the tale in his *Life of Gildas,* which predates Geoffrey's *History of the Kings of Britain:*

> He [Gildas] came to Glastonbury . . . , while king Melvas was reigning in the summer region. . . . Glastonbury, that is, the Glassy City, which took its name from glass, is a city whose name was originally in the British language. And it was besieged by the tyrant Arthur with a numberless multitude on account of Guennuvar his wife, raped and abducted by the above-mentioned evil king, and brought there for the protection afforded by its invulnerable situation because of the fortifications of river, swamp, and growths of reed. The rebellious king [Arthur] had sought the queen through the course of a year, and finally heard where she was dwelling. At that he roused the armies of all Cornwall and Devon; war between the enemies was prepared. When he saw this, the abbot of Glastonbury, with the clergy and Gildas the wise, intervened between the battle lines and peaceably advised his king Melvas to give back the abducted woman. Therefore she was given back who was to be given back, in peace and good will. When these things were done, the two kings gave the abbot a donation of many domains.
>
> [Ingressus est Glastoniam . . . Melvas rege regnante in aestiva regione. . . . Glastonia, id est Urbs Vitrea, quae nomen sumsit a vitro, est urbs nomine primitus in Britannico sermone. Obsessa est itaque ab Arturo tyranno cum innumerabili multitudine propter Guennuvar uxorem suam violatam et raptam a praedicto iniquo rege, et ibi ductam propter refugium inviolati loci propter munitiones arundineti et fluminis ac paludis causa tutelae. Quaesiverat rex rebellis reginam per unius anni circulum, audivit tandem illam remanentem. Illico commovit exercitus totius Cornubiae et Dibneniae; paratum est bellum inter inimicos. Hoc viso abbas Glastoniae comitante clero et Gilda Sapiente intravit medias acies, consuluit Melvas regi suo pacifice, ut redderet raptam. Reddita ergo fuit, quae reddenda fuerat, per pacem et benevolentiam. His peractis duo reges largiti sunt abbati multa territoria.] (Hugh Williams 1990 [1899]: 98–100)

Noteworthy is that Lancelot plays no part in this story, in which only Arthur is mentioned as the one seeking Guinevere's release. Glastonbury, the City of Glass, corresponds to Chrétiens Gorre (= *Voirre* 'Glass'), and Melvas to Meleagant the abductor, who is indeed depicted as evil in the romance. Gorre, like Valerin's castle in *Lanzelet,* is shown to be of particularly difficult access. In neither Chrétien nor Ulrich von Zatzikhoven, however, is the queen raped, nor does the search take a year. No role is given in the romances to the abbot of Glastonbury or to Gildas, who are associated with the tale of Guinevere's abduction only so that the narrator of the saint's life can convey reflected glory on them from their association with what must have been a well-known legendary event.

A more ancient version of the tale is implied in the Welsh dialogue poem "A Conversation Between Arthur and Guinevere," which is extant in two versions and is dated to around 1150 but seems to be based on a much older tradition (see the text, with translation and study, in Mary Williams 1938). In this poem, a stranger arrives at a feast in the court of Melwas of the Isle of Glass at which Guinevere and Cei are present. The queen mocks the stranger for his short stature in favor of the taller Cei. The stranger says to Guinevere that she has seen him before, drinking wine with his companions in Devon. Because in Welsh tradition the location of Arthur's court is in Devon, it is thought that the unnamed stranger is Arthur himself, come to fetch Guinevere back from Melwas's control. The poem in both its versions is obscure and highly allusive, but in the A version Melwas implies that the stranger is impotent. In neither version does Guinevere appear eager to leave the presence of Melwas. Perhaps in the version of the legend reflected in these poems Guinevere was a willing party to her abduction, leaving Arthur for a younger, more vigorous man.

Some form of the abduction of Guinevere was known on the Continent early in the twelfth century, as is witnessed by a scene sculpted in the archivolt of the north portal of the cathedral of Modena in northern Italy. The sculpture appears to have been executed before 1140, long before *Lancelot* was composed and perhaps even before Geoffrey's *History of the Kings of Britain.* At the top of the archivolt is a castle from which a woman looks out. She is flanked by two figures on foot. From either side progress toward the castle a series of mounted warriors. Over the figures, names are given. The woman is "Winlogee," a Breton form of the name Guinevere. The character on her left, as one views the scene, is unnamed and is on foot just outside the fortifications, wielding a pick. The man on her right, within the fortifications and also on foot, is "Mardoc," the Malduc of *Lanzelet.* The mounted figures, starting from the far left, are "Isdernus" (= Yder, Ydier), "Artus de Bretania" (Arthur of Britain), and "Burmaltus" (Durmart?). On the other side, starting from the far right, are "Che" (Keu), "Galvariun" (unidentified), and "Galvaginus" (Gauvain). All six of the mounted figures approaching the castle bear lances and shields, and all but Arthur are armed in hauberks. The attackers are all facing the castle except Arthur, whose face is turned from it. The sole armed knight defending the castle, on the right and placed in symmetry with the man bearing the pick, is "Carrado" (Caradoc). Just below the crenelated rampart of the castle is a stylized depiction of water.

That tales about French legends such as those of Roland and Oliver were presented to the public in northern Italian cities of this period is well known. The form Winlogee is evidence that Breton storytellers had carried the tale of Guinevere's abduction (but see Vàrvaro 1994: 7–11, and Sims-Williams 1998, who does not, however, discuss the forms of names in the archivolt) as far as Modena in the early twelfth century, where it was popular enough to be represented in the extraordinarily incongruous context of an entrance to the cathedral. The names show, however, that the version of Guinevere's rescue that is represented on the archivolt is quite different from Chrétien's. Yder is mentioned in *Lancelot,* but only as a participant in the tournament of Noauz (5802), whereas in the *Folie Tristan* of Bern he is cited as one who suffered pain and unhappiness on account of Guinevere, and in the *Roman d'Yder* (Adams 1983) he falls in love with and marries a woman named Guenloie. The name Guenloie is, like Winlogee, a variation on that of Guinevere, who also appears as a character in the *Roman d'Yder,* which, although it postdates Chrétien, is based on earlier legends about Ydier. Caradoc Briesbraz only appears in *Erec* for a brief mention (1715). "Burmaltus" may well be Durmart: the romance dedicated to his accomplishments, *Durmart le Gallois,* includes a rescue of Guinevere (see Loomis 1959d: 61). The figure who seems to be responsible for the abduction in the archivolt is Mardoc, however, whereas in *Durmart le Gallois* it is Brun de Morois.

In three early versions of the abduction of Guinevere—the "Conversation Between Arthur and Guinevere," *Lancelot,* and the tale reflected in the Modena archivolt—Keu plays a significant, albeit different role. In the *Life of Gildas,* the dialogue poem, and the archivolt, by contrast, Lancelot is not present, and even in *Lanzelet* he only shares the role of liberator with Arthur and other members of his retinue. Although Chrétien presents Maheloas, the lord of the Isle of Glass, as attending the marriage of Erec and Enide (*Erec* 1942–43), in *Lancelot,* the *Life of Gildas,* and the "Conversation" Guinevere is abducted by someone who is outside the court.

An interesting feature that *Lanzelet* and the Modena archivolt have in common is the presence in both of Malduc or Mardoc, a magician figure in *Lanzelet.* One might then expect *Lancelot* to have the same figure, but although Chrétien does list as the eighth in rank of the knights of the Round Table Mauduit the wise (*Mauduiz le sage, Erec* 1695), whose name corresponds to that of Malduc and whose epithet is appropriate to the role, this

Mauduit does not figure in *Lancelot*. The role of the helpful magician is, however, filled by Bademagu, whose name means the "magician of Bath" (see Chapter 2, above) and whose helpful role is unusual in that he is the villain's father. In the Christian context of the *Life of Gildas,* the helpful magician's role is assigned to another wonder-worker, Gildas himself, who intercedes between Arthur and Melvas.

In adding Lancelot to the tale of Guinevere's abduction as the queen's rescuer and lover, quite probably at the behest of Marie de Champagne, Chrétien transformed the legend completely by introducing the problematics of adultery between the lord's wife and his vassal and created a work that has shown itself to be of extraordinary and lasting popularity.

But in addition to its provenance as a variant on the traditional tale of Guinevere's abduction, *Lancelot* is also the story of a savior knight, one who redeems the people of his land from their captivity at the hands of an Otherworld figure, Meleagant. Gorre is a kingdom "from which no outsider ever returns" (*dont nus estranges ne retorne,* 641–42). Should one person from the outside succeed in leaving, however, all the rest could leave freely (2110–15). On his journey into Gorre, Lancelot comes to a church where an old monk shows him a number of tombstones awaiting the bodies of well-known nobles who are still alive, including Arthur and Yvain. The largest, most beautiful, and most recently carved is covered by a stone that seven strong men could not lift and bears an inscription to the effect that in it will lie the man who succeeds in lifting the stone by himself and who will deliver those who are imprisoned in Gorre. Lancelot lifts the tombstone effortlessly: he is thus not just the savior but the destined savior of the prisoners of Gorre. In *Lanzelet,* the hero visits the monastery of the Sorrowful Fief, where, he hears, he will be buried if he is killed by Iweret, but it is not a question in *Lanzelet* of the rescue of prisoners. The land from which no one returns in *Lancelot* is the Otherworld, as many analogous legends and folktales make clear, and for the inhabitants of Logres it is a land of permanent servitude according to the custom (2096). That the Otherworld takes on the same aspects of a land of the dead appears to be a particularly Breton phenomenon (Loomis 1941: 898). As the savior of those imprisoned in Gorre, and despite his decidedly un-Christian moral stance, Lancelot appears to assume certain qualities that figure those of Christ the savior: he suffers wounds in his hands and feet in crossing the Sword Bridge, Bademagu gives him the balm of the Three Maries to assist his recovery (3358), he lifts his own tombstone (see Le Rider 1991: 84–91).

Lancelot's discovery of his destiny from a tombstone reinforces the link with death. The defining moment of the romance, the scene from which Chrétien took his own title "Knight of the Cart" (*Chevalier de la charrete,* 24), sees Lancelot faced with the dilemma of whether to mount the shameful cart or to shun it and risk losing the queen. Chrétien digresses from his narrative to explain that carts in those Arthurian days were like pillories are in his own time, destined for murderers, betrayers, thieves, highway robbers, and those defeated in judicial combats. It was on this account, Chrétien continues, that people began to say that upon encountering such a cart one should bless oneself and be mindful of God, so that no misfortune occurs (341–44). The cart was used to carry criminals to torture or execution (410–13). Actually, convicted criminals were often transported to their places of execution on a cart, so that they could be seen clearly by the populace (Gonthier 1998: 91, 126–28). That this practice should make mounting on all carts inadvisable, however, does not make sense on the surface, for the cart, though certainly not a proper knightly conveyance, was essential for commerce and for both rural and urban labor. Chrétien's explanation appears to be a rationalization for fear of the Ankou's cart— in Breton *karriguel ann Ankou*—a vehicle driven by the personification of death (*ankou* 'anguish') to convey the bodies of the recently deceased, according to Breton folk beliefs that have survived into modern times. The long stick (*verge,* 349) that the dwarf holds is possibly a reminiscence of the scythe that is the attribute of the Ankou (see Le Braz 1928: ch. 3).

The means by which Lancelot finally penetrates the inner reaches of Gorre, the Sword Bridge, has antecedents in both Welsh and Irish. The Irish precedent is the Bridge of Leaps that is "sharp as a blade" and that appears in the Irish saga *The Wooing of Emer* (Hibbard 1913: 179n; see also Cross and Nitze 1930: 54n). The Welsh antecedent is the sword Bronllafn in *Culhwch and Olwen,* carried by Osla Great-knife (Cyllellfawr). Bronllafn is short and wide: "When Arthur and his men would come to the edge of a river, they would seek a narrow crossing over the water, and the knife in its sheath would be placed over the water; that would be bridge enough for all the armies of the three isles of Britain, their three adjacent islands, and their goods" (Ford 1977: 129). Bronllafn is a compound of *llafn,* "blade," and *bron,* "edge," and thus means "Edge of the Blade." Normally *bron* applies to the edge or bank of a torrent. Would similar connotations in Breton have led Chrétien to associate the sword with a torrent? The Welsh example is a bridge that is itself a sword, whereas the Irish example is sharp like the Sword Bridge in *Lancelot* on which the knight cuts his hands, knees, and feet, sweet though the suffering is for the lover Lancelot (*Lancelot* 3110–15).

The captives from Gorre are liberated after Lancelot's second combat with Meleagant. Some return to Logres with Keu while others wait with Guinevere until, reassured by the letter that supposedly comes from Lancelot, she, too, returns to Arthur's kingdom. The rescue of compatriots of the captive queen does not appear in the other versions of Guinevere's kidnapping. That Chrétien makes it such an important part of his romance indicates that he or his source, which is likely to have been of Breton origin, was combining two motifs, the queen's abduction and the freeing of mortal captives from the Otherworld.

Cross and Nitze long ago demonstrated (1930: 42–47) that the story of Guinevere's abduction was only one of many Celtic tales of the abduction of a ruler's wife. Sometimes these rulers are mortal kings, sometimes Otherworld figures. In *The Wooing of Etain,* Eochaid Aiream, high king of Ireland, falls in love with Etain, wife of the Otherworld figure Midir. She leaves Midir and becomes Eochaid's wife, but Midir wins her back by exacting a rash promise from Eochaid after winning a game of chess with him. To recover Etain, Eochaid destroys all the fairy mounds of Ireland. In *The Adventures of Cormac in the Land of Promise,* Manannán mac Lir exacts three rash gifts from Cormac, also a high king of Ireland, which turn out to be his wife, his son, and his daughter. When Manannán takes them away, Cormac follows and comes to three wondrous habitations, of which the third is Manannán's palace. Manannán surrenders the three members of Cormac's family and also gives the king a truth-testing cup (Cross and Slover 1969: 503–7; see also Dillon 1955: 146–48). Cross (Cross and Nitze 1930: 42–44) pointed out that *The Adventures of Cormac* is particularly relevant to *Lancelot* because it combines the motifs of the abduction and the journey to an Otherworld kingdom. It also involves the rescue of two people in addition to Cormac's wife.

An issue raised by these and other Celtic analogues is the category to which the traditional tale of the abduction of Guinevere belongs. Was Guinevere always merely the mortal wife of Arthur sought by the Otherwordly Melwas, or was she once an Otherworld woman who took up her union with Arthur and was then reclaimed by her Otherworld lover or husband? (See Cross's reconstruction of the tale pattern in Cross and Nitze 1930: 60.) The "Conversation Between Arthur and Guinevere," in which Guinevere does not appear eager to return from Melwas's Isle of Glass, supports the second possibility. *Guinevere*'s Welsh etymon is, after all, *Gwenhwyfar,* which means "white enchantress, white fairy." The first element, *gwen-,* could designate either the shining quality of a fairy, or whiteness, a sacred color in Celtic religion. If Guinevere is originally an Otherworld woman who appropriated Arthur or was appropriated by him, it is surprising that the literary tradition did not make greater use of this aspect of her person, which any intelligent storyteller could easily develop into a fascinating tale.

Yvain

Chrétien did not invent the central relationship among characters in *Yvain*. In the *Fragmentary Life of St. Kentigern,* a Latin text produced in Scotland before 1165 and thus before *Yvain* was written, Ewen, son of Queen Erwegende and King Ulien (the equivalent of Owein, son of Urien, and thus also of Yvain), seduces Thaney, daughter of King Leudonus of Leudonia (see Bromwich 1978: 320). This Leudonus is probably Loth of Lothian, the father of Gauvain according to Geoffrey of Monmouth, Wace, and Chrétien. Ewen courted Thaney, but she refused to marry him. In punishment, her father made her work as a swineherd's servant. Ewen sent a female intermediary to persuade Thaney to love him, but when persuasion did not achieve his ends, he disguised himself as a girl and approached Thaney near a fountain. He tricked her into accompanying him to an isolated place, where he raped her. Thaney conceived the son who would be Kentigern, patron saint of Glasgow. Ewen then abandoned Thaney. In punishment for her pregnancy, her father had her thrown from a mountaintop, but she survived and a clear fountain sprang up miraculously as a token of her innocence. Thinking that the swineherd was responsible for Thaney's pregnancy, Leudonus pursued him into a marsh but was himself killed. The association of Thaney with a fountain and a herdsman, the use of a female intermediary, Ewen's abandonment of the lady, and the killing of one of her close kin, along with correspondences of proper names including Laudunet and Lauduc (Laudine's father and his land, respectively—the forms of the French names vary from scribe to scribe—obviously connected with *Leudonus*), make it clear that Chrétien was drawing upon a Celtic source for important details of the central story pattern of *Yvain*. This source was cognate with that on which the *Fragmentary Life of St. Kentigern* depends. Chrétien's immediate source might well have been the lay that he mentions as attached to the memory of Laudine's father (*Yvain* 2155).

In *Yvain,* Chrétien places the magic fountain in the forest of Brocéliande (189, 695), today the forest of Paimpont in Brittany. Wace acknowledges in the *Roman de Rou,* lines 6395–6420, that he went to Brocéliande to see the fountain of Barenton that caused rain when water was poured on the stone:

. . . Broceliande,
about which the Bretons often tell tales,
a forest very long and wide
which is very much praised in Brittany.
The fountain of Barenton
springs up beside a stone.
In time of great heat, hunters
were in the habit of going to Barenton
and of taking the water in their horns
and wetting the top of the stone;
this way they used to have rain.
Thus it used to rain in former times
in the forest and its surroundings,
but I do not know why.
One is accustomed to see fairies there,
if the Bretons are telling us the truth,
and many other marvels.
There are nests of goshawks there
and a great number of large stags,
but the peasants have devastated it.
There I went in search of marvels,
saw the forest and saw the land;
I sought marvels but did not find them.
A fool I came back, a fool I went;
a fool I went, a fool I came back;
I looked for folly, I considered myself a fool.
[. . . Brocheliant
donc Breton vont sovent fablant,
une forest mult longue e lee
qui en Bretaigne est mult loee.
La fontaine de Berenton
sort d'une part lez un perron;
aler i solent veneor
a Berenton par grant chalor,
e a lor cors l'eve espuisier
e le perron desus moillier;
por ço soleient pluie aveir.
Issi soleit jadis ploveir
en la forest e environ,
mais jo ne sai par quel raison.
La seut l'en les fees veeir,
se li Breton nos dient veir,

e altres mer(e)veilles plusors;
aires i selt aveir d'ostors
et de grant cers mult grant plenté,
mais vilain ont tot deserté.
La alai jo merveilles querre,
vi la forest e vi la terre;
merveilles quis, mes nes trovai,
fol m'en revinc, fol i alai;
fol i alai, fol m'en revinc,
folie quis, por fol me tinc.]   (Holden 1973, 3: ll. 6373–98)

If the presence of fairies and the storm-producing qualities of the fountain as Wace describes it were not enough to convince us that Chrétien knew this passage, the matter is settled by the echo of Wace's words in what Calogrenant says:

"Thus I went, thus I came back,
On coming back, I thought myself a fool.
And I have told you, like a fool,
What I never wanted to tell."
["Ainsi alay, ainsi reving,
Au revenir pour fol me ting.
Si vos ai conté comme fox
Çou c'onques mais conter ne vox."]   (*Yvain* 575–78)

A local legend about a water fairy was thus known in Brittany before Chrétien composed *Yvain*. Because his tale of the fountain also features a hospitable host—the vavasor with his beautiful daughter (*Yvain* 197–275, 775–90)—and a giant herdsman, details found in Celtic lore but not in Wace, Chrétien either embellished what he knew from the *Roman de Rou* or, as seems more likely, knew the legend also through other sources.

The fountain in *Yvain* has various magical qualities. The hero is sent to it by the hideous club-wielding herdsman who exhibits a number of zoomorphic features: head as big as a packhorse's, ears as large as an elephant's, eyes like an owl's, nose like a cat's, mouth like a wolf's, teeth like those of a wild boar, and a garment of freshly skinned cowhide (292–311). Like a woodland deity, he masters wild beasts, through the exercise of his brute strength. The water in the fountain boils but is colder than marble. Above it stands the most beautiful pine ever fashioned by Nature. Beside the fountain are a gold basin hanging by a chain, an emerald block hollowed out in the form of a shell (see Gregory 1989) and topped by four rubies, and a small, beautiful chapel. Pouring water with the basin into the emerald block produces an awesome storm that destroys trees and chases animals from the wood. In a moment of peace following the storm, every branch of the tree is covered with birds singing in counterpoint. A mounted knight comes crashing through the brush, demanding to know who has damaged his wood and castle with lightning and rain.

The storm-producing stone is an item of folk belief that is widespread throughout the world. Typically water or some other liquid is sprinkled on the stone or it is dipped in water to produce the desired effects, and in Europe these practices were continued in some places into the Christian period but attached to the cults of saints (Frazer 1959: 26–27, 78).

Chrétien has certainly embellished whatever description of the storm-making fountain was in his source. The emerald or heliotrope, for example, is described in an early lapidary as a stone that can conjure rain:

Listen to the nature of the heliotrope
Which no one knows at all.
It has taken the color of the emerald,
But it does not have the same value;
It is spotted with red drops.
Now listen here to great wonders:
Whoever places this stone in water,
In a good vessel, beautiful and clean,
And places it in the sunlight,
The sun will become entirely red:
It will all be the color of blood,
No longer will it be beautiful or clear or white,
So that all those who see it
Will think there is an eclipse;
And the water in the vessel in which the stone lies,
Know that [the stone] will make it all boil,
And will make thunder in the air
And make it rain immediately all around.
[Oëz l'assens del Yotrophie,
Que tute gent ne sevent mie.
D'esmeralde a pres la colur,
N'a pas meïsmes la valur;
Estencelee est de gutes vermailles.
Ore escutez ci granz merveilles:
Ki cele pere en eawe met,
En un bon vessel bel et net,

E tut si en rai du solail,
Il devendra trestut vermail:
Tut ert coluré come sanc,
Ja tant n'ert beals ne cler ne blanc,
Si ke tuz ceus ky le verunt
A eclypse le jugerunt;
E l'eawe eu vaissel ou gerra,
Sachez ke tot boillir fera,
E f(e)ra par l'eir tenebror
E tantost ploveir par entor.]   (Paul Meyer 1909: 68)

The fountains that appear in Celtic mythological or folkloric sources are not associated with precious stones. The stone slab beside the fountain in the third branch of the *Mabinogi, Manawydan, Son of Llyr,* for example, is simply made of marble, although it does have a golden bowl next to it that is attached to chains rising into the sky (Ford 1977: 80).

That Laudine was originally a water fairy seems highly likely, and the choice of the eve of the Nativity of John the Baptist, June 23, for Arthur's arrival at the fountain is no accident because that was also celebrated as Midsummer Eve, a day propitious for fairies. Nitze linked the fairy and her fountain to the cult of the Arician Diana and the Celtic goddess Diona or Dibona, to which Ausonius refers in a poem on the fountain of Bordeaux (Nitze 1909: 151; 1955: 173–74). This reference points up the widespread localization of the cults of Celtic deities near water sources. To this day in France, archaeologists and sometimes even casual strollers find votive objects that were left in the Gaulish period at fountains, in wells, and at the sources of rivers in hope that local deities would answer the prayers of their suppliants. That such places were assigned a numinous quality for long periods of time is shown by the action of a priest of Concoret (in Breton, *Konkored* 'Valley of the Fairies'), a town near Brocéliande, who led a procession of his parishioners to the fountain of Barenton in 1835 in hope of ending a drought. The priest blessed the water, then dipped his holy water sprinkler into it and sprinkled the water on the stones surrounding the fountain (Villemarqué 1860: 235). A collection of medieval texts relating the storm-producing powers of this fountain was assembled by Foerster (1912: xxii–xxviii). One of these, by the Dominican Thomas of Cantimpré, who died in 1263, relates that an altarlike stone stood beside the fountain of Barenton on marble columns.

The thirteenth-century prose romance known as the Huth *Merlin* or the *Suite du Merlin* presents Morgan in the role of Yvain's mother, married to

Urien. In a Welsh triad enumerating the "Three Fair Womb-Births of the Island of Britain," Yvain's prototype Owein is said to be the son of Modron and Urien (Bromwich 1978: triad 70). As previously discussed, a tale surviving in Latin tells how Owein and his sister Morfudd were conceived in Modron at a ford. Although it is impossible on linguistic grounds to derive the name *Morgan* from *Modron,* Morgan seems to have taken the place of an earlier Modron in the hero's genealogy. Chrétien never names or even refers to Yvain's mother.

An attribute of Owein in Welsh tradition is that he is accompanied by a flight of ravens. *The Dream of Rhonabwy,* for example, tells how Owein's ravens destroyed Arthur's war band (Jones and Jones 1974: 146–50). This association of Owein with ravens is significant in light of Yvain's rescue by the lady of Norison, because *Norison* can be construed as O. F. *noir oison* 'black bird'. A figure from Celtic mythology whose name, like *Morgan* and *Modron,* begins with *Mo-* and ends in *-n* is the Morrígan, the "Great Queen" of Irish mythology, who sometimes takes on the form of Badb, 'crow, raven' (Mac Cana 1983: 86). Morgan is said in Geoffrey of Monmouth's *Life of Merlin* to transform herself into a bird (Clarke 1973: l. 923). Morgan (and all the more so Modron) cannot derive etymologically from Morrígan either, but a transfer of attributes between powerful divine or preternatural women whose names resemble each other in certain ways is not to be excluded (see Loomis 1956: ch. 8, "Morgain la fée and the Celtic Goddesses"). In the thread of the mythic tradition that underlay *Yvain,* the hero was probably rehabilitated not merely by an unguent that had been prepared by Morgan the Fay but by Morgan herself. Morgan may there have been presented as Yvain's mother, as she is in the *Suite du Merlin.*

The test that Calogrenant and Yvain undergo at the fountain includes elements that recall several parallels in other myths and legends, none of which correspond exactly. That Yvain replaces the dead Esclados le Roux suggested to Nitze (1909) the myth of the sacred grove of Diana at Lake Nemi in Italy, made famous by Sir James Frazer's *The Golden Bough* (1890), in which the priest-king, husband of the nymph Egeria, was periodically killed and replaced by his killer. Jessie Weston (1920) believed that the Grail was a remnant of ancient initiation rituals connection with a vegetation cult practiced in the British Isles.[9]

The role of Lunete, at one and the same time governess (*maistre*) and subordinate of Laudine, finds parallels in Celtic lore (Loomis 1949: 296–97, based on A. C. L. Brown). The closest is in the Irish saga *The Wasting Sickness of Cuchulainn* (translated in Gantz 1981: 155–78). There the great Irish hero sees in a dream two women who beat him severely with a whip so that he spends a year in bed convalescing. He is then persuaded by one of the women, the fairy Liban, to win the love of her sister, Fand. Killing three enemies to attain his goal, Cuchulainn sleeps with Fand, but after a month he leaves her to return to his wife, Emer, and Fand returns unhappily to her husband, Manannán mac Lir, god of the sea. Like Yvain, Cuchulainn then goes mad and lives in the wild until the druids cure his insanity with a drink of forgetfulness. In this saga Liban and Fand play roles that are analogous to those of Lunete and Laudine in *Yvain,* and Cuchulainn's situation—loving the fairy, leaving her, and then losing his mind—is parallel to Yvain's.

The fact that Cuchulainn is a figure of Irish myth and folklore does not mean that Chrétien, or even the sources on which he depends, derived this lore from Ireland. Just as Welsh and Irish mythology share a number of important figures, so the lost myths of the Bretons must have held many cognate features in common with Irish tradition.

Perceval

Analysis of the background of Celtic myth for *Perceval* centers on two scenes, Perceval's experiences in the Grail castle and Gauvain's in the castle of the Rock of Champguin, although other scenes also have Celtic antecedents.

After leaving the castle of Beaurepaire, Perceval journeys all day. That evening, in the midst of praying that God should let him find his mother, he comes to a deep, swift river on which he sees a boat descending with two men in it (*Perceval* 3000). The boat stops at anchor in the middle of the river. The man in the prow is fishing. Perceval asks if there is a bridge, and the fisherman tells him there is no way to cross the river but offers to put him up; he should climb the bank through a split rock to find the fisher's house in a valley. Following the directions, Perceval at first sees nothing but then makes out the top of a stone tower in a nearby depression. Riding on, he sees that the tall tower, beautifully made, is flanked by two turrets; in front are a hall and an entranceway. He enters the house by crossing a drawbridge, where four young men welcome him. Two take off his armor, one cares for his horse, and the fourth leads him to the entranceway. Two young nobles take him into the hall, which is square. He sees a handsome gray-haired man sitting in a bed and wearing a sable robe and a sable hat trimmed with purple. This is the fisherman he had previously seen on the river, Perceval later tells his cousin (3505–6). He is reclining on his elbow on a bed in the middle of the hall before a large wood fire that is burning amid four columns supporting a wide brass chimney. Four hundred men could have fit with ease around the fire. The fisher excuses himself from rising, which would be difficult for him, and asks Perceval to sit beside him. He asks where Perceval came from and learns it was from Beaurepaire. "You must have left before the watchman sounded dawn," says the fisher. "No," Perceval assures him, "it was after prime," that is to say, around six o'clock in the morning.

A young man enters the door of the house and hands a sword to the fisher, who is here called "the rich man." The fisher pulls it halfway out of its sheath and sees written on the sword the place where it was made and that it was of such good steel that it could not be broken, except through a single peril known only to him who forged and tempered it. The young man who brought the sword tells the rich man that the wealthy man's beautiful blond niece (3145–46) has sent it to him, to give to whomever he wishes, but she wants it to be used well. The smith who forged it has made only three swords in his life and will die before making another. The rich fisher immediately girds onto Perceval the sword, with its gold bridge and its orfrey sheath, because it was destined for him (3168). After drawing the sword from its sheath and balancing it in his hand, Perceval gives it to the young man who is taking care of his weapons, standing near the fire with other youths, then again takes his seat beside the rich man who is showing him so much honor.

In the room there is light as bright as any torches could project. While Perceval and his host are speaking, a young man walks into the hall from a bedroom carrying a white lance by the middle and walks between the fire and those who are sitting on beds around it. All who are there see the white lance with its white point, and a drop of blood oozes out of the point and flows down to the young man's hand. Perceval, too, sees this wonder but refrains from asking how it came about, for he remembers Gornemant's counsel not to speak too much and does not want to be considered impolite. Two other young men then enter the room carrying candelabras, each with at least ten candles in it. A beautiful young woman bearing in her hands a grail (3220) comes into the hall with the two young men, and with her enters a great light that makes the candelabras seem dim, as the rising sun or moon obscures the stars. Another young woman enters carrying a silver carving tray (3231). The Grail, which is in front, is of pure gold, inlaid with the most precious stones in the world (3238–39). Like the lance-bearer, those carrying the Grail and candelabras exit into a bedroom. Perceval does not dare ask who is being served by the Grail because he recalls Gornemant's advice that he should not speak too much.

The rich fisher has water and towels brought in. A one-piece ivory table with imperishable ebony supports and a white tablecloth is set up for a meal. The first course, a leg of venison in pepper sauce, is cut on the carving tray. With each course the Grail passes through again, completely visible, but each time Perceval refrains from inquiring whom it serves, although he intends to ask one of the young men of the court the next morning when he leaves. The abundant meal is fit for king or emperor and is followed by delectable fruits, beverages, and sweets. The rich man says his body has no power, and four men carry him to his bedroom (3342–43). Perceval sleeps in a bed in the hall, but when he awakens the next morning no servants are present and he finds all the bedroom doors locked. He has to dress and put on his armor by himself. The door to the hall is wide open and he finds his horse saddled and his lance and shield leaning against a wall. The drawbridge has been lowered. He crosses it, thinking that the young men have gone out to check their game traps; he intends to ask them why the lance bleeds and where the Grail is being carried (3399–3401). As he is approaching the end of the bridge, it begins to lift, and his horse has to jump over the gap. Perceval calls out to whoever lifted the bridge but receives no reply.

Few scenes in medieval French literature have elicited as much comment as the Grail procession in *Perceval*. Early in the twentieth century two interpretations were popular that now have few adherents: the Christian or liturgical theory, which focused on the detail that Perceval later learns from his hermit uncle, that the Grail contains a single communion wafer that keeps alive the father of the rich fisher (6422–25)—Heinzel, Peebles, Burdach, Bruce, Micha, Roques, and Henry and Renée Kahane—and the ritual theory, which centered on the information Perceval learns from his cousin, that if he had asked the right questions, the rich fisher, whom she calls a king, would have regained the use of his limbs and would have ruled the land (3586–90)—Weston 1906–9 and 1920 (the book that informed T. S. Eliot's "The Waste Land").

The lance is of prime importance for the liturgical theory. The legend of Longinus, the name assigned to the Roman soldier who, according to John 19.34, pierced Christ's side with his lance so that blood and water gushed out, was popular in the twelfth century (see Peebles 1911). The soldier was conflated with the centurion who is reported in Matthew 27.54 and Mark 15.39 to have converted to belief in Christ. *Longinus* is actually derived from the Greek word for lance, *longe,* and the soldier Longinus is first mentioned by name in the apocryphal Gospel of Nicodemus, according to which he would have converted and later died as a martyr. Subsequent versions of the legend held that Longinus was blind. Christ's blood would have flowed down the shaft of the lance to his hand; when Longinus rubbed his eyes with the bloody hand, he was miraculously cured of his infirmity. Almost a century before Chrétien composed *Perceval,* in 1098, the supposed lance of Longinus was recovered by a crusader, Peter Bartholomew, at Antioch, but it was discredited when Peter died as the result of an ordeal by fire that was supposed to demonstrate the implement's authenticity. Relics of the passion lance were also claimed by others before that date (Hibbard 1950: 250–51). If the lance of the Grail scene does represent Longinus's lance, one has to account somehow for the fact that its point is not just bloody but actually bleeding.

It has been suggested that the Grail and the cutting-tray represent the liturgical chalice and the paten, a thin metal disk on which the communion wafer is offered in the mass and that serves also to cover the chalice. The Grail has also been interpreted as a ciborium, the large chalice used to store consecrated communion wafers. Perhaps, say the partisans of this hypothesis, the Grail procession is a ceremony to bring viaticum, the last communion given to a dying person, to the Grail King, but in this case the role of the female Grail-bearer would be extremely unusual, although not strictly impossible, because women were not normally permitted to carry the eucharist. Chrétien says that the Grail King is spiritual and that the communion wafer in the Grail has sustained and comforted his life for twelve years—the Guiot manuscript has "fifteen years"—so that he requires nothing more to live on (6426–31). The wafer thus functions not as viaticum, the eucharistic provision for the soul's journey to the next life, but rather as food that, sanctified though it may be—Chrétien does not specify—has the decidedly physical and mundane effect of nourishing earthly life. That the cutting-tray is silver and the Grail gold has also to be explained, because the chalice and the paten have to be of the same substance according to liturgical practice. What above all does not fit into this hypothesis is the Bleeding Lance.

Some proponents of the liturgical theory invoked a ceremony of the Byzantine church, the Grand Entrance, in which the eucharistic bread and wine are prepared in a hidden area of the church, then carried into public view along with a knife symbolizing the lance with which the Roman centurion is reported to have pierced the side of the crucified Christ (Golther 1925; Burdach 1974). The officiating priest makes a mark on the host to represent the centurion's thrust. He then arranges the communion bread on the *diskos,* equivalent of the paten. There follows a procession in which are carried lighted candles, the chalice, the diskos, the holy knife, and evangelaries and reliquaries, in that order. This theory was unable, however, to explain two details in the Grail scene of *Perceval:* why the Grail is carried by a woman, which would be strictly forbidden in the Byzantine church (or in the Roman Catholic Church, for that matter, except under the most extreme circumstances), and why the lance precedes the Grail. In addition, that the lance in *Perceval* is bleeding constantly (6114–15), and not merely bloody, is a difficulty for any association with the lance of Longinus. Jean Frappier pointedly asked why, if the Grail has a liturgical meaning, none of the characters in the scene makes a religious gesture of any kind, such as genuflection or the sign of the cross (Frappier 1972a: 169; also Brown 1910: 6).

Mario Roques (Foulet 1970 [1947]: xix–xxii) attempted to conflate the two main variants of the liturgical theory—viaticum and the Byzantine ritual—but why would Chrétien be motivated to combine these two?

The ritual theory was based on the studies of Sir James Frazer (1890) concerning practices in which periodically a fertility king would be killed and replaced by his killer in order to maintain the fertility of the land. The communion wafer that is in the Grail fits into this hypothesis only with contrived difficulty.

The theory of Celtic antecedents for the Grail, also deriving from religion but from a pagan belief system, has attracted the most adherents. To begin with, Chrétien's debt to Celtic tradition is evident: his other romances are based on Celtic myth and folk beliefs with the exception of *Cliges,* and even the plot of that work takes place mostly in the Arthurian milieu. Any theory that is successful should explain as many elements of the mystery as possible: the Grail with its wafer, the Bleeding Lance, the candelabras, the cutting-tray, the Fisher King's invalid state and that of the Grail King, the unasked questions, the infertility of the Waste Forest, and the destined nature of Perceval. Of the theories that have been put forward, the Celtic thesis has shown the greatest explanatory power. Before going into it in greater detail, it is necessary to describe other texts of relevance for the issues at hand, texts that present the Grail and its mysteries with extraordinary diversity.

Chrétien's *Perceval* gave rise to a number of other medieval romances as well as an astonishingly rich postmedieval progeny. Among the medieval texts are Wolfram von Eschenbach's Middle High German *Parzival,* com-

posed between 1204 and 1212, the Welsh *Peredur* (late twelfth or early thirteenth century), and *Joseph d'Arimathie* and a 502-line fragment of a *Merlin,*
both by the Burgundian Robert de Boron. Robert was active between 1191
and around 1212 and is responsible for transforming the Grail, which Chrétien refers to only once as a "holy thing" (*Perceval* 6425), into the Holy Grail,
the chalice used by Christ at the Last Supper and in which Joseph of Arimathea collected the blood of the Savior when he took the body down from the
cross after the crucifixion. *Joseph d'Arimathie* tells how Joseph—mentioned
in the Gospels but especially in the apocryphal Gospel of Nicodemus—received the sacred vessel from Pontius Pilate and used it in a ceremony to
recall the Last Supper. In the Grail was placed a fish caught by Joseph's
brother-in-law Hebron or Bron. At the table those who have led a chaste
life and believe in the Trinity have all that they desire, but the sinners who
are present do not. One seat is reserved for Bron's future son. A voice fills
the room declaring that only Bron's grandson will be allowed to sit in the
seat. Bron is called the Fisher King because he caught the fish used in the
Grail service. His grandson, Alain, will carry the Grail west to Britain, to
the vale of Avaron.

A much deteriorated prose version of Robert's *Joseph d'Arimathie* and
Merlin survives that is followed in each of its two manuscripts by another
prose work called the Didot *Perceval,* after the owner of one of the manuscripts. The Didot *Perceval* (Roach 1941) is either the reworking of a lost
work by Robert de Boron or a continuation of his other works. It recounts
that Alain had a son, Perceval, who was destined to find Bron and heal him
of an infirmity. Perceval first had to go to Arthur's court, where he sat in the
Siege Perilous, a stone, at the Round Table. The stone roared out and split
beneath him, darkness issued from the earth, and a voice declared that because of Perceval's boldness in sitting in the seat, Bron would not be healed
of his illness, the stone would not be joined together again, and the enchantments of Britain would not be lifted until a knight who surpassed all others
in valor asked what the Grail was and whom it served. Perceval eventually reached the Grail castle, where he failed to ask the questions for fear
of displeasing his host. The Grail procession consisted of a damsel carrying two cutting-trays, a young man carrying the Bleeding Lance, and a second young man holding aloft the vessel of Joseph of Arimathea. The next
morning Perceval finds the castle deserted, leaves it, and meets the weeping young woman. He wanders for seven years, undergoing adventures and
forgetting God. He meets his uncle the hermit, confesses his sins, and does
penance. He eventually returns to the Grail castle and asks the right ques-

tion. The Fisher King, Perceval's grandfather Bron, is healed. At the bidding of the Holy Spirit, Bron instructs Perceval in the secrets of the Grail and entrusts him with it. Bron dies two days later. The integrity of the Siege Perilous is restored. Merlin announces to Arthur that the Grail quest has been carried out successfully and the enchantments of Britain are lifted. Merlin then dictates an account of the events to a certain Blaise, who writes it down. A section follows recounting the death of Arthur, based mostly on Geoffrey's *History of the Kings of Britain.* As in Geoffrey, Arthur is taken to Avalon to recover from his wounds. Arthur is said to have survived as a hunter, and the Bretons believe he will return. Merlin retires to a mysterious place called *l'esplumoir Merlin*—an *esplumoir* is a cage in which birds are kept while they are molting—and is not seen again. Most critics agree that Robert de Boron knew Chrétien's *Perceval* (see Pickens 1987–88). Robert's achievement was to tie the Grail myth to the story of Christ's redemption, a path taken by most of the writers that followed him and one that rendered more radical Chrétien's mild Christianization of what is essentially a pagan tale.

The early thirteenth-century *Parzival,* by the Bavarian knight Wolfram von Eschenbach, presents the Grail in a quite different light. Wolfram assigns names to characters whom Chrétien leaves anonymous, calling Parzival's father Gahmuret, his mother Herzeloyde, his cousin Sigune, the hermit Trevrizent, and the king of the Grail castle Anfortas. Chrétien's Blancheflor is called Condwiramurs, and she and Parzival make love on the third night they are together. Parzival's motivation for not asking the question is that he is indifferent to the king's suffering. When Gawan mentions God to him, Perceval replies: "Alas, what is God? asked the Waleis [Welshman]. Were He all-powerful—were God active in His almightiness— He would not have brought us to such shame! Ever since I knew of Grace, I have been His humble servitor. But now I will quit His service! If He knows anger, I will shoulder it" (Hatto 1980: 172). The Grail scene, in which no fewer than twenty-five women participate, is as follows:

> At the far end of the Palace a steel door was thrown open. Through it came a pair of noble maidens. . . . Each bore a golden candelabra. Their long flaxen hair fell in locks, and the lights they were carrying were dazzling-bright. . . . Two princely ladies were seen advancing in ravishing gowns. They carried a pair of knives keen as fish-spines, on napkins, one apiece, most remarkable objects. . . . After these came the Princess. Her face shed such refulgence that all imagined it was sunrise. Upon a green achmardi she bore the consummation of heart's desire, its root and its blossoming—

a thing called "The Gral," paradisal, transcending all earthly perfection! She whom the Gral suffered to carry itself had the name of Repanse de Schoye. Such was the nature of the Gral that she who had the care of it was required to be of perfect chastity and to have renounced all things false. . . . Whatever one stretched out one's hand for in the presence of the Gral, it was waiting, one found it all ready and to hand—dishes warm, dishes cold, new-fangled dishes and old favourites, the meat of beasts both tame and wild. (Hatto 1980: 125–26)

Wolfram has the hermit Trevrizent explain the Christian faith to Parzival, and also explain the Grail as a stone, called "small stone" (*lapis exillis*), whose name is possibly derived from the stone referred to as "a small object" (*substantia exilis*) in the *Journey of Alexander the Great to Paradise* (*Iter Alexandri Magni ad Paradisum*), a well-known medieval work. Chrétien uses *grail* as a common noun, whereas in Wolfram the Grail is the most precious thing outside of Paradise. Parzival fights his half-brother Feirefiz, who becomes a Christian and marries Repanse de Schoye. Wolfram has Parzival return to the Grail castle, which he calls Munsalvaesche, and take the throne as the king of the Holy Grail. Fans of Wagner's *Parzifal* will recognize that Wolfram's romance is the ultimate source of his version of the Grail legend.

Wolfram mentions "master Chrétien de Troyes" (*von Troies meister Kristjân*) at the end of the poem but names Kyot as the person who has presented him with the authentic tale:

The authentic tale with the conclusion to the romance has been sent to the German lands for us from Provence.

I, Wolfram von Eshenbach, intend to speak no more of it than what the Master uttered over there. (Hatto 1980: 410)

Elsewhere Wolfram writes: "Now Kyot laschantiure was the name of one whose art compelled him to tell what shall gladden no few. Kyot is that noted Provençal who saw this Tale of Parzival written in the heathenish tongue, and what he told in French I shall not be too dull to recount in German" (Hatto 1980: 213–14). Finally, elsewhere Wolfram gives as the source of Kyot a work by a half-Jewish astronomer, Flegetanis, on the history of the Grail, a book that Kyot found in Toledo, Spain. The term *Provençal* may refer to the town of Provins (there is evidence for this usage in Wolfram's *Willehalm*), and Kyot may be the poet Guiot de Provins, who lived in the late twelfth and early thirteenth century, or even the scribe of the same name who copied the most famous of the manuscripts of Chretien de Troyes's works. That Kyot as a writer on the Grail has been invented by Wolfram is entirely possible, even likely.

A comparison of Wolfram's text with Chrétien's makes it obvious that *Perceval* was Wolfram's main source, but he is thought to have drawn upon other sources, especially for the Gahmuret episode in books 1 and 2, devoted to Parzival's father, and the final three and a half books. From book 3 to the middle of book 13—there are sixteen books in all—*Parzival* compares closely with *Perceval.*

The lack of an ending to Chrétien's *Perceval* allowed four medieval authors to write continuations (edited in Roach 1949–83, Mary Williams 1922–25, and Oswald 1975).[10] Of these, the *First* and *Second Continuations,* both written before the end of the twelfth century, are the most interesting. In the *First Continuation,* devoted mostly to Gauvain's adventures, the Grail moves by itself and produces food for the guests in the Grail castle. In the *Second Continuation,* Perceval reaches the Grail castle again after a long sequence of adventures; the sword he received from the Fisher King breaks, but he mends it. The *Third Continuation,* by Manessier, written in the second quarter of the thirteenth century, sees Perceval reach the Grail castle, where the Grail again wondrously provides food. Perceval succeeds the Fisher King and achieves salvation upon his death, when the Grail, the Bleeding Lance, and the carving-tray are transported to heaven. Gerbert de Montreuil's *Fourth Continuation,* written between 1226 and 1230, is an interpolation between the *Second* and *Third Continuations.*

Two writers produced introductory narratives for *Perceval,* called the *Elucidation* and *Bliocadran.* Both survive together in manuscript Mons, Bibliothèque de l'Université de Mons-Hainaut 331/206, and *Bliocadran* is also found in London, British Library, Additional 36614. The *Elucidation,* a 484-line text, claims that the wasting of the kingdom of Logres and the disappearance of the Fisher King's castle can be ascribed to the brutality of a certain King Amangon, who along with his men raped well-maidens living in the forest and stole their gold cups. The title that has been assigned to the 800-line *Bliocadran,* really an insert in *Perceval* rather than a prologue proper, is the name this text confers on Perceval's father. He is said to have had eleven sons.

In the 1220s and early 1230s, these verse works were succeeded by a series of anonymous romances in prose, the Lancelot-Grail Cycle (also known as the Vulgate Cycle), which tells the story of Arthur from before his birth until the end of the Arthurian world in the battle of Camlan. Two of these works are devoted largely to the Grail: the *Story of the Holy Grail*

(*Estoire del saint graal*) and the *Quest for the Holy Grail* (*Queste del saint graal*), both of which incorporate the line of medieval reception that comes out of Robert de Boron. Of all the medieval versions, the *Quest* gives the most thoroughly Christian interpretation of the Grail myth, suffused with monastic values. The other romances of the Vulgate Cycle are *Merlin,* the *Lancelot* proper, and the *Death of King Arthur* (*La Mort le roi Artu*).

The *Lancelot* proper recounts that Lancelot has a son, Galahad, whose mother is the Grail maiden, daughter of the Rich Fisher King. Galahad is a descendant of both the biblical King David and Joseph of Arimathea. He is thus in the lineage of the Grail kings.

At the beginning of the *Quest,* the newly knighted Galahad is led into Arthur's palace at Camelot, where he passes the tests of the Siege Perilous and the Sword in the Stone, indications that as the best knight in the world he will fulfill the Grail quest. When the knights of the Round Table are seated in the hall, a clap of thunder sounds and they are all struck dumb. The Holy Grail, sent by God, floats into the room, and each guest is provided with whatever food he desires. Led by Gauvain, each of the knights pledges not to rest until he is seated once again in a palace where such dishes are served daily. The Grail is referred to as a "platter" (*escuele*). After a series of interlaced adventures in which most of the knights, including Lancelot and Lionel, fail in the quest because of their sinful lives, Galahad, Perceval, and Lancelot's cousin Bohort reach the Grail castle, called Corbenic. There they participate with nine other knights in a mass celebrated by Josephé, the son of Joseph of Arimathea, who has descended from heaven for the occasion, at a silver table on which angels have placed the lance beside the Grail. The host used in the mass takes on the appearance of a child, and the crucified Christ emerges from the Grail to give the knights communion. Galahad heals the wounded king by anointing him with blood from the lance. Having seen the beatific vision, Galahad, now king of the land, dies, as does Perceval a year later. The various components of the knights' quest for the Grail and the objects they encounter are assigned allegorical meanings in the context of Christian ideas of grace and salvation. These are often explained by monks dressed in the white habits of the Cistercian order whom the knights meet along the way and who expound ideas that can be linked to the writings of St. Bernard of Clairvaux. In the *Queste,* as in the *Estoire del saint graal* and the Didot *Perceval,* the bearer of the Grail is a young man rather than a young woman.

The prose romance *Perlesvaus* (translated in Bryant 1978) was written either shortly after the year 1200 (Nitze et al. 1932–37: 89) or between 1230

and 1240 (Bogdanow 1984). The romance claims to be based on a tale written by the Jewish historian Josephus and found in a monastery on the Isle
of Avalon, where Arthur and Guinevere are buried. *Perlesvaus* opens with
an account of Arthur's loss of enthusiasm for courtly values, caused by Perlesvaus's failure to ask the questions in the Grail castle, but the king is reinvigorated by a visit to the chapel of St. Augustine in Wales. A maiden looking for Perlesvaus gives an account of his boyhood exploits and lineage. He
is the son of the widow who is the niece of Joseph of Arimathea. Perlesvaus
is also called Parluifet and Perceval in the course of the romance. Three
knights, Gauvain, Lancelot, and Perlesvaus undertake quests to find the
Grail. Gauvain fails, although he does meet the Fisher King in the "Waste
Castle" (*Gaste Chastel*), where he sees the Grail and the Bleeding Lance but,
mesmerized by the drops of blood, fails to ask the questions. Lancelot also
fails because he cannot give up Guinevere. Keu kills Arthur's son Loholt,
leading Guinevere to die of unhappiness. Perlesvaus manages to return to
his mother and dispatch her enemy, the Lord of the Marshes. He then captures the Grail castle from the King of Castle Mortal, but fails to see any
Grail procession, since the Fisher King has died. During a mass, Arthur
himself enjoys the vision of the Grail under five forms, the last of which is
a chalice. Keu, Brian of the Isles, and Claudas have revolted against Arthur,
and Lancelot helps the king to suppress this rebellion. In the end, Perlesvaus becomes ruler of the Island of the Four Horns and one day hears a
voice that tells him that the Grail will not reappear in that place. A ship
bearing a white sail with a red cross on it comes for Perceval and for the
bodies of his mother and the Fisher King, and he is never seen again. *Perlesvaus* imposes a definite Christian interpretation on the Grail in the line
of Robert de Boron, with symbolic interpretations at every turn. In spite of
this spiritual cast, however, the romance contains many scenes of violence,
including beheadings, a suicide, and a horrendous execution.

When one views these early adaptations and developments of the Grail
story in the light of Celtic motifs, it becomes clear that some of the authors, despite their dependence on Chrétien's *Perceval*, were also drawing
on other sources that were either themselves Celtic or went back to Celtic
antecedents independently of Chrétien (see Newstead 1939: 185–86). Wolfram's *Parzival* and the Welsh *Peredur*, for example, share two details that
are not in Chrétien: when the Grail enters the hall, lamentations break out;
and the scene of the blood on the snow takes place outside the habitation
of a hermit (not the uncle in Chrétien: another hermit). Although these
are not important details, they are unlikely to have been invented indepen-

dently—especially the second of the two—and point to a source other than Chrétien.

The Bleeding Lance in *Perceval* is a wondrous weapon not just because drops of blood continuously issue from its point but because of its destined role, to which a vavasor of the king of Escavalon alludes:

> "And it is written that there will come an hour
> When the whole kingdom of Logres,
> Which once was the land of ogres,
> Will be destroyed by that lance."
> ["Et s'est escrit qu'il ert une hore
> Que toz li roiames de Logres,
> Qui jadis fu la terre as ogres,
> Sera destruis par cele lance."]   (*Perceval* 6168–71)

The lance of Longinus leads to its owner's conversion, thus to a spiritually beneficent end, whereas the Bleeding Lance will be the agent that destroys Arthur's kingdom. Wolfram von Eschenbach calls the lance poisonous and omits any connection with the lance of Longinus. With Geoffrey of Monmouth's and Wace's narrative of the battle of Camlan in mind, it is natural to conjecture that Arthur would be fatally wounded by the Bleeding Lance, although Chrétien never suggests that. In any case, the search for the antecedents to Chrétien's Bleeding Lance should lead in the direction of a threatening context, even though in nearly all the Grail romances after *Perceval* the Bleeding Lance is presented as the lance of Longinus. This medieval reception of the Bleeding Lance is the work of Robert de Boron, although Frappier (1972a: 171–72) was able to find no instance, from the discovery of the lance by Helen, the mother of Constantine the Great, to its alleged rediscovery at Antioch in the First Crusade, in which the lance of Longinus was described as bleeding.

The Celtic theory is able to produce an analogue to the Bleeding Lance that is lacking in the theories of Christian origin. This is the lance of the Irish Mac Cecht, which is described as "black-red, oozy" (O'Rahilly 1976: 66). In the *Book of Invasions* (*Lebor Gabala*), an important source of Irish mythological material, Mac Cecht is the husband of Fotla, a representation of the sovereignty of Ireland. The lance of Mac Cecht is one of a series of Irish mythological lances that were originally lightning-spears. A description of Mac Cecht in the Irish saga *The Destruction of Da Derga's Hostel* appears to link him to Bran. In the saga, Mac Cecht, reclining, is described thus: "The two lakes next to the mountain . . . , those were his two eyes next to his nose" (Gantz 1981: 84). In *Branwen,* the giant Bran wades across the Irish Sea. He is perceived as a mountain, and "the two lakes on either side of the ridge are his eyes alongside his nose" (Ford 1977: 67).

Unlike the ominous lance in character, the Grail is, Chrétien tells us, a dish in which one might well serve a salmon, a lamprey, or a pike (6421), thus a broad serving dish. Fortunately the word *grail* was defined by an author living only a bit later than Chrétien, Helinand of the monastery of Froidmont near Beauvais, who was active in the first quarter of the thirteenth century. Helinand was interested in reading a Grail text of which he had heard that was in the tradition of Robert de Boron.

> At this time in Britain a certain marvelous vision was shown through an angel to a certain hermit, about Saint Joseph the decurion, who took down the body of the Lord from the cross, and about that vessel or dish in which the Lord ate supper with his disciples. A story is told about this by the same hermit which is called "Of the Grail": *gradalis,* however, or *gradale* in French is a broad and slightly deep plate, in which precious courses are placed for the rich with their juice, gradually, one morsel after the other, in various orders, and it is called by the common name *graalz,* because that which is in it is welcome [*grata*] and acceptable to the person eating, both on account of the container, for it is of strong silver or other precious material, and on account of what is contained in it, that is the multiple ordering of the expensive courses. I have not been able to find this story written in Latin, but it is claimed that there are writings in French by certain high dignitaries, nor is it easy to find all of them. This Latin text, however, I have not yet been able to obtain to read, in spite of some assiduity. As soon as I am able, I will translate succinctly into Latin the more probable and more useful parts.
>
> [Hoc tempore in Britannia cuidam eremitae monstrata est mirabilis quaedam visio per angelum de sancto Joseph decurione, qui corpus Domini deposuit de cruce, et de catino illo sive paropside in quo Dominus coenavit cum discipulis suis. De qua ab eodem eremita descripta est historia quae dicitur "De Gradali." *Gradalis* autem sive *gradale* Gallice dicitur scutella lata et aliquantulum profunda, in qua pretiosae dapes cum suo jure divitibus solent apponi gradatim, unus morsellus post alium in diversis ordinibus; et dicitur vulgari nomine *graalz,* quia grata et acceptabilis est in ea comedenti: tum propter continens, quia forte argentea est, vel alia pretiosa materia; tum propter contentum, id est ordinem multiplicem pretiosarum dapum. Hanc historiam Latine scriptam invenire non potui, sed tantum Gallice scripta habetur a quibusdam proceribus, nec facile, ut aiunt, tota inveniri potest. Hanc autem nondum potui ad legendum sedulo ab aliquo

impetrare. Quod mox ut potuero, verisimiliora et utiliora succincte trans-
feram in Latinum.] (Migne, *Patrologia latina,* 212, col. 814–15)

This passage is strong evidence from a native speaker of Old French that
the Grail was still regarded several decades after Chrétien not as a chalice
but rather as a serving dish. The etymologies that Helinand proposes are
both based on seeming resemblances between the word in question and
other words that Helinand can plausibly associate with it—those for *grad-
ual* and *grateful*—an example of the type of popular etymologizing common
in this period.

Philologists have proposed two plausible etymologies for the Latin *gradale* 'vessel': it comes from either the Greek *kratalis* (*krater* 'mixing vessel',
through L. **cratale,* influenced by *gararium* 'vessel for mixing with *garum*', a
fermented fish-based sauce [Gossen 1959, following Hertz, Gröber, Wechs-
sler, Baist, and Bezzola]); or the Latin *cratis* 'grid, woven object, basket'
(Spitzer 1944). This second etymology draws upon the notion that the vessel the etymon originally designated was a woven receptacle and that the
sense later evolved to a more general 'serving dish, bowl'. Whatever its etymology, *gradale* occurs in Latin from the ninth century on, and its reflexes
are found beginning in 1030 in French, Franco-Provençal, Occitan, Italian,
and Ibero-Romance dialects both medieval and modern (see the attestations in Gossen 1959: 181–200). Although the word became popular enough
through Chrétien and his successors to figure in the lexicon of a number
of modern languages—for example, English, where the sense of *grail* as a
common noun (often *holy grail*) is 'object avidly sought'—its medieval uses
are by no means limited to literary works.

Proponents of the Celtic thesis (Nitze 1911, 1952–53; Nitze and Williams
1955; Newstead 1939; Brown 1943; Loomis 1949, 1956, 1959c; Marx 1952;
Dillon 1955, 1959, 1972, 1982) identify the objects that appear in the Grail
scene—the lance, the Grail, and the carving platter—as avatars of the talismans of the Tuatha Dé Danann, the people of the goddess Dana.

> The Túatha Dé Danann were in the northern islands of the world, study-
> ing occult lore and sorcery, druidic arts and witchcraft and magical skill,
> until they surpassed the sages of the pagan arts. They studied occult
> lore and secret knowledge and diabolic arts in four cities: Falias, Gorias,
> Murias, and Findias. From Falias was brought the Stone of Fál which was
> located in Tara. It used to cry out beneath every king that would take Ire-
> land. From Gorias was brought the spear which Lug had. No battle was
> ever sustained against it, or against the man who held it in his hand. From

Findias was brought the sword of Núadu. No one ever escaped from it once it was drawn from its deadly sheath, and no one could resist it. From Murias was brought the Dagda's cauldron. No company ever went away from it unsatisfied. (Gray 1982: 25)

This opening of *The Second Battle of Mag Tuired,* the most important single medieval text for the understanding of Irish mythology, introduces three of the most important gods: Nuadu, king and warrior; Lug, master of all the arts, who is, in addition, a warrior; and the "Good God" (Dagda), husband of the "Great Queen" (Morrígan; Gray 1982: 121) and associated with hospitality and fertility. The four talismans are also mentioned in other sources, are borrowed from the *Book of Invasions* into *The Second Battle of Mag Tuired,* and go back at least to the early tenth century (Hull 1930). The antecedents of the implements in Chrétien's Grail procession would be Lug's spear for the lance and the Dagda's cauldron for the Grail. The sword that the Fisher King gives Perceval would descend from Nuadu's sword. Significant in this regard is that the spear of Lug is ominous like the lance that will destroy Logres, whereas the Grail is beneficent like the Dagda's cauldron. That leaves the cutting platter (*tailleoir*), which might conceivably be based on the stone of Fál, although the semantics of this equivalence is not clear. One possible chain of reasoning is that *tailleoir* has a wider semantic range than 'cutting-platter', as an object on which one makes all kinds of cuts: *taillier* 'to cut', can apply to dressing stones as well as carving meat. The stone of Fál in any case has its correspondence in later Grail romances in the Siege Perilous that cries out or produces a voice from heaven in the Didot *Perceval* and the *Queste del saint graal.*

In *Perceval,* Triböet (3679) or Trabuchet (Méla 1992: l. 3617), a smith living on a lake under the Firth of Forth, is the maker of the sword that the Fisher King gave the young hero and the only person who can repair it. The form *Triböet* resembles *Tribruit,* the name of a river on whose banks Arthur is said by the *History of the Britons* to have fought his tenth great battle against the Saxons and which is also mentioned in the "Pa Gur" poem in the Black Book of Carmarthen. In some of its manifestations, the Celtic Otherworld is located underwater (see Patch 1950: 43–44). The Welsh term for the unified Otherworld with many entrances, Annwfn, in fact, appears to have as its etymons *wo-* 'under' and *dwfn* 'the deep' (Sims-Williams 1990: 62; Hamp 1977–78: 10). If *Triböet* does derive from *Tribruit,* a personal name would result from a place-name, which is not unheard of— two examples are *Manawydan,* which probably derives from the territorial place-name "Manaw" (Bromwich 1978: 441–42), and *Efrawg,* the name of Perceval's father in Welsh tradition, which means 'York'. The variant form Trabuchet, by contrast, suggests lameness (Old and Modern French *trébucher* 'to stumble, stagger, trip'), which makes one think of the Germanic Wayland Smith (O. F. Galant), the Greek Hephaistos, and the Roman Vulcan, all lame smiths. Goibniu, however, smith of the Tuatha Dé Danann (Ir. *goba* 'smith'), one of the three gods who makes the weapons for them in *The Second Battle of Mag Tuired* (O'Rahilly 1976: 313–17, 525–27), is not said to be lame, nor is his Welsh counterpart Gofannon.

The Grail is linked to the Dagda's cauldron and to other vessels of Celtic myth and folklore that are associated with kings and have magical properties related to nourishing and sustaining life (see Vendryes 1949: 11–14; Marx 1952: 117–20; Le Roux 1955, who distinguishes between beneficent and malefic Celtic mythological cauldrons; and Bromwich 1978: cxxxiii–iv). No one goes away unsatisfied from the Dagda's cauldron. The cauldron of Cormac mac Airt supplied cuts of pork and beef to those eating at Tara in accordance with the dignity and station of each of the diners (Loomis 1941: 909). A related but distinct manifestation is the cauldron of regeneration in *Branwen,* into which dead warriors are thrown with the result that the next morning they are restored to complete health but cannot speak (Ford 1977: 69; Jones and Jones 1974: 37; see also Le Roux 1955: 40–41). In *The Second Battle of Mag Tuired,* a well regenerates mortally wounded warriors (Gray 1982: 55).

Other containers are not cauldrons but still serve as vessels of plenty, such as the hamper of Gwyddneu Garanhir in *Culhwch and Olwen* that could feed all the people in the world with every food they desire (Ford 1977: 130), the horn of Bran, one of the thirteen treasures of Britain, of which it was said that it provided immediately whatever food or drink one asked for (Newstead 1939: 20), and the platter (*dysgl*) of Rhydderch, another of the thirteen treasures, that also produced instantly whatever food one desired (Loomis and Lindsay 1931: 69–71; Newstead 1939: 68; Loomis 1941: 911–13). The personage with whom this platter is associated in a late medieval tradition is Rhydderch Hael, a sixth-century king of Strathclyde. In the Grail scene in *Perceval,* the young hero and the Fisher King are served a lavish meal:

> The first course was a leg
> Of venison in hot pepper sauce.
> There was no lack of clear wines to drink. . . .

They were not stingy in bringing
Wines and dishes to the table
That are pleasant and delectable.
The meal was handsome and good;
Of all the dishes that king or count
Or emperor should have
The worthy man was served that evening,
And the young man along with him. . . .
And the servants prepared
The beds and the fruit to eat,
For there were very expensive ones:
Dates, figs, and nutmegs,
And cloves and pomegranates
And electuaries at the end
And Alexandrian ginger jam,
Now pleuris and narcoticum,
Resumptive and stomachum.
Afterward they drank many a drink:
Mulled wine with no honey or pepper,
And aged blackberry wine and clear syrup.
[Li premiers mes fu d'une hanche
De cerf de craisse au poivre chaut.
Vins clers a boire ne lor faut. . . .
L'en n'aporte mie a dangier
Les vins et les mes a la table,
Qui sont plaisant et delitable.
Li mengiers fu et biax et buens;
De toz les mes que rois ne quens
Ne empereres doive avoir
Fu li preudom servis le soir,
Et li vallés ensamble od lui. . . .
Et li vallet appareillierent
Les lis et le fruit a mengier,
Car il en i ot de molt chier:
Dates, figues et nois muscades
Et girofle et pomes grenades
Et laituaires en la fin
Et gigembras alexandrin,
Or pleuris et arcoticum,
Resontif et stomaticum.
Aprés ce burent de main[t] boivre:

Piument ou n'ot ne miel ne poivre,
Et viez moré et cler syrop.]   (*Perceval* 3280–82, 3312–19, 3322–33)

This menu indeed leaves little to be desired, and in fact the electuaries, pharmaceutical preparations meant to aid digestion and promote good health, have left both medieval scribes and modern editors perplexed. What is clear, however, is the extraordinary richness of the delicacies served in this castle that has appeared suddenly amid the bleakness of a waste landscape. With each dish, the Grail passes once again through the hall (3299–3301), and although the dishes served at the feast are never said to come in the Grail, they and the Grail appear in company with one another.

Perceval's failure to ask the questions concerning Grail and lance will, according to the Hideous Maiden, result in ladies being widowed, lands laid waste, and knights killed. Perceval's first cousin tells him that if he had asked the questions, the king would have been cured and restored to power. This is not the only association between a vessel and the principle of sovereignty in *Perceval:* when the Red Knight (*Chevalier vermeil*) of the forest of Quinqueroi steals Arthur's cup, he speaks of having challenged the king's power over his land (889–893). Of the Fisher King, Perceval's first cousin says:

But in a battle he was
Wounded and crippled without fail,
So that subsequently he could not manage,
For he was struck by a javelin
Through [*or* in the middle of] his two thighs.
[Mais il fu en une bataille
Navrez et mehaigniez sanz faille,
Si que puis aidier ne se pot,
Qu'il fu ferus d'un gavelot
Parmi les quisses ambesdeus. . . .]   (*Perceval* 3509–13)

Being wounded through the thighs is a circumlocution for castration—an insight of Jessie Weston (1920: 12; see also Brunel 1960, Frappier 1977)—and Perceval's mother mentions similarly that his father had been "wounded through the leg" (*par mi la jambe navrez,* 436), as a consequence of which his land and his treasure went into decline (441). In Marie de France's lay *Chaitivel,* one of the main character's lovers is wounded in the thighs, and it is made perfectly clear that he has been castrated (Rychner 1968: ll. 122–

24, 215–22). In searching for antecedents and analogues for the Fisher King, one should look for castrated kings.

Bran the Blessed, Bendigedvran, son of Llyr, who went to the Otherworld seeking the cauldron of regeneration, is just such an analogue. The Didot *Perceval* calls the Fisher King *Bron,* a form very close to *Bran.* In Welsh mythology, Bran was wounded through the thighs, and in *Branwen* (Derick S. Thomson 1976: 37; Jones and Jones 1974: 37; Ford 1977: 69) he is called "the man with holes in his thighs" (Morddwyd Tyllion), and his wounding is followed by the wasting of Britain. Both Bran and Nuadu, a sea-god pictured with tridents and fish, and thus a fisher king, were wounded gods. Nuadu was not wounded in the thighs, but he was deprived of his arm. Because a blemished king could not rule the land, he was replaced by Bres, but the physician Dian Cecht fashioned a silver arm for Nuadu and Dian Cecht's son Miach made his original arm whole once more, so Nuadu displaced Bres as king until he stepped down in favor of Lug (Gray 1982: 33). Nuadu was killed in the second battle of Mag Tuired. The Fisher King cannot rule his land, according to Perceval's first cousin, who associates the curing of the king's malady and his holding the land (*Perceval* 3588–89). Like the Fisher King, Bran was associated with feasting, notably a seven-year-long feast in Harlech and a feast of eighty years on the island of Gwales that was held in the presence of his severed head (Newstead 1939: 19).

The link between the king's state and the prosperity of his kingdom is a widely attested belief. In one of the foretales to the Irish *Cattle-Raid of Cooley,* King Conchobor is said never to have given a judgment before it was ready, for fear that it might be wrong and that the crops would then worsten (Kinsella 1969: 4). In a testimony contemporary with Chrétien, Walter Map in his *Courtly Trifles* (*De nugis curialium*), written around 1181, mentions that in the parish in which Alan, count of Brittany, was castrated, "no animals even today can bring forth young, but, when ripe for bearing, they go outside of the parish to deliver the offspring" (James 1923: 214). Gerbert de Montreuil, the author of the *Fourth Continuation of Perceval,* composed between 1226 and 1230, wrote that by answering the crucial question, the Grail hero would be restoring the kingdom as well as the king to health (Mary Williams 1922–25: ll. 488–501). *Sone de Nansay,* a romance written in the second half of the thirteenth century (Goldschmidt 1899), explains that the Fisher King is Joseph of Arimathea. When, to test Joseph, God wounded him "in the kidneys and below" (*es rains et desous,* 4775) as a punishment for marrying a pagan princess, the land of Lorgres (that is, Logres) fell under an enchantment:

For one does not sow there peas or wheat,
Nor is a child born to man,
Nor did a maiden have a husband,
Nor did a tree bear leaves,
Nor did any meadow grow green,
Nor did any bird have offspring,
Nor did any beast bear young,
As long as the king was crippled.
[Car on n'i seme pois ne blés,
Ne enfes d'omme n'i nasqué,
Ne puchielle n'i ot mari,
Ne arbres fueille n'i porta,
Ne nus prés n'i raverdia,
Ne nus oysiaus n'i ot naon
Ne se n'i ot beste faon,
Tant que li rois fu mehagniés.]   (*Sone de Nansay* 4846–53)

These medieval references reflect a pagan belief that the fertility of the land depended on the king's wholeness or effectiveness or potency or even fertility. The Waste Land is waste because of the king's deficiency, which can result from bad judgment, physical infirmity, or, in a Christian context, sin. I believe that the Fisher King, Perceval's father, is lame because he was punished for the sin of committing incest with his aunt, Perceval's mother. As a result, he cannot rule the land.

In *The Second Battle of Mag Tuired* the enemies of the Tuatha Dé Danann are the *Fomoire,* or Fomorians. Bres's name means 'Beautiful'. His father was the king of the Fomorians, Elatha, and his mother was Eriu of the Tuatha Dé, after whom Ireland is named. When he was conceived, his father specified his nature: "Let no name be given to him but Eochu Bres [that is, Eochu the Beautiful], because every beautiful thing that is seen in Ireland—both plain and fortress, ale and candle, woman and man and horse—will be judged in relation to that boy, so that people will then say of it, 'It is a Bres' " (Gray 1982: 29). Bres had been adopted by the wives of the Tuatha Dé, who proposed him for the kingship when Nuadu was blemished. He began to rule in Tara, but the Tuatha Dé found him ungenerous, unjust, and lacking in judgment; his rule was limited to seven years. During this time he went to the Fomorians and asked for warriors so that he could take Ireland back by force and not give up the position of king. In the meantime, Nuadu reassumed the kingship. Lug then arrived at Tara and took Nuadu's place on the throne to prepare for the battle against the Fomorians. To preserve him and his many skills, the Tuatha Dé tried to keep Lug out of the fighting, but he escaped from those watching over him and plunged into the battle. Nuadu was killed, but the Tuatha Dé Danann overcame the Fomorians. Bres was spared only after he gave advice essential to good agriculture.

Perceval's father was a knight, like the Fisher King wounded through the haunches, which made his land and treasure decline. This seems to have occurred when Perceval was two years old. He was from the "Isles of the Sea" (*Illes de mer*). Note that Rion, Clamadeu, and Perceval's mother are all also from the *Illes de mer*. In *The Second Battle of Mag Tuired*, the Tuatha Dé Danann come to Ireland from the northern isles, where they are said to have acquired arcane knowledge. Nuadu, their king, is a counterpart of the Fisher King. A persistent tradition from Caesar, Tacitus, and Plutarch to *The Second Battle of Mag Tuired* places the sources of Celtic religion and magic in islands to the west and north of Britain (Le Roux 1962). I believe that Perceval's kin are the avatars of the Tuatha Dé Danann.

Another king, however, rules in Chrétien's *Perceval,* the king of Escavalon, whom Chrétien calls beautiful (5716) and more handsome than Absolom (4792). His kingdom is close to Galloway, in southwestern Scotland. Escavalon has plausibly been identified as Avalon, the initial syllable *Esc-* representing an intensifier on the analogy of the sword-name *Escalibur* coming from *Caliburn* (Loomis 1949: 424; Nitze and Williams 1955: 272). This would be consistent with Gauvain's encountering a white doe (5677) just before meeting the king. The king of Escavalon, whom Chrétien unfortunately never names, was originally an Otherworld king of the same type as Bres: beautiful but ineffectual.

The king of Escavalon's tutor, Guingambresil, accuses Gauvain of having killed the former king in treachery (*traïson,* 4763), that is to say, without having first challenged him. This is a false charge, as it is specified later that Gauvain would not have survived the test of the Wondrous Bed if he had been guilty of treason (7559). Gauvain is to defend himself in Escavalon against Guingambresil's accusation and accordingly makes his way there to submit to the trial by combat, but the king of Escavalon, on the advice of a vavasor, puts off the trial for a year to give Gauvain time to find the Bleeding Lance, which he is to surrender if he obtains it. Apparently Gauvain's journey to Mont Esclaire is now postponed under the pressure of this constrained detour. Chrétien probably meant to have his readers assume that Gauvain did kill the old king, but not treacherously, for Gauvain never denies the fact of the killing. The king of Escavalon is, however, intensely interested in having the Bleeding Lance. Because the lance is destined to destroy the kingdom of Logres, that is to say, Arthur's kingdom, it seems distinctly possible that if *Perceval* had been completed, Gauvain would have found the lance and would have given it to the king of Escavalon, who would have employed it successfully against Arthur. In the beginning of the romance, Perceval's mother told him that his elder brother had gone off to be a knight with the king of Escavalon (463)—this must have been the king of Escavalon whom Gauvain killed—and had died in battle while on his way home. His eyes had been destroyed by crows (478), and his father had died of grief at his eldest son's death (481). Did Gauvain kill the king in the same battle in which Perceval's brother died?

The Fisher King's father is the Grail King, who has been an invalid for twelve years (6429)—fifteen, according to the Guiot manuscript. Was he the second of the men whom Perceval encountered on the river? This seems likely. Perceval's hermit uncle tells him that the old man has not left his bedroom for all those years, but his manifestation in the boat would be no stranger than that of the Fisher King who has given Perceval directions on how to get to his dwelling but is already there waiting when Perceval arrives. Both kings seem to have appeared magically in the boat. Perceval's cousin does not mention the Grail King when she refers to the curing of the Fisher King; and yet, Chrétien never gives any indication that the Grail King would not have been cured, and he is obviously informing the reader of essential details gradually. The nature of his malady is not discussed by his brother, the hermit uncle, who is the only person in the romance to call him an invalid. Chrétien does not name the Grail King.

On account of the subtlety of Chrétien's tale and its unfinished state, other theories have emerged—and will undoubtedly continue to emerge —to account for the Grail and its accompanying implements: it reflects Cathar beliefs (Olschki 1966) or it is a *roman à clef* based on the history of the Cathars at Montségur (Rahn 1964 [1933]; see also Bernadac 1994), or it goes back to Occitan, Aragonese, Catalan, and Spanish roots (Mandach 1992, 1995), or it derives from the cult of Osiris in ancient Egypt (Fiore 1967), or it is connected with the Hermetic corpus (Henry and Renée Kahane 1965) or with Jewish tradition (Holmes and Klenke 1959) or the tradition of alchemy (Duval 1979) or with Islam (Ponsoye 1957), or it arose among the Ossetians of the Caucasus (Littleton and Malcor 1994). In my view, in comparison with the theory of Celtic origins, each of these theories poses more problems than it solves.

In regard to its hero, *Perceval* is an initiation tale. Perceval, however, is also a destined hero, for the sword the Fisher King presents him is said to have been fated for him (3168). It comes to him by way of his lineage, given by the Fisher King, who received it from his niece. Given the key role of swords in coronation rituals and in the ceremony of dubbing a knight (see *Perceval* 1632–38, 9171–86), the sword Perceval received would seem to have a heavy significance of some kind. What is the destiny that dictated Perceval's possession of the sword? I think that Perceval was marked to take the place of his father, the Fisher King, who is already no longer living and, in the words of the Hideous Maiden, will not hold his land again (4674). First, however, Perceval was destined to avenge his father's death. Were Chrétien to have finished his text, Perceval would probably have encountered the Grail again, asked the right question about whom it serves, and assumed the kingship of the Grail castle as ruler of a now reinvigorated land. The prediction that the Bleeding Lance would lead to the destruction of the kingdom of Logres (*Perceval* 6168–71) makes it likely that a completed *Perceval* would have included a cataclysmic battle. Would Perceval then have fallen into a state of warfare with Arthur and his kin? Chrétien took the answer to this and many other questions to his grave.

An Irish saga that also tells of a hero's initiation, *The Boyhood Deeds of Finn*, bears some remarkable similarities to *Perceval*, as has long been recognized (Loomis 1949: 337–38), and involves a boy taking vengeance for his father's death. Demne is the son of Cumall, who was killed and beheaded by Goll and Aed at the battle of Cnucha in a struggle to occupy the chief stewardship of Ireland. Cumall's treasure-bag had been taken from him in that battle by the man who carried it for him, resulting in a hereditary feud between Demne and the sons of Morna. Demne was born to Muirne Fairneck after his father's death. For fear that his father's enemies would kill him, Demne was taken away to live in the forest of Slíab Bladma, where he was raised by druidesses. His first hunt involved shooting a duck on a lake. One day he went alone to a stronghold at Mag Life and bested the young men at hurling, on which occasion a man of the stronghold said that they should call him *Finn*, 'fair', and so they did. On another occasion he caught a deer by running after it and seizing it. Finn entered the military service of the king of Bantry without revealing his identity, but the king suspected who he was. He then went into the service of the king of Kerry, who realized that he was the son of Cumall and urged him to leave, lest he be killed in the king's presence. Finn then went to Cuillein of the Ui Cuanach, to the house of the chief smith, Lochan, where Lochan's daughter Cruithne slept with him. Lochan made two spears for Finn.

On his way into Connacht to seek his uncle Crimall, Finn met a woman weeping and spitting blood whose only son had been killed by a warrior whom Finn pursues and kills, taking from him Cumall's treasure-bag. The one Finn killed was the warrior who had first wounded his father in the battle of Cnucha. Finn then went into Connacht and found his old uncle living in a forest wilderness, showed him the bag, and told him his story. He went on to visit Finn the poet at the Boyne River, who taught him the art of poetry and gave him the salmon of knowledge to eat. He traveled to see the poet Cethern and wanted to marry a fairy woman living in the fairy mound of Ele, but if anyone courted her, a member of the courting person's retinue had to die. Cethern went to woo her, and a member of the wooing party was killed. Finn took this to heart as a disgrace upon himself. On the advice of Fiacail mac Conchenn, his aunt's husband, Finn went to the two Paps of Anu, fairy mounds. On Samain night (October 31), the two strong-holds between the mounds opened, and he saw a great fire in each. A voice came from one asking, "Is your hospitality good?" From the other, a voice responded, "Good, indeed!" The first asked, "Is there anything to be brought from us to you?" The answer was, "If something is brought to us, something will be brought to you in return for it." Finn saw a man coming out of the fairy mound with a kneading-trough in his hand and a pig, a cooked calf, and a bunch of wild garlic. As the man passed Finn on his way to the other fairy mound, Finn cast the spear of Fiacail at him, saying: "If the spear from us has reached anyone, I think I have avenged the death of my compan-ion." He killed with that cast Aed, who had killed his father at the battle of Cnucha. Lamenting was heard to issue from the fairy fortress, to the effect that unless the spear was thrown out of the mound, plague would take over the land. Fiacail gave Finn the spear to keep. (This summary is based on the translation in Nagy 1985: 209–21.)

The Boyhood Deeds of Finn is suggestive in abstract ways of the boyhood deeds of Perceval. Like Finn, Perceval does not know his father, who has died as the result of a battle. He is brought up in isolation in the forest, goes to a king's court without revealing his name, and leaves. He then goes else-where and sleeps with a woman. He receives a spear. He meets a woman lamenting a man, whom he pursues. He visits his uncle who lives in the for-est and tells him his story. He goes to a fortress where he does not ask two questions—in the case of Finn, the hero overhears two questions and their answers—concerning things being brought. He watches a person carrying a serving dish. Perceval is associated with a spear that can bring great de-struction. I do not think that *Perceval* is based on *The Boyhood Deeds of Finn*. It seems likely, however, that it is based on an analogous tale about the boy-

hood deeds and initiation of a hero, for it shares the narrative pattern of
the Irish saga. Such a tale would probably have been in Breton, although it
might have been in Welsh.

The motif of the unasked question, whose motivation Chrétien takes
pains to prepare in the advice the hero receives from Gornemant of Gohort,
may in Celtic tradition reflect the very common motif of the *geis,* a prohibition that is imposed on heroes and that they break only at their great peril
(Vendryes 1949: 20; on the geis in romance, see the thorough treatment in
Reinhard 1933). The geis is a device that contributes to the aura of fatality
surrounding the heroes of Irish saga: often the hero can achieve glory only
by an act that is specifically forbidden to him by the geis. Because the concept of geis would not have been comprehensible to Chrétien's audiences,
he would have had to rationalize it somehow and would have chosen the
expedient of the counselor's advice.

A moment in *Perceval* that has attracted much attention is the scene in
which the hero, catching sight of blood that has dripped onto the snow from
the neck of a goose that has been struck by a falcon, falls into a state of reverie about the color of Blancheflor's face (4202). Three knights try to rouse
him from this condition, but only the third, Gauvain, succeeds. The scene
in *Perceval* is reminiscent of a passage in the Irish saga *The Exile of the Sons
of Uisliu,* dating from before the tenth century. Deirdre, who is to be the
wife of Conchobor, king of Ulster, sees her foster-father skinning a calf one
day on the snow. A raven alights on the snow and drinks the calf's blood.
Deirdre remarks to the royal satirist Leborcham:

> "I could desire a man who had those three colors there: hair like the
> raven, cheeks like blood and his body like snow."
> "Good luck and success to you!" Leborcham said. "He isn't too far away,
> but close at hand—Noisiu, Uisliu's son."
> "I'll be ill in that case," she said, "until I see him." (Kinsella 1969: 11)

When Deirdre does see Noisiu, she not only falls in love with him but
shames him into abducting her. In Chrétien's scene, only two of the colors
are present: the red of blood and the white of snow, which remind Perceval
of Blancheflor's facial coloring. Chrétien could not use the color black in
this scene, as Blancheflor is, like virtually all heroines of medieval French
romances, a blonde (see Colby 1965: 30–34). The author of *Peredur,* who
must have known from Welsh lore a motif like one in *The Exile of the Sons
of Uisliu,* adds the raven back into the scene as recalling the color of the
woman's hair. In any case, Chrétien is here receiving and using a traditional

scene in which the colors resulting from a bird of prey's attack remind the hero of his beloved. That this is truly a literary borrowing and not a mere co-incidental occurrence of the same images is shown by the seasonal anach-ronism of Chrétien's scene, which takes place in the snow but at Pentecost, fifty days after Easter and thus in late spring when the presence of snow is highly implausible.

If Perceval is a hero with a destiny, so also is Gauvain, who is fated to pass the test of the Wondrous Bed. Gauvain's adventures after the hermit scene begin with his encounter with the wounded knight Greoreas, who warns him against crossing the boundaries of Galloway (*Galvoie*). Gallo-way is surely conceived here as an Otherworld kingdom, and the historian William of Malmesbury reports ca. 1125 that Gauvain ruled there (Mynors 1998, 1: §287). Gauvain later cures Greoreas—an act that is the opposite of Perceval's failure to cure—who mounts Gauvain's horse Guingalet on a pretext and then makes off with it. The reader then learns that Gauvain had previously shamed Greoreas for raping a girl by having him eat for a month with dogs, his hands tied behind his back.

On his adventures, Gauvain meets the hateful Orgueilleuse de Logres (Haughty Woman of Logres). Her stated purpose is to bring Gauvain pain and shame, and her speech is insulting. Her horse, which Gauvain gallantly recovers for her, bears the marks of Otherworldliness, for its head is white on one side and black on the other. She accompanies Gauvain in his meet-ing with Greoreas and secures a boat for Gauvain to pass over a broad river to the castle of ladies. While he is fighting and defeating Greoreas's nephew, however, both she and her boat disappear, and Gauvain must secure the services of a boatman who tells him that Orgueilleuse de Logres has led many a knight to his death. After his success in the Wondrous Bed, Gau-vain has the boatman take him across the river again, where after defeating Orgueilleus del Passage de l'Estroite Voie (Haughty Man of the Passage of the Narrow Way), whom he hands over to the boatman, he again meets Orgueilleuse. She asks him to cross the Perilous Ford to pick flowers for her, which he does with great difficulty, his horse just succeeding in reaching the far bank. Gauvain then meets Guiromelant, who tells him that he, too, had been the companion of Orgueilleuse until she took up with the knight whom Gauvain had recently defeated. Gauvain has now acquired the high-est reputation in the world (8586). From Guiromelant, Gauvain learns the name of Orgueilleuse and that she has now as her companion Orgueilleus del Passage de l'Estroite Voie, who guards the passes into Galloway. When Gauvain crosses the Perilous Ford again, Orgueilleuse asks his forgiveness, explaining that she has hated all knights since Guiromelant killed her lover, after which she linked up with Orgueilleus. Gauvain deflects her attempt to employ him as the agent of her death so that no young woman will ever say to other knights the shameful things she has said to him. She then accompanies Gauvain back to the castle of the Rock of Champguin, where the boatman takes him, and Chrétien mentions her no more.

Orgueilleuse resembles Celtic sovereignty figures who appear to heroes, often as ugly hags who are transformed into beautiful women when the hero successfully completes a test. The prime example is Eriu, the sovereignty of Ireland, who appears to both Niall and Lugaid (see the discussion above). In *Perceval,* however, the function of the sovereignty figure is obscure. Orgueilleuse meets Gauvain while he is on his way to a land of which he will become the sovereign, but he does not pass the tests of the battle against Orgueilleus and the Perilous Ford until after he has been recognized as the destined lord of the Rock of Champguin. Even more puzzling is that the sovereignty figure in the castle is Ygerne, who explicitly grants sovereignty (*seignorie,* 8116) to Gauvain.

The boatman claims the horse of Greoras's defeated nephew. Like the men Perceval met fishing in a boat, this boatman is helpful. He claims his reward, however, in the form of the two knights whom Gauvain defeats in his presence, who constitute his fee (*fief,* 7379) for transporting Gauvain. While ferrying Gauvain and his prisoner across the water, the boatman acts as a guide, informing Gauvain that he is entering a land of marvels, regaling him with a feast when they reach the other shore, putting him up for the night, and telling him about the castle's enchantments, the expectations of its inhabitants, and the qualifications of those who enter it. He asks for a rash pledge, which Gauvain grants but later refuses to honor when it turns out to be a request that the hero leave the castle without attempting the test of the Wondrous Bed. This is the only rash pledge that is not granted in Chrétien's romances. The boatman accompanies Gauvain past a man with a leg of silver encrusted with jewels and through the castle gates of ivory and ebony, but then goes off for a time without his client. After Gauvain passes the test, the boatman returns, tells him to remove his armor, as there are no other dangers to parry, warns him that the king of this land would never be able to leave the castle, and sits with him at a feast. He eventually takes Gauvain back across the river for his combat with Orgueilleus and ferries him again to the castle in the company of Orgueilleuse de Logres.

The boatman resembles Charon in book 6 of the *Aeneid.* That Chrétien had in mind Aeneas's passage across the River Styx to the Underworld is clear from his description of the gates of the castle of Champguin as made of ivory and ebony, corresponding to Virgil's gates of ivory and horn, which Chrétien could have learned about from the *Roman d'Enéas* (Petit 1997: ll. 3080–81). Charon and other boatmen ferrying passengers to the land of the dead traditionally require a sacrifice or the payment of a fee.

Gauvain's arrival in the castle of the Rock of Champguin is long awaited, for the social life of the inhabitants is suspended until someone arrives who can recover the property of the dispossessed widows, marry off the orphaned girls, and knight the young men. The perfect knight who can accomplish this would also suppress the enchantments. The castle is inhabited by five hundred women, but also by an equal number of men divided into age groups, which points up the ravages of death among those of all ages.

When Gauvain meets the man with the silver leg, the man is sitting on a bundle of rushes at the foot of the castle steps, sharpening an ash stick with a knife (7648–59). The boatman informs Gauvain that the silver-legged man is exceedingly rich and that he would have given Gauvain trouble had Gauvain not been properly accompanied. The silver-legged man thus plays the role normally assigned to a porter, but he pointedly does not speak. His silver leg recalls the silver arm that was fashioned for the god Nuadu in *The Second Battle of Mag Tuired* (see Ménard 1969: 396). Why an analogue of Nuadu would be functioning as a porter is, however, puzzling. Roger Sherman Loomis (1949: 445–46) explained the silver-legged man as a misunderstanding. The Old French word for "one-legged man" is *eschacier* (7651, 7660, 7670), while the word for "chessboard" is *eschaquier.* Loomis referred to the Welsh *Dream of Maxsen Wledig,* in which the Emperor Maxsen dreams of entering a beautiful castle and seeing a white-haired man sitting on an ivory throne decorated with golden eagles, with a chessboard in front of him. The man is carving chessmen from a rod of gold. The bundle of rushes (*de gles*) on which the one-legged man is sitting in *Perceval* Loomis explained as the counterpart of a throne decorated with eagles (*d'egles*), a misreading that would be facilitated by the fluidity of word division and the lack of apostrophes in medieval manuscripts. This explanation would have an important consequence: Chrétien's source for the scene would have been not only a written text but one written in the Old French language rather than in Latin or a Celtic language. Unfortunately, there is no way of testing whether Loomis's theory is correct. Paule Le Rider, following up on a study by Mac Fynn (1952), stresses the sinister character of the eschacier, who shares his one-leggedness with a number of figures in medieval iconography representing pagans or devils (Le Rider 1978a: 268–71). Charles Foulon (1983: 74) sees the one-legged man as a guardian figure and interprets his silence as a sign that Gauvain's personal qualities are sufficiently high to allow him entry to the castle. The critical tradition has seen in the man with the silver leg a mythological figure, of diverse provenance depending on the observer, but no consensus has emerged (see Döffinger-Lange 1998: 77–81).

In the middle of the castle hall, Gauvain and the boatman come to a bed made of gold with silver ropes and a satin coverlet, illuminated by four carbuncles—precious stones reputed in this period not merely to reflect light but to be luminous sources—one on each bedpost. The female inhabitants of the castle, including its two queens, can see Gauvain through windows, but he cannot see them. When Gauvain sits on the bed, bells ring and five hundred arrows and bolts shoot out from the windows and lodge in Gauvain's shield. He is wounded but manages to remove the missiles. A peasant or uncouth character (*vilain*) with a stake breaks open a door from which a lion leaps to attack Gauvain, who succeeds in beheading the beast and cutting off two of its paws. At that, a group of young ladies and a young man greet Gauvain as their awaited savior. A tall and beautiful young woman, later revealed to be Gauvain's sister Clarissant, tells him that the queen greets him as their rightful lord. The queen sends him an ermine robe. Gauvain then admires the view of the fertile land around the castle. This scene of contentment and fulfillment is broken only by the boatman's intervention to the effect that the king of this land can never leave the castle and that Gauvain consequently should not hunt in the land but only pass through it. The two queens dressed in white silk arrive, one with white tresses, who is Gauvain's grandmother Ygerne, and the other who is his mother. Although he is obviously now lord of the castle of the Rock of Champguin, Gauvain asks permission of the older woman to leave—pointing up her role as a sovereignty figure—which she grants reluctantly, not wishing him harm, on condition that he return at night. Gauvain does then leave.

Jessie Weston (1897: 36–38), followed by Loomis (1949: 444), linked Gauvain's visit to the castle of the Rock of Champguin with the Irish saga *The Voyage of Bran* (Kuno Meyer 1895–97: 1–99). Bran is visited by a woman who sings fifty quatrains of poetry to him and invites him to visit the island of women, which she describes as a surpassingly beautiful country. Bran and twenty-seven of his men embark on a sea voyage and see Manannán mac Lir driving his chariot over the sea as if it were a plain. Manannán sings thirty quatrains, then tells them that the island of women is near. Approaching the Land of Women, Bran is welcomed by its queen, who takes him and his men to her house, where there are twenty-seven beds and where they are treated to a feast in which nothing they wish for is lacking. Expressing a desire to leave, Bran is told that he will regret departing and that he and his men should be careful not to touch land. When they reach Ireland, Bran announces his identity, but the people tell him that there is no contemporary named Bran—Bran's voyage is part of their ancient lore. One of Bran's men leaps out onto the shore and immediately dissolves into a pile of ashes. Like Bran, Gauvain crosses a body of water to visit a beautiful land with the help of a guide; it is a land ruled by women; the queen welcomes him to a house with many beds and gives him a feast; he is told that he may leave the land but will regret it. In *Perceval* in the state in which we have it, however, Gauvain does leave the castle of women without any ill consequences.

Guiromelant informs Gauvain that a city they see in the distance is Orqueneseles, which is Guiromelant's freehold. Guiromelant is incredulous when Gauvain tells him he has passed the test of the Wondrous Bed, but he finally believes it. Guiromelant plays the role for Gauvain that Perceval's first cousin plays for him after he leaves the Grail castle, that of explaining the identity of kin whom the knight in question has just met in a mysterious castle. He tells Gauvain what the castle is called and that the queens are his grandmother Ygerne and his mother—here unnamed but called Norcadés in the *First Continuation* (Roach 1949–83, 1: 1. 285)—although Gauvain recognizes that both have long been dead. The women came to the castle after Uther Pendragon's death, which would have been the same time that Perceval's family came to the Waste Forest (although there is an obvious discrepancy in the chronology here, for in this episode Uther is said to have died sixty years before). Guiromelant is in love with Gauvain's sister Clarissant and expresses his hatred for Gauvain, whom he does not recognize, prompting Gauvain to remark that this is not the right sentiment to have toward one's lover's kin. Guiromelant says that Gauvain's father killed his own father and that Gauvain killed one of Guiromelant's first cousins. When Gauvain reveals his name, Guiromelant challenges him to a public duel that is to take place a week later in the presence of Arthur and his queen. In fact, this battle does not occur in *Perceval* proper but takes place in the *First Continuation.*

The adventures of Gauvain in the borderlands of Galloway are analogous in a number of ways to Perceval's adventures in the Grail castle. Whereas Perceval fails his maternal kin, however, Gauvain succeeds with his maternal kin, passing all the tests. In both cases two older kin are present, for Gauvain his mother and grandmother—two queens—and for Perceval his uncle and his cousin—two kings. But if the Fisher King, who has the same kind of wound as the hero's father, is in fact Perceval's father as well as being his cousin, then the symmetry would be closer, for in both cases it would be a parent and a grandparent.[11] Perceval and Gauvain both encounter men in boats who are instrumental in guiding them to their destinations. In both instances, questions are involved: the questions that Perceval does not ask and Ygerne's questions that Gauvain answers. Each knight speaks afterward with a person who explains the ordeals to which he has recently been subjected. In each scene the landscape is noteworthy: Perceval is in the Waste Forest, whereas Gauvain looks out from the rampart of the castle of the Rock of Champguin and sees a land of running waters, wide plains, and forests rich in game. These analogies and oppositions lead me to think that the Gauvain adventures are not based on an extended narrative the way the Perceval adventures follow the pattern of Celtic tales about the hero's boyhood deeds. Rather, Chrétien has himself invented a narrative for Gauvain that owes much to discrete tale patterns in the Celtic tradition and that he has shaped in significant ways into a mirror image of Perceval's experiences.

In *Perceval,* Chrétien was obviously using Celtic antecedents to an even greater extent than in any of his other romances, with the possible exception of *Erec.* Did his materials come directly from Celtic tradition or from the book that he received from Philip of Flanders? He mentions that a detail of his description of Keu, who is always associated with Arthur, is from the story—*Et l'estoire ensi le tesmoingne,* 2807—and I believe that this story was in Philip's book. He refers to the *conte* as saying that Perceval kissed Blancheflor seven times (709). These references and the syntax of Chrétien's claim,

> This is the tale of the Grail
> Of which the count gave him the book
> [Ce est li contes do greal
> Don li cuens li bailla lo livre]   (*Perceval* 66–67)

lead me to think that the Grail was the topic of Philip's book and that it was already placed in an Arthurian setting. That Chrétien added substantially to the material furnished him in the book by calling on other Celtic sources is, however, not to be excluded.

THE ROLE OF CELTIC MYTH IN CHRÉTIEN

Mythological figures in the Celtic tradition typically took on multiple identities. Gods and goddesses could appear under various manifestations and different names. Sometimes an epithet was used as a name, sometimes a god with various attributes was given names in accordance with the attributes, sometimes the identity of a god had merged with that of a local deity, and sometimes the god changed shape and apparent identity. Even when it is obvious that figures of Celtic mythology and Celtic story patterns are behind the text, the precise identification may be difficult and at times impossible. The interpretations of A. C. L. Brown and Roger Sherman Loomis often took on a precision that is not in keeping with the nature of the evidence. The aura of the matter of Britain is one of half-revealed forms seen as through a mist.

Chrétien's Celtic sources for *Erec, Lancelot,* and *Yvain* appear to have been primarily Breton, to judge by the forms of names such as Brien, Enide, Erec, Gauvain, Grislemier, Guilemer, Guivret, Karadués, Lancelot, Loholt, Morgain, Ydier, son of Nut, and Yvain. In the case of *Perceval,* the analogues are mostly Irish but may have been available to Chrétien in Breton forms. The issue of which branch of Celtic tradition Chrétien owes the most to, and through what intermediaries, is distorted by the virtual nonexistence of medieval sources in Breton, the significant but relatively modest quantity of surviving sources in Welsh, and the fairly abundant extant Irish tradition. The fact that many of the Celtic names in Chrétien take on greatly modified forms and that the antecedents of many cannot be explained has led Rachel Bromwich (1983: 44) to conclude that most of them come to him through oral sources.

The primary quality of Chrétien's romances is that they are stories that hold a reader's interest, and the incorporation of one or another strand of Celtic myth or folklore contributes enormously to their attraction. Not that Chrétien privileges the elements of mystery on the level of narrative: characters do not discuss why or by what mechanism pouring water on the stone beside the fountain in *Yvain* unleashes a violent storm and a chorus of bird song, why it is impossible to carry fruit out of the enclosure of the Joy of the Court, or why a maimed king would be healed by someone's asking the right questions. Such events, occasionally linked with necromancy, are simply a part of the conventions of the seamless world that Chrétien has created, and whatever pagan mythic or religious elements they represent never emerge as objects of treatment in the tales themselves. The "customs" are just there. In fact, Chrétien gives us no clue as to whether he himself understood those elements, perhaps because they were more valuable to him shrouded in a veil of ambiguity than as matters to be eluci- dated. Chrétien's natural tendency seems to have been to create a realistic ambiance in the fabric of which even the slightest suggestion of the preter- natural is enough to arouse fascination in his readers.

The embedding of mythic figures in history is a phenomenon known as euhemerization: thus Chrétien refers on the same level of narrative and in the same tone to a historically plausible emperor of Constantinople named Alexandre, the possibly but not verifiably historical—and certainly not royal—Arthur, and the mythical Gifflet or Nut, with the implication that all three once lived. This treatment of the wondrous as an element of the everyday experiences of characters is one of the attractions not only of Chrétien's tales but of the matter of Britain in general as it manifests itself first in French romance and lay and then in the literatures of England, Germany, Italy, Spain, and other regions of Europe. At the same time, it is essential to realize that the Celtic characters, themes, and motifs Chré- tien knew gave him access, before any other writer of sustained narrative, to a new stock of creative materials that took its place beside the stories of ancient history and mythology available in the matter of antiquity and the tales of Frankish and Carolingian provenance found in the chansons de geste. His integration of pagan mysteries into the weave of Arthurian narrative plays an essential role in his success.

Chapter 6

The Art of the Storyteller

Chrétien de Troyes was a master storyteller. He was also an innovator, creating a literary tradition, the Arthurian romance, that rose to popularity with his works, was continued in prose form soon after his death, and has lasted to this day in a variety of national literatures. Two stories that he was the first to tell in any surviving version have been retold in constantly varying forms: the quest for the Grail and the love between Lancelot and Guinevere (see Elisabeth Brewer 1987; and Lacy and Ashe 1988: 151–221). His romances are read by the educated public young and old, figure on school reading lists for courses in literature and history, are a major source of knowledge for details of everyday living in the twelfth century, and can still provide entertainment for those wishing temporary escape from life's pressures. The reasons for this success are many, and although it is impossible to exhaust the subject, as the vast volume of studies on Chrétien attests, this chapter explores a few of the more significant ones.

CHRÉTIEN'S CONCEPTION OF HIS ART

In all his romances, Chrétien sets a context: in relation to his previous works (*Cliges*), his sources, whether oral (*Erec*) or written (*Cliges, Perceval*), or his attitude toward themes (*Yvain, Perceval*) and other compositional aspects of the works. He is in this sense a self-conscious author, one who articulates and thematizes the material with which he works. Medieval writers of imaginative literature, unlike the jongleurs who are represented as singing chansons de geste without the aid of the written word, felt themselves under the obligation to justify their efforts according to philosophical or religious principles. Chrétien is no exception.

Chrétien views Greece as the font from which, through the intermediary of Rome, came both the learning that allows him to write and chivalry, the subject of his writings (*Cliges* 30–44). He expresses the wish that learning and chivalry should remain forever in France and that God should not withdraw them and place them elsewhere, as happened with Greece and Rome, whose glory is now dimmed. The notion that power and learning have been passed from the ancient to the medieval world is known as the transmission of empire and learning (*translatio imperii et studii*). Although this is an important idea, I take it not as a key to the interpretation of the romance in which it occurs but, rather, as Chrétien's summary and incidental expression of his view of the relation between the France of his time and the achievements of antiquity.

Like many of his contemporaries, Chrétien is fond of quoting or evoking proverbs (see the collection of his proverbs and sayings in *Erec, Yvain, Lancelot,* and *Perceval* in Grosse 1881: 193–200), which are cited in the prologues to *Erec, Yvain,* and *Perceval. Erec* begins with a dictum to the effect that often a thing is despised that turns out to be worth more than was thought. On that basis Chrétien justifies applying himself to Erec's story, which thus for him fits into the class of topics that is more beneficial than at first appears, implying a deeper significance than what is visible on the surface. He bases his romance on an adventure tale that he endows with a fitting together (*conjointure, Erec* 14) of loose parts that professional storytellers (those who want to make a living from telling tales, *cil qui de conter vivre vuelent,* 23), plying their wares orally in courts, typically performed separately and imperfectly (literally "are in the habit of breaking into pieces and corrupting," *depecier et corrompre suelent, Erec* 21). This task of his he sees as fulfilling the Christian's obligation to employ his talents well (see the parable of the talents, Matt. 25.14–32).

Recourse to what, if it is not an actual proverb, still mirrors the lapidary syntax of proverbs, occurs again in the prologue to *Yvain,* where, after reflecting on the superiority of those who lived in the Arthurian world and were skilled in the arts of love, Chrétien observes, "Still, a dead courtly man is worth more, in my estimation, / than a live churl" (*Encor vaut mix, che m'est a vis / Un courtois mors c'uns vilains vis, Yvain* 31–32). Calogrenant's exhortation that his audience in Arthur's court—and by implication the audience of the romance—make an effort to understand his tale not just with the ears but with the heart also fills the function of a prologue, because it is intended to apply to the whole romance and not just Calogrenant's story.

Proverbial concision also marks the first line of *Perceval,* which invokes

Christ's parable of the sower who harvests in abundance only if his seed
has fallen on fertile ground:

> Whoever sows little, harvests little,
> And whoever wants to harvest something,
> Let him sow his seed in such a place
> That it render him a hundredfold increase,
> For on land that is worthless,
> Good seed dries out and fails.
> [Qui petit seime petit quiaut
> Et qui auques recoillir viaut
> En tel leu sa semence espande
> Que fruit a cent doble li rande,
> Car en terre qui rien ne vaut
> Bone semence seiche et faut.]

This allusion is to the parable of the sower (Matt. 13.4–9, Luke 8.5–8) alerts
the reader to a religious note in *Perceval,* as Chrétien extends the metaphor
to himself. The author is a sower and his romance the seed that he sows
in the fertile ground, that is to say his patron, Philip of Flanders (*Perceval*
7–14).[1] Chrétien does not limit himself to this one reference to a biblical
passage but rather returns twice to the allusive mode in the same prologue,
invoking and then providing exegetical commentary on Christ's admonition that in almsgiving, one's right hand should not know what one's left is
doing (38–46; Matt. 6.3), and citing the dictum that he who lives by charity
lives in God and God in him, which he wrongly ascribes to St. Paul (47–50;
it is from the first epistle of John 4.16). In *Perceval,* then, Chrétien deviates
from the purely profane themes of his other prologues.

Chrétien states in *Erec* that he is drawing from an adventure tale (*conte
d'aventure*) a "very beautiful conjoining" (*mout bele conjunture,* 13–14). The
term *conjointure* is particularly important for Chrétien's conception of his
tasks as a writer who is calling upon and refashioning a variety of previously existing tales and myths. An analysis that is relevant for the interpretation of *conjointure* as Chrétien uses the word in the prologue to *Erec* comes
from his contemporary Alan of Lille's *Complaint of Nature.* Alan describes
junctura as a combining of history with the storytelling tricks of jongleurs
(*joculationibus fabulosis*) (cited in Luttrell 1974: 67). Chrétien's pejorative
reference in line 21 of *Erec* to the activities of professional performers of
tales shows that he wants to give the impression of holding a depreciatory
view of them. At the same time, however, he is profiting from what those

performers bring him by taking stories about Erec—performances of epi-sodes such as the Hunt for the White Stag, the Joy of the Court, and per-haps even the Test of the Sparrow-Hawk—and weaving them together into a sustained narrative endowed with a meaning (*sens,* 5). This combination produces a cohesion, a *conjointure,* and his story (*estoire,* 23) will result from this weaving together of tales.[2] The Test of the Sparrow-Hawk may have been performed as an independent narrative, depending on how one in-terprets an allusion in the *sirventes-ensenhamen* of the Catalan troubadour Guerau de Cabrera. Guerau, who was no longer alive in October 1170, re-proaches his jongleur Cabra for not knowing, among other tales, "how Erec conquered the sparrow-hawk outside his kingdom" (Riquer 1967: 344; Pirot 1972: 545–62). This may refer to the episode as told by Chrétien in *Erec,* in which case it would reveal an extremely early knowledge of the romance in Catalonia, or, as is more likely, it may allude to one of the shorter tales that Chrétien associates with professional storytellers in *Erec,* lines 21–23.

In the prologue to *Lancelot,* Chrétien uses other technical terms of the art of composition, notably *matiere* 'matter', and *sens,* which has two mean-ings, 'intelligence' (l. 23) and 'interpretation' (l. 26). For this romance, both the matter and the interpretation, he claims, were given to him by Marie de Champagne (*Lancelot* 26–27), whereas his contribution is limited to his thought, his effort, and his intention or plan (*antancïon,* 29). This statement has given rise to much commentary (see Nitze 1915–17, 1954; Hoepffner 1934; Robertson 1951; Lyons 1954; Kelly 1966; Rychner 1967, 1972; Frappier 1972b; Ollier 1974; Burrell 1985; Janssens 1986; Beltrami 1989). I believe that the matter Marie gave Chrétien was the tale of Guinevere's abduction and her rescue by the knight Lancelot. The *sens* was the interpretation of the relationship between knight and lady as an adulterous love.

Writers of Chrétien's time valued the old and established ways and were apprehensive about novelties, seldom boasting of their innovations and often claiming to tell the authentic version of a widely known tale. Chré-tien says that he derived *Cliges* from a book in the collection of the church of Saint-Pierre in Beauvais, which, he mentions, was very old, and thus all the more worthy of belief (*Cliges* 18–26). This valuing of the past is not, however, limited to sources. The prologue of *Yvain* evokes neither the cir-cumstances of patronage nor the metacommentary of compositional ter-minology but, rather, takes the whole Arthurian world as the example of a society in which love was practiced by many. In those days, its practition-ers, "the disciples of Love's convent" (*Yvain* 16), were acclaimed as courtly, accomplished, generous, and full of honor, but in Chrétien's time love has become the subject of lies told by those who boast that they love but are in fact devoid of feeling.

Chrétien does not highlight clearly in his prologues the themes of his romances or the interpretations he intends his audiences to adopt. The reader is left, then, with a set of suggestive indicators. In *Perceval*, Chrétien extols the charity of Philip of Flanders (*Perceval* 28–60), which some have taken to mean that charity is the dominant theme of the romance. In *Yvain*, he praises the time of King Arthur, when men and women knew how to love, a skill lost in his own time, according to him. These are possible thematic keynotes that, like the theme of the transmission of empire and learning in *Cliges*, have been pursued and adopted by some critics, but if they are the keynotes of the various romances, Chrétien never says so explicitly.

In considering closures to Chrétien's narratives one has only four texts to work with, because *Perceval* is unfinished and *Lancelot* was completed by Godefroy de Lagny. *Philomena*, which was imbedded in the *Ovide moralisé*, a process that may have affected its close, ends with a simple "About Philomena I will leave off here" (*De Philomena lairai ci*, 1468). Similarly, the final line of *Erec* is, "Now the tale ends here" (*Li contes fine ci a tant*, 6950). *Yvain* is provided with a short epilogue:

> Chrétien ends here his romance
> Of the knight of the lion.
> Never did he hear speak any more about him,
> Nor will you ever hear tell any more about him
> Unless someone wants to add a lie.
> [Del chevalier al lion fine
> Crestïens son romant issi.
> Onques plus dire n'en oï,
> Ne ja plus n'en orés conter
> S'on ne velt mençongne ajoster.]   (*Yvain* 6804–8)

These lines confirm that Chrétien derived the tale about Yvain from a source or sources and claim that further stories about the characters in the romance would not be truthful. This does not necessarily imply, however, that Chrétien believed in the historicity of the story as he received it.

The epilogue of *Cliges* is of still greater interest. Fenice, Chrétien tells us, was not closely guarded like the wives of subsequent emperors of Constantinople:

> For never since then was there an emperor
> Who did not fear, of his wife,

That she should deceive him,
If he heard tell
How Fenice deceived Alis
First by the potion that he drank
And then by the other treachery.
On this account, the empress,
No matter how rich or noble she should be,
Is guarded in Constantinople
As if she were in prison,
For the emperor does not believe her
As long as he remembers this one [Fenice].
He always has her guarded in her room,
More out of fear than to avoid the sun,
Nor will she ever have with her a male
Who is not castrated in his infancy,
On account of which there is no fear or apprehension
That Love is binding the two of them in its rope.
Here ends Chrétien's work.
[Qu'ainc puis n'i ot empereor
N'eüst de sa fame peor
Qu'ele nel deüst decevoir,
Se il oï ramantevoir
Comant Fenice Alis deçut
Primes par la poison qu'il but
Et puis par l'autre traïson.
Por ce einsi com an prison
Est gardee an Costantinoble,
Ja n'iert tant riche ne tant noble
L'empererriz, quex qu'ele soit,
Que l'empereres ne la croit
Tant com de cesti li remanbre.
Toz jorz la fait garder en chanbre
Plus por peor que por le hasle,
Ne ja avoec li n'avra masle
Qui ne soit chastrez en anfance,
De ce n'est criemme ne dotance
Qu'Amors les lit an son lien.
Ci fenist l'uevre Crestien.]   (*Cliges* 6683–6702)

If the emperors' fear of being cuckolded were generalized to the characters of all women, and if Fenice had not had ample justification for her actions, one might be justified in viewing this prologue as revealing a streak of anti-feminism in Chrétien. Such a conclusion would be strange, as few of the stereotypes that are typical of clerical antifeminism are found elsewhere in Chrétien's œuvre—but see, on the margin of clerical bias, Yvain's complaint that "a woman has more than a hundred whims" (*femme a plus de chent courages, Yvain* 1440) and, in the same romance, the observation that Laudine shares with other women the tendency of excusing her own follies and rejecting what she desires (1640–44). As it stands, however, the emphasis in the finale of *Cligès* is on a trait of local color—namely, the service of eunuchs at the court of Constantinople, which is presented as a consequence of the duping of Alis—rather than on any supposedly justified fear of female conduct in general. In addition, the consistently positive portrayal of Fenice and her refusal to become a second Ysolt make it clear that Chrétien does not disdain her.

Unlike some of his contemporaries and near-contemporaries, as for instance Thomas d'Angleterre in his *Roman de Tristan* or Marie de France in some of her lays, Chrétien does not employ the epilogue to impose an interpretation on his works.

POINT OF VIEW AND AUTHORIAL INTERVENTIONS

In considering the point of view from which the romances are told it is useful to distinguish the author-reworker from the narrator, following Sophie Marnette (1998). Chrétien tells his tales largely in the third person but occasionally intervenes as a first-person narrator, as in the opening of the narration proper of *Erec*, "From this point I will begin the story" (*Des or comencerai l'estoire*, 23), and *Yvain*, "For this reason it pleases me to recount . . ." (*Pour che me plaist a reconter . . .*, 33). To insert himself into the tale for the purpose of commenting on it, he then uses first-person singular forms of the verb,[3] with or without the first person pronoun, which is optional in medieval French, or the first-person object pronoun, as in, "Along with those whom you hear me name" (*Avec ces que m'öez nommer, Erec* 1941). Exceptionally, he has a character assume the task of reporting the story, notably Calogrenant in *Yvain*, who takes more than four hundred lines to tell about a series of events that happened to him six years before the scene in which he is speaking (*Yvain* 175).

Many literary works from medieval France, among them some of the finest quality, are anonymous—the *Vie de Saint Alexis*, the *Roman de Thèbes*, the *Roman d'Enéas, Aucassin et Nicolette, Flamenca,* the prose *Lancelot, La Mort le roi Artu,* the *Chanson de Roland, Raoul de Cambrai, Girart de Roussillon,* and in fact the vast majority of chansons de geste—so it is not a foregone conclusion that the person responsible for generating a literary text considers himself an author in the sense of claiming open responsibility for it by naming himself. Chrétien, however, not only claims his works as his own but takes great pride in them, if one is to judge by his boast in *Erec* that he tells a story that will be remembered as long as Christianity lasts (*Erec* 23–26). That *Erec* is also the romance in which, for the only time in his career, he identifies himself as Chrétien *de Troies* (9) is no accident. Each of the other romances treated in this book also bears his name (tautologically, as we have no other secure way of judging whether a work is by Chrétien): *Cliges* in lines 23, 45, and 6702; *Lancelot* in line 25 and, in the section written by Godefroy de Lagny, in lines 7105 and 7107; *Yvain* in line 6805; and *Perceval* in lines 7 and 60. The name Chrétien always occurs with a verb in the third person, a common authorial practice in French works of the period.

In spite of his pride in his work, however, Chrétien freely admits reworking the work of others, oral sources for *Erec* (19–22), books for *Cliges* (18–23) and *Perceval* (66–67), and materials of unspecified nature for *Lancelot* (26–27). The analysis of mythic and folkloric motifs in *Yvain* leads to the conclusion that this romance is also derivative, although the modalities of its dependence on previous material are indefinable. In keeping with the general notion, widespread in this period, that older is better, and with the common and honored practice of creative adaptation, there is no implication that Chrétien considered the lack of complete originality as detracting from his conception of himself as an author. He is thus, for himself and for us, an author-reworker, and does not hesitate to declare his ignorance of certain details, implying this status: Yvain and his lion stayed in the dwelling of a hospitable host "for I don't know how many days" (4702). In *Perceval,* he also uses transitional expressions such as "Here the tale ceases to speak of Gauvain and begins to speak of Perceval" (6214–16; see also 4813–15, 6514–18), assigning to his source the change of focus.[4]

The person who speaks in Chrétien's romances we will call the narrator, as distinct from the author-reworker, in keeping with Marnette's conceptualization. In addition to the framing function of his presence in the prologues to his works, Chrétien the narrator maintains an atmosphere of close communication with his audience during the narrative proper. The means he takes to sustain this ambiance are many: formulas of presentation such as exhortations that listeners should pay attention, exclamations that signal his sympathy with or antipathy against his characters, declarations of the intention to be brief, expressions of the type "if you had been there, you would have seen" (or "heard"), pleadings that the audience believe him or assertions that it should do so, rhetorical questions, expressions of opinion, declarations of his inability to do justice to an aspect of the tale, references to other parts of the story, first-person references to sources, changes of focus expressed in the first person, and the use of other first-person verbs. His protestations of ignorance about certain details— as in *Yvain* 5403, where he claims not to know whether those who welcome the hero to the castle of Ill Adventure with such enthusiasm are deceiving him—imply that he is merely retelling stories or that there is a deeper reality behind them than his own words, as if these characters are not just creatures of the author.[5] This is decidedly not the type of distant narrator who tells the story as an objective sequence of actions: on the contrary, Chrétien gives the impression of continuously grappling with both the audience and the tale.

At times Chrétien solicits the audience's collusion, flattering it for its expertise, as when he addresses those with experience in amatory matters:

You who consider yourselves wise with Love,
Who uphold faithfully
The customs and the practice of her court
And never broke her law
Whatever should befall you. . . .
[Vos qui d'Amors vos feites sage,
Qui les coustumes et l'usage
De sa cort meintenez o foi,
N'onques ne fausates sa loi
Que que vos en deüst cheoir. . . .]   (*Cligés* 3819–26)

When Lancelot is hiding his intention to go to the queen's bedroom, Chrétien slyly appeals to the readers' experiences in similar situations:

You can well understand and gloss,
You who have acted likewise,
That for the personnel of his hostel
He pretends to be tired and goes to bed.
[Bien pöez antendre et gloser,

Vos qui avez fet autretel,
Que por la gent de son ostel
Se fet las et se fet couchier.]   (*Lancelot* 4550–53)

The glossing in question is the process by which readers add to the romance
by their interpretations, as a medieval scholar might write comments in
the margins of the manuscript page of a Bible or law text by way of eluci-
dating its obscurities. Because glossing was a learned practice, once again
Chrétien is subtly flattering his audience.

On another occasion, Chrétien addresses his audience as if he is arguing
a philosophical point in a scholastic setting. When Gauvain and Yvain are
about to do combat with each other, each fighting on behalf of one of the
heiresses of Noire Espine but neither knowing the other's identity, the narrator argues at length in a disputatious style about whether the two knights
can be said to love each other (*Yvain* 5997–6066). His initial answer is "yes
and no," leading to a series of distinctions interspersed with rhetorical questions and punctuated by exclamations of "Yes," "Not he," "God," and "Ha."
Marnette (1998: 71) underscores the anomalous nature of Chrétien's direct
address to the audience in this passage—"'Yes,' I tell you, and 'no'" (*"Oïl,"
vous respont, et "nenil,"* 5998), "'No, I swear and certify'" (*"Nenil, jel vous jur
et affi,"* 6072). The impression is of a dialectician addressing his audience.

A use of the first-person plural pronoun in *Lancelot* led Gaston Paris to
believe that he could identify Chrétien's occupation. When Lancelot goes
to Noauz in preparation for the tournament, a herald recognizes him but
promises not to reveal that Lancelot is there. He cannot, however, keep
himself from crying out, "'Now he has come who will take the measure'"
(*"Or est venuz qui l'aunera,"* *Lancelot* 5563). Chrétien then intervenes in his
own voice:

And know that then was said for the first time:
"Now he has come who will take the measure!"
Our master in this was the herald
Who taught us how to say it,
For he said it first.
[Et sachiez que dit fu lors primes:
"Or est venuz qui l'aunera!"
Nostre mestre an fu li hyra
Qui a dire le nos aprist,
Car il premieremant le dist.]   (*Lancelot* 5570–74)

The expression here ascribed to the herald was indeed a common saying (Le Rider 1978b). That Chrétien should be identified as a herald on the basis of the passage is, however, doubtful. He consistently identifies the Arthurian milieu as a world in the distant past, and the "we" in question is the ensemble of those, including his audience and himself, who use the saying that the herald first invented.

IRONY

Distancing himself by his comments and interventions from the narration of events proper, Chrétien enables himself to recount the tale without espousing the viewpoints of the characters or the implication of the plot, developing a stance of narrative irony.

In treating the tropes of irony in *Cliges* and *Perceval,* Peter Haidu (1968) takes his cue from rhetorical treatises and distinguishes between *allegoria,* the trope of saying one thing while meaning another, and *significatio,* expressing by implication. *Allegoria* has as its subtypes *ironia* 'expressing by the contrary', *antiphrasis* 'one word irony, especially by contrary etymology', *aenigma* 'figurative paradox', *charientismos* 'saying harsh things in an agreeable way', *paroemia* 'using proverbs with a twist of meaning', *sarcasmos* 'mockery', and *asteismos* 'witty urbanity'.[6] *Significatio* can work by hyperbolic praise, by ambiguity, by practical conclusion, by implication of a conclusion, by innuendo, and by analogy. As a writer trained in the school, Chrétien is likely to have encountered these abundant and nuanced tropes of irony. The degree to which the reader perceives them, however, obviously depends very much on an overall interpretation of the sense of the work and of the immediate context of the passages in question, an interpretation not just of the obvious literal sense but also of the sense that the author might intend. Thus a certain circularity of thought is involved: one sees irony by perceiving a discrepancy between expressions and intentions, but one's expectations about the author's intentions derive from other expressions that are also open to interpretation. As with all such circular procedures, a hermeneutic process is at work, as the reader is constantly experiencing new perceptions about the romance and rethinking what has already been perceived in a different light.

A close reading of key passages makes it clear that irony is one of the dominant modes in Chrétien's romances. Nowhere is it more evident on a large scale than in *Lancelot,* whose prologue, in distancing the patron from the author-reworker—the patron being responsible for the matter and the interpretation and issuing commands about them, the author declaring himself responsible for the technique and implying little ultimate responsibility for the content—puts the audience on notice that not everything in the romance is necessarily to be taken at face value or with full authorial approval, however well the narrator does his job. Accordingly, Chrétien paints the character Lancelot in ridiculous colors as a knight who violates every norm of moderation in pursuing a love that he unwisely allows to dominate all other aspects of his life, including his honor and the decorum that is due when invoking pious contexts. Not that Marie de Champagne would have noticed this discrepancy, at least at first. Because irony consists of expressing an idea but intending something else, the greatest practical difficulty of the author who employs it is somehow to signal to the reader this contrary movement, without which what the author really means does not merely pass unnoticed but can pass in the guise of its opposite. When a performer speaks the text's words aloud—a female performer in the cases of *Yvain* and *Hunbaut:* see Chapter 1, above—she can convey the proper hint by a gesture or a change of intonation. For the reader of *Lancelot,* deprived of these auditory clues, the tip-off is provided not only by the distancing discourse of the prologue but by the context of Chrétien's other romances in which ideals are promoted that are completely at odds with the thrust of *Lancelot.* Chrétien's failure to complete *Lancelot* may have resulted from Marie's finally catching on to his ironic manipulation of the main character, her realization that her *san* was undercut by his *antancion* and that the narrator was at odds with Chrétien the author.

When irony operates on the level of the event, Chrétien may share with the audience knowledge of certain elements that the characters do not know. So Thessala describes to Cliges the drink she has concocted for Alis as one that the emperor will cherish for its expense, taste, and health-giving qualities, but the audience has already been let in on the real nature of the drink as a protection against Fenice's deflowering (*Cliges* 3235–62). Another instance is the audience's realization that Yvain, whom Lunete has depicted as so far away that she must send a fast messenger to fetch him, is already present in Laudine's castle (*Yvain* 1820–31). This type of irony contributes to a sense of complicity between narrator and audience, drawing the audience into the tale to share in the narrator's omniscience to which the characters do not have access.

Situational irony can sometimes generate humor. This is the case, for example, when Count Oringle of Limors, assuming that Erec is dead, has his body carried on a bier into the hall of his castle, where he has his chaplain marry Enide to him much against her will. He then proceeds to abuse Enide when she refuses to respond to him. Chrétien's readers know that Erec is not dead but has only fainted away because of the pain of his wounds. He revives from his faint to see the count strike Enide, leaps up, seizes his sword, and splits Oringle's head with a single blow. The count's retainers, thinking that they are being attacked by the devil himself, disperse screaming, "Flee! flee! It's the dead man." They run into one another in their rush to escape. Comic effects are frequently elusive, for few aspects of the relation between audience and subject are as deeply historically conditioned, or as hard to pin down, as humor, but the transformation of the courtesans from earnest participation in the scene of Oringle's forced marriage to headlong flight produces an effect of slapstick that I think was as effective in the twelfth century as it is today. Another, perhaps more questionable instance of humor is the attempted suicide of Yvain's lion (3502–21), which, seeing its master fall into a faint and cut himself with his sword, thinks he is dead. The beast carefully places the offending weapon against a log with his teeth, then puts another log behind it so that it will stay in place. He is hurtling toward the sword point "like a crazy pig" when the knight awakens and the lion halts mid-charge. The lion is acting here as an animal would in an episode of a beast epic such as the contemporary *Roman de Renart*.

Chrétien the narrator plays at times with his audience. One example is his statement, at the point in the narrative at which Erec, Enide, and Guivret come together to Arthur's court at Roais, that he is not going to tell his readers why Erec set out with Enide on their journey of adventures because he has already told them (*Erec* 6470–74). After three thousand lines with no discussion whatever of Erec's motivation, Chrétien can here be engaged only in ironic teasing. In this regard, Philippe Ménard identifies Chrétien as probably the first French narrator to speak to his public with a tone of amusement (Ménard 1969: 487). This tone would be possible only with an audience that is sophisticated enough to appreciate the nuances and subtleties of Chrétien's language, that is to say, in this period, a courtly audience.

Chrétien has been called the creator of the modern *roman*. The French term *roman*, which in its earliest uses simply means a work written in French rather than Latin, whether it be a tale, a history, a treatise, or another type of work, has a wider semantic range than the English "romance," encompassing also, in the postmedieval period, the semantic field of English "novel." Disillusionment is the hallmark of the realistic novel in the tradition stretching from *Don Quixote* to the modern era, but disillusionment is effective only in the hands of an ironic narrator. In this sense Chrétien is perhaps the first writer in French whose attitude toward his characters is consistently ironic on a number of levels.

THE ART OF VERSE-MAKING

Rhythm

Although Chrétien appears to have been fairly conservative in regard to his narrative material, to judge by the evidence available, he takes advantage of a feature of the art of narrating that was of recent invention in his time and that he exploits skillfully. Verse was composed in octosyllabic lines long before Chrétien by epic poets, in the chanson de geste *Gormont et Isembart.* In works employing the rhymed couplet, however, such as Geoffrey Gaimar's *Estoire des Engleis* (1137), Wace's *Roman de Brut* (1155), the *Roman d'Enéas,* and Benoît de Sainte-Maure's *Roman de Troie,* the rhymed couplet is not always a unit of sense, and occasionally the meaning is carried across the boundary of the second rhyme word. Chrétien contributes to breaking the barriers of the couplet (Frappier 1965), imparting an impression of ease and a suppleness of expression to the flow of narrative and rendering possible the stylistic effects of anticipation and retardation. Jean Frappier assigned a quality of surprise to the practice of breaking the couplet, at least during the first generations of poets to employ this device.

Frappier notes that in dialogue Chrétien frequently ends the speech of a character after the first line of a couplet and begins the reply of the interlocutor in the second line, thus linking the sequence of replies through the rhyme words and anticipating a technique found in the thirteenth-century French theater (Frappier 1964b: 5–7). Although Chrétien had other means at his disposal to signal the change of interlocutors, such as introductory or parenthetic verbs of speaking, vocative nouns such as "Sire" and "Lady," and interjections indicating a positive or negative response, he rarely uses the breaking of the couplet between interlocutors in the presence of these other devices. A break in the couplet also serves as the boundary between dialogue and narrative, as the passage between individual events in a sequence of actions, as a sign of change of time or place, and to set off a proverb, commentary, or conclusion.

Rhyme

An aspect of the poetics of the rhyming couplet is the avoidance of identical rhyme words in the same couplet. Identical forms were permitted, however, as long as the words were different parts of speech or had different meanings. Thus *Par qu'em puet prover et savoir / Que cil ne fait mie savoir* . . . ("By which one can prove and know / That he does not practice wisdom . . . ," *Erec* 15–16) is acceptable because the two instances of *savoir* at the rhyme are respectively the verb 'to know' and the infinitive of the same verb used as a noun meaning 'wisdom'. Such rhymes give the poet the opportunity to pun. This is not, however, always the case: for example, in the last twenty-six lines of *Erec,* Chrétien rhymes two couplets in *contes,* both times with the meanings 'count, lord of a county' in one line and 'count, tally' in the other (*Erec* 6925–26, 6941–42), but this consonance sets off no particular flash of recognition, insight, or humor and thus is not a pun properly so called. But when he opens the action of a romance "At that feast that so much costs / That one should well name it Pentecost" (*A chele feste qui tant couste, / C'on doit nommer le Penthecouste, Yvain* 5–6), the reader perceives that the morpheme *couste* of *Penthecouste* has for Chrétien resonances of costliness. The possibility then arises that he may well be criticizing the expense of feast days at court, albeit in a gentle and ambiguous way so as not to offend any high patron. Equivocal rhymes are fairly common in Chrétien and are one of the features that give his style a spark and make reading him in the original Old French such a pleasure. Keith Busby rightly calls Chrétien a "master rhymer" (1993b: lxiv).

Style

In the teaching of twelfth-century schools, literary texts were studied in the part of the curriculum known as the trivium—grammar, rhetoric, dialectic: the arts of language. The principal authors (*auctores*) treated were the Latin writers, including Ovid, Virgil, Cicero, Boethius, Sallust, Lucan, Statius, Juvenal, Horace, and Prudentius (see Curtius 1953: 48–54). Texts in the vernacular language were not studied, and what few treatises on poetic composition there are from the period, such as Matthew of Vendome's *Ars versificatoria* (early 1170s) and Geoffrey of Vinsauf's *Poetria nova* (early thirteenth century, and thus after Chrétien, but codifying earlier materials), concern themselves exclusively with literary expression in Latin. This was also true, of course, of the ancient treatises that were available, the most popular of which was the *Rhetorica ad Herennium* mistakenly as-

286 Art of the Storyteller

cribed to Cicero. What is known directly about the poetics of composition in twelfth-century French must thus be derived largely from analysis of the texts themselves rather than from theoretical works of the period. Teaching about poetic figures was indistinct from teaching about rhetoric. Chrétien naturally uses various tropes and figures in his works, some of which are found in the arts of rhetoric in relation to Latin.

One such figure is *praeteritio,* declaring that one passes over some matter in silence so as thereby to call attention to it. Thus Chrétien has other things to do than to enumerate for his readers all the plates that were served at Erec's coronation feast (*Erec* 6932–35) or, in *Cliges,* all the splendors of the wedding of Alexandre and Soredamor (2312–18) or that of Alis and Fenice (3200–3201) or the welcome that Cliges received on returning from Britain (5073–75). He will not say that, in comparison to Soredamor's throat, glass looks opaque (*Cliges* 834–35). Once his justification takes on a quality of extravagant exaggeration: Nature could never equal what she achieved in creating Fenice, and if Chrétien had a thousand years and his intelligence doubled each day, he still could not describe the woman's beauty in detail (*Cliges* 2688–99). In hearing about the tournament at Oxford in *Cliges* don't think the narrator is going to identify for you all the kings and counts who were present! (4572–75). Is this last a reaction to criticism Chrétien may have received for the long lists of knights of the Round Table and guests at Erec and Enide's wedding in his first romance, or is it simply a way of saying that very many high nobles were in attendance? These examples of prae-teritio are all found in the first two romances, and I cannot help thinking that, in trying to find the right pace for his tales, Chrétien feels an obligation to let his audience know that he describes only when description is neces-sary. Sometimes his refusal to tell does not seem to have the slightly ironic tinge of praeteritio: thus he will not describe the appointments of Enide's quarters in the castle of Brandigan (*Erec* 5563–71), or the scene of Alexan-dre's dubbing (*Cliges* 1203). In refusing to come right out and say that Marie de Champagne surpasses queens as a precious gem surpasses pearls and sardonixes—although, he claims, it is still true (*Lancelot* 16–20)—is Chré-tien being unduly coy so as to arouse the suspicions of his audience as to the countess's role in the genesis of this romance?

Comparisons—metaphors and similes—are another area of figurative language in which Chrétien seems to delight. Some of his comparisons evoke renowned classical or biblical characters as models that his heroes equal or surpass: thus Erec is as handsome as Absolom, as eloquent as

Solomon, and as generous as Alexander the Great (*Erec* 2262–66; compare 6665–68).

On the elemental level, Laudine's enthusiasm for Yvain, whom she had first rejected mentally as her husband's killer, is described in terms of fire:

> And by herself she lights up
> Like a log that smokes
> Until the flame takes hold
> Without anyone blowing on it or fanning it.
> [Et par li meïsmes s'alume
> Ausint com la buche qui fume,
> Tant que la flame s'i est mise,
> Que nulz ne la soufle n'atise.]   (*Yvain* 1777–80)

The "by herself" is occasioned by the knowledge shared by author and audience that Laudine's judgment is based more on her perception of self-interest than on any considerations of justice in spite of the trial that she has just conducted in her mind as to Yvain's responsibility for her husband's death. Similar associations of love with fire are found elsewhere: for example, lines 598–600 of *Cliges,* which compare the lover's desire to approach the beloved in search of relief to the fact that one who approaches too near to a fire will surely be burned. This semantic field of this metaphor is not unusual, however. In Marie de France's *Guigemar,* for example, the hero's unnamed lover burns for him with a fire that consumes her heart (in Ewert 1944: ll. 390–92). Such comparisons of love with fire may have been suggested by Ovid—*Metamorphoses* 7.79–83, for example.

Other comparisons in Chrétien are more original. Thus Alexandre is said to have received three joyous honors while at Windsor, of which the first two are his capture of the castle from Angres and Arthur's promise to give him the best kingdom in Wales as a fief. The third honor is the greatest, however, namely that Soredamor is now the queen on the chessboard on which he is king (*Cliges* 2330–31). Another unusual metaphor for the period, this time in the semantic field of martial endeavors, describes Cliges and the duke of Saxony as sounding out the music of a lay with the sword-blows they are giving to each other's helmets (*Cliges,* ll. 4–6 following 4014). Yet another is the comparison that emerges in the description of Guivret le Petit's horse, which as it gallops shatters rocks under its hooves more finely than a millstone grinds wheat (*Erec* 3704–5).

The most elaborate metaphor occurs in Alexandre's long internal monologue in *Cliges* the evening after he first sees Soredamor on the ship sailing for Brittany: his meditation on Love's arrow (766–853). In contemplating the feathers in the arrow, Alexandre notes that the notch and the feathers are close, divided only by a straight part; the yellow feathers are the blond tresses that he saw on his sea voyage—Soredamor's hair, although he refrains from mentioning her name all through the monologue. It is the arrow that makes him love! If he could have the notch and the feathers, he would not desire the rest at all. The metaphor then slips imperceptibly from the qualities of the arrow to Soredamor's attributes: if only he could gaze at that forehead more lovely than a jewel! Her eyes outshine candles. He remarks on the well-shaped nose, the clear face, the laughing mouth, the teeth, the chin, the eyes, the throat, the décolletage. Then the parts of the metaphoric arrow surface again, perhaps to maintain decorum as Alexandre's mind wanders toward more specifically erotic territory. His unhappiness would be assuaged if he could see the whole arrow and describe its shaft. But it was covered by the quiver: the shift and tunic in which the girl was dressed. This passage is really a triple metaphor: falling in love is caused by the metaphoric abstraction Love, which shoots an arrow, which is an image of the beloved's body. Its complications are characteristic of the Ovidian stage of Chrétien's career, of which *Philomena* and *Cliges* are the surviving products.

During the visit of Arthur and his court to Landuc, Chrétien, addressing his audience with a rhetorical question, mentions what he calls the acquaintance between the sun and the moon, that is to say, between Gauvain and Lunete (*Yvain* 2395–2440). Gauvain is the sun, for his renown is greater than any other knight's, and Lunete is the moon not just for her faithfulness and help but because her name means "Little Moon." Some have thought that there is more than just a metaphor at work here, as Gauvain is said elsewhere in tradition to grow stronger toward noon and weaker toward dusk (see, for example, *La Mort le roi Artu,* ed. Frappier 1964a: 154). A similar comparison sets Yvain above other fighters as a candle among candelabras, the moon among the stars, or the sun in comparison to the moon (*Yvain* 3245–49).

Not all metaphors are positive, however: Yvain is said to be almost cut in two in the entrance to Laudine's castle by the action of trip-levers that release the portcullis and catch him like a rat in a trap (*Yvain* 911–26). The pejorative cast of this image implies a criticism of Yvain's conduct in leaving Arthur's court clandestinely to undertake alone the test of the fountain.

Unsurprisingly in an author identified with the commercial center

Troyes, economic metaphors occasionally surface. Thus Gauvain, ignorant of the identity of his adversary, tells Yvain that if he has made him a loan—that is, of forceful blows—Yvain has rendered him an account of it for both the capital and the interest, for he was more generous in paying the blows back than Gauvain was in receiving them (*Yvain* 6248–52). A similar metaphor occurs in *Cliges* 4026–29, where Cliges and the duke of Saxony, exchanging blows, are said to render each other capital and interest. Critics who view such metaphors as evidence of bourgeois concerns seem to pass over the realities of aristocratic existence, in which borrowing at interest was common. To shame a knight by mistaking him for a merchant or a money changer (*Perceval* 5094), as the young women who discuss Gauvain with the Maiden of the Short Sleeves do, is quite another matter.

Description

Chrétien is a word-painter of vivid scenes that have lingered in the imagination of readers and writers. One of the most famous is Perceval's reverie on the colors of Blancheflor's face (*Perceval* 4164–4465), discussed in Chapter 5. Perceval has come upon a frozen meadow on which snow has fallen; Arthur and his court are encamped there. A falcon startles a flock of wild geese and swoops down on one of them, knocking it to the ground but then immediately flying away. The goose flies away as well. Seeing three drops of blood that have fallen from the goose's neck onto the snow, Perceval thinks of the hues of his lover's face and sits in a trance, leaning on his lance, for the entire morning. First Sagremor and then Keu go to fetch him into the court, but Perceval's lack of response provokes their attacks and he unhorses them in succession, breaking Keu's arm and unknowingly avenging the Laughing Girl whom Keu had abused on Perceval's account. Perceval returns to his contemplative state, yielding only to the invitation of Gauvain, who approaches him courteously and remarks that to fall into a pensive state is a mark of courtliness and gentleness (*Perceval* 4459). Chrétien has achieved a number of goals with this scene: he has shown that Perceval has moved far beyond his initial coarseness, reinforced the character of his sentimental attachment to Blancheflor, added actions typical of the characterizations traditionally assigned to Sagremor le Desreez, "the Impetuous," and Keu, had Perceval take his vengeance on Keu without appearing overly aggressive in doing so, and reintegrated Perceval into the court in anticipation of the Hideous Maiden's arrival and the launching of the quest for the Bleeding Lance and the Grail. At the core of the scene is not metaphor but metonymy: the colors stand for Blancheflor by association. That this scene was memorable in the Middle Ages as well as attractive to modern readers is shown by its occurrence as a subject of manuscript illuminations of *Perceval*. Manuscript Bibliothèque nationale, fonds français 12576, for example, copied in the third quarter of the thirteenth century and containing *Perceval* and the four *Continuations,* bears on folio 19 an illumination that includes the details of Perceval leaning on his lance and gazing at the three drops of blood on a snowbank (see Hindman 1994: 20, fig. 3; see also plate 7).

A much briefer scene that is also set off by a vivid detail is the reconciliation of Erec and Enide. After Erec revives from his seemingly dead state and kills Count Oringle, he and his wife are forced to flee Limors on a single horse. As they ride off, Erec embraces her and speaks comforting words, pardoning any offense she might have committed.

> Now Enide is not badly off
> Since her husband is hugging and kissing her
> And reassuring her of his love.
> They go off in the night at a great pace
> And it is a great sweetness to them
> That the moon sheds its clear light for them.
> [Or n'est pas Enide a malaise,
> Quant ses sire l'acole et baise,
> Et de s'amor la raseüre.
> Par nuit s'en vont grant aleüre,
> Et ce lor fait grant soatume
> Que la lune clair lor alume.]   (*Erec* 4927–32)

Is this an anticipation of the "pathetic fallacy," that nature sympathizes with the moods and sentiments of humanity? To conclude thus would be to read too much into the passage, to interpret it in view of modern rather than medieval mentalities. When nature interacts on an emotive level with characters in Chrétien, it is in the guise of the personified figure Nature, and because *alume* 'sheds light' is not necessarily a personal verb, there is no need to assume allegorization. Rather, Chrétien is providing illumination through the light of the moon for an unusual night ride in a society in which people normally do not venture out, much less ride, after dark if they can help it.

Perceval's initial view of knights is a scene that also struck the imaginations of illuminators (*Perceval* 69–136; see plate 10). The young Perceval, called simply "the son of the widow of the deep Waste Forest," goes mounted on a hunter and armed with three javelins to watch his mother's harrowers. Rejoicing in the springtime atmosphere, he lets his horse graze and is prac- ticing his javelin throws when suddenly five knights come through the woods. Perceval hears their shields and hauberks clanking and knocking against the trees before he sees them. Taking this as the sound of devils approaching, Perceval prepares to strike out with a javelin, but his audi- tory experience is displaced by the sight of the knights' gleaming hauberks and the many colors of their helmets and clothing. He reconsiders and con- vinces himself that what he is seeing is angels.

A less significant, but still telling, use of detail is the apparently unmean- ingful inclusion of a small element, such as the reference to a "robe of fine red wool, / Lined with squirrel fur marked in chalk" (*robe d'eskallaste vermeille, / De vair fourree a tout la croie, Yvain* 1886–87). The fact that the tailor's chalk has not yet rubbed off the robe suggests that the garment is newly made, and the mark lends a touch of realism to the scene in which Lunete is dressing Yvain to meet Laudine.

Blood drops on the snow, the moon lighting the way, the sounds of metal on wood, chalk marks on a new robe, such clear details anchor the medi- eval—and the modern—audience's imagination. These images result from choices of the verbal artist independent of the myths that stand behind the tales. One could add to them the bedroom scene and the first view of the Joy of the Court in *Erec*, the test of the fountain, the hero's entrapment, and the lion's rescue in *Yvain*, the love scene in *Lancelot*, the young Perceval's meeting with Orgueilleus de la Lande's mistress, his entry into Arthur's court on horseback, the Grail procession, the Good Friday encounter with the pilgrims, the episode of the Maiden of the Short Sleeves, and Gauvain's entrance into the castle of the Rock of Champguin in *Perceval*, as well as a number of other finely drawn scenes in the five romances. In this regard, Jean Frappier remarked that Chrétien tends to increase the frequency of realistic traits in episodes of heightened fantasy (Frappier 1982: 174).

An offspring of his age and milieu, Chrétien revels in scenes of magnifi- cence. Of these, perhaps the finest is Erec's coronation at Nantes, during which King Arthur dubs two hundred knights and gives a feast served at five hundred tables that is as great as was ever given by Caesar or any king of epic fame. Arthur and Erec are seated on ivory faldstools, gifts of Brian of the Isles, on which are carved leopards and crocodiles. Erec and Enide both wear crowns. The coronation ceremony is performed by the bishop of Nantes, but it is Arthur who gives the couple scepters. The centerpiece is Erec's robe of moiré silk and gold thread (6726–6801), woven by four

fairies and decorated with personifications of the four arts of the quadrivium: geometry, arithmetic, music, and astronomy. Geometry is pictured
measuring the world. Arithmetic counts the days and hours but also the
grains of sand, the stars, and the leaves of trees. Music governs musical instruments that produce delight. Astronomy consults the stars, the moon,
and the sun and is counseled by the other arts, for she knows all that was
and all that will be. The lining shows marvelous beasts called *barbiolettes,*
with white heads, black necks, red backs, spotted stomachs, and indigo
tails, which eat nothing but exotic spices. Amethysts and chrysolites, set
in gold, ornament the tassels. Chrétien claims to have gotten the description of this robe in Macrobius, author of a famous commentary on Cicero's
Dream of Scipio, but that book contains nothing of the kind,[7] so perhaps
it is only the art of describing it that is owed to Macrobius. In any event,
the four arts of the quadrivium are especially appropriate for a king, who
must take the measure of his kingdom and anticipate the future, and they
symbolize the maturity that Erec has acquired in the course of his long
ride with Enide. The magnificence of this scene, with its representation of
Erec in all the accoutrements of the ideal king (Maddox 1978: 185, 1991: 14)
reinforces the notion that Chrétien was drawing an unarticulated parallel
with the Christmas court of 1169 at which the Breton nobles paid homage
to Geoffrey, son of Henry II of England.

Erec's robe is, however, only the final piece of clothing to play a special
role in *Erec.* The young knight was quite concerned that Enide wear her
threadbare tunic to Arthur's court, and refused to let her accept the gift of
a dress from her cousin. When they arrive at court, Guinevere takes great
pleasure in dressing Enide in her own tunic and mantle (1583–1638). The
tunic is decorated with ermine, and jewels set in gold line the sleeve and
neck openings. The tunic alone is worth ten pounds of silver. The mantle is
also lined in ermine and covered in sable with gold tassels. These garments
symbolize the beauty of Enide's character as well as her rapidly increased
status as Erec's promised bride. Ironically, Erec will command her to put
on her best dress[8] for their solitary journey, but there it will be a matter of
baiting the covetousness of intruders rather than stressing nobility of heart.
Clothing plays yet again a symbolic role in the plot when King Guivret has
two beautiful robes made for Erec and Enide in his castle of Penuris (5217–
27), emblematic of their reconciliation: Enide's of blue material set off with
ermine, Erec's of striped fabric with squirrel fur. The description of this
luxurious clothing was no doubt of great interest to Chrétien's courtly audi-

ences. In none of his other romances does he approach this level of detail in dressing his protagonists.

THE ART OF NARRATION

Organization

Chrétien has a term for the larger divisions of a romance, "verse" (*vers*), and he calls the first section of the narrative of *Erec* "the first verse" (*li premerains vers,* 1840). This line of *Erec* is, however, the only time he uses the term in this sense, so it is up to the reader to conceptualize the divisions of each romance. Dividing the narrative is not an empty exercise but rather a function of how the reader conceives the meaning of each text. That Chrétien includes two "customs" in the first verse shows that he thinks of his romances as organized on a level higher than the individual episodes.

The narrative proper of *Erec* is structured in five large divisions: (1) *li premerains vers,* consisting of the Hunt for the White Stag, in which is imbedded the Test of the Sparrow-Hawk and which tells how Erec meets Enide and how she is welcomed to Arthur's court, lines 27–1840; (2) the wedding of Erec and Enide and the tournament at Edinburgh, lines 1841–2307; (3) the beginning of their married life in Carnant, the crisis of confidence, the journey with its six tests (against three knights, five knights, Galoain, Guivret, two giants, and Oringle), and the couple's reconciliation, lines 2308–4932; (4) the sojourn in Guivret le Petit's castle and the adventure in Brandigan, lines 4933–6403; and (5) the return to Arthur's court and Erec's coronation at Nantes as king of Estre Gales, lines 6404–6950. The romance tells how Erec's prowess and Enide's faithfulness were doubted and successfully put to the test and how Erec then assumed his rightful place as ruler of Estre Gales with Enide by his side.

Cliges is modeled on Thomas d'Angleterre's *Roman de Tristan,* which consists of the stories of two couples, the parents of Tristan, Rivalen and Blancheflor, and then Tristan and Ysolt. *Cliges* accordingly is divided into two parts. The first panel of the diptych tells of Alexandre's voyage to Britain, the love between him and Soredamor, their marriage, and the birth of Cliges, lines 45–2588. The second panel concerns Cliges and Fenice, their love, and their eventual marriage and enthronement in Constantinople, lines 2589–6676. A prologue, lines 1–44, and an epilogue, lines 6677–6702, frame the tale.

Because *Lancelot* was finished not by Chrétien but by Godefroy de Lagny, it is not certain that its ending is all that its first author would have desired. Nonetheless, as the romance stands, it is usefully divided into three main parts: the pursuit of Meleagant and the queen, punctuated by the appearance of the five damsels, all of whom appear to be manifestations of Meleagant's sister, lines 30–3137; the events in Gorre, including Lancelot's first two combats with Meleagant, liberation of the captives, Guinevere's rejection of Lancelot, the night of adulterous love, and Lancelot's imprisonment, lines 3138–5501; and the final events in Logres, namely, the tournament of Noauz, Lancelot's liberation, and his final victory over Meleagant, lines 5502–7097. As was the case with *Cligès,* the narration of *Lancelot* is framed by a prologue, lines 1–29, and an epilogue, written by Godefroy de Lagny, lines 7098–7112.

Yvain reverses the larger organization of *Lancelot* in that the multiple testings of the protagonist follow the pivotal action, the victory over Escla-dos, rather than preceding it. The narrative falls into three parts: Yvain's victory at the fountain and the events leading up to it, including Calo-grenant's tale, lines 42–2538, which is a rare flashback in Chrétien, involving as it does events that happened six years before the scene in which it is recounted; the crisis of faithfulness and Yvain's madness, lines 2539–3141; and the series of tests (Count Alier, rescue of the lion, Harpin de la Montagne, the defeat of Laudine's seneschal and his brothers, the castle of Pesme Avanture, and the duel between Yvain and Gauvain) resulting in Yvain's rehabilitation and his return to Laudine, lines 6500–6803. Once again a prologue, lines 1–41, and an epilogue, lines 6804–8, encase the narration, the prologue mixing the scene at Arthur's court with reflections on the inadequacy of lovers in Chrétien's day, the epilogue a simple sign-off.

Perceval's action is divided into two large parts: the youth and adventures of Perceval, who leaves home, acquires armor, is knighted, meets Blanche-flor, visits the Grail castle, and undertakes the quest to find the Grail again, lines 69–4815, and the adventures of Gauvain in Tintagel, Escavalon, and Galloway, lines 4816–9234, into which intrudes Perceval's visit with his hermit uncle, lines 6217–6518. Only slightly more than half of the narrative proper is devoted to Perceval, the rest being given over to the Gauvain episodes. Chrétien may have intended to balance the prologue, lines 1–68, with an epilogue.

Various critics have, however, pointed out discrepancies of chronology in *Perceval* (for a survey of the discussion, see Döffinger-Lange 1998: 35–71). Perceval first sees King Arthur in Carduel on a day unspecified in the text. From there he travels to Gornemant's castle, where he is initiated into knighthood. He goes on to the castle of Beaurepaire, defeating Clamadeu and dispatching him to Arthur's court, now at Disnadaron in Wales. Clamadeu arrives on Pentecost (l. 2785, the seventh Sunday following Easter) after journeying for three days. The day after his victory over Clamadeu, presumably then on the Friday preceding Pentecost, Perceval leaves Beaurepaire and makes his way to the Grail castle. On what must be Saturday, he speaks with his first cousin, then meets and defeats Orgueilleus de la Lande. Shortly after this, Arthur expresses a desire to meet Perceval again and takes his court on a journey with that purpose in mind. Two weeks after he first arrived in Arthur's court (4550), Perceval is again in Arthur's presence after his trance over the blood on the snow. All the action of the romance has thus far taken place, then, within a week or so on either side of Pentecost. The Hideous Maiden comes to the court and provokes the knights' dispersal on various quests, but before Gauvain can leave, Guingambresil arrives and challenges him to a judicial duel that will take place forty days later at Escavalon. Gauvain leaves and, although he stops to take part in a tournament at Tintagel, arrives at Escavalon before the forty days have elapsed. The king of Escavalon postpones the judicial duel for a year while Gauvain searches for the Bleeding Lance. The narrator now returns to Perceval, who has been seeking for five years (6220–38) to find the Grail castle again. Stressing this period of time, Chrétien mentions the five year time lapse no fewer than six times in eighteen lines. It is Good Friday, and Perceval stays with his uncle the hermit until Easter Sunday. The narrator then returns to Gauvain and his adventures in Galloway, which are presumably taking place within the year's delay that Gauvain has been granted. Unless one is to assume, absurdly, that to tell about Perceval's Good Friday experience the narrator jumped ahead five years, the chronology of years is confused. Furthermore, the romance ends with Arthur's court at Orcanie on Pentecost (8888–89, 9103). Thus even setting aside Perceval's visit to the hermit and only viewing time as it is calculated to be passing for Gauvain, two feasts of Pentecost occur in the same year, at a few weeks' distance from each other, so the chronology of the year is also confused.

Martín de Riquer argued (1957), partly on the basis of these inconsistencies, that the Perceval and Gauvain sections were written as separate romances and only joined after Chrétien's death, but Frappier (1958) responded that if Chrétien had lived to finish the text, he would have corrected it to reflect a plausible chronology. A surprising aspect of the inconsistencies of time in *Perceval*, however, is that unless they are calculated and pointed out, most readers do not notice them. Chrétien's story is so interesting that one becomes lost in it and is willing to lend him credence as to the details of his characters' lives. Another instance of improbable chronology is found in *Lancelot,* where the hero has his evening meal interrupted by a challenge after the first course has been served by candlelight (2559), goes to a field with the challenger, defeats him in combat, decapitates him after a second combat, and then returns to dinner. Chrétien never explains, nor does it ever occur to the average reader to want him to, how all this could take place in the dark! Perhaps Chrétien's greatest inconsistency is in situating Uther Pendragon's death either when Perceval was two years old (*Perceval* 442–458) or sixty years before Gauvain's entry into the castle of the Rock of Champguin (*Perceval* 9734–43), a difference of forty-eight years!

Portraits

In treating the physical description of characters, medieval poetic treatises recommend beginning with the head and then describing the rest of body down to the feet. Although this order is not invariably followed, it does describe a general tendency in literary portraiture of the period.

The qualities that were deemed beautiful in twelfth-century men and women do not always correspond to modern ideals. For example, in medieval French texts heroes and heroines alike are almost always blond, so there does not appear to have been an ideal of the female "dark beauty" or the male who is "tall, dark, and handsome." A small mouth was considered desirable for men. Furthermore, the color of the eyes is simply passed over in all the extended descriptions examined in Alice Colby's classic study of twelfth-century literary portraits (Colby 1965: 41).

The portrait of Erec when he first appears is limited to matters other than the physical details of his body (*Erec* 81–104): his name, his status as a knight of the Round Table, his popularity, his beauty and prowess, his youth, his horse, his clothing, his spurs, and his sword. In fact, Chrétien never describes Erec's body in detail. In the case of Cliges, by contrast, Chrétien announces that he is going to undertake a short description (*description . . . don molt sera briés li passages,* Cliges 2716–17)[9] but then of the possible physical details tells his audience only those of the hero's head and face:

> He was in the flower of his age,
> For he was almost fifteen.[10]

He was more handsome and attractive
Than Narcissus, who under the elm
Saw his form in the fountain
And loved it so much when he saw it
That he died of that, it's said,
Because he was unable to possess it.
He had great beauty and little wisdom,
But Cliges had much more,
As much as pure gold surpasses copper,
And even more than I am saying.
His hair resembled fine gold
And his face a budding rose.
His nose was well formed and his mouth handsome,
And he had as beautiful a line
As Nature was able to form,
For in him she put all together
That which she gives in parts to each one.
In him Nature was so generous
That she put everything in one package,
And she gave to him whatever pleased her.
This was Cliges, who in himself
Had wit and beauty, generosity and strength.
He had both the trunk and the bark.
He knew more of fencing and archery
Than Tristan, the nephew of King Mark,
And more about birds of prey and about dogs.
No virtue was lacking in Cliges.
[En la fleur estoit ses aages,
Car pres avoit ja de .XV. anz,
Plus biaus estoit et avenanz
Que Narcisus qui desouz l'orme
Vit en la fonteinne sa forme,
Si l'ama tant quant il la vit
Qu'il en fu morz si com en dit
Por ce qu'il ne la pot avoir.
Molt ot biauté et pou savoir,
Mes Cligés en ot plus grant masse,
Tant com fins ors le coivre passe,
Et plus que je ne di encor.
Si chevuel sembloient fin or,
Et sa face rose novele.
Nés ot bien fet et bouche bele,

Et fu de si bele estature
Com meuz le sot former Nature,
Que en lui mist trestout a .I.
Ce que par parz done a chascun.
En lui fu Nature si large
Que trestout mist en .I. charge,
Si li dona quanque li plot.
Ce fu Cligés, qui en lui ot
Sen et biauté, largece et force.
Cist ot le fust o tout l'escorce,
Cist sot plus d'escremie et d'arc
Que Tristanz li niés le roi Marc,
Et plus d'oisiaus et plus de chiens.
En Cligés ne failli nus biens.]   (*Cliges* 2718–47)

The description of Cliges is the most elaborate of any male character in Chrétien's romances. In contrast to the accomplished Erec, Yvain, and Perceval, whose physical qualities Chrétien does not supply except in fragmentary and abstract ways, we have before us Cliges's complexion, the color of his hair, and the perfection of his nose, his mouth, and his posture. The qualities of his character are enumerated, and he is compared favorably with literary figures whom the medieval audience would recognize as paragons of their type: Narcissus for beauty and Tristan for dexterity and skill in training animals to hunt. He is a masterwork of Nature, gold compared to copper. Why this degree of detail and intertextual reference? Cliges is a new and better Tristan, just as Fenice is a socially improved version of Ysolt, and Chrétien is at pains to bolster his model of the consummate knight at the expense of King Mark's nephew.

The hyperbole evident in the portrait of Cliges is also found in Chrétien's descriptions of female characters. Laudine could not have been made even if Nature had spent all her time at the task, so God made the lady himself to astonish Nature, and even he could not duplicate the achievement (*Yvain* 1502–10)! As much as the effort of fashioning Cliges was extraordinary, an even greater effort was needed in the case of Fenice, about whose creation Chrétien says that Nature could not duplicate the feat. Nor will Chrétien himself bother to describe her, for he would, he says, be incapable of the task (*Cliges* 2692–99). This is a commonplace of medieval rhetoric inherited from antiquity, the topos of inexpressibility (Curtius 1953: 159–60). True to his word, Chrétien then gives an account not of Fenice's physical attributes but of the effect of her beauty and of Cliges's, too:

The girl hastened until
She came to the palace,
Bareheaded and without a veil,
And the glow of her beauty
Gives forth as great a radiance in the palace
As four carbuncles would have done.
Before his uncle, the emperor,
Cliges, on his part, had taken off his cloak,
But they were both so beautiful,
Between the girl and him,
That a ray of light issued forth from their beauty
By which the palace shone
Just as if the sun were shedding
Its bright and golden rays.
[Tant s'est la pucele hastee
Que el palés en est venue
Chief descovert et face nue,
Et la luors de sa beauté
Rent el palés si grant clarté
Com feïssent .IIII. escharbocle.
Devant l'empereor son oncle
Restoit Cligés desafublez,
Mes tant estoient bel andui,
Entre la pucele et celui,
C'uns rais de lor biauté issoit
Dont li palais resplendissoit
Tout ensement com li soleuz
Raiast molt clers et molt vermeuz.]   (*Cliges* 2700–2714)

Carbuncles are large precious stones that medieval lapidaries, romances, and chansons de geste describe as giving forth their own light (see Lyons 1965: 108–9), a quality that Chrétien evokes again in *Perceval* (7702–5). The effect of Cliges and Fenice's presence is described only in terms of radiance, as if they were together a source of light. Later, Cliges is welcomed by the knights of Arthur's court with a related comparison, this time motivated not by his beauty but by his prowess:

"Just as the sun
Puts out the little stars in such a way
That their light does not appear among the clouds
When the rays of the sun appear,
So do our acts of prowess fade away

And so are they extinguished before your own. . . ."
["Tot autresi com [li] solauz
Estaint les esteiles menues
Que la clartez n'en pert as nues
La o li rai del soleil naissent,
Ausi estaignent et abaissent
Nos proeces devant les voz . . ."]   (*Cliges* 4944–49)

A similar luminosity, physical this time, marks Soredamor, whose eyes seem to those who look at them, according to Chrétien, to be burning candles (*Cliges* 809–10, a new metaphor in this period [see Colby 1965: 154]). Her teeth shine like ivory or silver and her throat makes crystal seem cloudy by comparison. Her breasts are whiter than newfallen snow (827–41). Enide, too, is described in terms of light, her face "illuminated" by the paleness of her complexion, her hair gleaming, and her eyes shining like stars (*Erec* 425–34). Similarly Laudine's hair gleams like gold, and no crystal or ice is as polished as her throat (*Yvain* 1466–88).

In his portrait of Perceval's lover Blancheflor, whose very name signifies "white flower," Chrétien descends from his habits of extreme hyperbole to mere exaggeration and retains the primary effect of gleaming illumination while also focusing on finer detail. He begins by referring self-consciously to his previous descriptions of women:

And if I ever made a description
Of beauty that God would have placed
In body of woman or in face,
Now it pleases me again to do so,
For never will I lie in a single word.
Her hair was loose
And it was such, if this could be,
That he who saw it would think
That it was all made of fine gold,
So intensely was it blond and gleaming.
Her forehead was high and pale and unlined
As if it were made by hand
And fashioned by human hand
Out of stone or ivory or wood.
With shapely eyebrows widely spaced,
The eyes in her head were
Flashing and laughing, clear and deep-set;
Her nose was straight and long,

And better did it become her face,
The rosiness set off against the white,
Than red upon a silver ground.
In order truly to steal people's hearts,
God made in her a surpassing wonder,
For never since did He make her equal
Nor had He ever made it before.
[Et se je onques fis devise
En biauté que Diex eüst mise
En cors de feme ne en face,
Or me replaist que une en face,
Que ja n'en me[n]tirai de mot.
Desfublee fu et si ot
Les chaveus tiex, s'etre poïst,
Que bien quidast qui les veïst
Que il fuissent tot de fin or,
Tant estoient luisant et sor.
Le front ot haut et blanc et plain
Come s'il fust ovrez a main,
Et que de main d'ome ovrez fust
De pierre ou d'yvoire ou de fust.
Sorciex bien fais et large entrueil,
En la teste furent li oeil
Vair et riant, cler et fendu;
Le nez ot droit et estendu,
Et miex avenoit en son vis
Li vermeus sor le blanc assis
Que li sinoples sor l'argent.
Por voir embler les cuers de gent
Fist Diex en li passemerveille,
C'onques puis ne fist sa pareille
Ne devant faite ne l'avoit.]   (*Perceval* 1805–29)

The forehead, eyes, nose, and complexion dominate the physical features
in this description, which gives attention to texture, shape, and hues. Color
is difficult to pin down, as medieval French civilization made distinctions in
the spectrum that were different from those of modern French or English:
what I have rendered as "rosiness" is *vermeil* 'red', whereas the "red" in
line 1825 is *sinople,* a term commonly used in heraldry. This may signify
that Chrétien is juxtaposing the hues of Blancheflor's face with the symbolic colors of coats of arms. In any event, it appears that Chrétien's tech-

nique evolves in the course of his career away from extreme dependence on effects of light toward a greater attention to line, contour, and details of physiognomy.

Is hyperbole a special characteristic of Chrétien's art of portrayal? According to Alice Colby, Chrétien makes use of hyperbole half again more frequently than other writers in the period 1098–1191 and more than two and a half times more frequently in combination with such stylistic devices as a rhetorical question, a metaphor, or a comparison, in what she terms "expressive hyperbole." This last is, then, a practice that sets Chrétien off from other narrators of his time. Faith Lyons linked his use of hyperbole to describe Cliges's martial prowess with the account of hyperbole in the *Rhetorica ad Herennium.* There the example of the trope hyperbole, termed *superlatio,* is: "Such was his splendor in arms that the gleam of the sun seemed darker" (Lyons 1965: 105).

Chrétien's art of human portraiture has a hyperbolic quality, but by contrast one of his greatest assets is the restraint he demonstrates on the level of the narrative. This restraint is most evident if one compares his treatments with those of other writers of romance (see Kelly 1987–88). The comparison with Ulrich von Zatzikhoven is particularly apt, for both he and Chrétien are drawing upon a tradition of tales about Lancelot. Ulrich seems to pile up incidents one after the other with no particular progression, three times having his hero come to a castle, kill its lord (Galagandreiz, Linier, and Iweret), and win the love of the lord's niece or daughter. Lanzelet is the lover of Galagandreiz's daughter, of the queen of Pluris, of Yblis, and perhaps of Ade. He becomes successively the king of Moreiz, Genewis, and Dodone. Chrétien, by contrast, subordinates the episodes of *Lancelot* to the central theme, the love between the hero and Guinevere, having Lancelot encounter a series of marvels and adventures, but all in a progression toward the queen. This organization of potentially disparate materials into an orderly sequence is the *bele conjointure* that Chrétien mentions in the prologue to *Erec.* It results in the effective subordination of easily multiplied episodes to a principal theme.

A quality critics associate with Chrétien is his finesse in choosing small and often seemingly insignificant details to lend an air of acute observation to his storytelling (see the discussion above). An example of this in his descriptive technique would be his placing Narcissus under an elm tree in the passage from *Cliges* cited above, when Narcissus is never associated with the elm in classical versions of the myth. In this light it is striking that his description of characters reflects, with the exception of a trait that can be taken for granted among the northern French nobility, namely blondness, an impressionistic gaze rather than an exact one.

Reported Speech

In telling a story, the author has to choose when to recount events in the narrator's voice and when to have the characters speak. How does Chrétien use speech in his narrative art? Two passages in *Yvain* are instructive in this regard.

The opening at Arthur's court is told in the narrator's voice. An unpleasant exchange among Keu, Guinevere, and Calogrenant serves to fix the characterization of Keu as a nasty and vituperative person, an end that could not have been achieved nearly so effectively without presenting Keu's own sarcastic words. Calogrenant then recounts the tale of his shaming for 436 lines. Imbedded in this speech is the humorous questioning of the hideous herdsman, whose responses are disarmingly straightforward: "'What kind of man are you?' 'Just as you see. . . .' 'And what do you do?' 'I stand here'" (*"Ques hom es tu? — Tes com tu vois. . . . —Et que fais tu? — Ychi m'estois,"* *Yvain* 329, 331). When Calogrenant has finished the tale, Yvain expresses his desire to avenge his cousin, and Keu intervenes again in a provocative tone for which the queen reproaches him. Arthur awakes and says he wishes to test the fountain, but this is told in the narrator's voice, using both indirect and free indirect discourse. Yvain tells his squire to prepare his horse so that he can depart, and the squire assents. There follow 230 lines in which the narrator tells of Yvain's testing of the fountain and his pursuit of Esclados. Chrétien needed to tell the same story twice, with a different outcome the second time, but he has deftly varied his presentation by couching the first narration in Calogrenant's words while placing the second in the narrator's voice, recalling quickly aspects of the journey that the audience is already anticipating because it has heard the first-person report of an eyewitness to the events.

In the second passage, Laudine is transformed from grieving widow to eager bride. The first lines spoken after Yvain's testing of the fountain are Lunete's conversation with him just after he has been trapped between the portcullises of Laudine's castle. The reader then hears the complaints of Esclados's men and Laudine about not being able to find the killer of their lord, who is protected by the ring of invisibility. Yvain asks Lunete to find him a vantage point from which to watch the funeral. Laudine pronounces her anguish over her husband's passing. Lunete once again cautions Yvain to be prudent. In a monologue Yvain regrets his inability to provide for Keu the proof that he has successfully undergone the test of the fountain. This is followed by a monologue in which Yvain estimates his chances of success with Laudine and rehearses her attractive features. He speaks with Lunete, who immediately understands that he is in love with Laudine and declares her intention to help. Lunete's two conversations with Laudine, persuading her to accept Yvain as a husband, then occupy center stage. Laudine engages in a short interior dialogue, putting Yvain through a moot court procedure and deciding that he is not guilty of murder (*Yvain* 1760–72). She subsequently speaks with Lunete and arranges for the accused party to present himself shortly and, when he is said to have arrived, summons him before her, and Lunete prepares Yvain for the conversational ordeal. Laudine and Yvain engage in dialogue over his responsibility for Esclados's death. The upshot is that she exculpates him, receives his promise to defend the fountain, and agrees to marry him. Laudine then leads her betrothed to meet her vassals, whose comments are reported as collective speech (2063–70). Laudine's seneschal addresses the barons and sketches out the dangers attendant on King Arthur's coming arrival; the vassals then ask their lady to do what she has already convinced herself and consented to do, namely, to marry Yvain. The narrator ends the scene by recounting that the marriage is concluded that same day.

Chrétien is justly admired for the skill with which he depicts the complete reversal of Laudine's attitude toward Yvain, from an eager desire for vengeance to an equally eager desire to unite with him in marriage. The key to this metamorphosis is the dialogue, with its prevarications, subtle hints at meanings other than the ones expressed, and gently ironic manipulation of the characters' sentiments. The change is orchestrated by the astute Lunete, of whom the narrator notes at one point, after she has played on the idea of imprisonment with Yvain, who runs the real danger of being incarcerated for murder:

> And she upsets him and reassures him,
> And speaks in allusive terms
> Of the prison in which he will be put,
> For no lover is out of prison.
> [Si l'esmarri, et l'aseüre,
> Et parole par couverture
> De la prison ou il ert mis,
> Que sans prison n'est nus amis.]   (*Yvain* 1939–42)

One can be sure that Chrétien, articulating here the nature of Lunete's metaphoric speech, had calculated all the subtleties and nuances of these conversations, which are among the best examples of a type in which he excels, the witty exchange of replies between intelligent and well-instructed participants in a sophisticated milieu.

In addition to dialogues in which the interlocutors are introduced by verbs of speaking, Chrétien often uses dialogues of short rapid responses without names (similar to the classical device of stichomythy, dialogue in alternating lines) as:

> "But who's this one? What is his birth?
> Who knows him?" "Not I." "Nor I.
> But it hasn't snowed on him!" (*Cliges* 4614–16)
> ["Mais qui est cist? Dont est naïs?
> Qui le conoit? —Ne gié. —Ne gié.
> Mais il n'a pas sor lui negié."]

This dialogue includes a pun on *ne gié,* "not I," and *negié,* "snowed." Another such dialogue, but in question-and-answer form with direct address to help as an occasional signpost and the repetition in the answers of words taken from the questions, is the conversation between Yvain and Laudine about the identity of the force that makes Yvain consent to all she requires (*Yvain* 2017–29), discussed in Chapter 4.

Quick exchanges keep the audience on the alert to identify who is speaking. In oral presentation the reader might assume different voices to correspond to the various protagonists, but in medieval manuscripts, in which there are no quotation marks and the reader perceives the difference between narration and dialogue only by the context, there is an even greater need for readerly engagement. One is reminded, anachronistically of course, of the form of a courtroom interrogation, but in this passage the prosecutor is certainly not interested in undercutting the defendant's responses. Although Chrétien does not always use the technique of short and quick replies primarily to create an effect of psychological realism—compare, for example, Perceval's dialogue with his cousin (*Perceval* 3548–71)—that is certainly his purpose in the dialogue between Yvain and Laudine. He did not invent the technique, which is already found in the *Roman d'Enéas* (see, for example, Petit 1997: ll. 1760–69, 1832–45, 7951–66, and elsewhere).

Suspense

The romance is a genre in which effects of suspense are not only possible but common. This may not seem surprising to the modern reader, but it is most often not the case with the contemporary rival to the romance, the chanson de geste. The reason for this appears to be the conditions under which chansons de geste were performed. Some of the finest examples of the genre were so popular that everyone in the audience, except for the youngest children, was thoroughly familiar with the plots to the extent of knowing their outcomes. A well-known example is the Oxford version of the *Chanson de Roland,* in which the audience is told early on, in line 178 of a 4,002-line poem, that the treason that is at the heart of the tale was committed by Ganelon. Anticipatory summaries of great swaths of the plot, analogous in nature and function to the movie trailer that reveals the most exciting moments of a film in order to draw an audience, are typical of the chanson de geste.

Not so with medieval romances, and *Yvain* is an outstanding example. The narrator not only remains silent about whether Yvain will succeed at the fountain but shapes the narrative in such a way as to imply that he may well not. Yvain delivers Lunete from execution, but he must first extricate himself from the commitment to defend the family of Gauvain's sister against Harpin de la Montagne—that is to say, he must struggle against the press of time. A similar situation occurs later, when Yvain agrees to champion the cause of the younger daughter of the lord of Noire Espine in a judicial duel to be held before King Arthur, but the episode of the castle of Pesme Avanture intervenes and Yvain arrives at Arthur's court only at midafternoon on the last day of the forty-day respite that the king has granted for the duel (*Yvain* 5886–87). *Yvain* appears to be the first work in French literature in which deadlines figure, not precise deadlines down to the minute in an age in which the concept of the measured minute had not yet developed, but deadlines nonetheless.

Once in *Erec,* however, Chrétien suggests the outcome in an otherwise suspenseful moment. Count Galoain is planning to kill Erec in order to have Enide, but Chrétien states in his first-person voice what he believes the outcome will be:

> But God can well aid him in this,
> And I think he will do so.
> [Mais Dex l'en porra bien aidier,
> Et je cuit que si fera il.]   (*Erec* 3424–25)

Another exception to the technique of suspense is found in *Yvain*. After telling of the one-year deadline for Yvain to return to Laudine, Chrétien writes, again in the first person:

> And I think that he will exceed it,
> For milord Gauvain will not
> Allow Yvain to leave him.
> [Et je cuit que le passera,
> Que departir nel leissera
> Mesire Gavains d'avec lui.]   (*Yvain* 2667–69)

These gentle suggestions will, of course, come to pass in the narrative. The anticipation is there, even though in both cases it is couched as a likelihood rather than a fact.

Chrétien not only keeps the reader in suspense in the vast majority of situations as to the outcome of his tales, so that it is impossible to say for certain how he would have ended *Perceval*, but he measures out in successive doses the essential information for unraveling relations that are a key to understanding the text. Thus in *Perceval*, the reader learns along with the hero, and early on in the romance, that Perceval's mother has fallen to the ground as Perceval leaves home and that the Grail is being carried out of the Fisher King's hall. It is only later, however, that the hero and the reader together learn that the mother had died as she fell, that the Grail's destination was important, and that the person for whom it was destined is Perceval's maternal uncle, kept alive by its contents.

At times Chrétien does not tell us all that we would like to know. In *Lancelot*, Count Guinable witnesses Guinevere's muttered comment that there is someone who would not let Keu lead her away without opposition, if only he knew what was happening (209–14), but this potentially inculpating detail is not followed through in the narrative, for Count Guinable is never again mentioned in the tale. That Chrétien would have reintroduced the count if he had finished *Lancelot* is always possible, but it is difficult to see what role a witness to such an ambiguous phrase would have played unless we are to imagine that Guinable informed Lancelot "off stage" of the queen's abduction.

A characteristic found in all the romances is the tendency to hide the names of significant characters until long after one would normally expect them to have been named, or even permanently. Thus the mother and father of Enide are only named in lines 6886–88 of *Erec*, and the land from which they come, and in which the Test of the Sparrow-Hawk takes place, is not given until line 6241. Perhaps tellingly, no one knows Enide's name until her wedding day, when it is necessary that it be revealed (*Erec* 2021–27). Mabonagrain's lady is never named, although we do learn that she is Enide's cousin. In these last two cases, the lack of naming may be a remnant of the motif that a fairy should not reveal her name lest someone with knowledge of it use the name to gain power over her. Yvain's name is well known, but after his madness he hides it under the designation "knight of the lion" (Duggan 1969). Chrétien gives Meleagant's name only in line 637 of *Lancelot,* long after he has appeared in Arthur's court. Lancelot refuses to reveal his name to the monk in the cemetery (*Lancelot* 1922) and is in fact named for the first time in the romance in line 3660, by Guinevere. Arthur's queen remains anonymous in *Cliges.* The most extreme examples of anonymity are in *Perceval,* where the names of Perceval's mother, father, cousin, and uncle and of the Fisher King and his father are not given and where Perceval does not know his own name and has to guess it when his cousin asks him what it is (3573–77). That knowledge of one's name exposed one to danger would explain why Enide's name is revealed only at her marriage, when she is presumed no longer to be vulnerable.

CHRÉTIEN'S ACHIEVEMENT AS A STORYTELLER

Chrétien's genius is that he was able to integrate, with skill and to great effect, the literary devices of romance—based on sources taught in the schools (Kelly 1992)—the Celtic materials deriving from Brittany and other Celtic lands, story elements found in oral tradition, and the aura of courtliness that suffused aristocratic French, Angevin, and Occitan circles in the late twelfth century. These are the principal currents that, coming together in his work, make up the distinctive characteristics of Arthurian romance. Many of his themes and motifs are of obscure provenance. As Guerreau-Jalabert has remarked (1983: 24), one of the difficulties that the romances of Chrétien place as obstacles to interpretation is precisely this author's remarkable capacity to disguise themes known from elsewhere in such a way as to render them almost unrecognizable.

Storytelling plays an essential role in society, as each generation has model characters placed before it whose conduct is described in a large variety of situations. In the twelfth century, values were imparted by kin groups to young people in idealizing tales that incorporated an aura of allure and mystery. Chrétien was a highly accomplished writer of such tales, whose authority he reinforced by placing them in the double setting of the court of a much admired figure from the distant past, King Arthur, and a world in which the unexpected was to be expected.

In Chrétien's period, when literature was performed at least as frequently as it was read and when jongleurs delivered chansons de geste, fabliaux, saint's lives, and lyric poetry to audiences both courtly and noncourtly, the matter of romance was also subject to oral presentation, either by being read out loud or by its presence in the repertories of jongleurs. In the mid-thirteenth-century Occitan romance *Flamenca,* itself a masterpiece of storytelling, the poet describes the performances of jongleurs at Flamenca's wedding feast and notes that among the many tales to be heard were those of the Round Table:

> The other told about Gauvain,
> And about the lion who was the companion
> Of the knight whom Lunete saved.
> One told about the Breton maiden,
> How she kept Lancelot in prison
> When he denied her his love.
> The other told about Perceval,
> How he came to the court on horseback.
> One told about Erec and Enide. . . .
> The other told about Fenice,
> How her nurse made her as if dead. . . .
> [L'autre comtava de Galvain,
> E del leo que fon compain
> Del cavallier qu'estors Luneta.
> L'us diz de la piucella breta
> Con tenc Lancelot en preiso
> Cant de s'amor li dis de no.
> L'autre comtet de Persaval
> Co venc a la cort a caval.
> L'us comtet d'Erec e d'Enida. . . .
> L'autre comtava de Feniza,   (Gschwind 1976: ll. 665–73,
> Con transir la fes sa noirissa. . . .]   677–78)

That all five of Chrétien's romances are included here—or extracts from them performed episodically—there can be no doubt. The author of *Flamenca* assigns to these works by a single poet a large portion of the jongleurs' repertory, an impressive tribute to the attractions of Chrétien's art.

It probably did not occur to him, however, that they would still play a dominant role in the repertory of romances read more than eight hundred years after his time.

With Chrétien, courtly rhetorical style reaches its highest expression in French. His genius raised the sights of audiences and created a new set of expectations for literature.

Chapter 7

Knights and Ladies

T he romance is an idealizing genre, and Chrétien fashions ideal characters to inhabit the world he has created. By the period in which he lived, knighthood was well on its way to becoming an institution, its sources in the Germanic and Celtic client-retainer relationship and the war band long forgotten. Like Geoffrey of Monmouth and Wace, Chrétien projects back onto the period reflected in Arthurian stories, the end of the fifth and beginning of the sixth century, the elements of his own twelfth-century civilization, with its courtly manners and codes of behavior, its tournaments and jousting, and its knightly customs. He posits Arthur as living in a time in which social practices were only somewhat different from those he, Chrétien, sees around him, but different enough to allow him to say that the cart was then a nefarious vehicle (*Lancelot* 321–44) and that in those days knights and ladies knew better how to love (*Yvain* 12–32).

At the focal point of each of his Arthurian romances is not King Arthur but one or several knights associated with him: Erec, Alexandre, Cliges, Lancelot, Yvain, Perceval, Gauvain. The knightly protagonists variously perform praiseworthy deeds, surviving the tests imposed by preternatural forces, defeating the cupidinous, the haughty, and those who attempt to satisfy their lust by force, protecting the vulnerable, freeing captives, and serving as champions in judicial duels. Does Chrétien's presentation of the ideals of knighthood and the conduct of his heroes and of other knights change between the beginning of his oeuvre and its abrupt end?

Erec, Lancelot, and Yvain are knights at the outset, so the occasions on which they were knighted are never described. The goal of Perceval's departure from home, however, which in turn is the occasion of his sin of leaving his mother, is to be knighted by King Arthur. Arthur promises to make the boy a knight, but in fact he is knighted only by Gornemant. In this Bildungsroman, Chrétien takes the opportunity to tell in some detail what a young man aspiring to knighthood is expected to learn by way of horsemanship, fighting skill, and moral precept. Gornemant stresses the importance and dignity of the knightly state, pronouncing the formula that

> he has given him
> With the sword the highest order
> That God has made and commanded:
> That is, the order of knighthood,
> Which should be without villainy.
> [donee li a
> Le plus haute ordene avec l'espee
> Que Diex ait faite et comandee:
> C'est l'ordre de chevalerie,
> Qui doit estre sanz vilonnie.]   (*Perceval* 1634–38)

This is one of the earliest uses of the term *order* to designate lay knighthood (as opposed to the military chivalric orders, such as the Knights Templars or the Knights of St. John; see Flori 1979: 39 but also Lodge 1979: 1. 585). Chrétien's formulation can be interpreted to imply the superiority of knighthood over clergy if one construes the phrase "with the sword" as modifying the verb "given," which is how Georges Duby reads it (Duby 1980: 303–4). It is also possible to take the phrase as modifying "order": that is, knighthood is the "highest military order," but this construction would be unusual in medieval French. Knighthood had already functioned as an order in the First Crusade, when Pope Urban II, in launching the enterprise at Clermont in 1095, appealed directly to the knights without passing through the intermediary of their secular lords (Keen 1984: 74). In what sense it had been "made and commanded by God" is unclear, but this phrasing may reflect the idea that knights formed the core of the second of the three orders into which society was divided: those who rule, those who fight, and those who pray (Duby 1980: 293–307).

In any case, this scene undercuts the indictment of chivalry found in the words and actions of Perceval's mother, whom Chrétien depicts as intent on keeping her son innocent of the very concept of knighthood because her husband and two older sons died as a consequence of knightly activities.

Because Perceval has acquired his equipment before meeting Gornemant, by stripping it from the Red Knight, the scene also implies that knighthood is not acquired simply by possession of arms and armor but must be conferred on the young man in a ceremony (Flori 1979: 31). Gornemant instructs Perceval in the knight's duties to show mercy toward defeated opponents, to advise orphans and women who are without other recourse (as he will soon do in the case of the orphaned Blancheflor), and to pray for divine protection in church, and he also gives him the social advice not to speak excessively or to say that his mother has taught him. The two most highly charged symbolic acts in Gornemant's conferral of knighthood in *Perceval* are the strapping on of Perceval's right spur[1] (*Perceval* 1624–28) and the girding on of his sword (1632–38). Gornemant also gives the new knight a ceremonial kiss (1633). No bath, such as Alexandre and his men take before being knighted (*Cliges* 1136–40), is mentioned here, nor is the symbolic light blow of the hand (*colee*) that was often given to a new knight. Of the three ceremonies of knighting depicted in Chrétien's works, this is the only one in which the knight is solitary; the other two, and most such ceremonies in this period, were social occasions on which a young noble heir and companions of his own age were knighted (Duby 1980: 300–301).

The most thorough depiction of a knighting ceremony in Chrétien's works comes late in *Perceval* (9171–86), when Gauvain, as ruler of the castle of the Rock of Champguin, confers knighthood on five hundred aspirants who had been waiting for the advent of a knight to perform the ceremony (*Perceval* 7586–89). The men bathe in individual tubs of hot water, dress in sumptuous clothing made of material interwoven with gold thread and lined with ermine, and conduct a vigil in church, standing all night in prayer. This is the first mention in any text of the standing vigil (Flori 1979: 37–38), which soon becomes the subject of a remark by the Cistercian Helinand of Froidmont in his book *On the Good Conduct of the Prince:*

> In certain places the custom also is for the knight who is to be consecrated the next day to spend the whole preceding night in vigil, and not to have permission either to lie down or to sit, unless the necessity of a sudden illness should require it, but rather to pray all night in a standing position. [In quibusdam etiam locis moris est, militem in crastinum consecrandum, totam noctem praecedentem pervigilem in orationibus ducere, et nec jacendi, ned sedendi habere licentiam, nisi forte repentinae infirmitatis necessitas coegerit, sed tota nocte stantem orare.] (Helinand de Froidmont 1855: col. 744)

Gauvain straps the right spur on each man, girds on the sword, and gives the colee. Descriptions of the ceremony of knighting are rare in this period. One of the earliest, along with the scene in *Perceval,* is a ceremony described in the *Chroniques des comtes d'Anjou* of Jean de Marmoutier (Halphen and Poupardin 1913: 179–80), composed around 1180 and thus in all likelihood slightly earlier than *Perceval.*

In the words of Jean Flori (1979: 43), with Chrétien "knighthood has acquired its own titles of nobility," in the sense that, from his works onward, 'to dub' (*adouber*) does not merely mean 'to equip' but has taken on the added sense of 'to knight', and the act of dubbing does not just confer a grade and a status on the recipient and promote him into an order that functions as a caste but does so with a series of gestures—the bath, the standing vigil, the blow on the shoulder, the conferral of spur and sword, the kiss, though not yet the oath of knighthood—that raise the event to the level of a ritual of passage, albeit still predominantly secular. Georges Duby identifies the 1170s as the decade in which "knighthood became a genuine institution" (1980: 293). Only in his last romance does Chrétien associate knighthood specifically with prayer and have the hermit associate the practice of religion with worldly reputation (*pris, Perceval* 6457) and link salvation to honor: "and you will have honor and paradise" (*S'avras honor et paradis,* 6458). In the one instance in which the knight is given a blessing, however, it is a layman, Gornemant, who makes the gesture as a sign of farewell (1694–95).

A key concept in Chrétien's vision of knighthood is that of a knight who is not just courageous, faithful, and open-handed but has developed an exemplary morality and a generous will, endowing his knighthood with a social and truly courtly sense (Köhler 1974: 148–59; Maranini 1970: 742). In *Cliges,* largesse is said to make a man a preudome, something that the attributes of high station, courtliness, wisdom, nobility, force, courage, and beauty are all insufficient to accomplish (*Cliges* 201–15). Bademagu tells his son that he could be the greatest knight in the world if he acted according to honor and service (*Lancelot* 3215–19), and in his reply, Meleagant protests that he does not wish to act like a preudome, thus providing a definition by contrast:

> "I am not such a hermit,
> Such a preudome or so charitable,
> Nor do I wish to be honorable to the extent
> That I should give up to him [Lancelot] the creature I most love. . . .
> Be a preudome as long as you wish,
> And leave me to be cruel."
> ["Je ne sui mie si hermites,
> Si prodom ne si charitables,
> Ne tant ne voel estre enorables

Que la rien que plus aim li doingne. . . .
Tant con vos plest, soiez prodom,
Et moi lessiez estre cruel."]   (*Lancelot* 3276–79, 3294–95)

A preudome is, then, a knight who serves others with his prowess, performs charitable acts, and avoids cruelty. That the preudome is not merely a literary construct but a notion that had a genuine social function is shown by the distinction that King Philip II "Auguste," Chrétien's contemporary, made, as reported a century later by Jean de Joinville in his *Life of St. Louis,* between a *preu homme* 'man endowed with prowess' and a *preudome,* both with the same linguistic roots. After calling a certain noble a *preu homme,* Philip was asked why he did not call him a *preudome.*

> "On this account, he said, that there is a great difference between preu homme and preudome. For there is many a knight in Christian and Saracen lands who is a preu homme who never believed in God or his Mother. Therefore I say to you, he said, that God gives a great gift and great grace to the Christian knight whom he permits to be physically valiant, and whom he permits to be in his service, guarding him from mortal sin. And one should call him who acts in this manner preudome, because this prowess comes to him from God's gift. And those of whom I spoke before can be called preu hommes, because they have physical prowess but do not fear God or sin."
>
> ["Pour ce, fist-il, que il a grant difference entre preuhomme et preudomme. Car il a maint preuhomme chevalier en la terre des crestiens et des Sarrazins, qui onques ne crurent Dieu ne sa Mere. Dont je vous di, fist-il, que Dieu donne grant don et grant grace au chevalier crestien que il seuffre estre vaillant de cors, et que il seuffre en son service en li gardant de pechié mortel. Et celi qui ainsi se demeinne doit l'en appeler preudomme, pource que ceste proesse li vient du don Dieu. Et ceux de qui j'ai avant parlé peut l'en appeler preuz hommes, pource que il sont preus de leur cors et ne doutent Dieu ne pechié."] (Corbett 1977: §560)

Philip seems here to be echoing the sentiments of Gornemant and Perceval's hermit uncle. Knighthood is a secular institution in Chrétien, but for the preudome it is a sine qua non to respect the church, fear God, and avoid sin. In light of the expressed ideals of knighthood and the concept of the preudome, it is of interest to take another look at each of Chrétien's protagonists, to see to what extent they measure up to these ideals.

Erec prudently pursues the haughty Ydier and defeats him in the Test of the Sparrow-Hawk. After the crisis scene with Enide, he defends himself against eight robber knights who are intent on gaining both wealth and his spouse by brutal means; he protects his wife from the lust of two counts, Galoain and Oringle; he parries the attack of a king, Guivret, his only adversary before the Joy of the Court episode who is not motivated by either cupidity or lechery. Erec's deeds are not, however, presented as conforming to an expressed set of ideals, in contrast to the code that Arthur articulates for himself as king in lines 1789–1810 of the romance, and all his deeds of arms can be viewed as self-defense until he measures himself against Mabonagrain. No precepts are associated with knighthood in *Erec,* although one might have expected Arthur to enunciate a few on the wedding day of Erec and Enide when he dubs a hundred young men, after having them bathe and distributing to them clothing, arms, and horses (*Erec* 2011–20). In the absence of articulated principles, the question is whether Erec's behavior toward Enide meets the standard that will be enunciated by Perceval's mother: "His honor must be dead / Who does not honor ladies" (*Qui as dames honor ne porte, / La söe honor doit estre morte, Perceval* 539–40). Surely the principles of chivalry do not leave Erec free to treat his own wife worse than he would any woman he was to meet on the road. As for respecting the church, fearing God, and avoiding sin, the issues are never raised.

In *Cliges,* the emperor of Constantinople offers to dub his son Alexandre a knight, but the young man refuses, accepting only to be knighted by King Arthur. Arthur's renown has raised him to the level of highest authority in matters of chivalry. Alexandre pledges not to engage in martial activities until King Arthur girds a sword on him (*Cliges* 112–21, 350–55), but first he requests that Arthur retain him and his companions in the king's service. After accompanying Arthur and Guinevere on a journey to Britain, Alexandre asks the king for knighthood, to which Arthur assents, equipping each young Greek with a horse, arms, and clothing. Before the ceremony, those who are about to be knighted all bathe in the sea (*Cliges* 1140). The ceremony itself is not described, but later (1292) Alexandre remarks that the new knights are suitably dubbed (that is, equipped for combat) and encourages them to joust with knights of the party of the rebellious Count Angres of Windsor. On behalf of Arthur, who is presented as blameless in this struggle with Angres, Alexandre captures the count and thereby proves himself worthy to marry into the lineage of the great king. His son Cliges, Greek on his father's side and British on his mother's but content to be knighted by his uncle Alis (*Cliges* 3966–84), defeats the duke of Saxony's nephew, then the duke himself, and finally rescues Fenice, all in defense of Alis's right to marry her. His action in cutting off Bertran's leg, however, when Bertran, with no ill intention, discovers Fenice and him in their forest hideaway, is difficult to justify as self-defense or altruistic in any sense. As with *Erec,* matters of religious belief and practice are not a part of the problematics of *Cliges.*

Lancelot is already a knight when the narrator first places him in scene. He fights on behalf of the king, in the sense that he is attempting to find Arthur's wife and bring her back to Logres, but he is already sentimentally devoted to Guinevere so that his pursuit has a decidedly self-serving aspect to it. He voluntarily undergoes shame by stepping into the cart, an action whose radically unknightly character is underscored not only by his own hesitation but most notably by Gauvain's refusal to climb in with him. Equally difficult to justify on the basis of the conduct expected of a knight is Lancelot's willingness to fight in the tournament of Noauz as poorly or as well as possible as his lady dictates. And yet, when Lancelot comes to the rescue of the Fourth Damsel, who appears to be threatened with rape, his motives are high-minded. He even resists the Fifth Damsel's request that he cut off the head of the knight who shames him in the manor house of the hospitable host (*Lancelot* 2836), but only half-heartedly, allowing the knight to fight on and then finally beheading him after vanquishing him a second time (*Lancelot* 2922). Here, however, Lancelot violates a principle of good knightly conduct, enunciated by one of Yvain's opponents in the castle of Pesme Avanture (*Yvain* 5676–77) and by Gornemant of Gohort (*Perceval* 1639–48)—namely, to give quarter to any defeated knight who asks for mercy. But no act is more reprehensible in the feudal context than Lancelot's adultery with his lord's wife, one of the worst of felonies. Meleagant, in referring to what he thinks is Keu's act of adultery with the queen but is really Lancelot's, appropriately uses the verb *traïr* 'to commit treason' (*Lancelot* 4854). In his treatise on knighthood *Libre del orden de cavayleria,* written a century after *Lancelot,* Ramon Lull lists three acts that a knight might commit that constitute treason: killing one's lord, lying with his wife, and surrendering his castle (Keen 1984: 10). Taking all his actions into account, Lancelot succeeds in his role of the savior of Guinevere and the captives from Logres who have been abducted into the kingdom of Gorre, but in the end fails to measure up to even modest standards of *preudomie.* Although the act of adultery is not viewed in an ecclesiastical context, it violates both feudal and religious principles.

Yvain, by contrast, is exemplary in following an implied knightly code— if one can assume that no such code proscribed forgetfulness toward one's wife. Not only does he undertake to avenge his kinsman Calogrenant: he also defends the lion, a beast that is noble (*gentil e franche, Yvain* 3375), against an ignoble serpent, defeats the aggressive Count Alier on behalf of the lady of Norison, whose offer of marriage he rejects, protects the family of Gauvain's sister against the giant Harpin, who seeks possession of her daughter, saves Lunete from the pyre by doing battle against three adversaries at once, and liberates the three hundred maidens who are forced to labor in the castle of Pesme Avanture. At the end of this last adventure, he turns down the offer to marry the daughter of the castle's lord and thereby to succeed him, obviously his reward for overcoming the two devils who held the maidens captive. His kindness is such that he undertakes to champion the younger daughter of the lord of Noire Espine even though he does not even know who she is (*Yvain* 5985).

That all those Yvain protects and rescues are either women or close dependents of women is not fortuitous. Yvain is portrayed acting in a distinctly charitable way, as one who, because he has lost his wife's confidence, has to reestablish his reputation and does so by defending women in need of help. This quality of Yvain may derive from the fact that he was himself saved from starvation by the hermit who helped him during his madness, whom Chrétien terms a *preudome* (*Yvain* 2839). If a knight who is also a preudome is not merely skilled but what we could now call empathetic, Yvain is the first protagonist in Chrétien's romances who is shown conducting himself consistently as a preudome, in his guise of Knight of the Lion, and perhaps the first in French literature. With the exception of his initial lack of commitment toward Laudine, he acts as if conscious of Perceval's mother's precept to honor ladies, particularly orphans (Perceval 531–38). On Yvain's journey of reconciliation, for the first time, the principle that a knight should defend women who are otherwise without recourse is raised to the level of a program. As moral ballast for the hero, this is a new development in Chrétien, because it places charitable conduct toward others at the center of the knight's concern. Chrétien, reacting at having to write *Lancelot* according to Marie de Champagne's design, composed at the same time a work in which the hero, Yvain, is the opposite of the self-absorbed and felonious Lancelot. Charity is not, however, articulated in *Yvain* as a religious ideal, however natural such a formulation might appear.

Charity is, however, expressed as a religious theme in the prologue to *Perceval,* which is also the romance of Chrétien that reveals the most acute consciousness of knightly principles. Once Perceval has confided to his mother his awareness that knights exist, she assures him that King Arthur will provide him with arms (*Perceval* 514–15)—expensive items—and counsels him to seek the company of preudomes and to speak with them (563–64), for they always give good counsel to their companions. Thus both her advice and that of the preudome Gornemant are aimed at Perceval's conduct as a knight. He is to honor women and do nothing with them that is against their will, know the names of any man he accompanies, pray to God in church, gain honor, and live an upright life. Gornemant, in addition to echoing the mother's advice by telling Perceval to pray in church and to help women, informs him that he is not to kill a vanquished knight who begs for mercy and admonishes him not to speak too much and not to invoke his mother to others as a source of how to behave. Perceval's third adviser, his uncle, says that he should honor priests by standing up when they approach and help widows and orphaned girls. He reinforces the religious advice Perceval has heard in the past by hearing his confession, imposing penance, giving him communion, and teaching him a secret prayer that invokes God's names. By the end of the romance as we have it, Perceval is well on his way to an even higher level of knighthood than that reached by Yvain: he has begun to act in the interests of orphans and women (his defense of Blancheflor's castle, his avenging of Keu's affront to the Laughing Girl), and he is on the threshold of a new stage in his adventures in which he will combine knightly deeds with an enhanced awareness of his religious duties, a stage of which the Laughing Girl gave a premonition when she foretold that Perceval would become the greatest of all knights.

The other protagonist of the *Perceval* is Gauvain, "he who had the reputation and renown / For all good qualities" (*Perceval* 4419–20: *Cil qui de totes les bontez / Ot los et pris*), the paragon of worldliness. From romance to romance, Gauvain never loses this reputation for perfection both in the pursuit of knightly ideals and in the accomplishment of knightly exploits. Like Lancelot, he penetrates the kingdom of Gorre in pursuit of the queen, taking the route of the Underwater Bridge. He serves as a yardstick of valor, and a knight who can measure up to him on the field of combat—Cliges, Yvain—has proven himself worthy of the highest praise. Gauvain is also a wise counselor, warning Arthur in *Erec* of the dangers that the Hunt for the White Stag poses for the tranquillity of his court, advising the king and other men to follow Meleagant and the queen, refusing to climb into the dwarf's ignominious cart in *Lancelot,* and persuading Yvain not to let marriage spoil his knightly skills in *Yvain,* although with unforeseen consequences. He also acts judiciously when diplomacy is called for, enticing Erec (*Erec* 4087–4150) and Perceval (*Perceval* 4418–4516) into Arthur's itinerant court, Perceval after Sagremor and Keu have provoked him to violence. Gauvain reminds Arthur of his own guidelines about not disturbing knights who have fallen into reverie (*Perceval* 4350–56). He not only speaks easily with women, such as Lunete, but he champions in *Yvain* the elder daughter of the lord of Noire Espine—an orphan who happens to be in the wrong—and sends the horse of a defeated opponent to the little Maiden of the Short Sleeves, for whom he fights in a tournament at Tintagel in *Perceval*. That he is without treachery is shown when he passes the test of the Wondrous Bed in that work. Chrétien evokes no other knight constantly from romance to romance and has Clarissant characterize him as "the best of all the preudomes" (*Perceval* 7935).

Among the good knights who are not protagonists of romances are the Greek Acorionde, who challenges Alis on behalf of Alexandre, forcing him to come to terms over the imperial crown and title, and the hapless Bertran of Thrace, who discovers Cliges and Fenice in their hideaway. Friendly knights include the hospitable host who puts up Lancelot for the night (*Lancelot* 2510–19). The knights whom the boy Perceval meets in the field are on the track of other five knights and three maidens, presumably to rescue the maidens from the knights. Kindly, wise, and peaceful vavasors are many in Chrétien's works: the knight whose sons guide Lancelot to the passage of stones leading to the Sword Bridge, the hospitable host who welcomes first Calogrenant and then Yvain on their journeys toward the fountain, Enide's father, Liconal, Gauvain's brother-in-law in *Yvain* (called a vavasor in Guiot's text), Gornemant of Gohort, Garin, the son of Berte, who lodges Gauvain in Tintagel, and three other unnamed vavasors, nine in all (Woledge 1969).

By no means, however, do all knights in Chrétien's works, or even most of them, conform to Gornemant's ideal that their order should be without villainy. On the contrary, there are far more villainous knights in the five romances than ones who follow Gornemant's principles. Rather than helping women, these men are prone to seize upon them as objects of prey: thus Count Galoain in *Erec*, Count Oringle, who compels Enide to marry him, and Meleagant, determined to force himself upon Guinevere. In *Yvain*, Count Alier oppresses the lady of Norison, and Clamadeu des Iles does the same to Blancheflor in *Perceval*. The lover of Perceval's cousin has been killed by a cruel knight (*Perceval* 3647), although the reader never learns why. Other knights are cupidinous and live off plunder (*Erec* 2793, 2927), as did some knights of history, such as the infamous Thomas of Marle, who, according to Suger of Saint-Denis, so ravaged the countryside around Laon,

Rheims, and Amiens earlier in the twelfth century, looting and destroying, that the papal legate stripped him of his knightly sword-belt in absentia (Waquet 1929: 176). Etienne de Fougères, writing between 1174 and 1178 in the circle of Henry II of England, complains in his *Livre des manières:*

> . . . Most [knights] are in the habit of avoiding their obligations,
> To such an extent that I hear people complain every day
> That there is nothing left
> That they can have or obtain.
> When the wretched people gape with hunger,
> Knights rob them and tax them,
> They oppress them, they work them over—
> The people have to perform many an unpaid task. . . .
> Chivalry was a high order,
> But now it is debauchery.
> [. . . Li plusor s'en solent feindre,
> Si ques en oi tote jor pleindre
> Qu'il ne lor pout chose remeindre
> que il pensent aveir n'ateindre.
> Quant li dolent de fein b[ä]aillent,
> Il les robent et il les taillent,
> Il les peinent, il les travaillent—
> Moltes corvees ne lor faillent. . . .
> Haute ordre fut chevalerie,
> Mes or est ce trigalerie.]   (Lodge 1979: ll. 541–48, 585–86)

Still others of Chrétien's knights are haughty: Ydier in *Erec,* who allows his dwarf to insult strangers, the knight who challenges Lancelot at the manor of the hospitable host (*Lancelot* 2642–44), the two knights in *Perceval* whose sobriquets mean 'haughty'—Orgueilleus de la Lande and Orgueilleus del Passage de l'Estroite Voie—and the Red Knight whom Perceval kills (pl. 10). The duke of Saxony in *Cliges* is a coward, hiding behind the pretext that to vanquish a young man would bring him little glory. Other knights, such as Angres of Windsor, who commits treason against King Arthur, and Meleagant, who poisons Keu's wounds (*Lancelot* 4043), are truly evil characters. Like Etienne de Fougères, Perceval's mother decries the state to which society has descended on account of the conduct of such knights:

> But the best have fallen,
> And one can well see in many places
> That misfortunes befall
> Worthy men who persevere

In great honor and prowess.
Cowardice, shame and laziness
Do not fall, for they cannot,
But the good must fall.
[Mais li meillor sont decheü,
S'est bien en pluisors lius veü
Que les mescheances avienent
As preudomes qui se maintienent
En grant honor et en pröece.
Malvestiez, honte ne pereche
Ne dechiet pas, qu'ele ne puet,
Mais les buens dechaoir estuet.]   (*Perceval* 427–34)

The frequency of private warfare, violence, oppression, and injustice in the five romances is probably a fair reflection of life in late twelfth-century France, where, in addition to the normal dangers of life in a land without uniform legal principles and consistently maintained public order, the populace had to deal with battles between local lords and rifts among allies of the Angevins and the Capetians.

If Gauvain is the ideal worldly knight, Arthur's seneschal Keu is the type of the boastful and discourteous knight. Keu strikes the Laughing Girl in *Perceval* and thereby demonstrates his lack of respect for women; his venomous tongue in the opening scene of *Yvain* shows that he lacks the good manners required in a courtly milieu. On an even more malicious note, Keu sends Perceval off to get the Red Knight's armor, and the audience is undoubtedly to suppose his motivation is that the boy will be killed in the process. Arthur unwisely gives in to Keu's extortion and allows him to fight Meleagant with the queen as stakes, which is seen to reflect badly on the king in both *Lancelot* (185–87) and *Yvain* (3703–7 and esp. 3919–21). For all his boasts, Keu never wins a joust. None of the seneschals in Chrétien's romances, in fact, are on the side of justice (see Woledge 1969). Engygeron, the seneschal of Clamadeu des Iles in *Perceval,* is portrayed as an evil and violent man (*Perceval* 2003). Laudine's unnamed seneschal is motivated by jealousy to accuse her falsely of treason toward her lady (*Yvain* 3665–74). Meleagant's seneschal (*Lancelot* 5425) is doing no more than carrying out his lord's wishes when he imprisons Lancelot, but at least Lancelot fares well at the hands of his wife, who lends him the seneschal's armor to fight at Noauz.

A number of knights in Chrétien's works are neither particularly good nor unusually bad but only concerned with finding the means to test their fighting qualities in the hope of gaining fame. When the hideous herdsman inquires of Calogrenant what he is looking for, he replies simply:

Adventures, to test
My prowess and my courage.
[Aventures, pour esprouver
Ma proesche et mon hardement.]   (*Yvain* 360–61)

This concern with one's reputation alone, yet without crossing the line toward criminal conduct, characterizes not just Calogrenant but also Yvain until he emerges from madness. Fame is also Gauvain's concern. Even Guivret le Petit, king of the Irish, who befriends Erec after Erec defeats him and whom Chrétien presents in a positive light, spends his time in his forest redoubt looking for passing knights whom he attacks gratuitously (*Erec* 3674–90). This mode of attacking without first defying one's adversary is precisely what Gauvain is accused of having done to the king of Escavalon (*Perceval* 4759–61). Enide's condemnation of Guivret's conduct may be an indictment not just of him but of a whole category of knights who impose their will by force and despise any stranger who comes their way (see Maranini 1970: 742). Nonetheless, Guivret is the most friendly knight whom the husband and wife meet on their journey until they arrive at Brandigan.

If the order of knighthood provides Chrétien with a standard of behavior toward which his heroes can aspire, no such secular order was available to women, and Chrétien seldom appeals to the moral standards of the Christian religion articulated as such. In judging the degree to which his female protagonists measure up to an ideal of conduct, then, one cannot appeal to an articulated set of concepts. Parallel to the concept of the preudome is, however, an archetype of female conduct, the *preudefeme* (*Perceval* 6460).

A wife's chastity and faithfuless are consistently praised in both secular and religious sources of the period. The ideal noble wife was expected to bear her husband children, boys in sufficient quantity to make it likely that at least one would survive to inherit the estate and girls who could be married off into powerful families. The concern for a wife's virtue was not, among nobles, simply an issue of abstract moral precept but, in a society in which fiefs had come to be inherited, an eminently practical matter. Were the lady's children also the children of the lord?

In respect to virtue, Enide's conduct is above reproach. Discovered by her future spouse while still under her parents' protection, Enide is a virgin until her marriage with Erec is consummated. She subsequently fends off advances from Count Galoain and Count Oringle of Limors, who goes so far as to coerce her to take part in a ceremony of marriage. The difference between her conduct and her cousin's behavior with Mabonagrain emphasizes that her relationship with Erec, confirmed by her kin and by the larger Arthurian society, meets current norms for marriage. Her faith in Erec never wanes, unless Chrétien intends his audiences to believe that she accepts his fellow knights' accusation of recreancy, which I do not believe is the case. She protects him steadfastly against dangers even at the cost of breaking his prohibition against her speaking to him. Soredamor, too, is morally blameless, not even falling under the shadow of a suspicion, disdaining love until Amor overcomes her, quickly bearing her husband a male heir, and dying of grief after Alexandre. Like Enide and Soredamor, Lunete appears to be a virgin, although her role in Laudine's castle would appear to expose her to the dangers evoked so expressively by Duby (1983; see, for example, pp. 259–64) for unmarried young women living in castles in this period. For Yvain she presents no sexual temptation, but she is shown dallying in private with Gauvain (*Yvain* 2395–2441), who offers himself as her knight "unless you think you can do better" (*se amender ne vous quidiés, Yvain* 2437).

Laudine is another matter. Like the widow of Ephesus in Petronius's *Satyricon* (see Huber 1990) to whom she is often compared, Laudine marries her husband's slayer shortly after becoming a widow. But in constructing the drama of this turnaround, Chrétien manages to justify what might be viewed as Laudine's unseemly conduct on the basis of her political need to have a husband who can take over the lordship of castle, land, and fountain. Blancheflor, similarly in need of a lord to defend Beaurepaire, engages in an undertaking even more unseemly, climbing almost naked into Perceval's bed in the middle of the night. Because he knows nothing yet of love, however, she leaves his bed in the morning with her virginity intact and succeeds in securing him as a defender in return only for her promise of love (*drüerie, Perceval* 2104).

Perceval's mother makes no attempt to protect the well-being of her land and kin by finding another husband, preferring the expedient of withdrawal from all contact with courtly society. Clarissant, like many of the other women in the castle that lacks a lord, is waiting for the appropriate man until Gauvain passes the test of the Wondrous Bed, but Gauvain will not be that long-awaited husband.

Fenice stands out from the rest. She does not hesitate to return Cliges's expressions of love but makes it clear more than once that she will not be another Ysolt and share her body with two men. When one views the whole of Chrétien's oeuvre, it turns out that Fenice is not just an anti-Ysolt but also an anti-Guinevere, as chaste a queen as the other is unchaste, as steadfast as the other is fickle, as faithful to her future husband as the other is faithless.

Women frequently play in Chrétien the role of protectors of men. In addition to Enide in the forest journey, women who take on this function are the lady of Norison and her companion, who cure Yvain's melancholy, Arthur's queen in *Cliges,* who arranges Alexandre's marriage, the seneschal's wife and Meleagant's sister in *Lancelot,* Lunete in *Yvain,* and, unsuccessfully, Perceval's mother. If the hackneyed image of the medieval woman "placed on a pedestal" was ever true, it certainly is not in the case of Chrétien's female creations, with the possible exception of Guinevere. The protective function of some of these women may stem from their origins as fairies in Celtic folklore and myth.

If most of the knights in Chrétien's romances are evil, the same is decidedly not true of his female characters. The elder daughter of the lord of Noire Espine is selfish in seeking to control all of the inheritance that she should share with her sister. Only one woman is thoroughly malicious, Orgueilleuse de Logres, who constantly seeks to shame Gauvain, but even her behavior is justified in a way that the conduct of Meleagant, Angrés, Galoain, and Oringle is not. Orgueilleuse regrets her treatment of Gauvain, telling him that she has sought so to outrage a series of knights that one of them would be motivated to kill her. She seeks death because the man she loved has been killed by Guiromelant. Chrétien thus allows the one vicious woman in all his romances to repent. The various women who serve as messengers, such as in *Perceval* the Hideous Maiden and in *Yvain* the Demoiselle Sauvage and the maiden on the black palfrey who shames the hero, are mere bit players for whom standards of conduct are not an issue.

Many ecclesiastical writers in Chrétien's society conceived of women as at one and the same time weak and dangerous, capable of seducing men on the model of Eve and Delilah (see Bloch 1991). This widespread sentiment, cloaked in scriptural and theological garb, does not seem to have taken hold in Chrétien's mind. The one time he flirts with it, he ascribes it to the motivations of the emperors of Constantinople who came after Cliges, who kept their wives locked up and guarded by eunuchs in fear of being treated the way Fenice treated Alis (*Cliges* 6680–6701).

There is little in Chrétien to reflect the brutal ways in which noble men often manipulated their kinswomen. Abduction of a potential bride was seldom practiced in his time, as it had been in the tenth and eleventh centuries, but young women were used to forge ties among men through marriage with little regard for their opinions, and betrothals sometimes took place among the higher nobility when the girls were still children, despite the church's insistence on consent. Widows were often sent back to their families, unless they had borne male offspring. Failure to produce a male heir could result in divorce, typically obtained under the guise of consanguinity or after an accusation of adultery. Women had little defense against such maneuvers unless the males in their families took offense and brought pressure to bear on their behalf. Women were objects of exchange, the means of passing on lineal currency from one kin group to another and of sealing peace through alliances. (See the illuminating treatment of these practices in Duby 1983.) With the exceptions of Meleagant's abduction of Guinevere and Fenice's betrothal to Alis, such abusive treatment of kinswomen is not depicted in Chrétien's romances.

The church was very much concerned about incestuous marriages, in this period those within the seventh degree of kinship. Marriages could be dissolved if they were found to be incestuous, and one precaution—if a precaution was desired—was to avoid the problem by searching for a wife outside one's region, where kinfolk abounded. This is the case with Erec, who finds Enide in Lalut; with Alexandre, who secures his bride in faraway Britain; with Alis and Cliges, successive husbands of a German woman. These are all men whose access to wealth and power is assured by their ancestry. Yvain, although the son of the renowned King Urien, is never seen returning to his father's kingdom but finds his own allodium by marrying a woman who is a widow (thanks to him!) in a principality that is not of easy access. In Perceval's relationship with Blancheflor the case for exogamy is not at all sure because of the obscurities surrounding the young man's ancestry. Tardy "discovery" of consanguinity could also provide a man with a legitimate, if unjust and exceedingly devious, method of dissolving a childless marriage, but this case never presents itself in Chrétien's romances.

Chrétien's principal subjects are love, loyalty, martial prowess, social and moral ideals, and justice. He does not challenge the nobility's dominance of the social order: on the contrary, the terms in which he tells of the cowardice displayed by the townspeople of Escavalon when they attack Gauvain (*Perceval* 5992–99) make it clear that his sympathies lie with the aristocracy. Morality as he formulates it in his romances is primarily adherence to a secular code of conduct, only secondarily to the teachings of the Christian religion into which that code had become imbedded. Prowess is often praised, even in its less sympathetic forms, when it is practiced by the protagonists for whom Chrétien generates sympathy. He treats love within the marital bond with great respect, straying from this path only in response to the wishes of a powerful patron.

Chrétien was not the inventor of the romance or of the adventure story told in rhyming couplets. But the adventure romance that flourished in the thirteenth and fourteenth centuries would not have existed as we know it had he not written (see Lacy, Kelly, and Busby 1987–88; Schmolke-Hasselmann 1998; and Trachsler 1997). He is the inventor of the quest as a grand subject for romance, and if he did not invent the Grail and the adulterous liaison between Lancelot and Arthur's queen, he certainly made them popular topics to a degree that later writers of romance could not ignore, for he created an audience demand for them. To us living more than eight centuries later, he reveals vividly a world different from our own not just in its physical aspects and its social habits but in its mental structures, its values and ideals, and its imaginative possibilities.

Notes

CHAPTER 1: CHRÉTIEN AND HIS MILIEU

1. As Yvain puts it before his combat with Laudine's seneschal and his two brothers, "God stays on the side of Justice, / For God and Justice think themselves friends" (*Dix se retient devers le droit, / Que Dix et Drois amis se tienent, Yvain* 4438–39). For the second of these lines, the Guiot manuscript appears to have a better reading: "God and Justice consider themselves as one" (*Dix et drois a .i. s'an tienent*). Line references for Chrétien's works throughout this book are to the following editions unless otherwise noted: for *Cliges*, Méla 1994a; for *Erec*, Fritz 1992b; for *Yvain*, Hult 1993; for *Lancelot*, Méla 1990; for *Perceval*, Roach 1959; for *Philomena*, Berthelot 1994a; and for the songs, Zai 1994. For convenience, the short titles of the romances will normally be used, followed by line numbers when appropriate. Chrétien gave other names to three of his works: *Le Chevalier au lion* to *Yvain*, *Le Chevalier de la charrette* to *Lancelot*, and *Le Conte du graal* to *Perceval*.

2. Holmes (1948) and Holmes and Klenke (1959: 51–61) suggested that "Chrétien" was likely to have been the name of a Jew who was converted, perhaps forcibly, to Christianity. Regardless of the significance of the name, they also posited influence on Chrétien from the Jewish communities of Champagne, particularly in regard to *Perceval*.

3. That Marie also enjoyed good relations with Richard Lion-Heart is shown by Richard's favorable mention of her (in contrast to her sister Alix) in the poem "Ja nus hons pris" that Richard wrote during his captivity in 1193–1194.

4. Rita Lejeune contests this interpretation, taking the phrase *an l'enpire de Rome* ("in the empire of Rome") to mean "in the civilized world."

5. Wilhelm Foerster, Gustave Cohen, Maurice Wilmotte, Arnulf Stefenelli, Maurice Delbouille, and Constance Bullock-Davies supported the attribution to Chrétien, while Jean Acher, Philip-August Becker, M. Dominica Legge, Jean Frappier, Carla Cremonesi, and the last two of the work's editors, Anthony J. Holden and Anne Berthelot, have opposed it. For an illuminating discussion of the problem, see Holden 1988: 14–35.

6. In addition to the forty-three Chrétien manuscripts, Nixon's list and description contain two manuscripts of works that are not by Chrétien, Brussels, Bibliothèque Royale IV 852, the *First Continuation* of *Perceval,* and Paris, Bibliothèque nationale, fonds français 1638, the manuscript of Pierre Sala's sixteenth-century adaptation of *Yvain.*

7. Manuscripts are identified by city, library, and shelf number. The core collection of French manuscripts in the Bibliothèque nationale in Paris is designated the *fonds français.* For nonspecialist readers, an explanation of certain other terms is here in order. *Codicology* designates the study of the book as a physical object, *paleography* the study of ancient and medieval writing, and *textual criticism* the art of establishing texts so as to give modern readers access to the literary work. The leaves of manuscripts are called *folios* ("f.," plural "ff."); the front of a folio is the *recto* ("r"), the back the *verso* ("v"). An *explicit* is a statement signaling that the text has ended, and a *colophon* is a note that the scribe writes after finishing the task of copying.

8. See the series of editions of the Guiot texts in the Classiques Français du Moyen Age, Roques 1952b (*Erec*), 1958 (*Lancelot*) and 1960 (*Yvain*), Micha 1957 (*Cliges*), and Lecoy 1973–75 (*Perceval*), and also Dembowski 1994a (*Erec*), Méla 1992 (*Lancelot*) and 1994a (*Cliges*), Nelson and Carroll 1968 (*Yvain*), Gregory and Luttrell 1993 (*Cliges*), Kajsa Meyer 1995 (diplomatic edition of *Yvain*), Poirion 1994b (*Lancelot*) and 1994c (*Perceval*), Uitti 1994 (*Yvain*), and Walter 1994 (*Cliges*).

9. The others are Edinburgh, National Library of Scotland, Advocates' 19. 1. 5. (*Perceval,* the *First* and *Second Continuations,* Manessier's *Third Continuation,* third quarter of the thirteenth century); Paris, Bibliothèque nationale, nouvelles acquisitions françaises 6614 (*Perceval* and all four continuations, fourth quarter of the thirteenth century); Mons Bibliothèque de l'Université de Mons-Hainaut 331/206 (the *Elucidation, Bliocadran, Perceval,* the *First* and *Second Continuations,* Manessier's *Third Continuation;* fourth quarter of the thirteenth century, basis for the Potvin edition [1865–73]); Paris, Bibl. nat., fonds français 1429 (*Perceval,* the *First* and *Second Continuations,* Manessier's *Third Continuation;* fourth quarter of the thirteenth century); and Paris, Bibliothèque nationale, fonds français 1453 (*Perceval,* the *First* and *Second Continuations,* and Manessier's *Third Continuation;* second quarter of the fourteenth century).

10. D. D. R. Owen (1966, 1971) has argued that *Le Chevalier à l'épée* and *La Mule sans frein* (edited in Johnston and Owen 1972) are both by Chrétien de Troyes, but this attribution has not been accepted.

11. Already in the sixth century Gregory of Tours, *Historia Francorum* 2: 17, tells about the bishop of Clermont's wife holding a book of tales concerning antiquity in her lap and pointing to illustrations that she wished to have painted on her walls (cited in Brenk 1984: 31).

CHAPTER 2: KINSHIP AND MARRIAGE

1. The unqualified Old French *cousin* was not always used precisely, but the sense of *cousin germain* is quite clear. Kullmann notes that the term *cousin* could extend even to lateral relatives of succeeding generations, although not to direct descendants, and *neveu* at times seems loosely to designate cousins (1992: 6 and nn.). *Neveu* could also mean grandson, the sense of its Latin etymon *nepos*.

2. Fritz 1992b and 1994: l. 1807, and Hult 1993 and 1994: l. 661. The text of *Erec* in the Guiot manuscript gives the less satisfactory "Pandragon" (Dembowski 1994a: l. 1775), as does fr. 1433, on which Hult bases his *Yvain*.

3. Loomis thought that Uther was not identified as Arthur's father in the pre-Geoffrey tradition (note in Webster 1951a: 216–17), but there is indirect evidence that he was. See Bromwich 1978: 521–22.

4. The tradition that Ygerna was Arthur's mother may go back farther than Geoffrey. See Bromwich 1978: 274–75.

5. Wright 1985: 98. Elsewhere in the tradition, Arthur's sister is called Morgana, Morgan the Fay, a designation perhaps hidden under Geoffrey's Anna, which corresponds to the last two syllables of Morgana.

6. Chrétien's neglect in naming Arthur's sister may reflect fluidity in the tradition. Geoffrey's *History,* for example, gives conflicting data about Gauvain's mother. Geoffrey first has Anna marry King Loth of Lodonesia (Wright 1985: 99). He then contradicts this by reporting that Loth was married to Ambrosius Aurelianus's sister, a woman who would have been Arthur's first cousin. This second woman is said to have borne Loth two sons, Gawain and Mordred (Wright 1985: 106). Twice later in the text, however, Geoffrey calls Gawain Arthur's nephew (*nepos;* Wright 1985: 123, 130), so his mention of Ambrosius Aurelianus must be an error for "Arthur." Wace, in fact, corrects the information accordingly (Arnold 1936–40: l. 9636; Baumgartner and Short 1993: 76–77 [l. 945] and 332 n. 6). Chrétien is the first to mention King Loth in French, as Loz in *Erec* 1733. Mordred (L. Modredus, W. Medrawt) is one of the oldest figures associated with Arthur, mentioned in the *Annals of Wales* under the year 537: "the battle of Camlann in which Arthur and Medraut fell" (*Gueith Camlann in qua Arthur et Medraut corruerunt*). See Bromwich 1978: 454–55. Morgue is the name of Arthur's sister in *Erec* 4214, and in 1950–53, but she is not linked there to either Lot or Gauvain. In fact, she is said to be the lover of Guilemer, line 1953. The earliest reference to her is under the form *Morgen* in Geoffrey of Monmouth's *Life of Merlin* (Clarke 1973: 920). In *Cliges,* the hero's mother Soredamor is Gauvain's sister, but her mother's name is not mentioned.

7. The toponym is given as Chanpguin in mss. *A* (Guiot) and *B.*

8. Hartmann thought similarly of Enide's relation to this lady because he says

that Imain of Tulmein is the brother of the lady's father and that the two women were both born in Lut (Hartmann's *Erec,* ll. 9719–24).

9. Celtic languages are divided into two branches, the P-Celtic (Welsh, Cornish, Breton) and the Q-Celtic (Irish, Manx, Scottish Gaelic), according to their treatment of Proto-Indo-European *k^w.

10. Baldwin (1994: 76) writes that Guinevere and Arthur give Soredamor to Alexandre "in the absence of male relatives from the family," but in fact Arthur is Soredamor's senior male relative and her brother Gauvain is also present.

11. This reading is given in four manuscripts of *Cliges,* including the Guiot text (Walter 1994: l. 2747), but four others make Cliges out to be seventeen (Méla 1994a: l. 2719). Foerster's great edition of 1884 gives the age as fifteen.

12. *Lanzelet,* unlike *Lancelot,* tells in detail the story of the hero's youth, how a fairy abducted him when he was a year old and raised him in her land of perpetual summer, populated by women in a constant state of joy (Spiewok 1997; Webster 1951a). See the discussion in Chapter 6, below. The story of Guinevere's abduction exists in a number of medieval versions (see Webster 1951b and Rejhon 1983), but in none of them except *Lancelot,* to our knowledge, does Guinevere commit adultery with one of Arthur's entourage.

13. The early Celtic tradition may have represented Cei (= Kay, Keu) as committing adultery with the queen during her abduction, but the matter is shrouded in ambiguity: see the "Conversation Between Arthur and Guinevere," published in Mary Williams 1938. A photograph of the Modena archivolt, which may represent a tradition recounted in *Durmart le Gallois* and the prose *Lancelot* of the Vulgate Cycle, is published as pl. 2 in Loomis 1959. Caradog of Llancarfan's account is found in Mommsen 1898: 109. That Guinevere was accepted as an adulteress in Welsh tradition is seen in triad 80, from a section of ms. National Library of Wales, Peniarth 47, that was copied in the fifteenth century (Bromwich 1978: xxxviii):

> Three Faithless Wives of the Island of Britain. Three daughters of
>   Culfanawyd of Britain:
> Essyllt Fair-Hair (Trystan's mistress),
> and Penarwan (wife of Owain son of Urien),
> and Bun, wife of Fflamddwyn.
> And one was more faithless than those three: Gwenhwyfar, Arthur's
>   wife, since she shamed a better man than any (of the others).
>   (Bromwich 1978: 200)

14. The initial *b* of 'Ban' has been devoiced, a phenomenon found in other literary names imported from Old French into Middle High German: see, for example, 'Paligan' for 'Baligant' in Konrad's *Rolandslied* (Kartschoke 1970: l. 7150, etc.). The name of the kingdom in Old French, Benoÿc, differs from Genewis in the sound represented in German by the initial *g.* Roger Sherman Loomis

believed that the Vulgate Cycle version of the place-name was closer to the original form. His theory was that the name Ban de Benoÿc was a variation on that of the legendary Celtic king, Bran the Blessed, which in Old French would be Bran le Benoïs (or Beneïs). See Webster 1951a: 157.

15. The lack of any mention of Calogrenant outside of *Yvain* accords with a theory of Roger Sherman Loomis (1949: 275), who disaggregated the name Calogrenant into *Ca* (that is, Cei, the figure behind the O. F. Keu) plus *lo grenant* 'the grumbler', an epithet that does indeed correspond to the character of Keu in the romances of Chrétien. Loomis gives other examples of Keu undertaking adventures that are analogous to Calogrenant's in *Yvain*. If one accepts this idea, Calogrenant would represent a folkloric doubling of Keu himself, who plays a subordinate role in the romance, although Chrétien does not seem to have been aware of this phenomenon.

16. Laudine is named in only three of the ten manuscripts, in the equivalent of line 2153 of the Hult edition. The other manuscripts, and the editions of Roques (1960), Nelson and Carroll (1968), and Hult (1993, 1994) call Yvain's lady simply *la dame de Landuc* (variants: Lauduc, Lenduc, Londuc). Foerster (l. 2151 in his 1887 and 1912 editions), Reid (1942, using Foerster's text), and Kibler (1985) opt for *Laudine de Landuc*. Woledge (1986: 136–37) shows that the preferred forms would be, for the lady, Laudune (*V*), for the place, Lauduc (*VF*), and for the father, Laudunet (*VR*), as these are the closest to the forms found in early independent references to the story pattern found in *Yvain*. The Welsh triads call the father Llewdun Lluydauc (Bromwich 1978: 320). The *Fragmentary Life of St. Kentigern,* written in Scotland between 1147 and 1164, and thus before Chrétien's *Yvain,* calls the father Leudonus of Leudonia (Forbes 1874: 243–52).

17. *Par mi la jambe* (l. 436 of Roach 1959 and Poirion 1994c), or "between the haunches" (*par mi les hanches,* 408 of the Méla 1990 edition, also found in mss. *MQRU; par mi la hanche* in mss. *BCHL*). Perceval's father remains unnamed in *Perceval* but receives a name in most of the works that take off from Chrétien's romance. See Wolfgang 1980–81.

18. This line is not in ms. *B,* the basis for Méla 1990, but Méla supplies it in his variants.

19. Another possibility is that Perceval's relationship to this *germaine cousine* is through his father (see below), in which case she would indeed be the niece of the Fisher King. The kinship relations of the young woman with whom Perceval falls in love in the castle of Beaurepaire, Blancheflor, are intriguing. She is the niece of Gornemant of Gohort or Gorhaut (1901), who is said in a section of *Peredur* that is allied to the *Conte du graal* to be the brother of the Fisher King. She refers to another uncle, a prior who sends her meager rations (1911). Were Chrétien to have posited Gornemant as the Fisher King's brother, Perceval would have fallen in love with, but not made love to, his own sister.

20. *Ferus d'un gavelot / Par mi les quisses ambesdeus,* Roach 1959: l. 3513; *navrez d'un javelot / Par mi les anches amedeus,* Méla 1990: ll. 3450–51; *feruz d'un javelot / Par me les hanches amedos,* Poirion 1994c: ll. 3512–13.

21. Fowler (1959: 28) came to this same conclusion, which is difficult to ignore. That two men of indeterminate lineage but of the same generation should be identified in the romance as wounded in this unusual way and should not turn out to be the same person would appear to be anomalous.

22. Patrick Ford (1983) has remarked on the occurrence of W. *gwyn,* f. *gwen,* 'pure, sacred, holy', in names associated with King Arthur. The people and objects so named—Arthur's knife Carnwennan, his ship Prydwen, his wife, Gwen-hwyfar, his mantle Gwenn, and his hall Ehangwen—all have their origins in the Otherworld. The Old Breton equivalent of *gwyn* is *guinn. Champguin,* if its first element derives from a form of Latin *campus,* would mean something like 'sacred encampment, sacred rampart', a fitting name for an Otherworld emplacement. W. *camp,* which becomes *champ* when undergoing initial aspi-rate mutation (a process whereby initial consonant sounds are transformed in certain circumstances) and can be either masculine or feminine, is attested only in the fifteenth century. Another possible etymon for the first element is the O. F. *champ* 'field'.

23. In this period, marriage between those related by common descent from an ancestor six or at times seven generations back was considered consanguin-ous. Perceval's mother and the Fisher King are presumably related at least in the third degree of kinship because they are descended from her parents and his grandparents, "presumably" because Chrétien gives us no information about the ancestral couple and there is no reason to assume that one of them was married more than once.

24. I see no reason, in the absence of indications to that effect in the text, to re-gard either Perceval's cousin or his hermit uncle as unreliable narrators or as intentionally misleading or manipulative in what they tell him (see Cazelles 1996: 138–40, 160–67).

25. Kullmann discusses this scene (1992: 203) but does not raise the possibility of incest in Perceval's kin group.

26. This figure of twelve years is also given in *B* (Méla 1990: l. 6355) and *FHRTV.* In Guiot's text it is fifteen years (Poirion 1994c: l. 6429), and in *CPSU* it is twenty.

27. These isles are mentioned later when a charcoal-maker whom Perceval meets tells him that Arthur is happy to have defeated King Rion of the Isles of the Sea (851–52). This designation recalls the kingship of Man and the Western Isles, attested in the twelfth century. Dorothea Kullmann believes it refers to the British Isles in contrast to the Continent (1992: 192–93), an interpretation with which I do not agree. Clamadeu, defeated and sent to Arthur's court by Perceval, is also called *des Illes* ("of the Isles").

28. Because Perceval wanders in search of the Grail castle for five years, he would

be about twenty years old when he meets his hermit uncle. Chrétien does not, however, show a strong interest in exact chronology.

29. I see no other way to read the hermit uncle's explanation in lines 6415–19 of *Perceval:*

> "He who is served is my brother;
> My sister and his was your mother;
> And I believe that the rich Fisher
> Is the son of that king
> Who has himself served with that grail."
> ["Cil qui l'en en sert est mes frere,
> Ma suer et soe fu ta mere;
> Et del riche Pescheor croi
> Qu'il est fix a icelui roi
> Qu'en cel graal servir se fait."]

The person who is served by the Grail is the brother of the hermit and of Perceval's mother, and that same person's son is the Fisher King, whatever Wolfram von Eschenbach and the author of *Perlesvaus* do with the kinship relations of the Grail King's family in their respective works. This interpretation is shared by Heinzel (1891: 12), Hilka (1932: 807), Frappier (1959: 188; 1972a: 155), Loomis (1949: 353; 1959c: 292), and Roach (see West 1971–72: 56 n. 11), but not by Busby 1993b: 542. The complications of the Fisher King's lineage are discussed in West 1971–72. Kullmann (1992: 195) believes that if Chrétien created two kings from one who would have functioned in the received tradition, he would have done so in order to represent Perceval's kin group as linear and vertical.

30. Guiromelant does marry Clarissant in the *First Continuation* (Roach 1949: ll. 1084–89). In that work he also duels with Gauvain, but the outcome is inconclusive.

CHAPTER 3: VALUES

1. The term *vertu* in Chrétien seems to signify primarily 'strength, force', as in *Erec* 839, 1727, *Cliges* 4579, *Lancelot* 1740, 4320, 6259, *Yvain* 3904, 3907, and *Perceval* 6406, but it can also designate what we would term 'virtue' (see *Cliges* 146, 194, 212, 2564). In some cases it is difficult to distinguish which of the two senses is intended. *Vertu* can also mean 'miracle' in other contexts. The more common term in Chrétien for virtue in the sense of 'good quality', however, is *bone teche,* and a bad quality is a *male teche.*

2. Erich Köhler (1964: 29, 1974: 26–43) took largesse as an essential element of court life, the keystone of his interpretation of courtliness and the varieties of love that it developed as phenomena that favored the nobles whom the growth

of central, Capetian authority weakened, as well as the knights who came to constitute the lower nobility. As the state of more or less permanent private warfare came under control, knights who had previously filled a military role found that they had become superfluous. It is at this stage in the social development of knighthood, between 1160 and preparations for the Third Crusade in 1190, that the ideal of a knight errant, wandering in search of adventures, would have been the most appealing (Köhler 1974: 79–80). The fief itself, Köhler pointed out, took the form of a gift, albeit one that entailed reciprocation in the form of fidelity and various types of service. How one is to account, in the framework of this elegant theory of courtliness as the vehicle of the lower nobility, for the courtly poems of the earliest troubadour whose works have survived, William IX of Aquitaine, is unclear. Köhler viewed William as merely the first high noble to sanction the courtly concepts proposed as an ideal by the lower nobles, but I see no justification in William's poems for this thesis.

3. An asterisk before a form signals that it is not attested but is, rather, reconstructed on the basis of the principles of historical linguistics.

4. In line 4387 of *Yvain, colpe* is also used in the expression *clamer sa colpe* 'to beat one's breast, exclaim *mea culpa*', an action performed by Lunete before the trial by combat that Yvain wins on her behalf.

5. *Honte* is also occasionally used in another sense, to designate a character's modesty, embarrassment, or confusion, thus *Erec* 1753, *Cliges* 602, 1601, 4242, *Yvain* 3021, *Perceval* 3786. *Vergogne* is used in the same sense in *Erec* 1751.

6. The notion of the wife as lover is found already in the *Roman de Troie,* ll. 2433–38, quoted in Luttrell 1974: 57:

   "I will marry you as my wife,
   Will love you above all.
   You will be my lady and my lover.
   You will have lordship over me:
   So much will I put my mind to serving you
   That I will do everything you wish."
   ["A femme vos esposerai,
   Sor tote rien vos amerai.
   Ma dame sereiz e m'amie,
   De mei avreiz la seignorie:
   Tant entendrai a vos servir
   Que tot ferai vostre plaisir."]

   The same idea is found in Gaimar's story of Havelok, as Luttrell points out.

7. That actions occurring in public take on an enhanced status in Chrétien is clear in an incident of *Lancelot* 1626–30 in which a young knight wants to fight with the hero in order to take from under his protection a woman whom the

knight loves. He regrets, however, that he cannot do battle with Lancelot before witnesses, so they all go to a clearing where damsels and young men are playing.

8. The line in which Lancelot is said to hesitate for the space of two steps is one of a couplet that is not in the Guiot manuscript, favored by most editors, but that was restored by Foerster in his edition (1899) on the basis of readings found in other manuscripts. The couplet is also absent from the Méla text (1992, 1994b), where it would come between ll. 360 and 361. The passage has been the subject of a series of studies: Vinaver 1969, Hult 1986, Uitti 1988, and Hult 1989a. Guinevere refers in l. 4487 to Lancelot's having hesitated for two steps.

9. For the second of these two lines, the Roach edition of Paris, Bibliothèque nationale, fonds français 12576, has a different sense: "He who speaks too much does wrong" (*Qui trop parole, il se mesfait*). This reading is not shared by other manuscripts, however, and it is likely that Chrétien's original text bore a reading close to that of the Méla edition, based on Bern, Bürgerbibliothek 356, in which the word *pechié* appeared. The Guiot manuscript, for example, has: *Qui trop parole pechié fet* (Poirion 1994c: l. 1654), "He who speaks too much commits a sin." Jean-Charles Payen made a convincing case that Perceval's sin of having caused his mother's death was compounded by the egotism and lack of charity that he demonstrated in forgetting God and not entering churches for five years, so that it was in the end a sin against the Holy Spirit. Chrétien would then here be rationalizing in the light of Christian beliefs what was formerly, in his Celtic source, a *geis* or magical prohibition that would have been imposed on Perceval. See Payen 1967: 397–99; and Reinhard 1933: 152–53.

10. For an example of such a prayer, see Payen 1984: 132.

11. This is the only place in *Perceval* in which the Grail is termed holy; Chrétien thus never refers to it as the "Holy Grail." Nevertheless the illuminators of the only two manuscripts of *Perceval* in which the Grail scene is the subject of a miniature (Montpellier, Bibliothèque interuniversitaire, Section Médecine H249, last quarter of the thirteenth century, and Paris, Bibliothèque nationale, fonds françis 12577, second quarter of the fourteenth century) have been influenced by the sanctification of the Grail that develops in works composed after Chrétien. See Baumgartner 1993.

12. Evil characters in *Perceval* are characterized by overweening pride, *orgueil:* Keu, Orgueilleus de la Lande, Orgueilleuse de Nogres, and Orgueilleus de la Roche a l'Estroite Voie.

13. Shame appears to play varying roles in the narratives and value systems of other authors of courtly romance from this period. In a section of 2,016 lines in Renaut de Bâgé's *Le Bel Inconnu,* for example, the word *honte* and its reflexes only occur three times, or once every 672 lines (Ferlampin-Acher 1996: 96), although that work is heavily influenced by Chrétien's *Erec,* which has

eighteen occurrences, averaging one every 386 lines. In Béroul's *Roman de Tristan,* the occurrences are even rarer, once every 747 lines (Andrieu, Piolle, and Plouzeau 1974: 129), perhaps because the lovers, under the influence of a potion, feel little shame for their actions. In the works of Jean Renart, by contrast, shame is more significant: in his *Roman de Guillaume de Dole, honte* and its reflexes are found on average once every 210 lines (Andrieu, Piolle, and Plouzeau 1978a: 245–47), and in his *Galeran de Bretagne* even more frequently, once every 137 lines on average (Andrieu, Piolle, and Plouzeau 1978b: 338–39). Reflexes of *honte* occur in the Lecoy edition of Guillaume de Lorris's *Roman de la rose,* where behavior is at issue—although not knightly behavior in particular—only nine times in 4,028 lines (Bertrand 1983, 1: 94, 2: 88). The subject bears investigation on a broader scale (see Robreau 1981).

CHAPTER 4: INTERIORITY AND RESPONSIBILITY

1. Possible influence of the School of Chartres on *Perceval* has been studied by Leo Pollmann (1965: 81–146).
2. In her study *La folie au moyen âge: XIIe–XIIIe siècles* (1991), Muriel Laharie interprets Yvain's madness as caused by a strong feeling of guilt, which I do not believe to be the case. Guilt is never mentioned in this scene, only Yvain's self-hatred for having deprived himself of marital joy and for his frustration at not being able to take vengeance on the perpetrator, who is himself. Shame is not mentioned specifically either, but Yvain has obviously been shamed by the public accusations of Laudine's messenger in Arthur's court.
3. Peter of Spain, who taught at Siena from 1245 and became pope under the name John XXI (1276–1277), associates silent behavior with melancholy as well: "Melancholy is a madness bringing on in silence illicit thoughts and acts" (*Melancolia est disipientia illicitas meditationes ac actus in taciturnitate procurans,* Alonso 1941: 515).
4. Jean-Marie Fritz (1992a: 99, 285, 295, 302) speaks of Yvain's frenzy; but Yvain's behavior corresponds more closely to the signs of melancholy. Nor is Yvain's madness the result of Laudine's absence (296): rather, it derives from his hatred of himself and the impossibility of taking vengeance on himself, as Fritz recognizes elsewhere (326). For a penetrating study of Keu in the light of the theory of the humors, see Merceron 1998.
5. I found this recipe by searching in the on-line *Patrologia Latina* database, maintained for the use of subscribers (individuals and libraries) by Chadwyck-Healey, Inc., for *melancholi**. This produced 99 occurrences in 42 works. The passages could then be scrutinized on-line. The recipe was found in the thirty-third work. The World Wide Web address of the database is < http://pld.chadwyck.co.uk/ >.
6. "Let the man whom melancholy affects crush fennel into a juice and anoint

the forehead, and the temples, and the breast, and the stomach often, and the melancholy will cease in him" (*Homo etiam quem melancholia laedit, foeniculum ad succum contundat, et frontem, et tempora, et pectus, et stomachum saepe perungat, et melancholia in eo cessabit,* Hildegard of Bingen 1862–65: ch. 66, "De feniculo").

7. Almost never. Gauvain refuses to grant the request of the boatman who ferries him to the castle of the Rock of Champguin, despite having promised him whatever he wishes (*Perceval* 7636–37). The request is that Gauvain return home, which the hero rejects because if he were to do so he would be shamed.

8. For a subtle and far-reaching critique of Köhler's treatment of the custom, see Maddox 1991, esp. 133–40.

9. Keu is the subject of a wide-ranging and informative study by Jacques Merceron (1998), who analyzes his character as choleric according to the theory of the four humors.

10. "Out of pity and generosity." The Guiot manuscript has "out of love" (*par Amors*) and another text, Paris, Bibliothèque nationale, fonds français 12560, has "out of alms-giving" (*par aumosne*). In all three a charitable motivation is specified.

11. Keith Busby (1984: 21) notes the seeming lack of motivation in Gauvain's actions compared with those of Perceval.

CHAPTER 5: CELTIC MYTH, FOLKLORE, AND HISTORICAL TRADITION

1. The most substantial early literary text in Breton is an Arthurian work of 247 lines from around the middle of the fifteenth century: the *Dialogue Between Arthur King of the Britons and Guinglaff* (*Dialog etre Arzur roe dan Bretounet ha Guinglaff,* Piriou 1985).

2. Three other manuscripts, *MPQ,* contain a similar passage, but only *L* gives the name Bleheri; *LMQ* mention the count of Poitiers, but only *L* says that the story was recounted to him.

3. The form *Mabinogion* results from a scribal misreading in a medieval manuscript, which Lady Charlotte Guest reproduced and popularized through her translation of Welsh tales (see Roberts 1984: 213–14). The proper term, *Mabinogi,* which actually includes only the four Welsh mythological tales or Four Branches of *Pwyll, Math, Manawydan,* and *Branwen,* probably means "the [collective] material pertaining to the god Maponos" (Hamp 1975). A reliable, though somewhat archaizing translation of the three Welsh romances is found in Jones and Jones 1974; a translation in contemporary language is that of Patrick K. Ford (1977).

4. R. M. Jones (1996: 222) has suggested Monmouth as a likely locus in which bilingual performers may have presented parallel versions of the romances.

5. Whether Arthur was a historical figure is a question that is beyond the scope of the present study. See Ashe 1985; Ashe et al. 1987; and Littleton and Malcor 1994.

6. "The elder Belin, the second Brenne" (*l'ainz nez Belin, li secunz Brenne,* Arnold 1938–40: l. 2315). The antecedent of Belinus in Celtic mythology is Beli Mawr, a deity from whom all the early Welsh dynasties traced their descent, perhaps cognate with the Gaulish god Belenos (Bromwich 1978: 281–83). This was recognized by the Welsh translator who produced *Brut y Brenhinedd,* the Welsh version of the *History of the Kings of Britain,* in the Llanstephan I manuscript, who substitutes Beli Maur, son of Manogan, for Geoffrey's Heli, son of Cligueillus. Brennius's mythological antecedent is the giant Bran ('raven') the Blessed, custodian of a cauldron of regeneration and said to be the grandson or the sister's son of Beli (Bromwich 1978: 284). On the dwarf king of the Antipodes and his giant brother, see Harward (1958: 33–42, 51–61).

7. Could the association with horses have been suggested by knowledge of a Breton counterpart of Enide, Etain Echraide, an Irish goddess whose epithet means 'horse-riding'?

8. The variants for this place-name are *Pencairic, Penevris* (Fritz 1992b: l. 5177 and variants)—both of which, like *Penuris,* contain the morpheme *Pen-* 'head, chief'—and the un-Celtic *Pointurie* (Dembowski 1994a: l. 5183).

9. The figure of Esclados himself bears resemblances to the Irish Cúroi, who is comparable to an Indian cowherd deity named Pushan who protects cattle, serves as a guide to the Otherworld, and helps the revolution of day and night (Mac Cana 1983: 99). For a study of the possible analogies of *Bricriu's Feast* with *Yvain,* see Loomis 1949: 278–89.

10. The existence of the continuations coupled with the lack of an articulated closure to *Perceval* led several scholars to question the end limit of Chrétien's composition. Philip-August Becker suggested that he was responsible for the text only up to the point at which Perceval leaves the Fisher King's castle (Becker 1935). Gustav Gröber (1888–1902, vol. 2, part 1: 504–5) and Stefan Hofer (1954: 210–14) ascribed Gauvain's adventures to a continuator, and Martín de Riquer (1957) believed that a redactor combined two unfinished works by Chrétien, one about Perceval and the other about Gauvain, into the romance we know. The authority of Jean Frappier (1958, 1960; see also Köhler 1959) has led to general agreement that Chrétien's composition extends to a point corresponding to the last line of the Roach edition of *Perceval* (1959).

11. Is this why Chrétien places two kings in the Grail castle (see ll. 6417–18 of *Perceval*)? Other early versions of the Grail legend (*Parzival, Peredur, Perlesvaus*) place only one king in the castle.

CHAPTER 6: THE ART OF THE STORYTELLER

1. Douglas Kelly (1992: 20) interprets the fertile ground as the book that Philip gave Chrétien, but I do not see how this conclusion can result from what is said in the text. Philippe Walter (1997: 10) has raised the possibility that the criticisms leveled in this prologue against those who listen to calumny, do not love churchmen, and boast about their generosity refer obliquely to Marie de Champagne, from whom Chrétien would have become disaffected. There is, however, no way of verifying this intriguing theory.

2. Jane Burns perceives a sexual denotation in Chrétien's use of *conjointure:* see Burns 1993: 162, 182. To designate the work he is composing, Chrétien uses, in addition to *estoire,* the terms *conte* 'tale' (*Erec* 6950, *Cliges* 8, 45, *Perceval* 6515), *roman* 'work in the vernacular language' (*Cliges* 23, *Lancelot* 2, *Yvain* 6805, *Perceval* 8), *livre* 'book' (*Lancelot* 25), and *œvre* 'work' (*Cliges* 6702, *Lancelot* 22). But he uses three of these terms to designate his source as well: *livre* (*Cliges* 20, 24, *Perceval* 67), *conte* (*Lancelot* 464, *Perceval* 63, 66, 709), and *estoire* 'story' (*Erec* 3586, 5730, 6728, *Cliges* 18, 22, 25, 46, *Perceval* 2807, 6217). See Ollier 1974: 27–29. Peter Damian-Grint has shown that *estoire* is most commonly used to designate historiographic narratives but passes too quickly over its occurrence in the romance, where it is occasionally self-referential (1997: 195), with an implication that the work in question is truthful. Surely *estoire* in line 23 of *Erec* refers to Chrétien's romance itself.

3. Occasionally Chrétien includes himself and his audience in a first-person plural: *Erec* 1242, *Lancelot* 5572–73. In the case of the source for Chrétien's description of Erec's coronation robe, where the introductory phrase is *Lisant trovomes en l'estoire* (*Erec* 6728), there is a rare authorial "we," as indicated by the reversion to the first-person singular two lines later: "And I take as my guarantor Macrobius" (*Si en trai a garant Macrobe,* 6730).

4. In the thirteenth-century prose romances expressions of this type refer to the romance itself: "Here the [present] tale ceases to speak of . . . ." I do not believe that Chrétien's usage is the same. See Marnette 1998: 44–45.

5. The various types of authorial intervention are enumerated in Grigsby 1979.

6. The "translations" of the Latin terms given here are my own interpretive attempts to capture the elusive nuances of the various tropes.

7. Luttrell (1974: 21–25) maintains that the description of the robe is more likely to show the influence of Martianus Capella's *Marriage of Philology and Mercury,* which gave to the Middle Ages the concept of the seven liberal arts. Similar portrayals of the arts are found in a poem by Baudri de Bourgueil, "Adelae comitissae," and in the *Roman de Thèbes.* But by far the closest parallel, according to Luttrell, is in Alan of Lille's *Anticlaudianus,* where the arts are depicted on a dress as in Chrétien, their processes rather than merely their physical instruments are described, and female deities provide the description.

8. This contrasts with the treatment of Enide's counterpart, Enid, in *Geraint,* who is made to wear her worst dress, to a Welsh audience symbolic of sovereignty besmirched.

9. For line 2717, the reading of mss. *CRT, don molt boen sera li passages,* "of which the passage will be very good," adopted by Méla, is colorless, banal, and inferior to that of mss. *PA,* preferred by Foerster (1884), Gregory and Stewart (1993), and Walter (1994), in which the adjective is *briés* 'brief'. The paradox, of course, is that, far from brief, the description is the longest devoted to any hero in Chrétien's works.

10. Méla keeps the reading of *BC,* which places Cliges's age at nearly seventeen, but his translation follows mss. *SAMP,* to whose reading I have emended here. The texts of Foerster (1884), Gregory and Stewart (1993), and Walter (1994) all make the hero out to be fifteen.

CHAPTER 7: KNIGHTS AND LADIES

1. Flori (1979: 34–35) believes the strapping on of the right spur may be Chrétien's innovation, since he takes pains to explain it as a custom from the days of King Arthur (*Perceval* 1626–28).

Bibliography

ABBREVIATIONS

BBSIA	*Bulletin Bibliographique de la Société Internationale Arthurienne*
CCM	*Cahiers de Civilisation Médiévale*
PRF	Publications Romanes et Françaises
CFMA	Classiques Français du Moyen Age
MA	*Le Moyen Age*
MÆ	*Medium Ævum*
MP	*Modern Philology*
PMLA	*Publications of the Modern Language Association of America*
RPh	*Romance Philology*
SATF	Société des Anciens Textes Français
SC	*Studia Celtica*
SP	*Studies in Philology*
TLF	Textes Littéraires Français
ZCP	*Zeitschrift für Celtische Philologie*
ZRP	*Zeitschrift für Romanische Philologie*

Adams, Alison. 1983. *The Romance of Yder*. Arthurian Studies, 8. Cambridge: D. S. Brewer.

Akehurst, F. R. P., trans. 1992. *The Coutumes de Beauvaisis of Philippe de Beaumanoir*. Philadelphia: University of Pennsylvania Press.

Alcock, Leslie. 1990. *Arthur's Britain: History and Archaeology, A.D. 367–634*. Harmondsworth: Penguin.

Allen, Rosamund, trans. 1992. *Lawman, Brut*. Translated with an introduction and notes. New York: St. Martin's.

Alonso, Manuel, ed. 1941. *Scientia libri de anima por Pedro Hispano*. Instituto Filosófico Luis Vives, ser. A, no. 1. Madrid: Consejo Superior de Investigaciones Científicas.

Andrieu, Gabriel, Jacques Piolle, and May Plouzeau. 1974. *Le Roman de Tris-*

tan de Béroul: Concordancier complet des formes graphiques occurrentes. Aix-en-Provence: Centre de Recherches et d'Etudes Linguistiques, Département de Littérature Française et Laboratoire de Traitement Automatique des Textes.

Andrieu, Gabriel, and Jacques Piolle. 1976. *Perceval, ou Le conte du graal de Chrétien de Troyes: Concordancier complet des formes graphiques occurrentes d'après l'édition de Félix Lecoy.* Aix-en-Provence: Centre de Recherches et d'Etudes Linguistiques.

———. 1978a. *Le Roman de la rose, ou de Guillaume de Dole de Jean Renart: Concordancier complet des formes graphiques occurrentes.* Paris: Champion.

———. 1978b. *Galeran de Bretagne de Jean Renart: Concordancier complet des formes graphiques occurrentes d'après l'édition de Lucien Foulet.* Paris: Champion.

Arnold, Ivor, ed. 1938–40. *Le Roman de Brut de Wace.* 2 vols. SATF, 81. Paris: SATF.

Arnold, Ivor D. O., and M. M. Pelan, ed. 1962. *La partie arthurienne du Roman de Brut.* PRF, Série B: Textes et Documents, 1. Paris: Klincksieck.

Ashe, Geoffrey. 1985. *The Discovery of King Arthur.* Garden City, N.Y.: Doubleday.

Ashe, Geoffrey, et al. 1987. *The Quest for Arthur's Britain.* With a new introduction by Geoffrey Ashe. Chicago: Academy Chicago.

Auerbach, Erich. 1957. *Mimesis: The Representation of Reality in Western Literature.* New York: Anchor.

Baldwin, John W. 1994. *Language of Sex: Five Voices from Northern France Around 1200.* Chicago: University of Chicago Press.

Bartrum, P. C., ed. 1966. *Early Welsh Genealogical Tracts.* Cardiff: University of Wales Press.

Baumgartner, Emmanuèle. 1993. "Les scènes du graal et leur illustration dans les manuscrits du *Conte du graal* et des *Continuations.*" In Busby et al. 1993: 489–503.

Baumgartner, Emmanuèle, and Ian Short, ed. and trans. 1993. *La geste du roi Arthur selon le Roman de Brut de Wace et l'Historia regum britanniae de Geoffroy de Monmouth.* Présentation, édition et traductions, 10/18. Paris: Union Générale d'Editions.

Becker, Philipp August. 1934. *Der gepaarte Achtsilber in der französischen Dichtung.* Abhandlungen der Philologisch-historischen Klasse der Sächsischen Akademie der Wissenschaften, 43. Leipzig: Hirzel.

———. 1935. "Von den Erzählern neben und nach Chrestien von Troyes." *ZRP* 55: 385–400.

Bédier, Joseph. 1928. "La tradition manuscrite du *Lai de l'ombre:* Réflexions sur l'art d'éditer les anciens textes." *Romania* 54: 161–96, 321–58.

Beltrami, P. G. 1989. "Lancelot entre Lanzelet et Enéas: Remarques sur le sens du *Chevalier de la charrette.*" *Zeitschrift für Französische Sprache und Literatur* 99: 234–60.

Bennett, Philip, ed. 1975. *Mantel et Cor, deux lais du XIIe siècle.* Exeter: University of Exeter.

Benton, John F. 1961. "The Court of Champagne as a Literary Center." *Speculum* 36: 551–91. Repr. in Benton 1991: 3–44.

———. 1968. "Clio and Venus: A Historical View of Medieval Love." In Francis X. Newman, ed., *The Meaning of Courtly Love,* 19–42. Albany: State University of New York Press. Repr. in Benton 1991: 99–121.

———. 1981. "Collaborative Approaches to Fantasy and Reality in the Literature of Champagne." In Glyn Burgess, ed., *Selected Proceedings of the Third Congress of the International Courtly Literature Society,* 43–57. Arca, 5. Liverpool: F. Cairns. Repr. in Benton 1991: 167–80.

———. 1991. *Culture, Power, and Personality in Medieval France.* Edited by Thomas N. Bisson. London: Hambledon.

Bernadac, Christian. 1994. *Montségur et le graal: Le mystère Otto Rahn.* Paris: France-Empire.

Berthelot, Anne, ed. and trans. 1994a. *Philomena.* In Poirion 1994a: 915–52, 1391–1410.

———. 1994b. *Guillaume d'Angleterre.* In Poirion 1994a: 953–1036, 1410–51.

———. 1994c. *Chansons courtoises.* In Poirion 1994a: 1037–49, 1451–57.

Bertrand, Roger. 1983. *Guillaume de Lorris, le Roman de la rose: Concordancier complet des formes graphiques occurrentes.* Aix-en-Provence: Publications du CUER MA.

Blacker, Jean. 1994. *The Faces of Time: Portrayal of the Past in Old French and Latin Historical Narrative of the Anglo-Norman Regnum.* Austin: University of Texas Press.

Blaess, Madeleine. 1978. "Perceval et les 'Illes de mer.' " In *Mélanges de littérature du moyen âge au XXe siècle offerts à Mademoiselle Jeanne Lods,* 69–77. Collection de l'Ecole Normale Supérieure de Jeunes Filles, 10. Paris: Ecole Normale Supérieure de Jeunes Filles.

Bloch, Marc. 1949. *La société féodale.* Vol. 1: *La formation des liens de dépendance.* Vol. 2: *Les classes et le gouvernement des hommes.* Paris: A. Michel.

———. 1960. *Les caractères originaux de l'histoire rurale française.* Nouvelle édition. Paris: A. Colin.

Bloch, R. Howard. 1991. *Medieval Misogyny and the Invention of Western Romantic Love.* Chicago: University of Chicago Press.

Blomme, Robert. 1958. *La doctrine du péché dans les écoles théologiques de la première moitié du XIIe siècle.* Universitas Catholica Lovaniensis, Dissertationes ad gradum magistri in Facultate Theologica vel in Facultate Iuris Canonici consequendum conscriptae, ser. 3, vol. 6. Louvain: Publications Universitaires de Louvain.

Bogdanow, Fanni. 1984. "Le *Perlesvaus.*" In *Grundriss der romanischen Literaturen des Mittelalters,* vol. 4, part 2: 43–67. Heidelberg: Carl Winter.

Bonnefois, Pascal, and Marie-Louise Ollier. 1988. *Yvain, ou Le chevalier au lion:*

Concordance lemmatisée. Collection ERA 642. Paris: Département de Recherches Linguistiques, Jussieu.

Bourciez, Jean. 1956. *Eléments de linguistique romane.* 4th ed. Paris: Klincksieck.

Boutémy, André, ed. 1946. "*La geste d'Enée* par Simon Chèvre d'Or (d'après le ms. Rawlinson G. 109 de la Bibliothèque Bodléienne)." *MA* 52: 243–56.

Brasseur, Annette, ed. 1989. *Jean Bodel, La Chanson des Saisnes.* 2 vols. Geneva: Droz.

Brault, Gerard J. 1972. "Chrétien de Troyes' *Lancelot:* The Eye and the Heart." *BBSIA* 24: 142–53.

Brenk, Beat. 1984. "Le texte et l'image dans la vie des saints au moyen âge: Rôle du concepteur et rôle du peintre." In *Texte et image: Actes du Colloque international de Chantilly (13 au 15 octobre 1982),* 31–39. Paris: Les Belles Lettres.

Brewer, Elisabeth. 1987. "The Figure of Guenevere in Modern Drama and Fiction." In W. Van Hoecke, Gilbert Tournoy, and Werner Verbeke, eds., *Arturus Rex,* 2: 478–90. Louvain: Louvain University Press. Repr. in Lori J. Walters, ed., *Lancelot and Guinevere: A Casebook,* 279–89. New York: Garland, 1996.

Bromwich, Rachel. 1955–56. "The Date of *Hirlas Owein." Bulletin of the Board of Celtic Studies* 16: 188–89.

———. 1961. "Celtic Dynastic Themes and the Breton Lays." *Etudes Celtiques* 9: 439–74.

———. 1975–76. "Concepts of Arthur." *SC* 10–11: 163–81.

———. 1983. "Celtic Elements in Arthurian Romance." In P. B. Grout et al., ed., *The Legend of Arthur in the Middle Ages: Studies Presented to A. H. Diverres by Colleagues, Pupils and Friends,* 41–55. Arthurian Studies, 7. Cambridge: D. S. Brewer.

———. 1991. "First Transmission to England and France." In Rachel Bromwich, A. O. H. Jarman, and Brynley F. Roberts, eds., *The Arthur of the Welsh: The Arthurian Legend in Medieval Welsh Literature,* 273–98. Cardiff: University of Wales Press.

———. 1997. "The Triads of the Horses." In Sioned Davies and Nerys Ann Jones, eds., *The Horse in Celtic Culture.* Cardiff: University of Wales Press.

Bromwich, Rachel, ed. 1978. *Trioedd Ynys Prydein, the Welsh Triads.* Cardiff: University of Wales Press.

Bromwich, Rachel, and D. Simon Evans, ed. 1992. *Culhwch and Olwen: An Edition and Study of the Oldest Arthurian Tale.* Cardiff: University of Wales Press.

Brook, G. L., and R. F. Leslie, eds. 1963–78. *Layamon, Brut.* Edited from British Museum Ms. Cotton Otho C.XIII. Early English Text Society Original Series, 250, 277. London: Oxford University Press.

Brown, Arthur C. L. 1910. "The Bleeding Lance." *PMLA* 25: 1–59.

———. 1943. *The Origin of the Grail Legend.* Cambridge, Mass.: Harvard University Press.

Bruce, James Douglas, ed. 1913. *Historia Meriadoci and De Ortu Waluuanii: Two*

Arthurian Romances of the XIIIth Century in Latin Prose. Hesperia, Ergänzungs-reihe: Schriften zur englischen Philologie, 2. Baltimore: Johns Hopkins University Press.

Bruce, James Douglas. 1928. *The Evolution of Arthurian Romance from the Beginnings Down to the Year 1300.* 2d ed., with a supplement by Alfons Hilka. 2 vols. Gloucester: Peter Smith.

Bruckner, Matilda Tomaryn. 1986. "An Interpreter's Dilemma: Why Are There So Many Interpretations of Chrétien's *Chevalier de la charrette?*" *RPh* 40: 159–80.

———. 1993. *Shaping Romance: Interpretation, Truth, and Closure in Twelfth-Century French Fictions.* Philadelphia: University of Pennsylvania Press.

Brundage, James A. 1987. *Law, Sex, and Christian Society in Medieval Europe.* Chicago: University of Chicago Press.

Brunel, Clovis. 1960. "Les hanches du Roi Pêcheur." *Romania* 81: 37.

Bryant, Nigel, trans. 1978. *The High Book of the Grail: A Translation of the Thirteenth-Century Romance of Perlesvaus.* Cambridge: D. S. Brewer.

Bullock-Davies, Constance. 1966. *Professional Interpreters and the Matter of Britain.* Cardiff: University of Wales Press.

———. 1981. "Chrétien de Troyes and England." *Arthurian Literature* 1: 1–61.

Burdach, Konrad. 1974 (1938). *Der Gral: Forschungen über seinen Ursprung und seinen Zusammenhang mit der Longinuslegende.* Mit einem Vorwort zum Neudruck von Johannes Rathofer. Darmstadt: Wissenschaftliche Buchgesellschaft.

Burgess, Glyn S. 1984. *Chrétien de Troyes, Erec et Enide.* Critical Guides to French Texts, 32. London: Grant and Cutler.

Burin, Elizabeth. 1993. "Pierre Sala's Manuscript of *Le Chevalier au lion.*" In Busby et al. 1993: 323–30.

Burns, E. Jane. 1993. *Bodytalk: When Women Speak in Old French Literature.* Philadelphia: University of Pennsylvania Press.

Burrell, Margaret. 1985. "The *Sens* of *Le Chevalier de la charrette* and the Court of Champagne." *BBSIA* 37: 299–308.

Busby, Keith. 1980. *Gauvain in Old French Literature.* Degré Second, 2. Amsterdam: Rodopi.

———. 1981. "The Enigma of Loholt." In Varty 1981: 28–36.

———. 1984. "Reculer pour mieux avancer: L'itinéraire de Gauvain dans le *Conte du graal.*" In *Chrétien de Troyes et le graal: Colloque arthurien belge de Bruges,* 17–26. Paris: Nizet.

———. 1993a. "The Scribe of MSS *T* and *V* of Chrétien's *Perceval* and Its *Continuations.*" In Busby et al. 1993, 1: 49–65.

Busby, Keith, ed. 1993b. *Chrétien de Troyes, Le Roman de Perceval, ou le Conte du graal.* Edition critique d'après tous les manuscrits. Tübingen: Max Niemeyer.

Busby, Keith. 1993c. *Chrétien de Troyes, Perceval (le Conte du graal).* Critical Guides to French Texts, 98. London: Grant and Cutler.

Busby, Keith, Terry Nixon, Alison Stones, and Lori Walters, eds. 1993. *Les manu-*

scrits de Chrétien de Troyes: The Manuscripts of Chrétien de Troyes. 2 vols. Faux
Titre, 71–72. Amsterdam: Rodopi.

Carey, John. 1999. "The Finding of Arthur's Grave: A Story from Clonmacnoise?"
In *Ildánach Ildírech: A Festschrift for Proinsias Mac Cana,* 1–14. Andover: Celtic
Studies Publications.

Carroll, Carleton W., ed. and trans. 1987. *Chrétien de Troyes, Erec et Enide.* With
an introduction by W. W. Kibler. Garland Library of Medieval Literature, 25.
New York.

Carron, Roland. 1989. *Enfant et parenté dans la France médiévale, Xe–XIIIe siècles.*
Travaux d'Histoire Ethico-politique, 49. Geneva: Droz.

Cazelles, Brigitte. 1996. *The Unholy Grail: A Social Reading of Chrétien de Troyes's
Conte du Graal.* Stanford, Calif.: Stanford University Press.

Chadwick, H. Monro, and Nora K. Chadwick. 1932. *The Growth of Literature.* Cambridge: Cambridge University Press.

Chambers, E. K. 1966 (1927). *Arthur of Britain.* New York: October House.

Chédeville, André, and Hubert Guillotel. 1984. *La Bretagne des saints et des rois,
Ve–Xe siècle.* Rennes: Ouest-France.

Chênerie, Marie-Luce. 1986. *Le chevalier errant dans les romans arthuriens en vers
des XIIe et XIIIe siècles.* PRF, 172. Geneva: Droz.

Chenu, Marie-Dominique. 1969. *L'éveil de la conscience dans la civilisation médiévale.* Conférence Albert-le-Grand 1968. Montreal: Institut d'Etudes Médié-
vales.

Clanchy, M. T. 1993. *From Memory to Written Record: England, 1066–1307.* 2d ed.
Oxford: Blackwell.

Clarke, Basil., ed. and trans. 1973. *Life of Merlin: Geoffrey of Monmouth, Vita Merlini.*
Cardiff: University of Wales Press.

Cline, Ruth H. 1971–72. "Heart and Eyes." *RPh* 25: 263–97.

Colby, Alice M. 1965. *The Portrait in Twelfth-Century French Literature: An Example
of the Stylistic Originality of Chrétien de Troyes.* Geneva: Droz.

Collet, Olivier, trans. 1994. *Chrétien de Troyes, Philomena.* Text of De Boer 1909. In
Chrétien de Troyes, Romans. Paris: Librairie Générale Française.

Corbett, Noel L., ed. 1977. *La vie de Saint Louis: Le témoignage de Jehan, seigneur de
Joinville.* Sherbrooke, Que.: Naaman.

Crick, Julia C. 1989. *The Historia Regum Britannie of Geoffrey of Monmouth, III: A
Summary Catalogue of the Manuscripts.* Cambridge: D. S. Brewer.

Cross, Tom Peete, and William Albert Nitze. 1930. *Lancelot and Guenevere: A Study
of the Origins of Courtly Love.* New York: Phaeton.

Cross, Tom Peete, and Clark Harris Slover, trans. 1969. *Ancient Irish Tales.* With a
revised bibliography by Charles W. Dunn. Totowa, N.J.: Barnes and Noble.

Curtius, Ernst Robert. 1953. *European Literature and the Latin Middle Ages.* Translated from the German by Willard R. Trask. Bollingen Series, 36. Princeton,
N.J.: Princeton University Press.

D'Alverny, Marie-Thérèse, ed. 1965. *Alain de Lille, Textes inédits*. Avec une introduction sur sa vie et ses œuvres. Etudes de Philosophie Médiévale, 52. Paris:
Vrin.

Damian-Grint, Peter. 1997. "*Estoire* as Word and Genre." *MÆ* 66: 189–06.

Davis, H. W. C. 1910. "Henry of Blois and Brian FitzCount." *English Historical Review*
25: 297–303.

Day, Mildred Leake, ed. and trans. 1984. *De ortu Waluuanii nepotis Arturi*. Garland
Library of Medieval Literature, 15. New York: Garland.

———. 1988. *Historia Meriadoci, Regis Cambrie*. Garland Library of Medieval Literature, 50. New York: Garland.

De Boer, Cornelis, ed. 1909. *Chrétien de Troyes, Philomena, conte raconté d'après
Ovide*. Paris: P. Geuthner. (Edition reproduced in Olivier Collet, trans., *Chrétien
de Troyes: Romans*, 1225–67. Paris: Librairie Générale Française, 1994.)

De la Borderie, Arthur Le Moyne. 1896–1913. *Histoire de Bretagne*. 6 vols. Rennes:
Plihon and Hommay.

Deist, Rosemarie. 1995. "Sun and Moon: Constellations of Character in Gottfried's
Tristan and Chrétien's *Yvain*." In Friedrich Wolfzettel, ed., *Arthurian Romance
and Gender: Masculin/féminin dans le roman arthurien médiéval*, 50–65. Selected
Proceedings of the Seventeenth International Arthurian Congress. Interna-
tionale Forschungen zur Allgemeinen und Vergleichenden Literaturwissenschaft, 10. Amsterdam: Rodopi.

Delcourt-Angélique, Janine. 1981. "Le motif du tournoi de trois jours avec change-
ment de couleur destiné à préserver l'incognito." In Varty 1981: 160–86.

Dembowski, Peter F., ed. and trans. 1994a. *Erec et Enide*. In Poirion 1994a: 1–169,
1053–1114.

Dembowski, Peter F. 1994b. "Textual and Other Problems of the Epilogue of *Erec
et Enide*." In Keith Busby and Norris J. Lacy, eds., *Conjunctures: Medieval Studies
in Honor of Douglas Kelly*, 113–27. Amsterdam: Rodopi.

Dillon, Myles. 1955. "Les sources irlandaises des romans arthuriens." *Les Lettres
Romanes* 9: 143–59.

Diverres, A. H. 1981–82. "*Iarlles y Ffynnawn* and *Le Chevalier au lion*: Adaptation
or Common Source?" *SC* 16–17: 144–62.

Döffinger-Lange, Erdmuthe. 1998. *Der Gauvain-Teil in Chrétiens "Conte du Graal":
Forschungsbericht und Episodenkommentar*. Heidelberg: Universitätsverlag
C. Winter.

Dörner, Heinrich, ed. 1907. *Robert Biquet's "Lai du Cor," mit einer Einleitung über
Sprache und Abfassungszeit*. Inaugural-Dissertation, Kaiser-Wilhelms-Universi-
tät Strassburg. Strasbourg: M. DuMont Schauberg.

Duby, Georges. 1977. "The Structure of Kinship and Nobility." In Duby, *The Chival-
rous Society*, 134–48. Translated by Cynthia Postan. Berkeley: University of California Press.

———. 1980. *The Three Orders: Feudal Society Imagined*. Translated by Arthur Goldhammer, with a foreword by Thomas N. Bisson. Chicago: University of Chicago Press. Originally published as *Les trois ordres, ou l'imaginaire du féodalisme* (Paris: Gallimard, 1978).

———. 1983. *The Knight, the Lady, and the Priest: The Making of Modern Marriage in Medieval France.* Translated by Barbara Bray. New York: Pantheon. Originally published as *Le chevalier, la femme et le prêtre* (Paris: Hachette, 1981).

Duggan, Joseph J. 1969. "Yvain's Good Name: The Unity of Chrétien de Troyes's *Chevalier au lion.*" *Orbis Litterarum* 24: 112–29.

———. 1977. "Ambiguity in Twelfth- and Thirteenth-Century French and Provençal Literature: A Problem or a Value?" In Hans R. Runte, Henri Niedzielski, and William L. Hendrickson, eds., *John Misrahi Memorial Volume: Studies in Medieval Literature,* 136–49. Columbia, S.C.: French Literature Publications.

———. 1986a. "The Experience of Time as a Fundamental Element of the Stock of Knowledge in Medieval Society." In Hans Ulrich Gumbrecht, Ursula Link-Heer, and Peter-Michael Spangenberg, eds., *Grundriss der Romanischen Literaturen des Mittelalters,* vol. 11: *La littérature historiographique des origines à 1500,* part 1: *Partie historique,* 127–34. Heidelberg: Carl Winter Universitätsverlag.

———. 1986b. "Medieval Epic as Popular Historiography: Appropriation of Historical Knowledge in the Vernacular Epic." In Hans Ulrich Gumbrecht, Ursula Link-Heer, and Peter-Michael Spangenberg, eds., *Grundriss der Romanischen Literaturen des Mittelalters,* vol. 11: *La littérature historiographique des origines à 1500,* part 1: *Partie historique,* 285–311. Heidelberg: Carl Winter Universitätsverlag.

———. 1989. "Oral Performance of Romance in Medieval France." In Norris J. Lacy and Gloria Torrini-Roblin, eds., *Continuations: Essays on Medieval French Literature and Language in Honor of John Lambert Grigsby,* 51–62. Birmingham, Ala.: Summa Publications.

———. 2000. "Vers une pragmatique textuelle de la chanson de geste." In *L'Epopée romane au moyen âge et aux temps modernes,* 427–48. Naples: Fridericiana Editrice Universitaria.

Dumville, David N. 1975–76. "'Nennius' and the '*Historia Brittonum.*'" *Studia Celtica* 10–11: 78–95.

Duval, Paulette. 1979. *La pensée alchimique et le Conte du graal.* Paris: Champion.

Dyggve, Holger Petersen, ed. 1951. *Gace Brulé, trouvère champenois: Edition des chansons et étude historique.* Mémoires de la Société Néophilologique de Helsinki, 16. Helsinki: Neuphilologischer Verein.

Ewert, Alfred, ed. 1932–33. *Gui de Warewic, roman du XIIIe siècle.* CFMA, 74–75. Paris: Champion.

———. 1939–71. *The Romance of Tristran by Béroul: A Poem of the Twelfth Century.* New York: Barnes and Noble.

———. 1944. *Marie de France: Lais.* Oxford: Blackwell.

Ferlampin-Acher, Christine. 1996. *La fée et la guivre: Le Bel Inconnu de Renaut de*

Beaujeu; Approche littéraire et concordancier. Concordancier établi par Monique Léonard. Paris: Champion.

Fichtenau, Heinrich. 1998. *Heretics and Scholars in the High Middle Ages, 1000–1200.* University Park, Pa.: Pennsylvania State University Press.

Fiore, Silvestro. 1967. "Origines orientales de la légende du graal." *CCM* 10: 207–19.

Flandrin, Jean-Louis. 1979. *Families in Former Times: Kinship, Household, and Sexuality in Early Modern France.* Translated by Richard Southern. Cambridge: Cambridge University Press.

Fleuriot, Léon. 1987a. "Langue et société dans la Bretagne ancienne." In Jean Balclou and Yves Le Gallo, eds., *Histoire littéraire et culturelle de la Bretagne,* 7–28. Paris: Champion.

———. 1987b. "Le patriotisme brittonique et l'histoire légendaire." In Jean Balclou and Yves Le Gallo, eds., *Histoire littéraire et culturelle de la Bretagne,* 105–19. Paris: Champion.

Flori, Jean. 1979. "Pour une histoire de la chevalerie: L'adoubement dans les romans de Chrétien de Troyes." *Romania* 100: 21–53.

Foerster, Wendelin, ed. 1884. *Cliges von Christian von Troyes.* In *Christian von Troyes sämtliche Werke,* vol. 1. Halle: Niemeyer.

———. 1887. *Der Löwenritter (Yvain).* In *Christian von Troyes sämtliche Werke,* vol. 2. Halle: Niemeyer.

———. 1890. *Erec und Enide.* In *Christian von Troyes sämtliche Werke,* vol. 5. Halle: Max Niemeyer.

———. 1896. *Kristian von Troyes: Erec und Enide.* Neue verbesserte Textausgabe mit Einleitung und Glossar. Romanischc Bibliothek, 13. Halle: Niemeyer.

———. 1899. *Der Karrenritter.* In *Christian von Troyes sämtliche Werke,* vol. 4. Halle: Niemeyer.

———. 1909. *Kristian von Troyes: Erec und Enide.* Neue verbesserte Textausgabe. Romanische Bibliothek, 13. Halle: Niemeyer.

———. 1910. *Kristian von Troyes: Cliges.* Textausgabe mit Variantenauswahl, Einleitung, Anmerkungen und vollständigem Glossar. 3d ed., rev. and improved. ("Kleine Ausgabe.") Romanische Bibliothek, 1. Halle: Niemeyer.

———. 1912. *Christian von Troyes: Yvain (Der Löwenritter).* Textausgabe mit Variantenauswahl, Einleitung, erklärenden Anmerkungen und vermehrte Auflage. 4th ed. ("Kleine Ausgabe.") Romanische Bibliothek, 5. Halle: Niemeyer.

Foerster, Wendelin, and Alfons Hilka, eds. 1901. *Christian von Troyes: Cligès.* Textausgabe mit Variantenauswahl, Einleitung, und Anmerkungen. 4th ed. Romanische Bibliothek, 1. Halle: Niemeyer.

Forbes, Alexander Penrose, ed. 1874. *The Lives of S. Ninian and S. Kentigern, Compiled in the Twelfth Century.* The Historians of Scotland Series, 5. Edinburgh: Edmonston and Douglas.

Ford, Patrick K. 1981–82. "Prolegomena to a Reading of the *Mabinogi: Pwyll* and *Manawydan.*" *SC* 16–17: 110–25.

————. 1983. "On the Significance of Some Arthurian Names in Welsh." *Bulletin of the Board of Celtic Studies* 30: 268–73.

Ford, Patrick K., trans. 1977. *The Mabinogi and Other Medieval Welsh Tales*. Berkeley: University of California Press.

Foster, Idris Llewelyn. 1959. "*Gereint, Owein,* and *Peredur.*" In Loomis 1959a: 192–205.

Foulet, Alfred. 1977. "Guinevere's Enigmatic Words: Chrétien's *Lancelot,* Vv. 211–213." In Hans R. Runte, Henri Niedzielski, and William L. Hendrickson, eds., *Jean Misrahi Memorial Volume,* 175–80. Columbia, S.C.: French Literature Publications.

Foulet, Alfred, and Mary Blakely Speer. 1979. *On Editing Old French Texts*. Edward C. Armstrong Monographs on Medieval Literature, 1. Lawrence: Regents Press of Kansas.

Foulet, Alfred, and Karl D. Uitti, eds. 1989. *Le Chevalier de la charrette (Lancelot)*. Classiques Garnier. Paris: Bordas.

Foulet, Lucien, trans. 1970 (1947). *Perceval le Gallois, ou le Conte du graal*. Préface de Mario Roques. Paris: Nizet.

Foulon, Charles. 1983. "Un personnage mystérieux du *Roman de Perceval le Gallois:* L'*eschacier* dans la Seconde Partie de *Perceval.*" In P. B. Grout et al., eds., *The Legend of Arthur in the Middle Ages: Studies Presented to A. H. Diverres by Colleagues, Pupils and Friends,* 67–75. Arthurian Studies, 7. Cambridge: D. S. Brewer.

Fourrier, Anthime. 1950. "Encore la chronologie des œuvres de Chrétien de Troyes." *BBSIA* 2: 69–88.

————. 1955. "Remarques sur la date du *Conte du graal* de Chrétien de Troyes." *BBSIA* 7: 89–101.

————. 1958. "Réponse à Madame Rita Lejeune à propos de la date du *Conte du graal* de Chrétien de Troyes." *BBSIA* 10: 73–85.

————. 1960. *Le courant réaliste dans le roman courtois en France au moyen-âge*. Paris: Nizet.

Fowler, David C. 1959. *Prowess and Charity in the Perceval of Chrétien de Troyes*. Seattle: University of Washington Press.

Frappier, Jean. 1958. "Sur la composition du *Conte du graal.*" *MA* 64: 67–102.

————. 1959. "Chrétien de Troyes." In Loomis 1959a: 157–91.

————. 1960. "Note complémentaire sur la composition du *Conte du graal.*" *Romania* 81: 308–37.

Frappier, Jean, ed. 1964a. *La Mort le roi Artu*. 3d ed. TLF, 58. Geneva: Droz.

Frappier, Jean. 1964b. "Sur la versification de Chrétien de Troyes: L'enjambement dans *Erec et Enide.*" *Romance Studies* 32: 41–49.

————. 1965. "La brisure du couplet dans *Erec et Enide.*" *Romania* 86: 1–21.

————. 1969a. "Le motif du 'don contraignant' dans la littérature du moyen âge." *Travaux de Linguistique et de Littérature* 7, no. 2: 7–46

———. 1969b. *Etude sur Yvain, ou le Chevalier au lion de Chrétien de Troyes.* Paris: Société d'Edition d'Enseignement Supérieur.

———. 1972a. *Chrétien de Troyes et le mythe du graal: Etude sur Perceval, ou le Conte du graal.* Paris: Société d'Edition d'Enseignement Supérieur.

———. 1972b. "Le prologue du *Chevalier de la charrette* et son interprétation." *Romania* 93: 337–77.

———. 1982 [1968]. *Chrétien de Troyes: The Man and His Work.* Translated by Raymond J. Cormier. Athens: Ohio University Press.

———. 1977. "La blessure du Roi Pêcheur dans le *Conte du graal.*" In Hans R. Runte, Henri Niedzielski, and William L. Hendrickson, eds., *Jean Misrahi Memorial Volume,* 181–96. Columbia, S.C.: French Literature Publications.

Frazer, James George. 1890. *The Golden Bough: A Study in Magic and Religion.* London: Macmillan.

———. 1959. *The New Golden Bough.* Edited and with notes and foreword by Theodor H. Gaster. New York: Anchor Books Doubleday.

Frescoe, Karen, ed. 1992. *Renaut de Bâgé, Le Bel Inconnu (Li Biaus Descouneüs; the Fair Unknown).* Translated by Colleen P. Donagher; music edited by Margaret P. Hasselman. Garland Library of Medieval Literature, ser. A, vol. 77. New York: Garland.

Fritz, Jean-Marie. 1992a. *Le discours du fou au moyen âge.* Paris: Presses Universitaires de France.

Fritz, Jean-Marie, ed. and trans. 1992b. *Chrétien de Troyes, Erec et Enide.* Lettres Gothiques, 4526. Paris: Librairie Générale Française.

——— 1994. *Erec et Enide.* In *Chrétien de Troyes, Romans.* Paris: Librairie Générale Française.

Gallais, Pierre. 1967. "Bleheri, la cour de Poitiers et la diffusion des récits arthuriens sur le continent." In *Actes du septième Congrès national de la Société française de Littérature comparée, Poitiers 27–29 mai 1965,* 45–79. Paris: Marcel Didier.

Gantz, Jeffrey, trans. 1981. *Early Irish Myths and Sagas.* Harmondsworth: Penguin.

Gerould, Gordon Hall. 1927. "King Arthur and Politics." *Speculum* 2: 33–51.

Goetz, Hans-Werner. 1993. *Life in the Middle Ages from the Seventh to the Thirteenth Century.* Notre Dame, Ind.: University of Notre Dame Press.

Goldschmidt, Moritz, ed. 1899. *Sone von Nausay.* Bibliothek des Literarischen Vereins in Stuttgart, 216. Tübingen: Laupp.

Golther, Wolfgang. 1925. *Parzival und der Gral, in der Dichtung des Mittelalters und der Neuzeit.* Stuttgart: Metzlersche Verlagsbuchhandlung.

Gonthier, Nicole. 1998. *Le châtiment du crime au moyen âge: XIIe–XVIe siècles.* Rennes: Presses Universitaires de Rennes.

Goody, Jack. 1983. *The Development of the Family and Marriage in Europe.* Cambridge: Cambridge University Press.

Gossen, Carl Theodor. 1959. "Zur etymologischen Deutung des Grals." *Vox Romanica* 18: 177–219.

Gowans, Linda. 1988. *Cei and the Arthurian Legend.* Arthurian Studies, 18. Cambridge: D. S. Brewer.

Gray, Elizabeth A., ed. and trans. 1982. *Cath Maige Tuired: The Second Battle of Mag Tuired.* Dublin: Irish Texts Society.

Gregory, Stewart. 1989. "La description de la fontaine dans l'*Yvain* de Chrétien de Troyes: Un problème d'interprétation." *Romania* 110: 539–41.

Gregory, Stewart, and Claude Luttrell, eds. 1993. *Chrétien de Troyes: Cligès.* Arthurian Studies, 28. Cambridge: D. S. Brewer.

Grigsby, John L. 1979. "Narrative Voices in Chrétien de Troyes—A Prolegomenon to Dissection." *RPh* 32: 261–73.

Grimm, Reinhold R. 1976. *Schöpfung und Sündenfall in der altfranzösischen Genesis-dichtung des Evrat.* Europäische Hochschulschriften: Französische Sprache und Literatur, Reihe 13, 39. Munich: Peter Lang.

Gröber, Gustav. 1888–1902. *Grundriss der Romanischen Literaturen des Mittelalters.* 2 vols. Strasbourg: Trübner, 1902.

Grosse, R. 1881. *Der Stil Crestiens von Troies.* Französische Studien, vol. 1, fasc. 2. Heilbronn: Henninger.

Grossel, Marie-Geneviève. 1994. *Le milieu littéraire en Champagne sous les Thibaudiens.* 2 vols. Orléans: Paradigme.

Gruffydd, W. J. 1912. "Bledhericus, Bleddri, Breri." *Revue Celtique* 33: 180–83.

Gschwind, Ulrich. 1976. *Le Roman de Flamenca: Nouvelle occitane du 13e siècle.* Bern: Francke.

Guadet, J., and N. R. Taranne, eds. 1836. *Sancti Georgii Florentii Gregorii, Historiae Ecclesiasticae Francorum Libri Decem.* 2 vols. Paris: Jules Renouard.

Guérard, Benjamin. 1850. *Cartulaire de l'église Notre-Dame de Paris.* 4 vols. Collection de Documents Inédits sur l'Histoire de France, Histoire Politique. Paris: Crapelet.

Guerreau-Jalabert, Anita. 1983. "Romans de Chrétien de Troyes et contes folkloriques." *Romania* 104: 1–48.

———. 1992. *Index des motifs narratifs dans les romans arthuriens français en vers (XIIe–XIIIe siècles).* PRF, 202. Geneva: Droz.

Guest, Charlotte. 1838. *The Mabinogion, from the Llyf Coch o Hergest and Other Manuscripts.* London: Longman, Orme, Brown, Green, and Longmans.

Guillaume de Saint-Thierry. 1895. *De philosophia mundi libri quatuor.* J.-P. Migne, ed., *Patrologia cursus completus,* Series latina, vol. 172. Paris: Garnier Frères.

Haidu, Peter. 1968. *Aesthetic Distance in Chrétien de Troyes: Irony and Comedy in Cliges and Perceval.* Geneva: Droz.

Halphen, Louis, and René Poupardin, eds. 1913. *Chroniques des comtes d'Anjou et des seigneurs d'Amboise.* Paris: Auguste Picard.

Hamp, Eric. 1975. "Mabinogi." *Transactions of the Honourable Society of Cymmrodorion,* Sessions 1974–75: 243–49.

————. 1977–78. "Intensives in British Celtic and Gaulish." *SC* 12–13: 1–13.

————. 1982. "*Lloegr:* The Welsh Name for England." *Cambridge Medieval Celtic Studies* 4: 83–85.

Harward, Vernon J., Jr. 1958. *The Dwarfs of Arthurian Romance and Celtic Tradition.* Leiden: Brill.

Hatto, A. T., trans. 1980. *Wolfram von Eschenbach, Parzival.* Harmondsworth: Penguin.

Haycock, Margid. 1983–84. "'Preiddeu Annwn' and the Figure of Taliesin." *SC* 18–19: 52–78.

Heinzel, Richard. 1891. *Über die französischen Gralromane.* Denkschriften der Kaiserlichen Akademie der Wissenschaften, Philosophisch-Historische Klasse, vol. 40, fasc. 3. Vienna: Tempsky.

Helinand de Froidmont. 1855. *De bono regimine principis.* J.-P. Migne, ed., *Patrologia Cursus Completus,* Series latina, vol. 212. Paris: J.-P. Migne.

Herlihy, David. 1985. *Medieval Households.* Cambridge, Mass.: Harvard University Press.

Hibbard, Laura. 1913. "The Sword Bridge of Chrétien de Troyes and Its Celtic Original." *Romanic Review* 4: 166–90.

Hibbard Loomis, Laura. 1950. "The Passion Lance Relic and the War Cry *Monjoie* in the *Chanson de Roland* and Related Texts." *Romanic Review* 41: 241–60.

Hildegard of Bingen. 1862–65. *Liber subtilitatum diversarum naturarum creaturarum.* J.-P. Migne, ed., *Patrologiae Cursus Completus,* Series latina, vol. 197. Paris: J.-P. Migne, through the *Patrologia Latina* on-line database available from Chadwyck-Healey, London < http://pld.chadwyck.co.uk/ >.

Hilka, Alfons, ed. 1912–16. *Li Romanz d'Athis et Prophilias (L'Estoire d'Athenes).* 2 vols. Gesellschaft für Romanische Literatur, 29, 40. Halle: Niemeyer.

————. 1932. *Der Percevalroman (Li contes del graal) von Christian von Troyes.* Unter Benutzung des von Gottfried Baist nachgelassenen handschriftlichen Materials. In *Christian von Troyes sämtliche erhaltene Werke nach allen bekannten Handschriften,* 5. Halle: Niemeyer.

————. 1966. *Chrétien de Troyes, Der Percevalroman: Li contes del graal.* 3d, improved ed. Sammlung Romanischer Übungstexte, 26–27. Tübingen: Niemeyer.

Hindman, Sandra. 1994. *Sealed in Parchment: Rereadings of Knighthood in the Illuminated Manuscripts of Chrétien de Troyes.* Chicago: University of Chicago Press.

Hoepffner, Ernest. 1934. "'Matière et sens' dans le roman d'*Erec et Enide.*" *Archivum Romanicum* 18: 433–50.

Hofer, Stefan. 1954. *Chrétien de Troyes: Leben und Werke des altfranzösischen Epikers.* Graz: Bohlau.

Holden, Anthony J., ed. 1973. *Le Roman de Rou de Wace.* 3 vols. SATF, 93. Paris: A. et J. Picard.

————. 1988. *Guillaume d'Angleterre.* TLF, 360. Geneva: Droz.

Holmes, Urban Tigner. 1948. *A New Interpretation of Chrétien's "Conte del Graal."* University of North Carolina Studies in the Romance Languages and Literatures, 7. Chapel Hill: University of North Carolina Press.

Holmes, Urban Tigner, and M. Amelia Klenke. 1959. *Chrétien, Troyes, and the Grail.* Chapel Hill: University of North Carolina Press.

Huber, Gerlinde. 1990. *Das Motiv der "Witwe von Ephesus" in lateinischen Texten der Antike und des Mittelalters.* Mannheimer Beiträge zur Sprach- und Literaturwissenschaft, 18. Tübingen: Gunter Narr.

Hugh of Fouilloy. 1880. *De medicina animae.* J.-P. Migne, ed., *Patrologiae cursus completus,* Series latina, vol. 176, cols. 1183–1202. Paris: Garnier Frères.

Hull, Vernam. 1930. "The Four Jewels of the Tuatha Dé." *ZCP* 18: 73–89.

Hult, David F. 1986. "Lancelot's Two Steps: A Problem in Textual Criticism." *Speculum* 61: 836–858.

———. 1988–89. "Lancelot's Shame." *RPh* 42: 30–50.

———. 1989a. "Steps Forward and Steps Backward: More on Chrétien's *Lancelot.*" *Speculum* 64: 307–16.

———. 1989b. "Author/Narrator/Speaker: The Voice of Authority in Chrétien's *Charrette.*" In Kevin Brownlee and Walter Stephens, eds., *Discourses of Authority in Medieval and Renaissance Literature,* 76–96. Hanover, N.H.: University Press of New England.

Hult, David F., ed. and trans. 1993. *Chrétien de Troyes, Le Chevalier au lion, ou, le Roman d'Yvain.* Edition critique d'après le manuscrit B. N. fr. 1433. Lettres Gothiques, 4539. Paris: Librairie Générale Française.

———. 1994. *Le Chevalier au lion, ou, le Roman d'Yvain.* In *Chrétien de Troyes, Romans.* Paris: Librairie Générale Française.

Hult, David F. 1996. "Gaston Paris and the Invention of Courtly Love." In R. Howard Bloch and Stephen G. Nichols, eds., *Medievalism and the Modernist Temper,* 192–224. Baltimore: Johns Hopkins University Press.

———. 1998. *Manuscript Transmission, Reception and Canon Formation: The Case of Chrétien de Troyes.* Morrison Library Inaugural Address Series, 13. Berkeley, Calif.: Doe Library.

Hunt, Tony. 1974. "Some Observations on the Textual Relationship of *Li Chevaliers au Lion* and *Iarlles y Ffynnawn.*" *ZCP* 33: 93–113.

———. 1981. "The Emergence of the Knight in France and England, 1000–1200." *Forum for Modern Language Studies* 17: 93–114.

———. 1986. *Chrétien de Troyes, Yvain.* Critical Guides to French Texts, 55. London: Grant and Cutler.

Huot, Sylvia. 1987. *From Song to Book: The Poetics of Writing in Old French Lyric and Lyrical Narrative Poetry.* Ithaca, N.Y.: Cornell University Press.

Imbs, Paul. 1956. "L'élément religieux dans le *Conte du graal* de Chrétien de Troyes." *Les Romans du graal dans la littérature des XIIe et XIIIe siècles,* 31–53. Paris: Editions du Conseil National de la Recherche Scientifique.

Jackson, Kenneth Hurlstone. 1959. "The Arthur of History." In Loomis 1959a: 1–11.

Jackson, Stanley W. 1986. *Melancholia and Depression: From Hippocratic Times to Modern Times.* New Haven: Yale University Press.

James, Montague R., trans. 1923. *Walter Map's De Nugis Curialium.* Cymmrodorion Record Series, 9. London: Honourable Society of Cymmrodorion.

Janssens, Jan. 1986. "Le prologue du *Chevalier de la charrette:* Une clef pour l'interprétation du roman?" *Bien Dire et Bien Aprandre* 4: 29–51.

Jarman, A. O. H. 1981. "The Delineation of Arthur in Early Welsh Verse." In Varty 1981: 1–21.

Jenkins, T. Atkinson, ed. 1909. *Eructavit.* Gesellschaft für Romanische Literatur, 20. Dresden: Gesellschaft für Romanische Literatur.

Johnston, R. C., and D. D. R. Owen, eds. 1972. *The Old French Gawain Romances "Le Chevalier à l'épée" and "La Mule sans frein."* Edinburgh: Scottish Academic Press.

Jones, Gwyn, and Thomas Jones, trans. 1974. *The Mabinogion.* London: Dent.

Jones, R. M. 1996. "Narrative Structure in Medieval Welsh Prose Tales." In C. W. Sullivan III, ed., *The Mabinogi: A Book of Essays,* 217–62. New York: Garland. Repr. from D. Ellis Evans, ed., *Proceedings of the Seventh International Congress of Celtic Studies,* 171–98 (Oxford, 1986).

Jones, Thomas, ed. 1955. *Brut y Tywysogyon, or, The Chronicle of the Princes, Red Book of Hergest Version.* Board of Celtic Studies, University of Wales. History and Law Series, 16. Cardiff: University of Wales Press.

Jones, Thomas. 1964. "The Early Evolution of the Legend of Arthur." *Nottingham Medieval Studies* 8: 3–21.

Kahane, Henry, and Renee Kahane. 1965. *The Krater and the Grail: Hermetic Sources of the Parzival.* In collaboration with Angelina Pietrangeli. Illinois Studies in Language and Literature, 56. Urbana: University of Illinois Press.

Kartschoke, Dieter, ed. and trans. 1970. *Das Rolandslied des Pfaffen Konrad.* Mittelhochdeutscher Text und Übertragung. Frankfurt am Main: Fischer Bücherei.

Keats-Rohan, K. S. B. 1989. "The Devolution of the Honour of Wallingford, 1066–1148." *Oxoniensia* 54: 311–18.

Keen, Maurice. 1984. *Chivalry.* New Haven and London: Yale University Press.

Kellogg, Judith. 1989. *Medieval Artistry and Exchange: Economic Institutions, Society, and Literary Form in Old French Narrative.* New York: Peter Lang.

Kelly, Douglas. 1966. *Sens and Conjointure in the Chevalier de la charrette.* Studies in French Literature, 2. The Hague: Mouton.

———. 1976. *Chrétien de Troyes, an Analytic Bibliography.* London: Grant and Cutler.

Kelly, Douglas, ed. 1985. *The Romances of Chrétien de Troyes: A Symposium.* Edward C. Armstrong Monographs on Medieval Literature, 3. Lexington, Ky.: French Forum.

———. 1987–88. "The Art of Description." In Lacy, Kelly, and Busby 1987–88, 1: 191–221.

————. 1992. *The Art of Medieval French Romance.* Madison: University of Wisconsin Press.

Kennedy, Elspeth, ed. 1991. *Lancelot.* In *Lancelot du Lac, roman français du XIIIe siècle.* Texte présenté, traduit et annoté par François Mosès d'après l'édition d'Elspeth Kennedy. Préface de Michel Zink. Lettres Gothiques, 4528. Paris: Librairie Générale Française.

Kibler, William W., ed. and trans. 1981. *Lancelot, or the Knight of the Cart.* Garland Library of Medieval Literature, I, ser. A. New York: Garland.

————. 1985. *The Knight with the Lion, or Yvain.* Garland Library of Medieval Literature, 48. New York: Garland.

Kinsella, Thomas, trans. 1969. *The Táin.* Translated from the Irish epic *Táin Bó Cuailnge.* With brush drawings by Louis Le Brocquy. London: Oxford University Press.

Koch, John Thomas. 1987. "A Welsh Window on the Iron Age: Manawydan, Mandubracios." *Cambridge Medieval Celtic Studies* 14: 17–52.

Koch, John Thomas, ed. 1997. *The Gododdin of Aneirin: Text and Context from Dark-Age North Britain.* Cardiff: University of Wales Press.

Köhler, Erich. 1959. "Zur Diskussion über die Einheit von Chrestiens *Li Conte del Graal.*" *ZRP* 69: 523–39.

————. 1960. "Le rôle de la 'coutume' dans les romans de Chrétien de Troyes." *Romania* 81: 386–97.

————. 1964. "Observations historiques et sociologiques sur la poésie des troubadours." *CCM* 7: 27–51.

————. 1974 [1956]. *L'aventure chevaleresque: Ideal et réalité dans le roman courtois; Etudes sur la forme des plus anciens poèmes d'Arthur et du Graal.* Translated by Eliane Kaufholz. Preface by Jacques Le Goff. Paris: Gallimard. Originally published as *Ideal und Wirklichkeit in der höfischen Epik.* Tübingen: Niemeyer, 1956.

Kullmann, Dorothea. 1992. *Verwandtschaft in epischer Dichtung: Untersuchungen zu den französischen chansons de geste und Romanen des 12 Jahrhunderts.* Beihefte zur *ZRP,* 242. Tübingen: Niemeyer.

Lacy, Norris J., ed. 1996. *Medieval Arthurian Literature: A Guide to Recent Research.* New York: Garland.

Lacy, Norris J., and Geoffrey Ashe. 1988. *The Arthurian Handbook.* New York: Garland.

Lacy, Norris J., Douglas Kelly, and Keith Busby. 1987–88. *The Legacy of Chrétien de Troyes.* 2 vols. Amsterdam: Rodopi.

Laharie, Muriel. 1991. *La Folie au moyen âge: XIIe–XIIIe siècles.* Paris: Le Léopard d'Or.

Laidlaw, James. 1984. "Shame Appeased: On the Structure and the *Sen* of the *Chevalier au lion.*" In Peter S. Noble and Linda M. Paterson, eds., *Chrétien de Troyes and the Troubadours: Essays in Memory of the Late Leslie Topsfield,* 195–219. Cambridge: St. Catherine's College, 1984.

Lambert, Pierre-Yves. 1997. *La langue gauloise: Description linguistique, commentaire d'inscriptions choisies.* Paris: Editions Errance.

Le Braz, Anatole. 1928. *La légende de la mort chez les Bretons armoricains.* 5th ed, rev. and augmented by Georges Dottin. 2 vols. Paris: Champion.

Leclanche, Jean-Luc, ed. 1997. *Le Roman de Dolopathos.* 3 vols. CFMA, 124–26. Paris: Champion.

Lecoy, Félix, ed. 1973–75. *Les romans de Chrétien de Troyes d'après la copie de Guiot (Bibliothèque nationale, fr. 794).* Vol. 5: *Le Conte du graal (Perceval).* CFMA 100, 103. Paris: Champion.

Lefay-Toury, Marie-Noëlle. 1979. *La tentation du suicide dans le roman français du XIIe siècle.* Paris: Champion.

Le Goff, Jacques. 1979. "Lévi-Strauss en Brocéliande: Esquisse pour une analyse d'un roman courtois." In *L'imaginaire médiéval, essais par Jacques Le Goff,* 151–87. Paris: Gallimard, 1985. Repr. from *Claude Lévi-Strauss,* 265–319. Paris: Gallimard.

Lejeune, Rita. 1954. "La date du *Conte du graal* de Chrétien de Troyes." *MA* 60: 51–79.

———. 1957. "Encore la date du *Conte du graal* de Chrétien de Troyes." *BBSIA* 9: 85–100.

Lemoine, Michel, ed. and trans. 1988. *Guillaume de Saint-Thierry: De la Nature du corps et de l'âme.* Paris: Société d'Edition "Les Belles Lettres."

Le Rider, Paule. 1978a. *Le Chevalier dans le Conte du graal de Chrétien de Troyes.* Paris: Société d'Edition d'Enseignement Supérieur.

———. 1978b. "*Or est venu qui l'auncra,* ou la fortune littéraire d'un proverbe." *Mélanges de littérature du moyen âge au XXe siècle offerts à Mademoiselle Jeanne Lods,* 1: 393–409. Collection de l'Ecole Normale Supérieure de Jeunes Filles, 10. Paris: Ecole Normale Supérieure de Jeunes Filles.

———. 1991. "Le dépassement de la chevalerie dans *Le Chevalier de la charrette.*" *Romania* 112: 83–99.

———. 1998. "L'épisode de l'épervier dans *Erec et Enide.*" *Romania* 116: 368–93.

Le Roux, Françoise. 1955. "Des chaudrons celtiques à l'arbre d'Esus, Lucain et les scholies bernoises." *Ogam,* n.s., 7: 33–58.

———. 1962. "Les Isles au nord du monde." In *Hommages à Albert Grenier,* 1051–62. Collection Latomus, 58. Brussels: Latomus.

Lewis, Archibald R. 1965. *The Development of Southern French and Catalan Society, 718–1050.* Austin: University of Texas Press.

Littleton, C. Scott, and Linda A. Malcor. 1994. *From Scythia to Camelot: A Radical Reassessment of the Legends of King Arthur, the Knights of the Round Table, and the Holy Grail.* New York: Garland.

Lloyd-Morgan, Ceridwen. 1991. "From Ynys Wydrin to Glasynbri: Glastonbury in Welsh Vernacular Tradition." In Lesley Abrams and James P. Carley, eds. *The*

Archaeology and History of Glastonbury Abbey: Essays in Honour of the Ninetieth Birthday of C. A. Ralegh Radford, 301–15. Woodbridge: Boydell.

Lock, Richard. 1983. *Aspects of Time in Medieval Literature.* New York: Garland.

Lodge, R. Anthony, ed. 1979. *Etienne de Fougères: Le Livre des manières.* Geneva: Droz.

Longère, Jean, ed. 1965. *Alain de Lille: Liber Poenitentialis.* Analecta Mediaevalia Namurcensia, 18. Lille: Librairie Giard.

Loomis, Roger Sherman, and Jean Stirling Lindsay. 1931. "The Magic Horn and Cup in Celtic and Grail Tradition." *Romanische Forschungen* 45: 66–94.

Loomis, Roger Sherman. 1941. "The Spoils of Annwn, an Early Arthurian Poem." *PMLA* 56: 887–936.

———. 1949. *Arthurian Tradition and Chrétien de Troyes.* New York: Columbia University Press.

———. 1956. *Wales and the Arthurian Legend.* Cardiff: University of Wales Press.

Loomis, Roger Sherman, ed. 1959a. *Arthurian Literature in the Middle Ages: A Collaborative History.* Oxford: Clarendon Press.

Loomis, Roger Sherman. 1959b. "The Legend of Arthur's Survival." In Loomis 1959a: 64–71.

———. 1959c. "The Origin of the Grail Legends." In Loomis 1959a: 274–94.

———. 1959d. "The Oral Diffusion." In Loomis 1959a: 52–63.

Lovecy, Ian. 1991. "*Historia Peredur ab Efrawg.*" In Rachel Bromwich, A. O. H. Jarman, and Brynley F. Roberts, eds., *The Arthur of the Welsh: The Arthurian Legend in Medieval Welsh Literature,* 171–82. Cardiff: University of Wales Press.

Lloyd, J. E. 1942. "Geoffrey of Monmouth." *English Historical Review* 57: 460–68.

Luscombe, D. E., ed. 1971. *Peter Abelard's Ethics.* Oxford: Clarendon Press.

Luttrell, Claude. 1974. *The Creation of the First Arthurian Romance: A Quest.* London: Edward Arnold.

Lyons, Faith. 1954. "*Entencion* in Chrétien's *Lancelot.*" *SP* 51: 425–30.

———. 1965. "Beauté et lumière dans le *Perceval* de Chrétien de Troyes." *Romania* 86: 104–11.

Mac Cana, Proinsias. 1983. *Celtic Mythology.* New York: Peter Bedrick Books.

Mac Fynn, S. 1952. "The *Eschacier* in Chrétien's *Perceval* in the Light of Medieval Art." *Modern Language Review* 47: 52–55.

Maddox, Donald. 1978. *Structure and Sacring: The Systematic Kingdom in Chrétien's Erec et Enide.* French Forum Monographs, 8. Lexington, Ky.: French Forum.

———. 1991. *The Arthurian Romances of Chrétien de Troyes: Once and Future Fictions.* Cambridge: Cambridge University Press.

Maître, Léon, and Paul de Bertou, ed. 1896. *Cartulaire de l'abbaye de Saint-Croix de Quimperlé (Finistère).* Paris: Librairie des Provinces.

Malato, M. T., and U. de Martini, eds. and trans. 1959. *Constantino l'Africano, Della Melancolia.* Rome: Istituto di Storia della Medicina dell'Università Roma.

Mandach, André de. 1992. *Le Roman du graal originaire.* Vol. 1: *Sur les traces du mo-*

dèle commun "en code transpyrénéen" de Chrétien de Troyes et Wolfram von Eschenbach. Göppinger Arbeiten zur Germanistik, 581. Göppingen: Kümmerle.

Manselli, Raoul. 1963. "I Passagini." *Bulletino dell'Istituto Storico Italiano* 75: 189–210.

Maranini, Lorenza. 1970. " 'Cavalleria' e 'cavalieri' in Chrétien de Troyes." In *Mélanges de langue et de littérature du moyen âge et de la Renaissance offerts à Jean Frappier,* 2: 737–55. 2 vols. Geneva: Droz.

Marnette, Sophie. 1996. "Réflexions sur le discours indirect libre en français médiéval." *Romania* 114: 1–49.

———. 1998. *Narrateur et points de vue dans la littérature française médiévale: Une approche linguistique.* Bern: Peter Lang.

Marx, Jean. 1952. *La légende arthurienne et le graal.* Paris: Presses Universitaires de France.

Méla, Charles, ed. and trans. 1990. *Le Conte du graal, ou, le Roman de Perceval.* Edition du manuscrit 354 de Berne. Lettres Gothiques, 4525. Paris: Librairie Générale Française.

———. 1992. *Chrétien de Troyes, Le Chevalier de la charrette, ou, le Roman de Lancelot.* Edition critique d'après tous les manuscrits existants. Lettres Gothiques, 4527. Paris: Librairie Générale Française.

———. 1994a. *Chrétien de Troyes, Cligès.* In *Chrétien de Troyes, Romans.* Translation by Olivier Collet. Paris: Librairie Générale Française.

Méla, Charles, ed. 1994b. *Le Chevalier de la charrette.* In *Chrétien de Troyes, Romans.* Paris: Librairie Générale Française.

Ménard, Philippe. 1969. *Le Rire et le sourire dans le roman courtois en France au moyen âge (1150–1250).* Geneva: Droz.

———. 1981. "Le don en blanc qui lie le donateur: Réflexions sur un motif de conte." In Varty 1981: 37–53.

———. 1984. "Problèmes et mystères du *Conte du graal.*" In *Chrétien de Troyes et le graal,* 61–76. Paris: Nizet.

Merceron, Jacques. 1998. "De la 'mauvaise humeur' du sénéchal Keu: Chrétien de Troyes, littérature et physiologie." *CCM* 41: 17–34.

Meneghetti, Maria Luisa. 1987–88. "Signification et fonction réceptionnelle de *l'Elucidation* du *Perceval.*" In Lacy, Kelly, and Busby 1987–88, 2: 55–69.

Meyer, Kajsa, ed. 1995. *La Copie de Guiot, fol. 79v–105r du manuscrit f. fr. 794 de la Bibliothèque nationale, "le chevaliers au lyeon" de Crestien de Troyes.* Faux Titre, 104. Amsterdam: Rodopi.

Meyer, Kuno. 1895–97. *The Voyage of Bran, Son of Febal to the Land of the Living.* An Old Irish saga now first edited, with translation, notes, and glossary, with an essay upon the Irish vision of the happy Otherworld and the Celtic doctrine of rebirth by Alfred Nutt. 2 vols. London: David Nutt.

Meyer, Paul. 1909. "Les plus anciens lapidaires français." *Romania* 38: 44–70, 254–85, 481–552.

Micha, Alexandre. 1939. *La tradition manuscrite des romans de Chrétien de Troyes.* Paris: Droz.

Micha, Alexandre, ed. 1957. *Les romans de Chrétien de Troyes d'après la copie de Guiot (Bibliothèque nationale, fr. 794).* Vol. 2: *Cligès.* CFMA, 84. Paris: Champion.

Miller, Jennifer. 1998. "Layamon's *Brut* and English Historiography." D. Phil. Thesis, Faculty of English Language and Literature, University of Oxford, Magdalen College.

Middleton, Roger. 1991. *"Chwedl Geraint ab Erbin."* In Rachel Bromwich, A. O. H. Jarman, and Brynley F. Roberts, eds., *The Arthur of the Welsh: The Arthurian Legend in Medieval Welsh Literature,* 147–57. Cardiff: University of Wales Press.

Morice, Hyacinthe. 1968 [1742–46]. *Histoire ecclésiastique et civile de Bretagne.* Westmead, Farnborough: Gregg International.

Mynors, R. A. B., ed. and trans. 1998. *William of Malmesbury, Gesta Regum Anglorum, The History of the English Kings.* Completed by R. M. Thomson and M. Winterbottom. Vol. 1. Oxford: Clarendon Press.

Misrahi, Jean. 1959. "More Light on the Chronology of Chrétien de Troyes?" *BBSIA* 11: 89–120.

Mommsen, Theodor, ed. 1898. *Chronica Minora.* Vol. 3. Monumenta Germaniae Historica, Auctores Antiquissimi, 13. Berlin: Weidmann.

Morawski, Joseph. 1925. *Proverbes français antérieurs au XVe siècle.* Paris: Champion.

Mullally, Evelyn, 1984. "The Order of Composition of *Lancelot* and *Yvain*." *BBSIA* 36: 217–29.

Munz, Peter. 1969. *Frederick Barbarossa: A Study in Medieval Politics.* London: Eyre and Spottiswoode.

Nagy, Joseph Falaky. 1985. *The Wisdom of the Outlaw: The Boyhood Deeds of Finn in Gaelic Narrative Tradition.* Berkeley: University of California Press.

Nègre, Ernest. 1991. *Toponymie générale de la France: Etymologie de 35,000 noms de lieux.* 3 vols. PRF, 194. Geneva: Droz.

Nelson, Jan, and Carleton W. Carroll, ed. 1968. *Chrétien de Troyes, Yvain, ou le Chevalier au lion.* New York: Appleton-Century-Crofts.

Newstead, Helaine. 1939. *Bran the Blessed in Arthurian Romance.* Columbia University Studies in English and Comparative Literature, 141. New York: Columbia University Press.

Nitze, William A. 1909. "The Fountain Defended, II." *MP* 7: 1–20.

———. 1911. "The Castle of the Grail—An Irish Analogue." *Studies in Honor of A. Marshall Elliott,* 1: 19–51. 2 vols. Baltimore: Johns Hopkins University Press.

———. 1915–17. " '*Sans et matière*' dans les œuvres de Chrétien de Troyes." *Romania* 44: 14–36.

———. 1952–53. "The Fisher King and the Grail in Retrospect." *RPh* 6: 14–22.

———. 1955. "Yvain and the Myth of the Fountain." *Speculum* 30: 170–79.

Nitze, William A., et al., ed. 1932–37. *Le haut livre du graal, Perlesvaus.* 2 vols. Chicago: University of Chicago Press.

Nitze, William A., and Harry F. Williams. 1955. *Arthurian Names in the Perceval of Chrétien de Troyes: Analysis and Commentary.* University of California Publications in Modern Philology, vol. 38, no. 3: 265–98. Berkeley: University of California Press.

Nixon, Terry Lynn. 1989. "The Role of Audience in the Development of French Vernacular Literature in the Twelfth and Early Thirteenth Century, with a Descriptive Catalogue of Manuscripts." Ph.D. diss., University of California, Los Angeles.

———. 1993a. "List of Manuscripts." In Busby et al. 1993, 1: 9–15.

———. 1993b. "Romance Collections and the Manuscripts of Chrétien de Troyes." In Busby et al. 1993, 1: 17–25.

———. 1993c. "Catalogue of Manuscripts." In Busby et al. 1993, 2: 1–85.

Oesterle, Jean, trans. 1995. *St. Thomas Aquinas, On Evil.* Notre Dame, Ind.: University of Notre Dame Press.

Ollier, Marie-Louise. 1974. "The Author in the Text: The Prologues of Chrétien de Troyes." *Yale French Studies* 51: 26–41.

———. 1989. *Lexique et concordance de Chrétien de Troyes d'après la copie Guiot, avec introduction, index et rimaire.* Traitement informatique par Serge Lusignan, Charles Doutrepont et Bernard Derval. Dernière édition, revue et corrigée. Paris: Vrin.

Olschki, Leonardo. 1966. *The Grail Castle and Its Mysteries.* Translated from the Italian by J. A. Scott and edited, with a foreword, by Eugène Vinaver. Berkeley: University of California Press. Originally appeared as "Il castello del Re Pescatore e i suoi misteri nel *Conte del Graal* di Chrétien de Troyes," *Atti dell'Accademia Nazionale dei Lincei,* 1961.

O'Rahilly, Thomas. 1976. *Early Irish History and Mythology.* Dublin: Dublin Institute for Advanced Studies.

Oswald, Marguerite, ed. 1975. *Gerbert de Montreuil, La Continuation de Perceval.* (3d vol. of the edition begun by Mary Williams.) CFMA, 101. Paris: Champion.

Owen, D. D. R. 1966. "Païen de Maisières—A Joke That Went Wrong?" *Forum for Modern Language Studies* 2: 192–96.

———. 1971. "Two More Romances by Chrétien de Troyes?" *Romania* 92: 246–60.

Padel, Oliver J. 1994. "The Nature of Arthur." *Cambrian Medieval Celtic Studies* 27: 1–31.

Paris, Gaston. 1881. "Etudes sur les romans de la Table ronde." *Romania* 10: 465–96.

———. 1883. "Etudes sur les romans de la Table ronde: Lancelot du Lac." *Romania* 12: 459–534.

Parry, John Jay, trans. 1964. *Andreas Capellanus, The Art of Courtly Love.* New York: Ungar.

Patch, Howard Rollin. 1927. *The Goddess Fortuna in Mediaeval Literature.* Cambridge, Mass.: Harvard University Press.

———. 1950. *The Other World, According to Descriptions in Medieval Literature.* Cambridge, Mass.: Harvard University Press.

Payen, Jean-Charles. 1967. *Le motif du repentir dans la littérature française médiévale (des origines à 1230).* PRF, 98. Geneva: Droz.

———. 1984. "Encore la pratique religieuse dans le *Conte du graal.*" *Chrétien de Troyes et le graal: Colloque arthurien belge de Bruges.* Paris: Nizet.

Peebles, Rose J. 1911. *The Legend of Longinus in Ecclesiastical Tradition and in English Literature and Its Connection with the Grail.* Bryn Mawr College Monographs, 9. Baltimore: J. H. Furst.

Pelan, Margaret M. 1931. *L'influence du Brut de Wace sur les romanciers français de son temps.* Paris: Droz.

Petit, Aimé. 1985. *Naissances du roman: Les techniques littéraires dans les romans antiques du XIIe siècle.* Paris: Champion-Slatkine.

Petit, Aimé, ed. and trans. 1997. *Le Roman d'Enéas.* Edition critique d'après le manuscrit B. N. fr. 60, traduction, présentation et notes. Lettres Gothiques, Le Livre de Poche, 4550. Paris: Librairie Générale Française.

Pickens, Rupert T. 1987–88. "Histoire et commentaire chez Chrétien de Troyes et Robert de Boron: Robert de Boron et le livre de Philippe de Flandre." In Lacy, Kelly, and Busby 1987–88, 2: 17–39.

Pickens, Rupert T., ed. 1990. *Chrétien de Troyes, The Story of the Grail (Li Contes del graal) or, Perceval.* Translated by William W. Kibler. Garland Library of Medieval Literature, 62. New York: Garland.

Pickford, C. E., ed. 1968. *Erec, roman arthurien en prose.* Publié d'après le ms. 112 de la B. N. Geneva: Droz.

Pickford, C. E. 1981. "The Good Name of Chrétien de Troyes." In Varty 1981: 389–401.

Piette, J. R. F. 1965. "Yr Agwedd Lydewig ar y Chwedlau Arthuriaidd." *Llên Cymru* 8: 187.

Piggott, Stuart. 1941. "The Sources of Geoffrey of Monmouth. I. The 'Pre-Roman' King-List." *Antiquity: A Quarterly Review of Archeology* 15: 269–86.

Piriou, Jean-Pierre. 1985. "Un texte arthurien en moyen-breton: Le dialogue entre Arthur roi des Bretons et Guynglaff." In Charles Foulon et al., eds., *Actes du 14e Congrès International Arthurien, Rennes, 16–21 Août 1984,* 2: 473–99. Rennes: Presses Universitaires de Rennes.

Pirot, François. 1972. *Recherches sur les connaissances littéraires des troubadours occitans et catalans des XIIe et XIIIe siècles.* Memorias de la Academia de Buenas Letras de Barcelona, 14. Barcelona: Academia de Buenas Letras de Barcelona.

Planiol, Marcel, ed. 1896. *La très ancienne coutume de Bretagne avec les assises, constitutions de Parlement et ordonnances ducales, suivies d'un recueil de textes divers antérieurs à 1491.* Rennes: Plihorn et Hervé.

Poirion, Daniel, ed. 1994a. *Chrétien de Troyes, Œuvres complètes.* Bibliothèque de la Pléiade, 408. Paris: Gallimard.

Poirion, Daniel, ed. and trans. 1994b. *Lancelot, ou Le Chevalier de la charrette.* In Poirion 1994a: 505–682, 1235–99.

———. 1994c. *Perceval, ou le Conte du graal.* In Poirion 1994a: 683–911, 1299–1391.

Pokorny, Julius. 1950–51. "Zu keltischen Namen." *Beiträge zur Namenforschung* 2: 33–39.

Polak, Lucie. 1974. *"Tristan* and *Vis and Ramin." Romania* 95: 216–34.

———. 1982. *Chretien de Troyes, Cligés.* Critical Guides to French Texts, 23. London: Grant and Cutler.

Pollmann, Leo. 1965. *Chrétien de Troyes und der Conte del Graal.* Beihefte zur *ZRP,* 110. Tübingen: Niemeyer.

Ponsoye, Pierre. 1957. *L'Islam et le graal.* Paris.

Poole, Austin Lane. 1951. *From Domesday Book to Magna Carta, 1087–1216.* Oxford: Clarendon Press.

Potvin, Charles, ed. 1865–73. *Chrétien de Troyes: Perceval le Gallois, ou, le Conte du graal.* Société des Bibliophiles Belges, 21. Mons: Desquesne Masquillier.

Press, A. R. 1969. "Le comportement d'Erec avec Enide." *Romania* 90: 529–38.

Price, Glanville. 1984. *The Languages of Britain.* London: Edward Arnold.

Putter, Ad. 1994. "Finding Time for Romance: Mediaeval Arthurian Literary History." *MÆ* 63: 1–16.

Pütz, Franz. 1892. "Zur Geschichte der Entwicklung der Artursage." *Zeitschrift für Französische Sprache und Literatur* 14: 161–210.

Raffel, Burton, trans. 1987. *Chrétien de Troyes, Yvain: The Knight of the Lion.* With an afterword by Joseph J. Duggan. New Haven and London: Yale University Press.

———. 1996. *Chrétien de Troyes, Erec et Enide.* With an afterword by Joseph J. Duggan. New Haven and London: Yale University Press.

———. 1997a. *Chrétien de Troyes, Cligès.* With an afterword by Joseph J. Duggan. New Haven and London: Yale University Press.

———. 1997b. *Chrétien de Troyes, Lancelot.* With an afterword by Joseph J. Duggan. New Haven and London: Yale University Press.

———. 1998. *Chrétien de Troyes, Perceval: The Tale of the Grail.* With an afterword by Joseph J. Duggan. New Haven and London: Yale University Press.

Rahn, Otto. 1964 (1933). *Kreuzzug gegen den Graal: Die Tragödie des Katharismus.* Stuttgart: Hans E. Günther.

Raynaud, Gaston, ed. 1879. *Elie de Saint-Gilles, chanson de geste.* Paris: Firmin Didot.

Raynaud de Lage, Guy, ed. 1976. *Gautier d'Arras, Eracle.* CFMA, 102. Paris: Champion.

Reid, T. B. W., ed. 1942. *Yvain (le Chevalier au lion).* The critical text of Wendelin Foerster with introduction, notes and glossary. Manchester: Manchester University Press.

Reid, T. B. W. 1976. "Chrétien de Troyes and the Scribe Guiot." *MÆ* 45: 1–19.

Reinhard, John Revell. 1933. *The Survival of the Geis in Medieval Romance.* Halle: Niemeyer.

Rejhon, Annalee C. 1983. "Hu Gadarn: Folklore and Fabrication." *Celtic Folklore and Christianity: Studies in Memory of William W. Heist,* 201–12. Patrick K. Ford, ed. Santa Barbara, Calif.: McNally and Loftin.

———. 1985–86. "The Mute Knight and the Knight of the Lion: Implications of the Hidden Name Motif in the Welsh *Historia Peredur vab Efrawc* and Chretien de Troyes's *Yvain ou le Chevalier au lion.*" *SC* 20–21: 110–22.

Resler, Michael. 1987. *Erec by Hartmann von Aue.* Translated with an introduction and commentary. Philadelphia: University of Pennsylvania Press.

Riquer, Martín de. 1957. "Perceval y Gauvain en *Li Contes del Graal.*" *Filología Romanza* 4: 119–47.

———. 1967. *Les Chansons de geste françaises.* 2d ed. Translated by Irénée Cluzel. Paris: Nizet.

Roach, William, ed. 1941. *The Didot Perceval, According to the Manuscripts of Modena and Paris.* Philadelphia: American Philosophical Society.

———. 1949–83. *The Continuations of the Old French Perceval of Chrétien de Troyes.* Vol. 1: *The First Continuation, Redactions of Mss. TVD.* Vol. 2: *The First Continuation, Redactions of Mss. EMQU,* edited with Robert Henry Ivy, Jr. Vol. 3, part 1: *The First Continuation, Redaction of Mss. ALPRS.* Vol. 3, part 2: *Glossary of the First Continuation,* by Lucien Foulet. Vol. 4: *The Second Continuation.* Vol. 5: *The Third Continuation by Manessier.* Philadelphia: American Philosophical Society.

———. 1959. *Le Roman de Perceval, ou le Conte du graal, publié d'après le MS fr. 12576 de la Bibliothèque nationale.* 2d rev. ed. TLF, 71. Geneva: Droz.

Roberts, Brynley F. 1977. "*Owein* neu *Iarlles y Ffynnon.*" *Ysgrifau Beirniadol* 10: 124–43.

———. 1983. "The Welsh Romance of the *Lady of the Fountain (Owein).*" In P. B. Grout et al., eds., *The Legend of Arthur in the Middle Ages: Studies Presented to A. H. Diverres,* 170–82, 250. Arthurian Studies, 7. Cambridge: D. S. Brewer.

———. 1984. "From Traditional Tale to Literary Story: Middle Welsh Prose Narratives." In Leigh Arathoon, ed., *The Craft of Fiction: Essays in Medieval Poetics,* 211–30. Rochester, Mich.: Solaris.

———. 1991. "Geoffrey of Monmouth, *Historia Regum Britanniae* and *Brut y Brenhinedd.*" In Rachel Bromwich, A. O. H. Jarman, and Brynley F. Roberts, eds., *The Arthur of the Welsh: The Arthurian Legend in Medieval Welsh Literature,* 97–116. Cardiff: University of Wales Press.

Robertson, D. W., Jr. 1951. "Some Medieval Literary Terminology, with Special Reference to Chrétien de Troyes." *SP* 48: 669–92.

Robreau, Yvonne. 1981. *L'honneur et la honte: Leur expression dans les romans en prose du Lancelot-Graal (XIIe–XIIIe siècles).* PRF, 157. Geneva: Droz.

Roncaglia, Aurelio. 1958. "*Carestia.*" *Cultura Neolatina* 18: 121–37.

Roques, Mario. 1952a. "Le manuscrit fr. 794 de la Bibliothèque nationale et le scribe Guiot." *Romania* 73: 177–99.

Roques, Mario, ed. 1952b. *Les romans de Chrétien de Troyes d'après la copie de Guiot (Bibliothèque nationale, fr. 794).* Vol. 1: *Erec et Enide.* CFMA, 80. Paris: Champion.

———. 1958. *Les romans de Chrétien de Troyes d'après la copie de Guiot (Bibliothèque nationale, fr. 794).* Vol. 3: *Le Chevalier de la charrette.* CFMA, 86. Paris: Champion.

———. 1960. *Les romans de Chrétien de Troyes d'après la copie de Guiot (Bibliothèque nationale, fr. 794).* Vol. 4: *Le Chevalier au lion.* CFMA, 89. Paris: Champion.

Ross, Anne. 1967. *Pagan Celtic Britain: Studies in iconography and tradition.* London: Routledge and Kegan Paul.

Rossi, Luciano. 1983. "A propos de l'histoire de quelques recueils de fabliaux, I: Le Code de Berne." *Le Moyen Français* 13: 58–94.

Rouse, Richard H., and Mary A. Rouse. 1989. "Wax Tablets." *Language and Communication* 9: 175–91.

———. 1990. "The Commercial Production of Manuscript Books in Late Thirteenth- and Early Fourteenth-Century Paris." In Linda L. Brownrigg, ed., *Medieval Book Production: Assessing the Evidence,* 103–15. Los Altos Hill, Calif.: Red Gull Press, and Oxford: Anderson-Lovelace.

Rutledge, Amelia A. 1980–81. "Perceval's Sin: Critical Perspectives." *Œuvres et Critiques* 5: 53–60.

Rychner, Jean. 1967. "Le prologue du *Chevalier de la charrette.*" *Vox Romanica* 26: 1–23.

———. 1972. "Encore le prologue du *Chevalier de charrette.*" *Vox Romanica* 31: 263–71.

Rychner, Jean, ed. 1968. *Les lais de Marie de France.* CFMA, 93. Paris: Champion.

Saenger, Paul. 1972. "Silent Reading: Its Impact on Late Medieval Script and Society." *Viator* 13: 367–414.

Salisbury, Joyce. 1994. *The Beast Within: Animals in the Middle Ages.* New York: Routledge.

Salmon, Amédée, ed. 1899–1900. *Philippe de Beaumanoir, Coutumes de Beauvaisis.* 2 vols. Collection de Textes pour Servir à l'Enseignement de l'Histoire, 24, 30. Paris: Picard.

Salverda de Grave, Jean-Jacques, ed. 1929–31. *Eneas, roman du 12e siècle.* CFMA, 44, 62. Paris: Champion.

Saly, Antoinette. 1994. *Image, structure et sens.* In *Etudes arthuriennes,* 353–61. Senefiance, 34. Aix-en-Provence: Publications du CUER MA.

Savignac, Jean-Paul. 1994. *Les Gaulois, leurs écrits retrouvés: "Merde à César."* Paris: Editions de la Différence.

Schmidt-Chazan, Mireille. 1979. "Un Lorrain de cœur, le champenois Calendre." *Les Cahiers Lorrains* 1979: 65–75.

Schmolke-Hasselmann, Beate. 1998. *The Evolution of Arthurian Romance: The Verse*

Tradition from Chrétien to Froissart. Translated by Margaret and Roger Middleton. Cambridge: Cambridge University Press. Originally published in 1980 as *Der arthurische Versroman von Chrestien bis Froissart: Zur Geschichte einer Gattung.* Beihefte zur *ZRP,* 177. Tübingen: Niemeyer.

Schultz, James A. 1983. *The Shape of the Round Table: Structures of Middle High German Arthurian Romance.* Toronto: University of Toronto Press.

Schulze-Busacker, Elisabeth. 1985. *Proverbes et expressions proverbiales dans la littérature narrative du moyen âge français.* Paris: Champion.

Shirt, David. 1975. "Godefroi de Lagny et la composition de la *Charrette.*" *Romania* 96: 27–52.

———. 1977. "How Much of the *Lion* Can We Put Before the *Cart?*" *French Studies* 31 (1977): 1–17.

Short, Ian. 1979–80. "On Bilingualism in Anglo-Norman England." *RPh* 33: 467–79.

———. 1992. "Patrons and Polyglots: French Literature in Twelfth-Century England." In Marjorie Chibnall, ed., *Anglo-Norman Studies XIV: Proceedings of the Battle Conference, 1991,* 229–49. Woodbridge: Boydell.

———. 1994. "Gaimar's Epilogue and Geoffrey of Monmouth's *Liber Vetustissimus.*" *Speculum* 69: 323–43.

Short, Ian, ed. 1997. *Chanson de Roland.* Lettres Gothiques, 4524. Paris: Livre de Poche.

Sims-Williams, Patrick. 1990. "Some Celtic Otherworld Terms." In A. T. E. Matonis and Daniel F. Melia, eds., *Celtic Language, Celtic Culture: A Festschrift for Eric P. Hamp,* 57–81. Van Nuys, Calif.: Ford and Bailie.

———. 1991. "The Early Welsh Arthurian Poems." In Rachel Bromwich, A. O. H. Jarman, and Brynley F. Roberts, eds., *The Arthur of the Welsh: The Arthurian Legend in Medieval Welsh Literature,* 33–71. Cardiff: University of Wales Press.

———. 1998. "Did Itinerant Breton Conteurs Transmit the *Matière de Bretagne?*" *Romania* 119: 72–111.

Spiewok, Wolfgang, ed. and trans. 1997. *Ulrich von Zatzikhoven, Lanzelet mittelhochdeutsch/neuhochdeutsch.* Greifswald: Reineke.

Spitzer, Leo. 1944. "The Name of the Holy Grail." *American Journal of Philology* 65: 354–63.

Stanger, Mary D. 1957. "Literary Patronage at the Medieval Court of Flanders." *French Studies* 11: 214–29.

Stirnemann, Patricia. 1993. "Some Champenois Vernacular Manuscripts and the Manerius Style of Illumination." In Busby et al. 1993, 1: 195–226.

Stones, Alison. 1993. "The Illustrated Chrétien Manuscripts and Their Artistic Context." In Busby et al. 1993, 1: 227–322.

Sturm-Maddox, Sarah. 1984. "*Tenir sa terre en pais:* Social Order in the *Brut* and in the *Conte del Graal.*" *SP* 81: 28–41.

Tatlock, J. S. P. 1933. "The English Journey of the Laon Canons." *Speculum* 8: 454–65.

————. 1950. *The Legendary History of Britain: Geoffrey of Monmouth's Historia Regum Britanniae and Its Early Vernacular Versions.* Berkeley: University of California Press.

Thiolier, Jean-Claude. 1989. *Pierre de Langtoft, Le Règne d'Edouard Ier.* Vol. 1. Paris: Université de Paris XII—Créteil.

Thompson, Albert Wilder. 1931. *The Elucidation, a Prologue to the Conte del Graal.* New York: Institute of French Studies.

Thomson, Derick S., ed. 1976. *Branwen uerch Lyr.* The Second of the Four Branches of the Mabinogi. Dublin: Dublin Institute for Advanced Studies.

Thomson, R. L., ed. 1957. *Pwyll Pendeuic Dyuet.* The First of the Four Branches of the Mabinogi edited from the White Book of Rhydderch with variants from the Red Book of Hergest. Dublin: Dublin Institute for Advanced Studies.

Thomson, R. L. 1991. *"Owain: Chwedl Iarlles y Ffynnon."* In Rachel Bromwich, A. O. H. Jarman, and Brynley F. Roberts, eds., *The Arthur of the Welsh: The Arthurian Legend in Medieval Welsh Literature,* 159–69. Cardiff: University of Wales Press.

Thorpe, Lewis, trans. 1966. *Geoffrey of Monmouth, The History of the Kings of Britain.* Harmondsworth: Penguin.

————. 1974. *Gregory of Tours, The History of the Franks.* Harmondsworth: Penguin.

————. 1978. *Gerald of Wales, The Journey Through Wales, The Description of Wales.* Harmondsworth: Penguin.

Thurneysen, Rudolf. 1910–12. Review of Mary Williams, *Essai sur la composition du roman gallois de Peredur* (Paris: Champion, 1909). *ZCP* 8: 185–89.

Topsfield, Leslie. 1981. *Chrétien de Troyes: A Study of the Arthurian Romances.* Cambridge: Cambridge University Press.

Trachsler, Richard. 1997. *Les romans arthuriens en vers après Chrétien de Troyes.* Bibliographie des Ecrivains Français, 11. Rome: Memini.

Tyssens, Madeleine. 1970. "Les sources de Renaut de Beaujeu." *Mélanges Jean Frappier,* 2: 1043–55. 2 vols. Geneva: Droz.

Uitti, Karl D. 1988. "On Editing Chretien de Troyes: Lancelot's Two Steps and Their Context." *Speculum* 63: 271–292.

Uitti, Karl D., ed. and trans. 1994. *Yvain, ou le Chevalier au lion.* Traduit, présenté et annoté par Philippe Walter. In Poirion 1994a: 337–503, 1170–1234.

Van Coolput, Colette-Anne. 1987–88. "Références, adaptations et emprunts directs." In Lacy, Kelly, and Busby 1987–88, 1: 333–42.

Van Hamel, Anton Gerard, ed. 1885. *Li romans de carité et miserere, du Renclus de Moiliens.* 2 vols. Bibliothèque de l'Ecole des Hautes Etudes, Sciences Philologiques et Historiques, 61. Paris: Vieweg.

Varty, Kenneth, ed. 1981. *An Arthurian Tapestry: Essays in Memory of Lewis Thorpe.* Glasgow: French Department of the University of Glasgow, on behalf of the British Branch of the International Arthurian Society.

Vàrvaro, Alberto, ed. 1960. *Rigaut de Berbezilh, Liriche.* Bari: Adriatica Editrice.

――――. 1994. *Apparizioni fantastiche.* Tradizioni folcloriche e letteratura nel medioevo: Walter Map. Bologna: Mulino.

Vendryes, Jean. 1949. "Les éléments celtiques de la légende du Graal." *Etudes Celtiques* 5: 1–50.

Vigneras, Louis-André. 1934–35. "Chrétien de Troyes Rediscovered." *MP* 32: 341–42.

Villemarqué, Hersart de la. 1860. *Les romans de la Table ronde et les contes des anciens Bretons.* 3d ed. Paris: Didier.

Vinaver, Eugène. 1969. "Les deux pas de Lancelot." Paul Valentin and Georges Zink, ed. *Mélanges pour Jean Fourquet,* 355–61. Paris: Klincksieck. Repr. in Christopher Kleinhenz, ed., *Medieval Manuscripts and Textual Criticism,* 160–66. North Carolina Studies in the Romance Languages and Literatures, Symposia, 4. Chapel Hill: University of North Carolina Press, 1976.

Vitz, Evelyn Birge. 1990. "Chrétien de Troyes: Clerc ou menestrel? Problèmes des traditions orale et littéraire dans les cours de France au XIIe siècle." *Poétique* 8: 23–42.

――――. 1999. *Orality and Performance in Early French Romance.* Cambridge: D. S. Brewer.

Waquet, Henri, ed. 1929. *Suger, Vie de Louis VI le Gros.* Paris: Champion.

Wallensköld, Axel, ed. 1921. *Les chansons de Conon de Béthune.* CFMA, 24. Paris: Champion.

――――. 1925. *Les chansons de Thibaut de Champagne, roi de Navarre.* SATF. Paris: Champion.

Walter, Philippe. 1997. *Chrétien de Troyes.* Que sais-je? 3241. Paris: Presses Universitaires de France.

――――. 1999. "Erec et le *cocadrille:* Note de philologie et de folklore médiéval." *ZRP* 115: 56–64.

Walter, Philippe, ed. 1994. *Cligès.* In Poirion 1994a: 171–336, 1114–70.

Walters, Lori. 1985. "Le rôle du scribe dans l'organisation des manuscrits de Chrétien de Troyes." *Romania* 106: 303–25.

――――. 1991. "The Creation of a 'Super-Romance': Paris, Bibliothèque Nationale, fonds français, MS 1433." *Arthurian Yearbook* 1: 3–25.

Webster, Kenneth G. T., trans. 1951a. *Ulrich von Zatzikhoven, Lanzelet.* A Romance of Lancelot translated from the Middle High German. Revised and provided with additional notes and an introduction by Roger Sherman Loomis. New York: Columbia University Press.

Webster, Kenneth G. T. 1951b. *Guinevere: A Study of Her Abductions.* Milton: Turtle.

Weiss, Judith, ed. and trans. 1999. *Wace's Roman de Brut: A History of the British.* Exeter: University of Exeter Press.

West, G. D. 1971–72. "Grail Problems, II: The Grail Family in the Old French Verse Romances." *RPh* 25: 53–73.

Weston, Jessie L. 1897. *The Legend of Sir Gawain*. Studies upon its original scope and significance. Grimm Library, 7. London: Alfred Nutt.

———. 1906–9. *The Legend of Sir Perceval*. Studies upon its origin, development, and position in the Arthurian cycle. 2 vols. London: D. Nutt.

———. 1920. *From Ritual to Romance*. Cambridge: Cambridge University Press. Repr. Princeton: Princeton University Press, 1993.

———. 1924–25. "Who Was Brian des Illes?" *MP* 22: 405–11.

Whitman, Jon. 1987. *Allegory: The Dynamics of an Ancient and Medieval Technique*. Cambridge, Mass.: Harvard University Press.

Williams, Gruffydd Aled. 1999. "The Feasting Aspects of *Hirlas Owein*." *Ildánach Ildírech: A Festschrift for Proinsias Mac Cana*, 289–302. Andover, Mass.: Celtic Studies Publications.

Williams, Harry F. 1958. "Crestiiens li Gois." *BBSIA* 10: 67–71.

Williams, Hugh, ed. and trans. 1990 [1899]. *Two Lives of Gildas*. Felinfach: Llanerch Enterprises. (Originally published in the Cymmrodorion Record Series.)

Williams, J. E. Caerwyn. 1991. "Brittany and the Arthurian Legend." In Rachel Bromwich, A. O. H. Jarman, and Brynley F. Roberts, eds., *The Arthur of the Welsh: The Arthurian Legend in Medieval Welsh Literature*, 249–272. Cardiff: University of Wales Press.

Williams, Mary. 1937. "More About Bleddri." *Etudes Celtiques* 2: 219–45.

———. 1938. "An Early Ritual Poem in Welsh." *Speculum* 13: 38–51.

Williams, Mary, ed. 1922–25. *Gerbert de Montreuil, La Continuation de Perceval*. 3 vols. CFMA, 28, 50. Paris: Champion. (See Oswald 1975.)

Wimmer, Georg, ed. 1888. *Li Tornoiemenz Antecrit von Huon de Mery*. Ausgaben und Abhandlungen aus dem Gebiete der Romanischen Philologie, 76. Marburg: Elwert.

Wind, Bartina, ed. 1960. *Les fragments du Roman de Tristan de Thomas*. Geneva: Droz.

Winters, Margaret, ed. 1984. *The Romance of Hunbaut: An Arthurian Poem of the Thirteenth Century*. Davis Medieval Texts and Studies, 4. Leiden: Brill.

Woledge, Brian. 1969. "Bons vavasseurs et mauvais sénéchaux." *Mélanges Rita Lejeune*, 2: 1263–77. Gembloux: Duculot.

———. 1986. *Commentaire sur Yvain (le Chevalier au lion) de Chrétien de Troyes*. 2 vols. PRF, 170. Geneva: Droz.

Wolfgang, Lenora D. 1980–81. "Perceval's Father: Problems in Medieval Narrative Art." *RPh* 34: 28–47.

Wright, Neil, ed. 1985. *The Historia Regum Britannie of Geoffrey of Monmouth*. *I. Bern, Bürgerbibliothek, MS. 568*. Cambridge: D. S. Brewer.

Zai, Marie-Claire. 1974. *Les chansons courtoises de Chrétien de Troyes*. Europäische Hochschulschriften, ser. 13, vol. 27. Bern: Peter Lang.

Zai, Marie-Claire, ed. and trans. 1994. *Chansons*. In *Chrétien de Troyes, Romans*. Paris: Librairie Générale Française.

Index

Ménard, Philippe, 283

Merlin, 35; in Geoffrey of Monmouth, 31, 201; in *Perceval,* 244

mesnie: defined, 48

Micha, Alexandre, 240

Middleton, Roger, 203

Misrahi, Jean, 59

Modena: cathedral of, 70, 205

Modron, 61, 204

monologues: in *Cliges,* 142–44; in *Erec,* 141–42; and female characters, 148; in *Lancelot,* 144–46; in *Perceval,* 148; in *Yvain,* 147–50

Mordred, 58; adultery of, 114; first mention of, 199; not in Chrétien, 57, 201

Morgan the Fay, 117, 126; ambivalence of, 99; as "Anna" or "Enna," 201–2; and Celtic tradition, 236–37; in *Yvain,* 159, 160, 163

Mort le Roi Artu, La, 35, 278

mother, Perceval's, 77, 79, 81, 83, 84, 85; counsel of, 120–21; death of, 119, 122, 124, 128, 178–79; incest of, 80, 257; on knighthood, 312, 321–22, 324

motivation, 168; and ambivalence, 99; and interiority, 164–80; in *Lancelot,* 171–74; in *Perceval,* 178–80; in *Yvain,* 174–78

Mule sans frein, La, 41

Mullally, Evelyn, 16

myth, Celtic: in *Cliges,* 220–22; in *Erec,* 212–22; and geography, 209–10; influence in Chrétien, 3, 182, 183–270; in *Lancelot,* 222–32; and names, 196–208; and plots, 211–68; transmission of, 185–86; Welsh romances, 189–96

Nantes, 11, 59

narrative: art in Chrétien, 293–308;

organization, 293–96; and portraits, 296–303; and reported speech; and suspense, 306–8

narrator: in Chrétien's works, 278–81

"Nennius": *Historia Brittonum (History of the Britons),* 30

Neo-Platonic science, 160–61

nephew. *See* avunculate

Newstead, Helaine, 218

Nicolas of Clairvaux, 17

niece: and granddaughter, 78–79, 83

Ninienne, 71

Nitze, William A., 231, 237

Nixon, Terry, 19, 34, 46

nobility: and consanguinity, 53; and customal rights, 166; and fosterage, 87; and primogeniture, 47–48, 89–90; role of in society, 47–48

Nodons, 62, 205; as "Nut" in *Erec,* 61

Norison, lady of, 123, 162, 163, 176, 237; and count Alier, 165; motivations of, 99; rehabilitates Yvain, 117, 159–60

Normandy, 208, 209

Normans, 184

nourris: defined, 52; and fosterage, 87

Nut: avatar of Nodons, 61; father of Ydier, 90

Occitania: lack of primogeniture in, 47

Olschki, Leonardo, 124–25

Orgueilleus de la Lande, 79, 119, 121, 125, 148, 165; and Perceval, 178, 179

Orgueilleus del Passage a l'Estroite Voie, 127

Orgueilleuse de Logres or Nogres, 86, 99, 152; and Gauvain, 126–28, 263–64